ADVANCE PRAISE FOR
Chomsky and Dershowitz:
On Endless War and the End of Civil Liberties

"With unfailing accuracy, Howard Friel has shown why he is nearly without peer in analyzing the ideological conflicts of the day, from the news media's coverage of war-making to climate change. Here he examines the Chomsky-Dershowitz rivalry and a myriad of important issues with the eyes of a teacher and a journalist who seeks truth."
—**Marcus G. Raskin, co-founder, Institute for Policy Studies**

"Howard Friel has drawn a fascinating contrast between the scholarship of MIT's Noam Chomsky and Harvard's Alan Dershowitz. Friel traces Dershowitz's transformation from a civil libertarian in the 1960s and 1970s to a supporter today of national ID cards, preventive detention, roving wiretaps, extra-judicial killing, and torture in extreme cases. This book is a must read for those who seek to understand some of the most critical issues of our time."
—**Marjorie Cohn, professor, Thomas Jefferson School of Law and former president of the National Lawyers Guild**

"Howard Friel has written with courage and conviction about two major figures in American intellectual life—Noam Chomsky and Alan Dershowitz. Friel's constructive polemics provide nuance and detail that could surprise readers into re-thinking the positions they hold on crucial concerns, from the Israel-Palestine conflict and human rights to perpetual war and civil liberties."
—**Robert F. Barsky, Professor of French and Comparative Literature, Vanderbilt University**

"Howard Friel's *Chomsky and Dershowitz* is a forensic dissection of the intellectual complicity of one American intellectual—Alan Dershowitz—and the courage and conviction of another—Noam Chomsky. The book provides a full assessment of building careers on behalf of power (Dershowitz) and askance of power (Chomsky). The test cases here are U.S. foreign policy, Israel-Palestine, international law, and civil liberties."
—**Vijay Prashad, George and Martha Kellner Chair in South Asian History and Professor of International Studies, Trinity College**

PRAISE FOR HOWARD FRIEL'S
The Lomborg Deception:
Setting the Record Straight about Global Warming

"Facts, John Adams once said, are stubborn things. Unfortunately for Bjorn Lomborg, this book is full of them. *The Lomborg Deception* sets the record straight with a rigorous, readable body blow to climate complacency."
—**Senator John Kerry**

"*The Lomborg Deception* by Howard Friel presents a troubling history of how a cleverly contrived claim—that hundreds of scientists and dozens of scientific institutions have gotten climate change and environmental science badly wrong over several decades—is way off base, unlike the well-established conclusions hammered out over decades in peer-reviewed assessments. Bjorn Lomborg's claims that environmental scientists mislead society into wasting money on nonexistent problems is based on hundreds of citations taken out of context, dozens of straw men, selective inattention to inconvenient science, and the illusion of careful scholarship. Friel documents this deception brilliantly."

—**Stephen M. Schneider, Melvin and Joan Lane Professor for Interdisciplinary Environmental Studies and Senior Fellow, Woods Institute for the Environment, Stanford University**

"For those interested in the future of polar bears and Arctic sea ice, *The Lomborg Deception* by Howard Friel clearly documents the inaccurate and utterly inadequate arguments that Bjorn Lomborg uses to erroneously suggest climate warming will have little negative impact on this bellweather mammal. The far greater tragedy is that misleading presentations such as those proffered by Lomborg may help to foster uncertainty in the public at large about the severity of the human causes of climate warming, and thus further delay the urgent need for the entire world to respond quickly to reduce our collective output of greenhouse gases."

—**Ian Stirling, Fellow of the Royal Society of Canada, Research Scientist Emeritus, Environment**

"Scientific discourse, born of the honest skepticism and unquestioned integrity of its participants, has been the lifeblood of scientific inquiry for centuries. False scientific debate over well-established results, born of the repeated interventions by voices whose skepticism is not honestly articulated, can be extremely dangerous—both to the conduct of scientific research and to the well-being of a planet that depends on responsible stewardship for its very existence. Since this danger is particularly acute for issues like climate change that have been politicized beyond reason, one can only hope that Howard Friel's careful documentation of persistent and pervasive misrepresentations will diminish significantly the credibility and thus the influence of Lomborg's assertions."

—**Gary Yohe, Woodhouse/Sysco Professor of Economics, Wesleyan University**

"In this work, Howard Friel does what nobody has done before, namely to systematically examine Lomborg's work citation by citation. This is no small task, so it is not surprising that this has not been undertaken until now... Friel has used real scholarship to reveal the flimsy nature of the scholarly foundation of Lomborg's work."

—**Thomas Lovejoy, Biodiversity Chair, The H. John Heinz III Center for Science, Economics and the Environment**

"Friel's book should give satisfaction not just to those who would like to see Lomborg marooned on a shrinking ice floe but to anyone who believes that scientific debate should be bound by scientific evidence."

—**Richard Girling, *The Times* (London)**

"Friel uses a detailed analysis of the systematic misrepresentations and partial accounting that are at the core of climate skepticism to reveal an enlightening pole-to-pole review of some of today's most urgent climate concerns."

—*Environmentalist*

CHOMSKY AND DERSHOWITZ
On Endless War and the End of Civil Liberties

by HOWARD FRIEL

OLIVE
BRANCH
PRESS

An imprint of Interlink Publishing Group, Inc.
www.interlinkbooks.com

First published in 2014 by

OLIVE BRANCH PRESS
An imprint of Interlink Publishing Group, Inc.
46 Crosby Street, Northampton, Massachusetts 01060
www.interlinkbooks.com

Library of Congress Cataloging-in-Publication Data

Friel, Howard, 1955-
Chomsky and Dershowitz : on endless war and the end of civil liberties / by Howard Friel.
    pages cm
Includes bibliographical references and index.
ISBN 978-1-56656-942-2 -- ISBN 978-1-56656-974-3
1. Chomsky, Noam--Political and social views. 2. Dershowitz, Alan M.--Political and social views. 3. Politics and war. 4. Politics and war--United States. 5. Civil rights. 6. Civil rights--United States. 7. Carter, Jimmy, 1924- 8. Falk, Richard A. 9. Goldstone, Richard. I. Title.
P85.C47F75 2013
940.53'2443091767--dc23
                    2013023663

Cover design: Pam Glaven, Impress, Northampton, MA
Front cover illustration: Luke Jaeger
Book design and production: Pam Fontes-May

Printed and bound in the United States of America

To request our complete 48-page, full-color catalog, please call us toll free at 1-800-238-LINK, visit our website at www.interlinkbooks.com, or send us an e-mail: info@interlinkbooks.com

CONTENTS

PART I
INTRODUCTION(S)

I

METAPHORS

In December 2005, the Kennedy School of Government at Harvard University hosted a debate between Noam Chomsky and Alan Dershowitz. The event began with a collegial opening statement from Dershowitz:

> It's a great honor for me to be participating in a debate with a man who has been called the world's top public intellectual. My connections to Noam Chomsky go back a long time. In the 1940s, I was a camper and he a counselor in a Hebrew-speaking Zionist camp in the Pocono Mountains called Camp Massad. In the 1960s we both worked against the Vietnam War. In the 1970s we had the first of our many debates about the Arab-Israeli conflict. I advocated ending the Israeli occupation in exchange for peace and recognition of Israel; he advocated a one-state solution, modeled on Lebanon and Yugoslavia. We debated again in the 1980s and the 1990s. I have the text. I hope that our once-a-decade encounter will continue for many decades to come, though I doubt we will agree with each other.

Dershowitz went on to advocate an Israel-Palestine final-status peace agreement based on a mutual compromise of Israeli and Palestinian rights:

> The time has come for compromise. My friend Amos Oz, the great novelist and leader of the Israeli peace movement, has said there are two possible resolutions to a conflict of this kind: the Shakespearian and the Chekhovian. In a Shakespearian drama, every right is wronged, every act is revenged, every injustice is made right, and perfect justice prevails, but at the end of the play, everybody lies dead on the stage. In a Chekhov play, everybody is disillusioned, embittered, heart-broken, disappointed, but they remain alive. We need a Chekhovian resolution for the Arab-Israeli

tragedy. This will require the elevation of pragmatism over ideology. It will require that both sides give up rights. Rights! Giving up rights is a hard thing to do. It will require that each side recognizes and acknowledges the pain and the suffering of the other. And it will require an end to the hateful attitudes and speech that some on each side direct against the other.[1]

In a similar fashion, near the beginning of his 1983 book *Fateful Triangle: The United States, Israel, and the Palestinians*, Chomsky described "certain assumptions" that would inform his analysis in that book and beyond:

> The first of these is the principle that Israeli Jews and Palestinian Arabs are human beings with human rights, equal rights; more specifically, they have essentially equal rights within the territory of the former Palestine. Each group has a valid right to national self-determination in this territory. Furthermore, I will assume that the state of Israel within its pre-1967 borders had, and retains, whatever one regards as the valid rights of any state within the existing international system. One may formulate these principles in various ways, but let us take them to be clear enough to serve as a point of departure.[2]

Similarly, in a recent book, *Knowing Too Much: Why the American Jewish Romance with Israel Is Coming to an End*, Norman Finkelstein—a Dershowitz adversary and a Chomsky ally—wrote: "If Israel does, or appears to, confront an existential crisis when its physical existence is literally at stake, American Jewry will almost certainly rally, and *should* rally, to its defense. The physical destruction of any society is a criminal act and sane people will contemplate such a prospect with horror" (emphasis in original). Finkelstein then wrote that "the choice between Israel's survival and Palestinian rights is a false one."[3]

All of this is to emphasize that this volume is aligned with the broad goals and principles that are advocated in each of the statements above from Dershowitz, Chomsky, and Finkelstein with respect to the Israel-Palestine conflict; however, it questions the fidelity of Dershowitz's scholarship and public commentary to his own articulated principles, as he listed them at Harvard in 2005. For example, to avoid a Shakespearean ending and to achieve a Chekhovian one, Dershowitz stressed that *both* the Israeli and Palestinian sides must give up rights. But I have read little in Dershowitz's work that proposes a compromise of any Israeli rights and much that supports the abandonment of Palestinian rights.

And which Israeli rights, exactly, would be implicated in an Israel-Palestine peace agreement, given Israel's core policies toward the Palestinians? These policies feature six decades of belligerent occupation of the Palestinian West Bank, extensive settlement of parts of Israel's population into the West Bank, the construction of a separation wall on West Bank territory, and a total economic embargo of the 1.5 million inhabitants of the Gaza Strip. Given these practices, which are grounded in no recognized rights of Israel, it isn't clear to which rights of Israel Dershowitz referred when he advocated a mutual compromise of Israeli and Palestinian rights as the best path to a permanent peace agreement.

In his debate with Chomsky, Dershowitz also observed that Israel "should end its occupation of all Palestinian cities and population centers on the West Bank."[4] A passing glance at those words might convince many readers of Dershowitz's moderation. But there is more to the West Bank than its cities and population centers, including its agricultural lands, water aquifers, air space, transportation system, and so on. The odd specificity of Dershowitz's appeal to end the occupation "of Palestinian cities"—as opposed to West Bank territory—seems to imply that he supports a continuation of the Israeli occupation in other areas of the West Bank, including an extension of official permanent status to the major Israeli settlements that encircle Jerusalem to the east and that were built in the West Bank across the Green Line from Tel Aviv.

Indeed, in his 2005 book *The Case for Peace: How the Arab-Israeli Conflict Can Be Resolved*, and years later, Dershowitz sketched ways for solving the conflict, including an assertion of an implied Israeli right to annex sizeable portions of Palestinian territory on which major Israeli settlements are located.[5] But there are no such rights of settlement and territorial annexation. There may be compelling grounds from a "pragmatic" standpoint to negotiate "relatively small" border adjustments during final-status negotiations, as Dershowitz also wrote.[6] But this is a different thing altogether from an assertion of an Israeli right to annex Palestinian territory on which Israeli settlements were built in violation of the Fourth Geneva Convention.

Finally, and consistent with Dershowitz's announced standard of Israeli-Palestinian mutuality, any Palestinian concessions on settlements and West Bank territory should be reciprocated on a one-to-one basis—that is, an exchange of roughly equal amounts of roughly comparable land—as the unofficial but credible Geneva Accord on Israel-Palestine stipulated: "In accordance with UNSC Resolution 242 and 338, the border between the states of Palestine and Israel shall be based on the June 4th 1967 lines with reciprocal modifications on a 1:1 basis."[7] But Dershowitz makes no such one-to-one stipulation, while rejecting what he refers to as "the indefensible 1967 lines"[8]—even though the 1967 lines legally allot 78 percent of historic Palestine to Israel and leave only 22 percent to the Palestinians (assuming that the Palestinians are able to hold onto all of the West Bank at the conclusion of a peace agreement).

This catalog of nonexistent Israeli rights does not invalidate Israel's recognized and legitimate rights. As a UN member state, Israel has the same rights and obligations under the United Nations Charter and other sources of public international law as any other state. Israel thus has a right to its internationally recognized borders (the June 4, 1967 borders) which do not incorporate East Jerusalem or any part of the West Bank—a legal fact that has been affirmed repeatedly by the UN Security Council, the UN General Assembly, the International Court of Justice, and the major human rights organizations.

Israel has a legitimate right to self-defense against an armed attack under Article 51 of the United Nations Charter. However, Israel has regularly violated the UN Charter's prohibition against the threat and use of force by states—Article 2(4), regarded as the cardinal rule of international law—by mis-casting its serial aerial bombardments, ground invasions, and armed reprisals in the region as "self-defense." Dershowitz consistently supports Israel's illegal military actions by improperly citing the self-defense exception to the cardinal rule that prohibits force, while persistently neglecting to mention the overarching rule itself.

As a UN member state, Israel also enjoys a legitimate expectation of recognition by other UN member states, including by the governing authorities of Arab and Muslim countries. Although the human rights records of several such states—Saudi Arabia, Iran, and Azerbaijan, for example, which refuse to recognize the state of Israel—are far worse than Israel's with respect to how those countries treat their domestic populations, the six decades of Israel's settler/annexationist occupation of the West Bank is unique to the contemporary world, and explains why Israel has been deprived of broader recognition internationally by Arab and Muslim states. Overall, with respect to his stated peace formula of the mutual compromise of rights, Dershowitz is a mostly uncompromising advocate of Israel's rights who detracts from Palestinian rights.

On the other side of the rights ledger, while the Palestinians possess a right of self-determination within the territorial borders of the West Bank and Gaza Strip, they possess no legal right today to territory within Israel's internationally recognized 1967 borders. Thus, the claim by some Palestinians to territory "from the (Jordan) river to the (Mediterranean) sea" has no basis in contemporary law. The Palestinians also possess no right to kill or injure Israeli civilians by resorting to terrorist acts or the indiscriminate firing of rockets into Israel. The major human rights organizations—Amnesty International, Human Rights Watch, and B'Tselem—have correctly and consistently deplored such acts. For his part, while Dershowitz deplores Palestinian terrorism, he writes and speaks in support of a much larger scale of Israeli state violence against the Palestinians. In short, when Dershowitz gave his support to a Chekhovian-style solution to the Israel-Palestine conflict—the formula for which is the mutual compromise of rights—he neglected to identify what those rights are, and thus to give some substance to his road map for peace.

And despite calling for "an end to the hateful attitudes and speech" in the debate over Israel-Palestine, Dershowitz paradoxically has identified scholarly critics of Israel's policies that violate Palestinian rights as "enemies" of Israel, including in his 2008 book *The Case against Israel's Enemies: Jimmy Carter and Others Who Stand in the Way of Peace*. In that volume, Dershowitz cited former President Carter, Noam Chomsky, Richard Falk, Richard Goldstone, Norman Finkelstein, the Presbyterian Church, and the pope, among others, as enemies of Israel. Yet, unlike Dershowitz with respect to Palestinian rights, none of these critics support the violation of Israel's rights, and they recognize the state of Israel within the June 4, 1967 borders. It is, therefore, simply false to claim that liberal or left scholarly critics of Israel support the destruction of the state of Israel, as Dershowitz suggested on the occasion of the death of former New York City mayor Ed Koch.[9]

Contrary to Dershowitz, who in his high-profile defense of Israel's illegal policies seems to have compromised an apparent earlier commitment to international law (when he signed published petitions opposing the war in Vietnam), human rights (when he supported Soviet dissidents), and civil liberties (when he opposed the Nixon administration's assault on the Bill of Rights), Chomsky's commitment to those sources of law and civilized conduct has never faded. From the outset, for example, and perhaps most prominently, Chomsky has challenged the right of any nation-state, including the United States and Israel, to resort to the threat and use of force in violation of UN Charter Article 2(4), or to intervene unilaterally in the internal affairs of other countries. In the introduction to his first book about U.S. foreign policy, published in 1969, Chomsky challenged the U.S. right to wage war in Vietnam: "The primary reason for opposition to the war is its costs to us. A second cause is the feeling that the cost to its victims is too great. At first glance, this reaction seems to be at a higher moral level than the first, but this is questionable. The principle that we should retract our claws when the victim bleeds too much is hardly an elevated one. What about opposition to the war on the grounds that we have no right to stabilize or restructure Vietnamese society?"[10] In the same volume *American Power and the New Mandarins*, which introduced a new critical paradigm of U.S. foreign policy by challenging the right to threaten and wage illegal war, Chomsky observed that "what is striking is the implicit assumption that we have a right to continue our efforts to restructure the South Vietnamese government in the interests of what we determine to be Vietnamese nationalism."[11] And in the same book: "Notice how perverse is the entire discussion of the 'conceptual framework' for [U.S.] counterinsurgency [in South Vietnam]. The idea that we must choose between the method of 'winning hearts and minds' and the method of shaping behavior presumes that we have the right to choose at all. This is to grant us a right that we would surely accord to no other world power."[12] Also:

> A striking feature of the recent debate on Southeast Asian policy has been the distinction that is commonly drawn between "responsible criticism," on the one hand, and "sentimental" or "emotional" or "hysterical" criticism, on the other. There is much to be learned from a careful study of the terms in which this distinction is drawn. The "hysterical critics" are to be identified, apparently, by their irrational refusal to accept one fundamental political axiom, namely, that the United States has the right to extend its power and control without limit, insofar as is feasible. Responsible criticism does not challenge this assumption, but argues, rather, that we probably can't "get away with it" at this particular time and place.[13]

That Chomsky has never retreated from this principled approach to U.S. foreign policy is not debatable. Citing the July 1955 worldwide appeal from Bertrand Russell and Albert Einstein to "renounce war," Chomsky wrote in his 2006 book *Failed States*: "The world has not renounced war. Quite the contrary. By now, the world's hegemonic power accords itself the right to wage war at will, under a doctrine of 'anticipatory self-defense' with unstated bounds. International law, treaties and rules of world order are sternly imposed on others with much self-righteous posturing, but dismissed as irrelevant for the United States—a long-standing practice, driven to new depths by the Reagan and Bush II administrations."[14]

Chomsky has applied the same principled, rights-based criticism to Israeli policy. Writing in 1983 in the first pages of *Fateful Triangle*, Chomsky wrote that "these remarks will be critical of Israel's policies: its consistent rejection of any political settlement that accommodates the national rights of the indigenous population," that is, the Palestinian inhabitants of the West Bank and Gaza Strip.[15] Chomsky similarly defended the rights of the indigenous populations in Latin America: "One of the most exciting developments of the past few decades is the revival of indigenous cultures and languages, and the struggles for community and political rights. Throughout the hemisphere and elsewhere there are indigenous movements seeking to gain land rights and other civil and human rights that have been denied them by repressive and often murderous states."[16]

In summary, there is an evident tension between Chomsky's approach to rights, whereby Chomsky and his allies apply rights universally, including to the United States and Israel, and Dershowitz's approach, where he and his allies apply rights selectively to shield Israel's U.S.-backed policies from criticism in the United States.

A major theme of this book is that U.S. and U.S.-supported violations of international law and human rights abroad has led to an erosion of civil liberties at home—one of "the costs and consequences of American empire," as Chalmers Johnson wrote in his 2000 book *Blowback*.[17] Among the costs and consequences here are the devastating loss of public wealth in the United States to excessive national-security spending (more than the rest of the world combined), an increased threat of terrorism to the United States, and the post–9/11 increase in intrusive security measures and electronic surveillance by the executive branch.

Jonathan Turley, a professor of law at the George Washington School of Law, wrote in the *Washington Post* in 2012 that the post–9/11 assertions of executive-branch security powers—which he listed as assassination of U.S. citizens, indefinite detention, arbitrary justice, warrantless searches, secret evidence, the secret and unaccountable FISA court, immunity from judicial review, continual monitoring of citizens, war crimes, and extraordinary renditions—"form a mosaic of powers under which our country could be considered, at least in part, authoritarian." Turley commented further: "Americans often proclaim our nation as a symbol of freedom to the world while dismissing nations such as Cuba and China as categorically unfree. Yet, objectively, we may be only half right. Those countries do lack basic individual rights such as due process, placing them outside any reasonable definition of 'free.' But the United States now has much more in common with such regimes than anyone may like to admit" and "the list of powers acquired by the U.S. government since 9/11 puts us in rather troubling company."[18] How did the post–World War II United States, a country that made incredible progress in civil rights and liberties, transition to a post–9/11 quasi-authoritarian state—with no evident path on which to walk back the ubiquitous focus on security and the accumulation of unchecked executive power?

One answer is that postwar U.S. foreign policy, which has cast aside human life and human rights and the rights of other nations, ultimately has boomeranged back into our own country with an increased threat of terrorism and a corresponding disregard for the basic constitutional rights of Americans.

One remedy—the one advanced in this volume—is relatively simple: respect international law and human rights abroad, and the security mandate to trim civil liberties at home will ease. Within this framework, then, the survival of civil liberties in the United States depends to a great extent on the observance of international law and human rights in the conduct of U.S. foreign policy.

I have chosen to illustrate the problems and remedies cited above and throughout this book through the metaphors of the work of Harvard professor Alan Dershowitz (who poses as the problem) and MIT professor Noam Chomsky (who represents the remedy). Whereas Dershowitz arguably once supported human rights abroad and civil liberties at home, since at least 9/11 he has appealed for a review of the traditional meaning of both areas of law. In contrast, Noam Chomsky has consistently supported human rights abroad and civil liberties at home. Thus, the Dershowitz metaphor in effect tracks the modern rise and fall of civil liberties in the United States, while the Chomsky metaphor is presented as the antidote, and the road, so to speak, not taken. One outcome, ironically, is that while American leaders have long proclaimed our nation as a shining beacon of the Chomskyan paradigm of human rights and civil liberties (if not labeled as such), what the American people are getting instead is the Dershowitzian model of a civil libertarianism turned to authoritarianism.

2

CHOMSKY AT MIT, 1965–1973

The first public notice that Noam Chomsky was opposed to the U.S. war in Vietnam was published in the *Washington Post* on March 22, 1965, in "An Open Letter to President Johnson." The letter was signed by 130 members of the faculty of the Massachusetts Institute of Technology, who expressed concern about the war's impact on the people of Vietnam. The letter to the president began:

> Dear Mr. President:
>
> The military policy of your administration in Viet-Nam is consistent nei-ther with our national interest nor with the interests of the Vietnamese people. We are appalled by the unilateral and continuing escalation of the war in Viet-Nam. This action has aroused widespread dissent at home and has been met with dismay abroad. The reason given to justify this es-calation—that we are only replying to aggression by North Viet-Nam—is not convincing.

The letter urged President Johnson to seek a cease-fire in South Vietnam and to end hostilities against North Vietnam.[1]

The campaign to draft the letter, and to have it signed and published, was organ-ized by Hilary Putnam, a professor of philosophy, and Warren Ambrose, a professor of mathematics, both at MIT. In addition to Chomsky, among other MIT professors who signed the letter were Jule Charney, a professor of atmospheric science; Louis Kampf, professor of literature and women's studies; Salvador Luria, professor of bi-ology; and Huston Smith, professor of religion. Not only was this antiwar letter the first one signed by Chomsky, it was the first such letter from college or university faculty in the United States to oppose the war in Vietnam. And it was organized and published quite early in the open combat phase of the war.

The chronology of major events leading up to March 1965, and the onset of the air and ground war by U.S. forces in Vietnam, by now are well known. In July 1954, the Eisenhower administration rejected the Geneva Accords on Vietnam, which ended the French colonial war and would have ended war altogether in a unified Vietnam had the United States supported the accords, as France, Britain, the Soviet Union, and China all did.

Since the U.S.-backed South Vietnam refused to participate in unification elections, and after the United States ignored the second major stipulation of the Geneva Accords, which was to demilitarize Vietnam, by January 1961 President Eisenhower had sent seven hundred "military advisers" to South Vietnam.[2] By the end of the Kennedy administration in November 1963, the number of U.S. "advisers" had increased to twelve thousand;[3] by August 4, 1964, the date of the Gulf of Tonkin incident and the U.S. bombing of North Vietnamese coastal territory that immediately followed, officially there were still no American combat forces in Vietnam.

Months later, on February 7, 1965, South Vietnamese National Liberation Front ("Vietcong") guerrillas attacked two U.S. airbases near Pleiku in South Vietnam, causing extensive damage to U.S. aircraft, and killing seven U.S. military personnel and wounding over a hundred.[4] That same day, the Johnson administration described the attacks as "provocations ordered and directed by the Hanoi regime" in North Vietnam.[5] This charge, like Johnson's claim that two U.S. destroyers were attacked in the Gulf of Tonkin on August 4, turned out to be false.[6] Nevertheless, the president immediately ordered reprisal bombings of North Vietnam, causing "considerable" damage, as the *New York Times* reported on February 8,[7] and escalating the "penny ante game" of U.S. war actions.[8] Due to Johnson's decision to bomb North Vietnam, an aide to U.S. National Security Adviser McGeorge Bundy observed that "the die was cast," and that "the war was about to be changed in kind rather than in degree."[9]

On February 10, the NLF (Vietcong) attacked another U.S. base in South Vietnam, killing twenty-three U.S. soldiers.[10] With no evidence of North Vietnamese involvement, on February 13 President Johnson ordered the "Rolling Thunder" bombing campaign of North Vietnam, described at the time as "a program of measured and limited air action," but which continued for three and a half years.[11]

On March 8, 3,500 U.S. Marines arrived in Vietnam—these were the first official U.S. combat troops sent to Vietnam.[12] Two weeks later, on March 22, the MIT faculty's "Open Letter to President Johnson" was published in the *Washington Post*, wherein they also stated that "we daily receive reports which contradict the reasons your administration has given for its actions in Viet-Nam."[13] By the end of 1965, President Johnson would have nearly 200,000 U.S. combat troops in Vietnam.[14]

The war, obviously, did not stop there. There are two credible estimates of the number of Vietnamese killed during the era of direct U.S. intervention and war.

One estimate—3.6 million—is given in a 1997 article in the *New York Times* by Robert McNamara, who in turn cited North Vietnamese General Nguyen Dinh Uoc as his source.[15] In a 1999 book, McNamara described the general as "Vietnam's outstanding authority on the vexing issue of casualties."[16] And in 2008, a major survey published in the *British Medical Journal* estimated "violent war deaths" in Vietnam (but not "all excess deaths attributable to war") at 3.8 million.[17] Regarding Cambodia, and prior to the Khmer Rouge taking power, Benedict Kiernan, a historian at Yale University and director of the Yale Genocide Studies Program, estimates that "up to 150,000 civilian deaths resulted from the U.S. bombing campaigns in Cambodia from 1969 to 1973."[18] With respect to Laos, a 1975 report in the *New York Times* estimated that "some 350,000 men, women, and children have been killed" between 1953 and 1975, which the *Times* at the time attributed euphemistically to "fratricidal strife that was increased to tragic proportions by warring outsiders."[19] This estimate was cited by Edward S. Herman and Noam Chomsky in *Manufacturing Consent*, their classic work on the U.S. news media.[20] Thus, adding the totals, a credible estimate of the number of people killed during the U.S. wars in Vietnam, Cambodia, and Laos would be 4.1–4.3 million. This is what the protest movement against these wars in essence was about—to stop the military escalation and the mass killing of men, women, and children that had no conceivable moral or legal justification.

The antiwar movement developed slowly at first, with much of it, once it got going, flowing out of Boston. Upon reading the *Boston Globe* archives, for example, one finds mostly brief notices of events in 1965, such as, "Only 100 Turn Out for M.I.T. Teach-In," published in May 1965, about Vietnam and the Johnson administration's armed invasion of the Dominican Republic in late April.[21] The notice reported: "Speakers at the teach-in, which ran from 11 AM to 6 PM included Prof. Noam Chomsky of MIT; Prof. Ruhl Bartlett of the Fletcher School of International Law and Diplomacy at Tufts; Prof. William S. Barnes, Harvard; Prof. Cyrus Levinthal of MIT; Robert Zevin, teaching fellow at Harvard; Prof. Milton Vanger of Brandeis and Prof. George Kahin of Cornell University."[22]

In July, a brief announcement in the *Boston Globe* titled "Author Mailer to Speak at Teach-In Here," announced:

> Controversial novelist Norman Mailer and journalist I.F. Stone are to speak at a teach-in on Wednesday night at Sanders Theater, Harvard University. Key factors in focus: Presidential administration policies for the Dominican Republic and for Viet-Nam. Teach-in sponsors include: Students for a Democratic Society; MIT Committee Opposing War in Viet-Nam; Boston Area Faculty Group on Public Issues; Massachusetts

Political Action for Peace; May 2 Committee; B.U. Students for Peace. Other speakers slated for the night-long session include: Profs. Noam Chomsky, Salvador Luria, both of MIT; Staughton Lynd of Yale; Robert Zevin of Berkeley; Banks McDowell of B.U.; Martin Peretz and Alan Gilberti, both of Harvard.[23]

The first major event in Boston against the war happened on the Boston Common on October 16, 1965, as part of a national day of protest, with a rally attended by three thousand people.[24] Michael S. Foley, who wrote a book published in 2003 about the draft resistance movement during the Vietnam War years, described what happened:

A total of 3,000 people had assembled at three separate locations—the Cambridge Common, the Massachusetts Institute of Technology (MIT) administration building on Massachusetts Avenue ("Mass. Ave.," to locals), and Boston University's Marsh Plaza on Commonwealth Avenue ("Comm. Ave.," to locals)—before marching to Boston Common, where they met at the Parkman Bandstand. At the Mass. Ave. Bridge, six Harvard freshmen held a banner that read, "We Support LBJ in Viet Nam." The six followed the marchers to the Common, where they joined another group, numbering 300, the core of which were members of the conservative student group Young Americans for Freedom; they waited until the marchers settled in front of the bandstand and the speakers took their seats before making their move. This smaller crowd, made up largely of students who came from Boston University, Harvard, MIT, Northeastern University, Boston College, and Emerson College, then pushed their way through the demonstrators until they positioned themselves directly in front of the platform. To the relief of the speakers, fifty police patrolmen had already posted themselves at the bandstand, with six men guarding the steps. The counter-protestors carried signs that said "Stay in Viet Nam," "Draft the Pinkos," "Drop the Bombs," and "Send the Draft Dodgers to Viet Nam." Seeing the signs, the antiwar marchers began to chant, "We want peace in Vietnam. We want peace," only to have the counter-demonstrators respond with "We want victory in Vietnam. We want victory." Russell Johnson of the American Friends Service Committee attempted to speak, but he could outshout the insurgents only briefly. State representative Irving Fishman from Newton and MIT linguistics professor Noam Chomsky could not match Johnson's performance, and police ended the rally before it turned violent. Chomsky later remembered that he "wasn't happy that there was a large contingent of police, who didn't like what we were saying . . . but didn't want to see people murdered on the Common."[25]

As the U.S. war in Vietnam continued to escalate throughout 1966—President Johnson would have a total of nearly 400,000 U.S. combat troops there by the end of that year[26]—opposition in the United States grew, especially among students and faculty at U.S. colleges and universities.

The bombing of Vietnam, both North and South, escalated with the troop deployments. According to McNamara, "between 1965 and 1967, U.S. and South Vietnamese air forces dropped over a million tons of bombs on the South."[27] In a recent study published by Yale University Press, German author Bernd Greiner reported that "between 1966 and 1968 the war planes of the United States and its allies dropped 2,865,808 tons of bombs on Vietnam, Laos and Cambodia—at least 800,000 tons more than in all theaters of the whole Second World War." Greiner reported that "by 1975 the U.S. armed forces had exploded seven million tons of bombs and artillery grenades in North and South Vietnam," and that "a country of 330,000 square kilometers, somewhat smaller than Germany, was left at the end of the war with twenty-six million bomb craters."[28]

Opposition to the American bombing among faculty members at American colleges and universities was published in display advertisements in major U.S. newspapers during the height of Johnson's war escalation, paid for collectively by the faculty members themselves. In addition to the "Open Letter to President Johnson" in the *Washington Post* in March 1965, signed by MIT faculty, which urged Johnson "to seek a cease-fire in South Viet-Nam and to end hostilities against North Viet-Nam," a massive petition signed by six thousand "Members of the Academic Community" and "Members of the Professional Community" was published in the *New York Times* in June 1966, which called upon the Johnson administration "to cease all bombing, North and South, and all other offensive military operations immediately." The faculty petition also urged the president "to encourage in every way, and in no way to interfere with, the free exercise of popular sovereignty in Vietnam," and "to evaluate seriously whether self-determination for the Vietnamese as well as our own national interests would not be best served by termination of our military presence in Vietnam."[29]

The petition included signatures from 130 members of the faculty at the University of California at Berkeley, 38 from Stanford University, 48 from Yale University, 170 from Harvard University, 95 from MIT, 23 from the University of Massachusetts, 32 from Tufts University, 50 from Brandeis University, 14 from Amherst College, 34 from Wellesley College, 30 from Smith College, 60 from Princeton University, 90 from Rutgers University, 80 from the Albert Einstein College of Medicine, 140 from City College, 190 from Columbia University, and 165 from New York University.[30]

Roughly as many members of the professional community signed the June 1966 antiwar petition as members of the academic community. These included "Architects and City Planners" (21), "Dance" (15), "Curators and Gallery Directors" (12), "Film" (27), "Literature" (210), "Music" (60), "Painting and Sculpture" (324), "Photography" (19), "Theater" (66), "Educators" (32), "Library Science" (14), "Teachers" (348), "Law" (33), "Social Work" (112), "Dentists" (45), "Physicians" (264), and "Psychology, Psychoanalysis, and Psychotherapy" (280).[31]

Seven months later, in January 1967, as the war and the bombing continued to escalate, approximately six thousand faculty members again put their names to two paid advertisements in the New York Times (January 15 and January 22) that boomed in bold type: "Mr. President: Stop the Bombing."[32] On January 16, the day after the first advertisement appeared, the Harvard Crimson reported that the ad was organized by the "Ad Hoc Faculty Committee on Vietnam," which itself "was organized by the Boston Area Faculty Group on Public Issues."[33] A cofounder of the group, MIT biologist Salvador Luria, observed years later on a Web page of the National Library of Medicine of the National Institutes of Health that newspaper ads as a political technique were ideal for an academic constituency because they did not require membership in an organization, the operation was inexpensive if each signer contributed a small amount to the cost of the ad, and ads in major newspapers were often picked up and reprinted in local papers, adding to their visibility. According to Luria, the Boston Area Faculty Group on Public Issues had developed a large efficient network that could activate the collection of signatures on a hundred or more campuses within one or two days. The group's last major ad—protesting President Nixon's reelection campaign as well as the war in Vietnam—was published in 1972.[34]

One month after the massive newspaper protest of President Johnson's war in Vietnam in the New York Times in January 1967 by faculty at the nation's colleges and universities, the New York Review of Books published an essay by Noam Chomsky titled "The Responsibility of Intellectuals,"[35] which, in addition to his political activities, transformed a professor of linguistics at MIT into the intellectual leader of the antiwar movement. Up to this point, February 1967, the New York Review of Books had published some oppositional analysis and commentary on the U.S. military involvement in Vietnam, including by I. F. Stone,[36] Bernard Fall,[37] and Jean Lacouture.[38] For example, in April 1965, in his review of two books about Vietnam by the American journalists Malcolm Browne and David Halberstam, Stone wrote:

> The morning I sat down to write this review, the Washington Post carried
> the news that Malcolm W. Browne had been arrested and held for two hours
> by South Vietnamese Air Force officers at the big U.S. air and missile base at
> Da Nang. The incident is symbol and symptom of the steady degeneration

in the conduct of the Vietnamese war. These two books by two newspaper-men who won Pulitzer Prizes last year for their coverage of the war, Browne for the Associated Press, and David Halberstam for the *New York Times*, record the agony of trying to report the war truthfully against the opposition of the higher-ups, military and civilian. The books appear just as the war is entering a new stage when honest reporting is more essential than ever, but now restriction and censorship are applied to black it out.[39]

In his review of a book about Senator Fulbright, Stone wrote: "Like most of his Senate colleagues, J. William Fulbright was slow to become a critic of our involve-ment in Indochina. In 1954, when [vice president] Nixon was canvassing the Senate privately for intervention, the only Senator to speak up against 'sending American GI's into the mud and muck of Indochina' was the late Ed Johnson of Colorado. One question some future biographer of Fulbright should try to answer is why so informed and enlightened a Senator was so slow to recognize what was really happening." As Stone reported, "Fulbright did not oppose intervention when Eisenhower almost embarked upon it in 1954, or when Kennedy began it in 1961. . . . As recently as the spring of 1964 Fulbright was still far from ready to translate liberal generalities into concrete dissent on foreign policy."[40]

The war correspondent Bernard Fall wrote in March 1967, in a review of two books published in French about the war in Vietnam, that "the best and most balanced reporting on Vietnam today is written by French-speaking writers," because "books which derive from direct contacts with the French-speaking Vietnamese are likely to have a degree of authority and insight which is often quite lacking in much American reporting."[41] The French correspondent Jean Lacouture, in his review of a 1966 book (and film) by James Cameron, *Here Is Your Enemy*, wrote that "Cameron was the first Western correspondent admitted to Hanoi since the beginning of the bombings" to report its effects on the people, society, and economy of North Vietnam. About the film, Lacouture wrote: "On the screen an old peasant woman stands amidst devastated houses and fields; like twenty-five million men and women in both parts of her country she wears black silk pajamas. Her left sleeve hangs empty." About the same woman, who lived in a village near a strategically important bridge, Cameron wrote: "The bridge as far as we know still stands, but the old lady had her left arm blown off by one of the bombs that went astray. She was more fortunate than her daughter, who was killed." In the *New York Review of Books*, Lacouture wrote: "No doubt Cameron's book will be dismissed—as his articles [in the *New York Times* and the *London Evening Standard*] were dismissed by *Time*—as a 'conduit for North Vietnamese propaganda.'"[42]

Thus, by early 1967—with 130 members of the MIT faculty accusing President Johnson of misrepresenting his publicly stated reasons for escalating the war in Vietnam, followed by thousands of U.S. college and university faculty members publicly exhorting the president to "cease all bombing" of Vietnam, to "negotiate with the National Liberation Front," and to "in no way interfere with the free exercise of popular sovereignty in Vietnam,"[43] and with leading political commentators and war correspondents writing about the "self-delusion" of American policymakers on Vietnam,[44] and accusing leading liberal members of Congress of hypocrisy for going along with the war policies of the president[45]—there was palpable public opposition in some quarters to the war in Vietnam when Chomsky published his 13,000-word essay in February 1967.

Writing about the role of intellectuals, Chomsky argued that "intellectuals are in a position to expose the lies of governments, to analyze actions according to their causes and motives and often hidden intentions." And: "In the Western world, at least, they have the power that comes from political liberty, from access to information and freedom of expression. For a privileged minority, Western democracy provides the leisure and the training to seek the truth lying hidden behind the veil of distortion and misrepresentation, ideology and class interest, through which the events of current history are presented to us."

Applying these principles to the Vietnam situation, Chomsky exhorted his readers to "return to the war in Vietnam and the response that it has aroused among American intellectuals," who were viewed either as "responsible" critics for not challenging the presumptive American right to wage war, or "sentimental" or "emotional" by virtue of "their irrational refusal" to accept that "right." Chomsky satirically observed that these "nasty types"—that is, the "irresponsible" or "hysterical" antiwar critics—"are often psychologists, mathematicians, chemists, or philosophers (just as, incidentally, those most vocal in protest in the Soviet Union are generally physicists, literary intellectuals, and others remote from the exercise of power), rather than people with Washington contacts."

Upon rejecting the notion that government officials and foreign policy experts are best qualified to make judgments about when to go to war, Chomsky wrote: "There is no body of theory or significant body of relevant information, beyond the comprehension of the layman, which makes policy immune from criticism. To the extent that 'expert knowledge' is applied to world affairs, it is surely appropriate—for a person of any integrity, quite necessary—to question its quality and the goals it serves."[46]

Two years to the month after the inauspicious protest against the war at the Boston Common in October 1965, the *Boston Globe* published an account of a major antiwar rally scheduled to happen at the Common:

> More than 10,000 Greater Boston and New England college students and teachers are expected to attend the Boston version of a 40-city, nation-wide,

anti–Vietnam War rally on Monday, Oct. 16. Expected to be the largest anti-war demonstration in the city's history, the protest will include a mass rally on Boston Common and a march to the Arlington Street Church for a "Service of Conscience and Acceptance" at which several hundred students are expected to "turn in their draft card." The latest in a series of anti-war protests from the nation's college campuses, the program was announced here Wednesday by a quartet of students. . . .

Speaking at a hastily called press conference at Arlington Street Church, "the quartet [Michael Ferber and William Dowling, graduate students at Harvard University; Neil Robertson, a "Dartmouth dropout"; and Alex Jack, a student at Boston University School of Theology] stressed that they are all currently out of the immediate reach of the draft board [and that the protest at the Common] is one of the major protests against the Selective Service system." It was announced that "the transfer of draft cards from the demonstrations in 40 major cities across the country will be handled by clergymen cooperating with the National Committee of Clergy and Laymen Concerned about Vietnam," and that the "local chairman of the Committee of Religious Concern for Peace is Rev. Harold R. Fray Jr., minister of the Eliot Church in Newton." Speakers at the Boston Common 11 AM rally included Howard Zinn, professor of government at B.U., Noam Chomsky, linguistics professor at Massachusetts Institute of Technology, and Nick Egleson, former president of Students for a Democratic Society.[47]

In his book on the movement to resist the military draft, *Confronting the War Machine: Draft Resistance during the Vietnam War*, Foley described the antiwar rally at the Boston Common:

October 16 [1967] dawned clear and bright. . . . By 10:00 AM, small groups of young people began approaching Flagstaff Hill [on the Boston Common] from all directions. When speeches began at 11:00, over 5,000 people stood or sat on the now-dry grass, listening. Buses filled with students from Dartmouth, Yale, Brown, the University of Rhode Island, the University of Massachusetts, and nearly every Boston-area college circled the Common looking for parking spots. . . . Dozens of people held signs. Some of the slogans included, "Suppose They Gave a War and Nobody Came?"; "The Resistance: Don't Dodge the Draft, Oppose It"; "Wars Will End When Men Refuse To Fight"; "The Resistance Shall Not End"; "UMB [UMass-Boston] Veterans Against the War"; "They Are Our Brothers Whom We Kill"; "No Draft—Don't Enlist—Refuse To Kill." Everyone who addressed the crowd emphasized morality, conscience, and the responsibilities of citizens. Rev. Harold Fray of the Eliot Church in Newton and chair of the Committee of

Religious Concern for Peace stood first before the vast crowd in his clerical robe. "What does it profit a nation," he asked, "to impose its military might upon peoples of the world, while in so doing it loses its soul?". . . Boston University government professor and World War II veteran Howard Zinn strode to the microphone. Zinn, like Noam Chomsky, was by then a well-known critic of the war. He frequently participated in antiwar teach-ins on area campuses, and his recently published book, *Vietnam: The Logic of Withdrawal*, attracted a wide readership. . . . Zinn derided policy makers for trying to save people everywhere from Communism, "whether the people want to be saved or not, and even if they have to kill them all to save them."[48]

William Sloan Coffin, Yale University chaplain and a founder of Clergy and Laity Concerned about Vietnam, also spoke at the rally, and called the U.S. war in Vietnam a crime under international law: "Let us be blunt. To us the war in Vietnam is a crime. And if we are correct, if the war is a crime, then is it criminal to refuse to have anything to do with it?"[49]

Five days later, on October 21, 1967, the legendary antiwar protest commenced against the Pentagon—"the true and high church of the military-industrial complex . . . the eye of the oppressor, greedy stingy dumb valve of the worst of the Wasp heart . . . morally blind . . . destroying the future of its own nation with each day it augmented in strength."[50] In his brilliant account of the one-day siege of the Pentagon—*The Armies of the Night*—in addition to the words just quoted, and re-calling his arrest and time in jail due to his involvement in the protest, Norman Mailer wrote:

> Definitive word came through. The lawyers were gone, the Commissioners were gone: nobody out [of jail] until morning. So Mailer picked his bunk. It was next to Noam Chomsky, a slim sharp-featured man with an ascetic expression, and an air of gentle but absolute moral integrity. Friends at Wellfleet had wanted him to meet Chomsky at a party the summer before—he had been told that Chomsky, although barely thirty, was considered a genius at MIT for his new contributions to linguistics—but Mailer had arrived at the party too late. Now, as he bunked down next to Chomsky, Mailer looked for some way to open a discussion on linguistics—he had an amateur's interest in the subject, no, rather, he had a mad inventor's interest, with several wild theories in his pocket which he had never been able to exercise since he could not understand what he read in linguistics books. So he cleared his throat now once or twice, turned over in bed, looked for a preparatory question, and recognized that he and Chomsky might share a cell for months, and be the best and most civilized cellmates, before the mood would be proper to strike the first note of inquiry into what was obviously the tightly

packed coils of Chomsky's intellections. Instead they chatted mildly of the day, of the arrests (Chomsky had also been arrested with [David] Dellinger), and of when they would get out. Chomsky—by all odds a dedicated teacher—seemed uneasy at the thought of missing class on Monday.[51]

The day after the march on the Pentagon, the *Boston Globe* published a brief news item, "M.I.T. Prof. Arrested on March." It read: "Prof. Noam Chomsky of M.I.T., outspoken opponent of the Vietnam War, was arrested on Saturday during the march in Washington. A Justice Department spokesman said Chomsky had been charged with disorderly conduct. . . . At the professor's home, Mrs. [Carol] Chomsky told The Globe her husband had phoned after his arrest. 'All he said was that he had spent many hours sitting in a police van,' Mrs. Chomsky said."[52]

People in the United States who have opposed aggressive war and the violations of human rights that inexorably go with it have often gone to prison. Two such noteworthy persons are the Berrigan brothers, Philip and Daniel, both Catholic priests. On October 27, 1967, Philip Berrigan, with three others—Thomas Lewis, an artist and organizer of Baltimore Artists Concerned about Vietnam; David Eberhardt, secretary of the Baltimore Interfaith Peace Mission; and James Mengel, a United Church of Christ minister—poured duck's blood, obtained from a Polish market, on Selective Service records in Baltimore in protest against the U.S. war in Vietnam. The same article in the *New York Times* that reported this incident also reported that "last Saturday . . . the Rev. Daniel Berrigan was among scores of persons arrested at the Pentagon for demonstrating against the Vietnam War." In response to the incident involving Philip Berrigan, the Baltimore Archdiocese of the Catholic Church issued a statement, which read in part: "We believe that such actions may be interpreted as disorderly, aggressive and extreme and that they are likely to alienate a great number of sincere men in the cause of a just peace."[53] Philip Berrigan was sentenced to six years in federal prison.[54]

Three years later, in August 1970, and writing about Daniel Berrigan's involvement in another incident, Noam Chomsky, Howard Zinn, and Robert S. Cohen, a professor of philosophy at Boston University, published a letter in the *New York Times*, which began as follows: "Father Daniel Berrigan has been taken away to prison for setting fire to draft board records and declaring, 'Thou Shalt Not Kill.' He was captured by a Government which, in violation of that Commandment, the Constitution, and international law, is carrying on a large-scale slaughter in Southeast Asia." The professors continued: "A government which does not hold sacred the right of its own and other people to life, liberty, and the pursuit of happiness no longer deserves allegiance. This describes the present Government, as it wastes this country's enormous wealth on war, and puts in jail those who protest most strongly. This is why Daniel Berrigan would not submit to its authority, why he calls himself 'a criminal for peace.' We honor him for his deeds of conscience."[55]

Prison in fact did loom for many Americans who "protested the war most strongly." In his political biography of Chomsky, Robert F. Barsky quoted Chomsky's own ruminations about the extent of his antiwar activism, and possibly going to prison:

> I knew that I was just too intolerably self-indulgent merely to take a passive role in the struggles that were then going on. And I knew that signing petitions, sending money and showing up now and then at a meeting were not enough. I thought it was critically necessary to take a more active role, and I was well aware of what that would mean. It is not a matter of putting a foot in the water, now and then, getting it wet and then leaving. You go in deeper and deeper. And I knew that I would be following a course that would confront privilege and authority.[56]

In fact, as Barsky wrote: "Chomsky was to spend long nights in custody and was threatened with lengthy jail terms."[57] One such night occurred on April 17, 1972, as the *New York Times* reported: "Noam Chomsky, an antiwar activist and linguistics professor at Massachusetts Institute of Technology, was among 60 persons arrested today during a peaceful demonstration in front of United Aircraft's Sikorsky Division plant here. They were part of a group of about 200 people—many of them Yale students—protesting Sikorsky's production of transportation and assault helicopters used by American forces in Vietnam. The police carried a number of the protesters to nearby police vans after they ignored orders to refrain from blocking the plant's main entrance."[58]

A month later, ninety-four persons, including Chomsky, were arrested inside the Capitol building in Washington "when they refused to leave in both symbolic and physical protest against the Indochina War." The *Washington Post* reported that "the arrests came at the end of a carefully orchestrated exercise in antiwar street theater designed to show that prominent, middle-aged artists and professionals—not just college students and street freaks—are now willing to be arrested to dramatize their discontent with the war." Those arrested, according to the *Post*, were "folksinger Judy Collins, baby doctor Benjamin Spock, MIT professor Noam Chomsky, actor Howard DaSilva, Mr. and Mrs. Robert Lifton, Yale psychiatry professor and his writer wife, painter Larry Rivers, antiwar activist Marcus Raskin, actress Barbara Harris, poet Kenneth Koch, fashion photographer Richard Avedon, columnist Judith Viorst, and columnist Garry Wills."[59]

The shadow of imprisonment lived with Chomsky, and Princeton professor of international law Richard Falk and Harvard professor Samuel Popkin, throughout the two-year U.S. government prosecution of Daniel Ellsberg under the Espionage Act of 1917 for leaking the Pentagon Papers to the *New York Times*. Ellsberg was a Pentagon and Rand Corporation analyst of the war in Vietnam and, at the time of his arrest, was working at the Center for International Studies at MIT. On June 29, 1971, about two weeks after the *Times* began to publish excerpts and analysis of the Pentagon's secret history of the U.S. war in Vietnam, the *Boston Globe* reported that federal agents had apprehended Ellsberg:

> M.I.T research associate Daniel Ellsberg surrendered to Federal authorities yesterday, and admitted he had distributed copies of a secret Pentagon study of the Vietnam War to the press. "I delivered the Pentagon papers to the Senate Foreign Relations Committee and to the people through the American press," Ellsberg said as he entered the Federal building yesterday morning. He admitted that all these actions were clearly in contradiction of security regulations, secrecy regulations, and, even more, the information practices of the Department of Defense. "Nevertheless, I felt as an American citizen, a responsible citizen, I could no longer cooperate in concealing this information from the American people. I took this action on my own initiative and I am prepared for the consequences."[60]

During or shortly after Ellsberg's trial, which began on January 3, 1973, it was disclosed that Nixon White House operatives G. Gordon Liddy and E. Howard Hunt had burglarized the office of Ellsberg's psychiatrist, Lewis Fielding,[61] that the FBI had wiretapped Ellsberg's telephone communications without a court order,[62] and that John Ehrlichman, President Nixon's chief domestic adviser, in April 1973, had twice met during the Ellsberg proceedings—once in San Clemente and also in Santa Monica—with Matthew Byrne, the federal judge hearing the case against Ellsberg, to offer Byrne the position of director of the FBI.[63] Due mainly to these events, on May 11, 1973, Judge Byrne dismissed all charges against Ellsberg and Anthony Russo, his codefendant.[64]

Between the start and end of his trial, Ellsberg received substantial moral support from the academic community in Cambridge. On October 12, 1971, the *Boston Globe* reported that "four associates of Daniel Ellsberg, including MIT professor Noam Chomsky, have been subpoenaed to testify before a Federal grand jury here [Boston]." The *Globe* continued: "Chomsky, Harvard professor Samuel L. Popkin, Princeton professor Richard Falk, and Howard Webber, director of the MIT Press, will appear tomorrow and Thursday before the grand jury, which is investigating the disclosure of the Pentagon papers."[65] Chomsky and Falk refused to testify on First Amendment grounds. Two days later, on October 14, the *Globe* reported: "Daniel Ellsberg, under indictment for his role in releasing the Pentagon papers, returned to MIT last night with what he described as 'an anarchic and seditious message.' 'If there is one message I have gotten from the Pentagon Papers,' the MIT research associate said, 'it is to distrust authority, distrust the President, distrust the men in power, even Americans in power, because power does corrupt, even Americans.' In his first public appearance at MIT since the publication of the once-secret Pentagon study, Ellsberg was applauded enthusiastically by an audience of more than 1,000."[66]

On October 23, the *Globe* reported that "members of the Cambridge academic community are mounting a First Amendment defense against the threat of involuntary testimony before the Ellsberg grand jury." "Twenty prominent Harvard professors," the newspaper continued, "have prepared affidavits opposing any effort to question Samuel L. Popkin, a Vietnam scholar and known associate of Daniel Ellsberg, unless an overriding interest in his testimony can be shown."[67] In an article two days later, the *New York Times* described Popkin as "a 29-year-old specialist in Vietnamese village life" who "has been to Vietnam three times" and is writing a book about "social forces and peasants" in that country. The *Times* reported that in gathering material for his book, Popkin had interviewed "countless" junior- and senior-level officials in sensitive posts in Washington and Vietnam, and "to appear before a grand jury without restrictions, he contends, would make it very difficult for him to obtain such confidential but legal information in the future."[68] Popkin never did agree to respond to open-ended questioning from the grand jury, was imprisoned for a few days in both March and November 1972, and was released when the federal grand jury in Boston was discharged on November 28.[69]

In January, the Harvard University Faculty Council unanimously condemned the government's interrogation of academics on grounds that "an unlimited right of grand juries to ask any question and to expose a witness to citations for contempt could easily threaten scholarly research."[70] On November 29, the *Globe* reported that "one factor in the decision [to discharge the grand jury in Boston] may have been a meeting in Washington on Friday [November 24] between Assistant Attorney General A. William Olson and Daniel Steiner, general counsel of Harvard University and adviser to [Harvard] President Derek Bok."[71] Upon his release, Popkin said, "I have no more idea today why I was called or what anyone hoped I would say than I did a year ago."[72]

Chomsky and Falk were similarly threatened with contempt-of-court sentences and imprisonment during the life of the grand jury in Boston. After Ellsberg was apprehended and charged in June 1971, the Boston grand jury was impaneled a few months later, and a grand jury in Los Angeles that had already indicted Ellsberg continued to investigate him further. Although, at first, the investigative focus of the grand juries was not clear, a motivation appeared to evolve over time, eventually pointing strangely toward Chomsky and Falk. In January 1972, the *Boston Globe* published a story under the headline, "Justice Dept. May Try to Link Ellsberg to Hanoi," by Sanford J. Ungar, who reported:

The Justice Department introduced a new element of intrigue into the Pentagon papers case 10 days ago when it named a former South Vietnamese ambassador to Washington as an alleged "co-conspirator" in disclosure of the top secret Defense Department history of the Vietnam War. Although it charged him with no crime, a federal grand jury in Los Angeles said that Vu Van Thai, 52, had "confederated" with Daniel Ellsberg and two others to reveal classified information.

The appearance of Thai's name in the new Ellsberg indictment also revived speculation that some of the subpoenas issued by another grand jury investigating the Pentagon papers in Boston may be based on the government's efforts to establish connections with a "foreign power."

Two of the witnesses called to testify there—Noam Chomsky, a linguistics professor at the Massachusetts Institute of Technology, and Richard A. Falk, a professor of international law at Princeton—have had frequent contacts with the North Vietnamese and NLF in Hanoi and Paris.

Both of them are friends of Ellsberg, but have refused to testify before the grand jury about whether they had any knowledge of the Pentagon papers. . . .

Additional indictments in the Pentagon papers case are anticipated in Boston, however, and there, too, the government would presumably be permitted to establish the "intent" of disclosure in part on the basis of inferences that might be drawn from Ellsberg's relationship with Falk and Chomsky.[73]

The investigative "inference" behind the two grand juries was that Ellsberg had engaged in a conspiracy with Chomsky, Falk, and Popkin—all of whom had contacts in the government of North Vietnam and within the National Liberation Front in South Vietnam—with intent to damage the security interests of the United States by leaking the Pentagon Papers to the news media.

Without evidence to support this theory, the government set out to question the three academics before the Boston grand jury without restriction. As a result, all three refused from the outset to testify, even under the threat of imprisonment for contempt of court, as the *Boston Globe* reported: "Popkin, Falk, Chomsky, and others have resisted subpoenas to appear before the grand jury, which they charge is being used to 'fish' for evidence against Ellsberg and to harass his antiwar colleagues."[74] No evidence ever emerged to support the government's theory that Ellsberg had "confederated" with Chomsky and Falk to damage the interests of the United States, nor did the two professors ever testify before the grand jury in Boston.[75]

In fact, there wasn't much in the way of any American interests in Vietnam to damage, as conceded by a key defense department official in the published accounts of the Pentagon Papers. In March 1965, the month in which President Johnson fatefully escalated U.S. military involvement, Assistant Secretary of Defense John McNaughton described 70 percent of the purpose of U.S. military policy in Vietnam as being "to avoid a humiliating U.S. defeat (to our reputation as a guarantor)," 20 percent "to keep SVN [South Vietnam] (and then adjacent) territory from Chinese hands," and 10 percent "to emerge from crisis without unacceptable taint from methods used."[76] At that time, George Ball, an undersecretary of state, prophetically advised that the United States should withdraw its forces "in order to avoid the uncertain but not unlikely prospect of a military defeat at a higher level of involvement."[77] Military withdrawal was precisely the policy advocated by Ellsberg, Chomsky, and Falk, though on legal and humanitarian grounds. One of the ironies of Chomsky's critique of the "New Mandarins"—American university intellectuals and technocrat experts who help devise policy for government officials—is that legalism and humanitarianism more often than not best represent U.S. interests, that is, if those interests include avoiding cataclysmic wars at enormous expense to the public.

Unlike in more recent years, when the United States was engaged in two major wars in Iraq and Afghanistan, Chomsky's work and activities in the late 1960s and early 1970s often received favorable coverage in the *New York Times* and *Boston Globe*. In October 1968—nine months after the January Tet Offensive—the *Times* published a lengthy article titled "A Linguistics Expert Believes That Academics Should Also Be Activists." It began: "In his twenties Noam Chomsky revolutionized linguistics. In his thirties he has been trying to revolutionize society. By his forties—which begin two months from now—there will be few worlds left for him to change. Common to his revolution is the belief that scholars are members of the world around them—and should do something about it." The article by the *Times*' Israel Shenker—a reporter on the metropolitan staff who was described as "a scholar trapped in a newsman's body," and who had also interviewed for the *Times*, in addition to Chomsky, the likes of Jorge Luis Borges, M. C. Escher, John Kenneth Galbraith, Marcel Marceau ("who spoke" as the *Times* noted), Groucho Marx, Vladimir Nabokov, Pablo Picasso, and Isaac Bashevis Singer[78]—continued:

> "Should universities be ivory towers," a visitor asked [Chomsky] recently. "That's like asking 'should professors be human beings?'" he replied. "If they're not human beings they shouldn't be professors. I don't see how a civilized human being in the United States cannot be involved in issues which are tearing society apart and which could destroy the world."
>
> Dr. Chomsky, a professor of linguistics at the Massachusetts Institute of Technology, wrote a seminal article last year in the *New York Review*

of Books entitled, "The Responsibility of Intellectuals." He argued that intellectuals should actively oppose the Vietnamese war.[79]

Shenker's article quoted Chomsky at length, including the following:

"I don't think I should conceal from my students what I am," [Chomsky] says. "[In addition to linguistics,] I also teach undergraduate courses in political and social change. I couldn't possibly teach this course without reflecting my own views. Very often it's a hard decision on whether some form of social act relates to one's university role. One of the reasons I started to teach courses on political and social issues was because my interests and energy were flowing in that direction and I wanted to teach what interested me."

He continued: "I think that a university should look quite favorably on a professor who makes a greater commitment to such matters. The university as an institution should be relatively free of commitment, but individuals in the university should work individually or together for social involvement. This work can contribute to the central goals of a university—which are intellectual and cultural. I don't think the university should encourage us. All we ask is that it give us freedom, and by and large it does."

[Chomsky] is not in favor of total freedom for total political dedication. "If I wanted to spend the dominant part of my time on resistance [against the war], I would leave the university. Similarly, if someone says that he wants to work principally on bombs or counterinsurgency, I think he should leave."

Professor Chomsky has been delighted with the growth of activist student movements, which he feels have "revitalized" the universities. "I think the kids are much more socially involved than the faculties," he said. "I think very healthy things have been going on in the student movements for the past five years, and we owe an enormous debt to the students."[80]

In April 1970, when Chomsky flew to Laos and North Vietnam, the *New York Times* published a report on his trip, beginning as follows: "For four years Noam Chomsky, the scholar in linguistics and antiwar crusader, has filled publications and campus lecture halls with relentless argument against United States involvement in Asia and exhortations to American intellectuals to oppose the war. . . . After repeated invitations from Hanoi, Professor Chomsky made the journey last month, along with Prof. Douglas Dowd of Cornell and the Rev. Richard Fernandez of Clergy and Laity Concerned about Vietnam." Concerning the university in Hanoi at which he spoke (for seven hours), Chomsky said: "I was intrigued and surprised to find the university people did not want to talk about the war, but linguistics—they are still people trying to carry on a normal life. They were eager to know about the math curriculum at M.I.T. and what kind of training was given to graduate students."[81]

From 1969 to 1973, Chomsky published three books about the U.S. war in Indochina—*American Power and the New Mandarins* (1969), *At War with Asia* (1970), and *For Reasons of State* (1973). These books engendered a total of six reviews, mostly favorable, in the *New York Times*.[82] In a March 1969 review of *American Power and the New Mandarins*, Jan Deutsch, a professor of constitutional law at Yale, wrote:

> Noam Chomsky is the Ferrari P. Ward Professor of Modern Languages and Linguistics at M.I.T., and his previously published books include such scholarly titles as *Syntactic Structures*, *Aspects of the Theory of Syntax*, *Cartesian Linguistics*, and *Language and Mind*. He is better known to the public at large and to the readers of *Ramparts*, the *New York Review of Books*, *Liberation* and the *Harvard Educational Review* . . . as one of the most articulate spokesmen of the resistance against the Vietnam War. In the essays on "Objectivity and Liberal Scholarship," "Some Thoughts on Intellectuals and the Schools," and "The Responsibility of Intellectuals," Chomsky develops the nexus between "scholar-experts"—the new mandarins—and the abuse of United States power. Chomsky's concern is not simply that social scientists have participated widely in designing and executing war-related projects. What he finds disturbing are the consequences of access to power by intellectuals; the difficulties involved in retaining a critical stance toward a society that makes the reward of power available.

In his review, Deutsch described Chomsky as "desperately opposed to the war and wholeheartedly committed to the resistance," and quotes Chomsky from the first paragraph of his essay, "The Logic of Withdrawal": "The simple fact is that there is no legitimate interest or principle to justify the use of American military force in Vietnam."[83]

In a review of *American Power and the New Mandarins* published two days later, Thomas Lask of the *Times* wrote:

> The central fact in this collection of historical and political essays and, it would appear in the life of the author, is the Vietnam War. Unlike many others, even those who oppose the war, Noam Chomsky can't stand it and his hatred of what we are doing there and his shame, as well as loathing for the men who defend and give it countenance, are tangible enough to touch. This attitude makes "American Power and the New Mandarins" a

book of unusual temper. Although the evidence against American impe-rialism and its ideology is assembled with cool professorial skill, and the voice is deliberately kept down, the thought is passionate with feeling. And conversely, the feelings of reproach, guilt and frustration found in the book have the force and power of thought.

Although the argument is sophisticated, the author's attitude could not be more simple: we do not belong in Vietnam, we are systematically destroying the Vietnamese people and we should get out. . . . His greatest criticism is aimed not against the military nor the simplistic-minded jin-goists, nor against the commercial interests with stakes in military expenditures or foreign markets. He expects them to behave as they do; it's the nature of the organism. A man like Gen. Curtis LeMay who wants to bomb Vietnam back into the Stone Age receives only passing mention. No, his anger is saved for the "intellectuals," the social and behavioral sci-entists, the academic historians, the policy-planners who defend America's right to impose its conception of order and stability on any spot on the globe and to do it by force.

Lask writes that Chomsky "is especially severe on men like Arthur Schlesinger, Walt Rostow, Roger Hilsman and others, who were close to Washington and played the devil's game."[84]

Almost two years later, in January 1971, Chomsky's second book on U.S. for-eign policy, *At War With Asia*, was reviewed in the *New York Times* by Hans J. Morgenthau, a political scientist at the University of Chicago and an influential proponent of political realism, which is an approach to international relations that emphasizes national security and national interests above moral and legal-istic concerns. Morgenthau had publicly opposed the war in Vietnam since at least April 1965, when he published a lengthy exposition of his views in the *New York Times Magazine*, in which he argued that President Johnson's escalation of the war to North Vietnam would prove ineffective in containing the military and political influence of Communist China on the mainland of Asia, which Morgenthau viewed as the chief U.S. policy goal of the Vietnam intervention. Morgenthau also argued that an American guerrilla war waged against the National Liberation Front in South Vietnam "cannot be won without the active support of the indigenous population, short of the physical extermination of that population."[85] Thus, like Chomsky, Morgenthau was one of the earliest, prominent opponents of the war in Vietnam, although Morgenthau's opposition was grounded in his view that the war could not serve what he deemed to be American interests in Asia, while Chomsky was opposed to any asserted right or national interest as a justification for waging war on the peasant populations of South and North Vietnam.

Accordingly, Morgenthau sympathized with Chomsky's opposition to the war, but harbored a different perspective about the grounds for opposition. Morgenthau thus began:

> American participation in the Indochina war can be opposed from three points of view: the absolute moral one that this kind of indiscriminate destruction of man and nature cannot be condoned on any ground; the deterministic one that this kind of war inevitably derives from a particular economic and political system which must be changed in order to bring that war to an end and prevent new ones of a similar nature; and the pragmatic one that this particular war happens to be indefensible on moral, political and military grounds. The position Noam Chomsky takes here is that of moral absolutism, supported at least by a degree of economic determinism. [Chomsky's] book is an outcry against the absurdity and immorality of the war rather than a sustained argument against it.[86]

Morgenthau appreciates Chomsky's opposition to the war but not his analysis, and thus both praises and disapproves of Chomsky's work. On the upside, as he saw it, Morgenthau wrote:

> The better part of the book consists of three chapters, previously published in the *New York Review of Books*, that report what the author saw and heard on trips to Cambodia, Laos and North Vietnam. These chapters make very interesting reading indeed; for the author is a good listener and observer and an articulate reporter. He gives a vivid and shocking account of senseless destruction rained upon a people of stoic equanimity. . . . [Chomsky] is supported by the factual evidence in his suspicion that the war will go on indefinitely after being made palatable to the American people, that our military presence in South Vietnam is also indefinite, and that the ultimate result of that presence may well be a military confrontation with China. Finally, he is on safe ground in assuming that only massive popular resistance will sway the Administration from its course; but while he seems to end on a note of hope, I despair of that possibility.

On the downside, Morgenthau objected, with little elaboration, to what he called Chomsky's "vulgar economic determinism." He also identified a "moral absolutism that is the driving force of [Chomsky's] book," which "colors his factual reporting," leading to a picture of a political world that is "black and white," and where "vice and virtue are clearly separated and there is never any doubt where they are located." Morgenthau continued: "This simplicity of moral judgment is of course a mere replica of the division of the world into good and evil nations on which ideological anti-Communism thrives, only that the location of the attributes is here reversed."[87]

However, referring to these comments, there is no mention in *At War With Asia* that Chomsky traveled to Cambodia, as Morgenthau claimed. Morgenthau also did not substantiate the alleged black and white, *good v. evil*, outlook in Chomsky's book, beyond Chomsky's principled opposition to the killing and maiming of millions of people in Indochina. And to support the claim of Chomsky's "absolutism," Morgenthau implied that Chomsky had naively endorsed the statement by North Vietnam's prime minister, Pham Van Dong—who met with Chomsky and his colleagues in North Vietnam during Chomsky's trip—that "Hanoi would be permanently satisfied with a neutral non-Communist government in Saigon."[88] But this position was first proposed by South Vietnam's National Liberation Front in 1962, and was modeled after the 1962 Declaration on the Neutrality of Laos (signed by the United States) and the largely successful effort by Cambodia to remain neutral throughout the 1960s. Given the absence at the time of any U.S.-backed blueprint for the reunification of Vietnam, neutrality for South Vietnam, combined with an end to the war, was a desirable and achievable proposition.[89] And by proposing a pull-out of U.S. forces himself—thus leaving only neutrality or unification as realistic political options—Morgenthau held a de facto position similar to Chomsky's on this count.[90]

In his assessment of Chomsky's 1973 book *For Reasons of State*, Christopher Lehmann-Haupt, the prolific reviewer of books at the *New York Times*, broke with the precedent set by the previous reviewers by leading with his criticism of Chomsky and his new book. In doing so, Lehmann-Haupt substituted sarcastic comments for substantive ones, edited Chomsky's lengthy excerpt from Michael Bakunin and by doing so transformed a fiercely eloquent statement into a somewhat hackneyed one, and confuses Chomsky's censure of a privileged intellectual class for its complicity in a war that would kill nearly four million Vietnamese with a reference to trash-toting mortgage-paying householders as if they were the targets of Chomsky's criticism. Thus, in his review titled "The Burden of Reading Noam Chomsky," Lehmann-Haupt began:

> It's a heavy duty reading Noam Chomsky's latest book, a collection of nine essays gathered under the title "For Reasons of State" (which is taken from a statement by Michael Bakunin excoriating the inhuman deeds committed "under no other pretext than those elastic words, so convenient and yet so terrible: 'for reasons of state'"). Heavy duty—because, for example, in an essay examining the conduct of the Berrigan brothers, "On the Limits of Civil Disobedience," Professor Chomsky's logic seems irristible [*sic*]. One may wish to protest that while one disapproved of the war, one had other priorities—there was the family to look after, the mortgage payments

to meet, the garbage to be put out—but Chomsky leaves one feeling like a moral pygmy for not having gone out and destroyed a few draft files.

Furthermore, the *Times'* readers, according to Lehmann-Haupt, were "already familiar with most of the points [Chomsky] makes" in his 140-page opening chapter on the Pentagon Papers. While complaining about the length of Chomsky's chapter and the number of endnotes (237), Lehmann-Haupt also claimed: "We were already aware that the war may well have been illegal constitutionally, that international laws were probably also broken, and that war crimes were perhaps committed. We have heard the argument put dozens of times that Vietnam was a civil war until the Western powers interceded. It does not require all of Chomsky's 140 pages and 237 footnotes to remind us of these points."[91]

In fact, Chomsky's chapter "The Backroom Boys," about the Pentagon Papers, was original and wide-ranging, Lehmann-Haupt's comments to the contrary notwithstanding. In his remarks to start off "The Backroom Boys," Chomsky bundled and itemized as follows the lengthy list of issues that he was about to address:

> The issues raised by the Pentagon Papers fall into several categories. There are, in the first place, questions relating to the public release of the material and the government response: the matter of executive privilege, the scope of the First Amendment, the rights and duties of a citizen (section II). The contents of the study also bear directly on problems of law and conscience and legitimate social action (section III). It is also important to explore the broader lasting value of this collection of documents and analyses as a contribution to the historical record (section IV) and to the understanding of the objectives of American global strategy (section V), as well as for the insight it provides into the mentality of the planners and the functioning government (section VI). All of these matters merit extensive study. I would like to comment on each of them, in the sequence indicated.[92]

Thus it seems that Lehmann-Haupt may have oversimplified the focus of Chomsky's chapter on the Pentagon Papers.

Having put up his complaints, Lehmann-Haupt then moved to post his praise: "Yet, who would deny that [Chomsky] was among the first, and most persistent and profound, critics of the war? Who can ignore that the daily news has been confirming his claims concerning 'The Wider War' [a chapter in Chomsky's book] in Laos and Cambodia—that 'In Laos as in South Vietnam, the United States has been bringing modernization and social and political development with cluster bombs and napalm and bribes for the rich,' and that 'it appears that [this] tragedy . . . is being re-enacted in Cambodia.'" Concluding, Lehmann-Haupt writes that Chomsky "continues to challenge our assumptions long after other critics have gone to bed," and: "He has become the foremost gadfly of our national conscience.

And so, heavy though it may be, it continues to be our duty to read him."[93]

An unsurprising element of these reviews was the resentment from Lehmann-Haupt and Morgenthau about Chomsky's legal and moral opposition to a presumptive American right to militarily attack other countries—a presumption that somehow survived the human catastrophes and the financial costs of the Vietnam War era. Along with other prominent commentators at the time, including Richard Falk[94] and the British philosopher Bertrand Russell,[95] Chomsky viewed the U.S. military actions in Indochina as aggressive war, which is a "crime against peace" and the "the supreme international crime" under the precedent of the prosecution and conviction at Nuremberg of major Nazi war criminals. Writing against the war in Vietnam and the killing of Vietnamese civilians, Chomsky wrote the essay "The Logic of Withdrawal," parts of which first appeared in *Ramparts* in September 1967, with an expanded version published in *American Power and the New Mandarins* in 1969:

> Since 1954 there has been one fundamental issue in Vietnam: whether the uncertainty and conflict left unresolved at Geneva will be settled at a local level, by indigenous forces, or raised to an international level and settled through great-power involvement. Alone among the great powers, the United States has insisted on the latter course. It seems clear that if the United States persists on this course, then either the issue will be settled unilaterally through the exercise of American power, in the manner of Nazi Germany in Poland or the Soviet Union in Hungary, or it will develop into a great-power conflict, with unimaginable consequences.
>
> This is the situation to which Howard Zinn [author of the 1967 book *Vietnam: The Logic of Withdrawal*] has addressed himself in a lucid and compelling study which advocates, very simply, that the United States accept the principle advocated by the other great powers at Geneva in 1954 and agree to turn Vietnam over to the Vietnamese. "The daily toll in Vietnam of innocent people is so terrible that the cessation of our military activity—the bombings, the burning and the shelling of villages, the search and destroy operations—has become no longer debatable or negotiable, but a matter of urgent and unilateral action" [Zinn]. And the only action on our part that can mitigate the torture, that can avert the still greater catastrophe that lies in wait, is to remove the military force that bears the primary responsibility. Since, happily, this is the one policy that we can successfully implement, there is a feasible alternative to devastation of Vietnam or a global conflict.[96]

Had Presidents Johnson or Nixon followed this "simple" advice from two "radical" Boston-area professors, literally millions of innocent lives in Indochina would have been saved, in addition to tens of thousands of American lives; hundreds of millions of dollars of American money would not have been spent to underwrite the killings of the millions that did occur.

Needless to say, the United States did not withdraw from Vietnam in 1967, as Chomsky and Zinn advised. Accordingly, and as Chomsky wrote:

> The savage battering of the Vietnamese continues without pause; in scale, it is unique in the history of warfare. We learn that aerial bombardment alone exceeds 100 pounds of explosives per person, 12 tons of explosives per square mile, distributed almost equally between North and South Vietnam. Hundreds of thousands of acres have been subjected to defoliation, with what ultimate consequences no one knows. Refugees in South Vietnam are counted in the millions. Why have they left their homes? . . . The reason why the people are forced to abandon their villages and their homes is because, in most cases, practically all of the homes are completely burned to the ground by the American forces. However, the people still try to cling to their scorched land, and are removed only by compulsion. . . . Numerous eyewitness reports have given the lie to the cynical pretense that our targets in North Vietnam are purely military, targets of "steel and concrete." The chief editorial writer of *Asahi Shimbun* [a leading newspaper in Japan] writes: "I myself walked around and inspected the bombed remains of schools, hospitals, churches, temples, market places, and other peaceful public facilities."[97]

Chomsky also quoted Ton That Thien, managing editor of the *Vietnam Guardian*, as reported by Christopher Lydon of the *Boston Globe* in one of a series of articles based on Lydon's trip through Vietnam: "You [Americans] cannot defeat the other side militarily unless you devote the next 30 or 40 years to it. You can win if you keep killing for a generation. You simply exterminate all the Vietnamese—the way you killed the Indians in America—and there will be no more war." Lydon himself reported: "This agony, if not utter desperation, among what seemed to me the most sensitive and patriotic Vietnamese, about the burden of American arms on their country, is the overriding impression I carry back from this tortured capital." Chomsky also cited Bernard Fall, who, "in one of his last articles" warned that "it is Viet-Nam as a cultural and historic entity which is threatened with extinction" as "the countryside literally dies under the blows of the largest military machine ever unleashed on an area of this size."[98]

In his 1970 book *At War With Asia*, Chomsky wrote a chapter titled "After Pinkville" about the 1968 My Lai massacre in South Vietnam. As Seymour Hersh reported in 1969 in his original published accounts of the massacres in the *St. Louis*

Post-Dispatch, "Pinkville" was the name given by the U.S. military to the South Vietnamese village Song My, "a Viet Cong stronghold."[99] (Song My was a Vietnamese village containing four hamlets, including My Lai, in which the My Lai massacre took place.) About the American designation for the village, Chomsky wrote that "more than two decades of indoctrination and counterrevolutionary interventions have created the possibility of a name like 'Pinkville'—and the acts that may be done in a place so named."[100] About the massacre, Chomsky wrote:

> Orville and Jonathan Schell have pointed out what any literate person should realize, that this was no isolated atrocity but the logical consequence of a virtual war of extermination directed against helpless peasants: "enemies," "reds," "dinks." But there are, perhaps, still deeper roots. Some time ago, I read with a slight shock the statement by Eqbal Ahmad that "America has institutionalized even its genocide," referring to the fact that the extermination of the Indians "has become the object of public entertainment and children's games." Shortly after, I was thumbing through my daughter's fourth-grade social science reader. The protagonist, Robert, is told the story of the extermination of the [Connecticut] Pequot tribe by Captain John Mason:
>
> > His little army attacked in the morning before it was light and took the Pequots by surprise. The soldiers broke down the stockade with their axes, rushed inside, and set fire to the wigwams. They killed nearly all the braves, squaws, and children, and burned their corn and other food. There were no Pequots left to make more trouble. When the other Indians saw what good fighters the white men were, they kept the peace for many years. "I wish I were a man and had been there," thought Robert.
>
> Nowhere does Robert express, or hear, second thoughts about the matter. The text omits other pertinent remarks: for example, by Cotton Mather, who said that "It was supposed that no less than six hundred Pequot souls were brought down to hell that day." Is it an exaggeration to suggest that our history of extermination and racism is reaching its climax in Vietnam today?[101]

As Chomsky observed at the time, and could also have said about the recent U.S. destruction of Iraq as a cultural and historical entity: "It is not a question that Americans can easily put aside."[102]

3

DERSHOWITZ AT HARVARD, 1967–1973

An early reference to Israel in the writings of Alan Dershowitz, using history as the chronological standard, is a brief account of the acts of "self-defense" by British soldiers involved in the Boston Massacre of 1770. Dershowitz has often defended Israel's military actions in the Middle East, including those that have led to civilian fatalities, by citing "self-defense" on behalf of the Israel Defense Force, as he did in this instance in support of the British occupation forces in Boston.

On March 5, 1770, British soldiers—sent by the King of England to occupy the town of Boston, Massachusetts, a British colony—shot and killed five civilians and wounded six others. No British soldiers were killed or seriously wounded either before or during the shooting. Historians have studied whether the soldiers committed murder, manslaughter, or whether they fired in self-defense in fear of their lives due to the provocations that night by a crowd of Bostonians. This event, known as the Boston Massacre, was ignited by the prerevolutionary, antioccupation ardor that had ripened in the town in the seventeen months since the king's soldiers first sailed into Boston Harbor.

However, in a recent study published by Oxford University Press, historian Richard Archer reported evidence that the lives of the British soldiers were not seriously threatened at the time of the shooting and concluded that "eight armed men [the British soldiers], with nearly a thousand reinforcements close by, deployed in front of an unarmed crowd of 125 that was rapidly diminishing, were not in danger of their lives."[1]

Using Paul Revere's street plan of the massacre, Archer constructed a diagram of the shooting victims on King Street. Crispus Attucks, a sailor and probably the most famous victim of the Boston Massacre, unarmed and "leaning on a stick as he stood on King Street, ten to fifteen feet from the soldiers," was killed with two musket shots to the chest from British grenadiers. Samuel Gray, a rope maker in

Boston, "standing peacefully with his hands inside his coat," was shot in the head and killed "about four or five yards" from the shooters. In a deposition, Bostonian Charles Hobby testified that one of the British grenadiers "pointed his piece directly for the said Gray's head and fired." James Caldwell, a Boston mariner, "was standing diagonally across King Street from the Custom House" from where the British soldiers were shooting "when two bullets struck him in the chest" with fatal wounds. Seventeen-year-old Samuel Maverick, "a bystander" to the events that night, was killed "by an errant bullet" from a British soldier that apparently "ricocheted before striking its victim." Maverick was about one hundred feet from the soldiers. Thirty-year-old Irish immigrant Patrick Carr, while crossing King Street, was shot in the hip and died ten days later.[2]

As for the six wounded Bostonians, Christopher Monk was shot in the back "about 4 inches above the left kidney, near the spine." Edward Payne, a merchant, who "had been standing on the steps of his home, across King Street and slightly east of the Custom House and the soldiers," was shot in the arm. Robert Patterson, a sailor, was shot in the arm as he "stood in the middle of King Street about to place a hat on his head." Tailor John Green and another man, David Parker, were shot in the thigh. Seventeen-year-old John Clark was shot in the groin. Three Bostonians—Edward Hill, Ebenezer Brigham, and Joseph Hilyer—all testified that one of the soldiers aimed at "a lad that was running down the middle of the street, and kept the motion of his gun after him a considerable time, and then fired" but missed.[3]

Upon providing many more details about the shooting by the British soldiers, Archer wrote: "In none of these cases can we know with certainty what a soldier was thinking when he fired his weapon. . . . Perhaps some did believe they were defending their lives or obeying a command, and perhaps a few discharged their weapons immediately after an adjacent comrade had fired. It is just as likely that several of them, without any premeditation, seized the opportunity to vent their frustration and anger at the hostile residents or to attain revenge. Whatever the case, the massacre on King Street was a soldiers' riot."[4]

This is one view of the Boston Massacre; a scholarly one presented throughout in careful and exhaustive detail. Alan Dershowitz, in a 2004 book, *America on Trial: Inside the Legal Battles That Transformed Our Nation*, presented another view, with few details, and which argued that the British occupation forces had fired their guns that night in "self-defense":

> The manner in which an event is characterized by history often determines our collective attitudes toward the culpability of the participants. The so-called Boston Massacre is a case in point. Every American schoolchild learns that British soldiers "massacred" several Bostonians by shooting into a crowd of patriotic protestors. It was the "real" beginning of the American Revolution, the first shots heard round the world.

A review of the actual trial records—there were two trials, the first of the commanding officer, the second of the soldiers—shows anything but an unprovoked massacre. It was much closer to an instance of arguable self-defense by a handful of frightened soldiers, cornered by a violent mob threatening to injure or kill them. Situations like this have arisen throughout history—most recently in Israel and Iraq—where soldiers fire on provocateurs who engage in, or threaten, violence. The term *massacre* should be reserved for cases of unprovoked mass killing against innocent people. To be sure, the Boston case was a close one, but close cases are supposed to be resolved in favor of the defendants—at least by a court of law. The verdict of history may well be different, as it was in this case. History, especially patriotic history, thrives on mythology. And the "Boston Massacre" emerged as one of the canonical myths of prerevolutionary America.[5]

About the Boston Massacre and in the same section on "Colonial America," and paraphrasing while appearing to support what he attributed to the attitude of John Adams, Dershowitz also referred to "the lower-class zealots who had provoked the British officers."[6] Dershowitz also wrote: "The community was divided, and many upstanding citizens of Boston understood that the 'rabble' that gathered in Dock Square on that cold March night with cudgels, ice balls, and other makeshift weapons comprised provocateurs who invited the violence that ensued."[7] The Boston community was indeed divided—between "Patriots" against the British occupation and "Loyalists" to the king—and Loyalists did in fact generally view Patriots as rabble and provocateurs.

Retracing the particulars in these comments: (a) the British soldiers in question were not "British officers," as Dershowitz wrote while invoking the "lower-class" of their victims, but soldiers below the rank of officer, with the exception of Captain Thomas Preston, who did not fire. Thus, Dershowitz mistakenly elevated the social class of the British soldiers who shot eleven unarmed Bostonians, whom he depicted as "lower-class," "rabble," "provocateurs," and "zealots"—designations for Dershowitz that apparently were relevant to his sparse recounting of the facts surrounding the massacre; (b) close cases should be decided in favor of the defense in a court of law out of deference to the presumption of innocence and as a safeguard against the prosecutorial power of the state; yet Dershowitz argued here that we should judge the use of deadly force, as a matter of principle, in favor of the British occupying power, which suffered no casualties of its own; and (c) the notion that Bostonians had provoked the British troops into shooting in "self-defense"—just as Israeli and American soldiers are provoked into shooting Palestinians and Iraqis, respectively, in self-defense—reflects a tendency in Dershowitz's work that gives the benefit of the doubt to those occupying armies over the people they shoot and kill. Furthermore, the sole reference that

Dershowitz cited in his five-page chapter on the Boston Massacre was a book published in 1870[8]—from which Dershowitz extracted mainly a few excerpts of ornate oratory by John Adams—while ignoring the more scholarly work that was available to him at the time, Hiller Zobel's *The Boston Massacre* (1970).[9]

While not wholly unsympathetic to the tactical position of the soldiers relative to the taunts from the Boston crowd that night, Zobel nevertheless described a mass shooting by British soldiers on unarmed Bostonians on the night of March 5, 1770:

> A club arched through the moonlight, squarely catching [British private Hugh] Montgomery. Down on his backside he went, his musket dropping to the ice. Rising to his feet, in agony, rage, frustration, and fear, "Damn you, fire!" he roared, and pulled his trigger. . . . No one seemed to be hit. . . . Between that first shot and the others which followed, there was a definite pause, long enough to order "Recover," which would have stopped the shooting. The estimates of that interval, however, varied from six seconds to two minutes. . . . [Boston town watchman Edward] Langford and [Samuel] Gray standing together watched [British private Matthew] Kilroy raise his weapon. "God damn you don't fire," said Langford. Without aiming, Kilroy fired. Gray, his hands in his jacket pockets, spun around and fell on Langford's left foot. [Bostonian] John Hickling ran to help him; feeling through the gushing blood, Hickling found a hole in Gray's head "as big as my hand." Another shot. Two bullets struck Michael Johnson's [i.e., Crispus Attucks's] chest. He dropped his stick and fell, gasping and struggling, his head in the little gutter running just before the line of Redcoats. Someone suggested going in on the soldiers to prevent their firing again. The mob advanced. More guns fired. The sailor [James] Caldwell was standing in the crowd somewhere toward the middle of King Street. A bullet passed through his body; another lodged in his shoulder. He dropped on the spot. [Robert] Patterson, the veteran of Richardson's siege, caught a bullet in the wrist of his raised right hand. The Irish mob expert, Patrick Carr, was just crossing King Street with shipmaster Charles Connor, heading toward the barber shop on the corner of Quaker Lane. A shot "went through his right hip & tore away part of the backbone & greatly injured the hip bone." As young [Samuel] Maverick fled at top speed toward the Town House, a bullet bounced crazily off some object and somehow struck his chest. He fell, dying. Edward Payne, standing inquisitively in his open doorway, took a bullet in the right arm. . . . Enraged, [British Captain Thomas] Preston asked his men why they had fired. They said they had heard the word "fire," and thought he was ordering them to shoot.[10]

Despite a few concessions to the British shooters—for example, that the British private Kilroy did not aim when he shot Samuel Gray in the head, contrary to Hobby's deposition and the reported fact that Gray was standing a mere ten to fifteen feet in front of Kilroy at that moment—Zobel's account of the relative positions and dispositions of the Bostonians who were shot, like Archer's, indicate that they posed no mortal threat to the British soldiers at the Custom House in Boston. Though Zobel's book was the most scholarly and detailed account of the Boston Massacre available to Dershowitz in 2004, Dershowitz ignored it while claiming that British soldiers shot eleven men in "self-defense."

As for the verbal provocations and petty violence directed at the British soldiers by the crowd of Bostonians on the night of the massacre: several undisputed massacres that have taken place in the West in the twentieth century—including the Bloody Sunday massacre of Irish citizens by British troops in Derry, Ireland, in 1972;[11] the shooting of college students at Kent State, Ohio, in 1970 by Ohio's National Guard;[12] and the government massacre of college students and bystanders at Tlatelolco Plaza in Mexico City in 1968[13]—involved in essence unarmed civilian protests against entrenched injustice, including some level of verbal provocation and nonlethal violence, which was met with deadly fire by the military or police forces at the scene.

Furthermore, Dershowitz provided little context for what led to the confrontation on King Street on the night of March 5, 1770. While he referred to the "rabble" and "provocateurs" who confronted the British soldiers on that night, he did not mention, let alone elucidate, the harsh impacts of the succession of tax laws imposed by the British—the Sugar Act (1764), the Stamp Act (1765), and the Townsend Acts (1767)—without representation in the British Parliament. Nor did Dershowitz mention the Quartering Act (1765), which permitted the billeting of British soldiers in the American colonies, nor the forced impressments by the British navy of American seamen to serve on British naval vessels. The broader context is ably summarized by David Hackett Fischer, a major historian of the American colonial period: "Many Americans most deeply feared and loathed the tyranny of a standing army in their midst. This was specially the case in Boston, where on October 1, 1768, a fleet of British warships anchored in a ring around that unruly seaport, and three regiments of British infantry marched ashore with bayonets fixed. Town-born Bostonians perceived these redcoated regulars as invaders, and saw them as a double threat to liberty from arbitrary power, and freedom to govern themselves as they had always done."[14] Also providing the context of what Bostonians were confronted with prior to the Boston Massacre, Archer wrote: "During the British occupation, one man in three was a [British] soldier. Redcoats were everywhere, on duty and off. Theirs was not a casual or unobtrusive presence. In the streets, along the ropewalks, in the taverns, directly outside the Town House where the main guard was located, at checkpoints, on the [Boston] Common, daytime and night, the people of Boston encountered the representatives of British power."[15] Perhaps given this and other accounts provided by the historians of early New England, if not the one given by Dershowitz, one might make a valid comparison after all between the British occupation of Boston and the Israeli occupation of the Palestinian territories.

One hundred and forty years before the Boston Massacre, the eleven-ship fleet of the Massachusetts Bay Colony, filled with English Puritans, began landing in 1630 near what would become the city of Boston. The founding of the Massachusetts Bay Colony closely followed the establishment of the English colonies at Plymouth in 1623 and Jamestown in 1607. Even before King Philip's War, fought in 1675 and 1676 between New England's Native Americans and the English settlers of New England, the so-called Pequot War—"the first in the long series of New England's Indian wars"[16]—was fought from 1634 to 1638 between the Massachusetts Bay Colony and the Pequot tribe, which had long inhabited the southern Connecticut River Valley.

On May 26, 1637, a Connecticut captain, John Mason, and a Massachusetts captain, John Underhill, with a combined number of several hundred armed men, initiated a brutal and decisive attack on an undefended Pequot village at Mystic, Connecticut. Neal Salisbury, a Smith College scholar of early New England, wrote that "the war's outcome was determined in a pre-dawn surprise attack in the Pequot's Mystic River village while most of the men were away, leaving it in the hands of between 300 and 700 women, children, and old men. Despite the sleeping villagers' inability to mount an effective resistance, Connecticut's captain John Mason ordered the wigwams burned, while the English and their allies sur-rounded the village so as to cut down those trying to flee."[17] Alfred A. Cave, a historian of the Pequot War, wrote that "most of the residents of Fort Mystic were burned alive," with Mason estimating "six or seven hundred" Pequots killed that morning.[18] Another major scholar, Francis Jennings, wrote that "massacre can accomplish the same end [as battle] with less risk, and Mason had determined that massacre would be his objective."[19] Ultimately, as Salisbury wrote, "under the terms of the Connecticut-dictated Treaty of Hartford (1638), the Pequot nation was declared dissolved," and "for many settlers, the Pequot slaughter was the ideological as well as military turning point in the war and in their conquest of New England."[20]

While Dershowitz asserted a right of self-defense of British soldiers to shoot the rebellious "rabble" in Boston, Noam Chomsky, in contrast, has long-defended the rights of the indigenous American population, whose status wasn't merely "lower class" but was barely human as viewed by the English and European settlers and as having almost no rights to their land or lives. For example, about the massacre of the Pequots, which marked the beginning of a 250-year genocidal campaign against the indigenous populations of North America, Chomsky wrote:

> Surely every American child who pledges allegiance to our nation "under God" is instructed as to how the Puritans borrowed the rhetoric and imagery of the Old Testament, consciously modeling themselves on His Chosen People as they followed God's command, "smiting the Canaanites and driving them from the Promised Land" (Salisbury). Who has not shown *hansei* while studying the chroniclers who extolled our revered forebears as they did the Lord's work in accord with the admonitions of their religious leaders, fulfilling their "divine mission" with a pre-dawn surprise attack on the main Pequot village while most of the men were away, slaughtering women, children, and old men in true Biblical style? In their own words, the Puritans turned the huts into a "fiery oven" in which the victims of "the most terrible death that may be" were left "frying in the fire" . . . while the servants of the Lord "gave the praise of God, who had wrought so wonderfully for them."[21]

About the demise of the Native Americans, from the Pequot War forward, Chomsky continued:

> To Theodore Roosevelt, the hero of George Bush and the liberal commentators who gushed over Bush's sense of "righteous mission" during the 1991 Gulf slaughter, "the most ultimately righteous of all wars is a war with savages," establishing the rule of "the dominant world races." The hideous and cowardly Sand Creek massacre [at an encampment of Cheyenne and Arapaho Indians, mostly women and children] in Colorado in 1864, Nazi-like in its bestiality, was "as righteous and beneficial a deed as ever took place on the frontier." The metaphors of "Indian fighting" were carried right through the Indochina wars. The conventions retain their vibrancy, as we saw in early 1991 [in Iraq] and may again, before too long.[22]

"Before too long"—Chomsky wrote these words in 1993—the Clinton administration would bomb Iraq again in 1998. President Bush would invade Afghanistan in 2001 and Iraq in 2003. President Obama would bomb Pakistan, beginning in 2009, and Libya in 2011. Israel, with U.S. political and military support, would bomb the Gaza Strip and Lebanon in 2006, and bomb and invade the Gaza Strip again in December 2008. In each of these contemporaneous episodes, the people who were bombed, invaded, and occupied, and who were killed, were not indigenous Americans but Muslims.

A clear difference between Chomsky and Dershowitz is that Chomsky has sought to make U.S. foreign and military policy—including U.S. policy toward

Israel—conform to U.S. obligations under international law, more specifically, the United Nations Charter, which prohibits the use of force by states, and the Fourth Geneva Convention, which protects civilians in the settings of armed conflict and military occupation. In contrast, in recent years Dershowitz has sought to reinterpret international law to suit the military and occupation-related preroga- tives of the United States and Israel. Chomsky also supports the right to self-determination under the UN Charter, and the right to a nationality under the Universal Declaration of Human Rights, including as applied in both instances to the Palestinians in Israel-occupied territory.

Consistent with his defense of the rights of Native Americans and Palestinians, Chomsky also has defended the humanitarian and human rights of civilian populations around the world. Dershowitz, on the other hand, is in the vanguard of a campaign to modify human rights and humanitarian law to give the United States and Israel—the two countries that he mentions most frequently in this context—more legal and military discretion to target civilian populations, inevitably Muslim populations, in the "war against terrorism." In addition to proposing modifications to humanitarian law and human rights law to suit the strategic policies and military conduct of the United States and Israel, Dershowitz also seeks to weaken fundamental constitutional rights, with the reported goal being to prevent terrorist acts.

It is worth noting that Dershowitz's position today, with regard to international law and U.S. domestic law, is quite different than it was forty years ago, when he supported international law as applied to the U.S. war in Vietnam, defended the Bill of Rights, and opposed the enactment of preventive measures in the United States to thwart crime and terrorism, including opposition to the establishment of preventive detention in Israel, even in the context of a serious threat of Palestinian terrorism. His overall assessment of the issue at the time in an article in *Commentary* magazine is of interest, especially since the same article also led to his first public confrontation with Chomsky and to the contentious rivalry that ensued.

In December 1970, Dershowitz published a lengthy article for *Commentary* titled "Terrorism & Preventive Detention: The Case of Israel." The article to a considerable extent was informative and was delivered in a more deliberative and less accusatory tone that many of Dershowitz's readers today might fail to recog- nize. Dershowitz's position back then on preventive detention was arguably also different. In the *Commentary* piece, he concluded by opposing Israel's twenty-year practice (at the time) of preventively detaining suspected terrorists: "On balance, I favor repeal of the Emergency Defense Regulations [a carry-over law in Israel from the British Mandate that permitted preventive detention]. If Israel feels that it cannot live with the normal rules of evidence in cases of suspected terrorists, then the Knesset [Israel's legislative body] should enact special rules of evidence for a narrowly circumscribed category of cases during carefully defined periods of emergency. All other safeguards should be provided, as in ordinary cases. In the last analysis, such a system might result in the release of some who are now detained. It is in the nature of any judicial system that in order to prevent confinement of the innocent, it must sometimes release the guilty. And those released might engage in acts of terrorism. But risks to safety have always been the price a society must pay for its liberty."[23]

The civil libertarianism expressed by Dershowitz in 1970—for example, that risks to safety are a price a society pays on occasion for its liberty—is a view that he apparently no longer holds. Thirty years later, in a 2002 book *Why Terrorism Works: Understanding the Threat, Responding to the Challenge*, published shortly after the terrorist acts against the United States on September 11, 2001, Dershowitz invoked a long-standing criminal justice standard articulated by the eighteenth-century English jurist William Blackstone, who said: "It is better for ten guilty criminals to go free than for even one innocent person to be wrongfully convicted."[24] Consistent with this notion, Dershowitz observed that "the Supreme Court has repeatedly interpreted the due process clause to require that the prosecution must prove guilt beyond a reasonable doubt," and that "the justices have invoked the [Blackstone] maxim and explained its underlying rationale." Dershowitz also wrote that the Blackstone maxim "has become enshrined among the principles that distinguish nations governed by the rule of law from nations governed by the passions of persons."[25] However, in the context of "rethink[ing] our general approach to balancing security and liberty" as he wrote in 2002, the more contemporary Dershowitz, arguing now for the practice of preventive detention of suspected terrorists, asserts that "with the advent of terrorists using weapons of mass destruction, the calculus may have changed." He thus proposes not only a broad exception to Blackstone's maxim, but to elementary principles of humanitarian law as they pertain to the protection of civilians in the setting of armed conflict (parentheses in original):

> It remains true, in my view, that it is better for ten guilty criminals (even murderers) to go free (and perhaps recidivate on a *retail* basis) than for even one innocent person to be wrongfully convicted. But it does not necessarily follow from this salutary principle that it is also better for ten potential mass terrorists to go free (and perhaps recidivate on a *wholesale* basis) than for even one innocent person to be detained for a limited period of time, sufficient to determine that he is not a potential terrorist. (Nor does it necessarily follow that it is better for ten acts of terrorism to occur than for the home of one innocent supporter of terrorism to be

destroyed.) Numbers do matter, even in principled decisions. It is clearly right to shoot down a commercial jet with hundreds of innocent passengers in it, if the jet is being flown toward a fully occupied large building that cannot be evacuated. It is less clearly right to shoot down that same jet if it is being flown toward the Washington Monument at midnight when only a night watchman is in it. By the same reasoning, it is proper to bomb a military target close to a small number of civilians, but less proper to bomb a similar target adjacent to a large and fully occupied civilian hospital. It is also less unjust to destroy a house in a village in which 95 percent of the residents actively support terrorism than in a village where there is far less support.[26]

Thus, one can see in this preliminary discussion that advocacy of preventive detention may have become a plank of Dershowitz's counterterrorist jurisprudence after all. And a reader might also detect the intellectual defects and ethical unhinging of Dershowitz's "preventive state," with the shooting down of civilian airplanes and all, and the bombing of houses with civilians likely to be inside or nearby.

In his article in *Commentary*, and in addition to describing the circumstances that led him to visit Israel to investigate the case of the preventive detention of Fawzi al-Asmar, an Israeli Arab intellectual, Dershowitz provided a definition of "preventive detention" as "the detention of persons who have not been convicted of any crime." Dershowitz also noted that during the British Mandate, "the Jews bitterly opposed preventive detention" because "many Jewish freedom fighters— including Golda Meir, Moshe Dayan, and others in the present Israeli government—were detained between 1937 and 1948." Dershowitz reported that "the Federation of Hebrew Lawyers convened a protest convention" and vowed, in the words of the lawyers, "to abolish the emergency regulations and restore the elementary rights to the individual." However, in 1948, "when Israel was established as a state, the emergency regulations [from the British Mandate]—including preventive detention—remained on the books, to be used sporadically until the Six-Day War of 1967 and more extensively after Israel's victory and the resulting occupation." Dershowitz continued: "Having long opposed preventive detention in America, I was greatly troubled when I learned of its use by the Israeli authorities. While in Israel, therefore, I decided to try to interview Fawzi and to learn all I could about why he and the other Israeli Arabs were being detained."[27]

Although Fawzi had been in preventive detention without charges for thirteen months when Dershowitz interviewed him in a prison cell in Israel, and although Fawzi denied in his interview with Dershowitz that he was a terrorist, Dershowitz wrote, pursuant to his own personal inquiry, that "I am personally convinced, for whatever that is worth, that Fawzi al-Asmar is the leader of a terrorist group." Contrary to Dershowitz's privately issued findings, Israel released Fawzi two months after his interview with Dershowitz, Fawzi was never arrested or detained thereafter, and there is no public evidence that Fawzi, who is still living as of this writing, ever committed or otherwise played any role in an act of terrorism.[28]

In a letter published in *Commentary* in June 1971, Fawzi disputed the accuracy of much of Dershowitz's article as it pertained to him.[29] So did Felicia Langer, identified by Dershowitz as Fawzi's "Jewish Communist" lawyer in Israel,[30] who wrote in a letter to *Commentary* that she was not Fawzi's lawyer.[31] But the key letter in *Commentary* for our purposes was written by Israel Shahak, chair of the Israeli League for Human and Civil Rights, who submitted a lengthy rebuttal that was sharply critical of Dershowitz's article. To all three letters, Dershowitz's published responses were substantive, but his response to Shahak was the most pointed—a quid pro quo—given that Shahak's letter to *Commentary* was the most contemptuous in its criticism of Dershowitz. In his letter, Shahak concluded:

> Contrary to what Mr. Dershowitz says, the Israeli practice of preventive detention is much worse than the British one. . . . I most emphatically deny Mr. Dershowitz's contention that the "rules" he says he was given about the use of preventive detention (he admits that they are secret) describe the situation. Either he has faked the rules he describes . . . or somebody faked them for him. The advisory committee he refers to [that oversees decisions by the Israeli military about preventive detention] is chosen by the military authorities from among the most abject yes-men . . . mere rubber stamps who almost automatically approve everything that is brought before them and who habitually disregard the gravest and best-founded accusations of beatings and torture. . . . Although I could cite many more examples of Mr. Dershowitz's hypocrisy, lack of knowledge, and even outright distortions, I shall end my rebuttal here. Mr. Dershowitz is not really important in himself, but unfortunately his attitude is typical of several American Jews I have encountered in Israel; their liberalism is, and always was, a fake. . . . In closing, therefore, I should like to say to American Jews: You cannot continue in this way. . . . If you believe in the same justice for Arabs that you demand for yourselves and for your brothers in the USSR, raise your voices and fight for human rights of the Arabs in Israel in exactly the same way. If not, go and worship military force, bow low to [U.S.] Phantoms and tanks, accumulate money—and go to hell.[32]

After responding to specific complaints, Dershowitz concluded his published rebuttal to Shahak as follows:

One final word: In my article I tried to present a fair picture of how a democratic society faced with real danger from within and without has coped with the task of balancing the interests of liberty and security. I concluded by disagreeing with some of the measures adopted by Israel, but—at the same time—by recognizing that no country had ever preserved so much liberty while facing comparable dangers. Dr. Shahak writes as if there were no threat of terrorism—as if the explosions at Machane Yehuda [an outdoor market in Jerusalem] and the Supersol [a supermarket] were contrived by the government for the purpose of curtailing liberties. Some Israeli government officials, on the other hand, speak as if there were no restrictions on civil liberties. Neither view is correct. Civil liberties have, in fact, been curtailed in the face of a genuine threat of terrorism. And it is essential, in my view, that civil libertarians continue to advocate an expansion of freedoms even during these times of crisis. The tragedy is that shrill and intemperate voices—like that of Dr. Shahak—often drown out the voices of reasoned criticism.[33]

Nearly two years later, on April 18, 1973, when the *Boston Globe* published an article based on an interview with Shahak in Cambridge, Massachusetts, Dershowitz responded with a letter to the *Globe* (April 29) that continued the Shahak-Dershowitz debate begun in *Commentary*. Chomsky, a friend of Shahak's, responded to Dershowitz with a letter to the *Globe* (May 17). Dershowitz responded to Chomsky (May 25), to which Chomsky replied (June 5). Thus began the four-decade public rivalry between Chomsky and Dershowitz about Israel-Palestine and related matters.

In the original article (April 18), the *Globe* reported that "the Israeli government is guilty of racial discrimination against non-Jews, Dr. Israel Shahak, chairman of the Israeli League for Human and Civil Rights, charged yesterday," and "chief victims of racial discrimination and harassment are 400,000 Palestinian Arabs, 20,000 Jews and Christians united in mixed marriages, and oriental Jews, according to 40-year-old Shahak, an associate professor of organic chemistry at Jerusalem's Hebrew University." Shahak told the *Globe* that couples in mixed marriages in Israel "are subject to strong harassment," and "in small communities, mobs are encouraged to stand in front of their homes and to shout 'Gentiles and goyim out.'" Shahak also stated that American Jews and the U.S. government "have a responsibility for the racist nature of Israeli society," and that "tax-exempt American dollars raised through the United Jewish Appeal are used by the Jewish National Fund to buy land from the Israeli government, land which is rented only to Jews."[34]

In his April 29 letter, Dershowitz wrote in response to the *Globe*, beginning as follows:

On April 18, you published an interview in which Israel Shahak characterized Israel as a "racist" society. Your reporter described Dr. Shahak as "chairman of the Israeli League for Human and Civil Rights." Shahak is not the chairman of that organization. In 1970, he was overwhelmingly defeated for reelection to that post. When he was chairman of the League, it was a tiny organization composed primarily of members of two Maoist organizations, Matzpen and Rakach (though Shahak himself belongs to neither). As soon as the membership was permitted to expand and include a broader political spectrum—over Shahak's vehement protests—Shahak and his clique were ousted. I suspect that it was not your reporter's fault that he characterized Shahak as current chairman of the League, since Shahak has continued to misinform the public about his status since his ouster.[35]

In the May 17 letter titled "Shahak, a Man of Honor and Principle," Chomsky wrote that Shahak was indeed still chair of the Israeli League for Human and Civil Rights, citing a campaign by Israel's Labor Party to expand the ranks of the League with Labor Party members in order to influence its political orientation and organizational leadership. Chomsky then cited a decision by an Israeli court that declared those party efforts null and void, thus preserving Shahak's position as chair. Chomsky noted that these were the events that Dershowitz had erroneously interpreted when he claimed that the League membership was permitted to expand to include a broader political spectrum and that Shahak thereafter had been ousted as chair.[36] On May 25, Dershowitz responded:

I was not surprised at the belligerent tone of Noam Chomsky's response (May 17) to my letter regarding Israel Shahak (April 29). Though Chomsky and I have been allies in numerous cases, I have seen over the years that Chomsky will stop at nothing in attacking those who support Israel or in defending those who attack it. As evidence of that, consider his statement that the Israeli courts declared the League for Human Rights election void and that "the leadership of the League remains as before under Israeli law." That is totally false. The truth is that the Tel Aviv District Court, in an opinion by Judge Levenberg [sic], ruled that the election was legal and that Shahak had been validly defeated. I challenge Chomsky to cite me any documentary evidence to the contrary![37]

Chomsky replied by quoting directly from the documentary record, which is what Dershowitz had challenged him to do:

In a further attempt to discredit the Israeli League for Human Rights and its chairman, Israel Shahak, Alan Dershowitz asserts (May 25) that "the Tel Aviv District Court, in an opinion by Judge Lovenberg, ruled that the election (of Nov. 16, 1972) was legal and that Shahak had been validly defeated." He challenges me to cite "any documentary evidence to the contrary." I quote from the opinion of Judge Lovenberg, Nov. 26, 1972: "The meeting called for Nov. 16, 1972, in the opinion of the Court, was not held properly, and no conclusions or actions are to be drawn from it." On April 8 [1973], Judge Lovenberg reaffirmed that the results of the November meeting "were not recognized as binding by this Court." . . . I have the Court documents in my possession, and will gladly show them to any interested person.[38]

This response ended the Chomsky-Dershowitz letter exchange in the *Boston Globe*, with Chomsky having met Dershowitz's challenge to prove that Shahak at the time still chaired the Israeli League for Human Rights. In his autobiography *Chutzpah*, published in 1991,[39] Dershowitz does not mention this exchange of letters with Chomsky in the *Boston Globe*. But in his first biographical study of Chomsky and his work, *Noam Chomsky: A Life of Dissent*, Robert Barsky wrote about the aftermath of the exchange of letters in the *Globe*:

> Chomsky became the lightning rod for the pro-Israel lobby: he was seen as the anti-Zionist, the pro-Arab, the anti-Semite. This, of course, was not all. His criticism of American policies in Vietnam and Cambodia had alienated him from establishment intellectuals and politicians; his condemnation of Cold War policies had led to his ostracization by the proponents of America's "free world" vision. Those bent on questioning or ignoring him persisted in their efforts. Edward Herman claims that, as a consequence of his refusal to toe the line, Chomsky's work was "subjected to an ongoing and intense scrutiny for any literal errors or bases of vulnerability, a scrutiny from which establishment experts are entirely free. This search was perhaps more intense in the United States and among its allies in the late 1970s and early 1980s, with a growing body of hard-liners anxious to overcome the Vietnam syndrome, revitalize the arms race, strengthen support for Israel's rejectionism and policy of force and involve the United States in more aggressive actions towards the Soviet bloc and Third World."[40]

Barsky also cited a 1992 reference by Chomsky to the exchange of published letters with Dershowitz in the *Globe*, where Chomsky wrote that Dershowitz has "been on a personal jihad [against Chomsky] for the last twenty years, ever since I exposed him for lying outright in a vicious personal attack on a leading Israeli civil libertarian. Despite pretenses, he's strongly opposed to civil liberties."[41] The exchange of letters in the *Globe* thus marked the beginning of a Cambridge-based academic rivalry—not merely in personal terms but, more importantly, in the mutually antagonistic substance of their work.

While Dershowitz observed in the *Boston Globe* in 1973 that he and Chomsky "ha[d] been allies in numerous cases," there is little public evidence to support that claim, although both Chomsky and Dershowitz opposed the U.S. war in Vietnam and elsewhere in Indochina, but did so in different venues and in different ways. They rarely crossed paths or cooperated in protests against the war. In a detailed and lengthy book on the draft resistance movement by Michael S. Foley *Confronting the War Machine: Draft Resistance during the Vietnam War*, which is focused to a significant degree on the Boston area in the 1960s, Chomsky is featured while Dershowitz is not mentioned.[42] In Barsky's two biographies of Chomsky, *Noam Chomsky: A Life of Dissent* (1997) and *The Chomsky Effect: A Radical Works Beyond the Ivory Tower* (2007), there is no mention of any collaboration between Chomsky and Dershowitz. Nor is there mention of any such collaboration in Dershowitz's *Chutzpah*.

Nevertheless, there is substantial evidence that Dershowitz opposed the U.S. war in Vietnam, and that he had engaged in high-profile opposition to what was widely viewed as an assault by the Nixon administration on constitutional rights and liberties. From October 1969 to March 1971, Dershowitz signed at least three petitions and one open letter, in each case with other Harvard law professors or Boston-area lawyers, calling for an end to American combat operations and a full withdrawal of U.S. military personnel from Vietnam, and later from Cambodia and Laos.

In October 1969, nearly seven hundred "members of the legal profession in greater Boston," including Derek Bok, Stephen Breyer, Archibald Cox, Robert Drinan, Laurence Tribe, Hiller Zobel, and Dershowitz, paid for and signed a full-page ad in the *Boston Globe*, which declared: "The time has come to end American combat operations and to withdraw the American military presence in Vietnam." Referring to the nationwide demonstrations against the war, the ad stipulated: "We join the NATIONAL MORATORIUM ON VIETNAM, OCTOBER, 15, 1969, protesting continued prosecution of the War, and urge upon our Government the following views, which all of the undersigned share." These views included that "military victory cannot be our goal in Vietnam" and "hope that a face-saving formula may emerge from the Paris Talks cannot justify further fighting and deaths in Vietnam."[43] An estimated two million people participated in the "Moratorium to End the War in Vietnam" in 1969, including a hundred thousand demonstrators on the Boston Common.[44]

Six months later, on April 22, 1970, the same number of "Lawyers of Greater Boston," including Dershowitz, in a full-page ad in the *Globe*, proclaimed that "[o]ur Government should put into effect at once a plan for the orderly cessation THIS YEAR of all American military operations in Vietnam and neighboring countries."[45]

Less than one month later, on May 14, 1970, "approximately 90 percent of the Faculty of the Harvard Law School," including Dershowitz, signed an open letter to the U.S. Congress, published in the *Globe*, which demanded that the United States "Quit Vietnam." The letter stated in part:

> The recent American military action in Cambodia and the recent new bombing of North Vietnam has further eroded our confidence and deepened our concern. . . . As both teachers and parents we have watched the progressive disillusionment of a generation who have received no convincing answer to the question why they should be required to kill and be killed in Vietnam. As citizens we have witnessed the substantial distraction of the energies of young and old away from urgent needs at home and abroad. As lawyers we have observed the alarming damage that accumulating frustrations over Vietnam and its consequences have begun to inflict on traditions of respect for law and mutual forbearance.

The Harvard lawyers thus asked the members of Congress to support pending legislative proposals that "promote a speedy, consistently pursued withdrawal of American forces from Indo China."[46]

As the war continued, Boston-area lawyers again paid for and signed another display ad in the *Boston Globe*, this one in March 1971. As in previous petitions published in the *Globe*, Dershowitz endorsed this ad, which read in full:

> We, the above signed members of the LEGAL PROFESSION in Greater Boston, urge that the Administration:
> • Stop enlarging the war area;
> • Stop all U.S. participation in new ventures which cause war casualties, American or Vietnamese;
> • STOP THE WAR by announcing an early, fixed withdrawal deadline for all U.S. military personnel in Indochina.
> *We urge* the Congress to use all of its Constitutional powers to these ends.
> *We endorse* the following statement:
> "We cannot condone a policy which merely withdraws ground troops while we are continuing to wage a war by other means which are less vis-ible to the American public but nonetheless devastating to the people who are being bombed and whose countries are being destroyed. The U.S. does not have the right to use firepower to determine who shall govern in Vietnam, Cambodia, or Laos. We see no justification for using aerial bom-bardment throughout Indochina, sacrificing Asian lives to save our prestige while shielding our sensibilities from the moral consequences of our war policy."[47]

Dershowitz also came within range of the views of a group of U.S. legal scholars, led by Richard Falk, Albert G. Milbank Professor of International Law and

Practice at Princeton University, who opposed the U.S. war in Vietnam on international law and constitutional grounds. The group of U.S. legal scholars on Vietnam, in addition to Falk, included Hans Morgenthau (University of Chicago), Quincy Wright (University of Chicago), Wallace McClure (Duke University), William G. Rice (University of Wisconsin), Richard S. Miller (Ohio State University), Burns H. Weston (University of Iowa), and John H. E. Fried (City University of New York).

In 1967, these professors issued *Vietnam and International Law*, a study of the legality of the U.S. war in Vietnam. After concluding that U.S. military actions in and against Vietnam violated the prohibition in the UN Charter against the use and threat of force by states, the law scholars argued further, as follows, that the war also violated the U.S. Constitution: "The United States Constitution considers ratified treaties to be the supreme law of the land and therefore considers any violation of such a treaty a violation also of the Constitution." Given that the threats and use of force against Vietnam violated the UN Charter—a treaty ratified by the United States—the law scholars argued that neither the president nor the Congress could declare or conduct a war that was illegal under the charter without also violating the U.S. Constitution. The law scholars thus observed:

> We have argued that the war actions of the United States in North and South Vietnam violate treaties to which the United States has become a party by due constitutional process. Above all, these war actions violate the Charter of the United Nations, of which the United States was a principal architect. Because these actions violate the supreme law of the land, the question as to which branch of the Government may authorize them, or whether one branch of the Government may delegate to another branch legal powers to authorize them, becomes irrelevant. No branch of Government is permitted directly or indirectly (by delegation) to violate the Constitution.[48]

Three years later, in March 1970, Dershowitz, along with nineteen other legal scholars, including all those listed previously (Falk et al.), endorsed a bill sponsored by State Representative James Shea of Newton, Massachusetts, that challenged the constitutionality of the U.S. war in Vietnam on grounds, as stated by Hans Morgenthau, that "the President, no less than the humblest citizen, should have to obey the law." The bill "would give any Massachusetts citizen the right to ask the state attorney general to act to prevent his assignment to a combat zone in the absence of a declaration of war."[49] In addition to Dershowitz, the Shea-sponsored bill was supported by the two Democratic candidates for governor of Massachusetts that year, Kenneth O'Donnell and Boston mayor Kevin White, and was signed (after it passed the Democrat-controlled state legislature) by the Republican governor of Massachusetts, Francis Sargent.[50] This alignment between

Dershowitz and the leading international law scholars listed earlier, including Richard Falk, was only temporary. Later, as he did with Chomsky, Dershowitz would lash out at Falk about his views on the Israel-Palestine conflict, although it wasn't the legal and political views of Chomsky and Falk that had changed.

Although, to my knowledge, Dershowitz never issued a scholarly assessment of the U.S. war in Vietnam in the context of international law and the U.S. Constitution—certainly not one to rival the exhaustive and important legal analysis issued by the aforementioned law scholars, chaired by Falk—it is worth pointing out that of the nearly seven hundred "members of the legal profession in Greater Boston" who paid for and signed a full-page ad in the *Boston Globe* in October 1969, stating their opposition to the war in Vietnam, Dershowitz was one of only two Boston-area lawyers from that number (the other was Peter Donovan of Boston College) to support the Massachusetts state challenge in March 1970 to the constitutionality of the American war in Vietnam.[51]

Finally, in addition to signing the antiwar petitions and open letters, and supporting the Massachusetts constitutional challenge, Dershowitz, according to *Time* magazine, founded a course at Harvard Law School on the war. On March 1, 1968, *Time* reported:

> "Viet Nam is the most significant social, political, and legal issue of the day," said Harvard Law Professor Alan Dershowitz last week. "And a law school should be concerned with the issues of the day." Dershowitz had just finished giving the first class in a brand-new, ten-week Harvard course entitled "The Role of the Law and the Lawyer in the Viet Nam Conflict." It has no exam or grades, offers no credit, and involves a good deal of reading over and above the students' already regular work load. But it has a record enrollment of more than 400—one-quarter of the student body—and is one of the most popular courses in the 150-year history of the school. The course will cover such questions as the international-law aspects of the war, the division of war-making responsibility between the President and Congress, free speech and dissent, the draft and the rights of an inductee, and the status of a conscientious objector to a specific war.

The *Time* article concluded by reporting that "a notably quiet antiwar petition is currently being circulated at a number of law schools, urging lawyers 'to work for a change in every legitimate way they can,'" and that one of the petition signers was Dershowitz, "founder of Harvard's Viet Nam course."[52]

In addition to opposing the war in Vietnam, Dershowitz publicly opposed government efforts to violate the civil liberties of antiwar activists. Not long after the draft-resistance convictions of Dr. Benjamin Spock and his alleged "Boston

Five" coconspirators—William Sloane Coffin, Mitchell Goodman, Michael Ferber, and Marcus Raskin—were overturned (Raskin was never convicted),[53] Dershowitz wrote a review of a book about the affair for the *New York Times*. Spock and his codefendants were prosecuted by the Nixon administration for aiding and abetting resistance to the draft in violation of a 1965 law that, among other things, prohibited the burning of draft cards.[54] Though the defendants were charged with conspiracy, they apparently didn't know each other very well. In his review of the book by Jessica Mitford, *The Trial of Dr. Spock*, Dershowitz wrote "even after the indictment, when the five defendants met for the first time to plan their legal strategy, Leonard Boudin, Spock's brilliant and courageous lawyer, felt it necessary to introduce the 'conspirators' to each other."[55]

Quoting Mitford, Dershowitz concisely summarized her view of the trial: "The conspiracy prosecution of Dr. Benjamin Spock, author and pediatrician, was a national disgrace." Dershowitz agreed, and generally supported Mitford's notion that the prosecution was politically motivated with the intention of weakening U.S. opposition to the war in Vietnam by undercutting the First Amendment rights of the war's opponents. Dershowitz himself concluded:

> The fact that five men who barely knew each other were indicted for a contrived conspiracy, the nature of the indictment and the various comments of the prosecutor, in the trial and to the press, all lend credence to the theory that an intended effect of the conspiracy charge was to stifle organized public opposition to the war. The Spock prosecution represented a deliberate effort to frighten away scores of opponents of the war who might consider signing statements like the "Call [to Resist Illegitimate Authority]," attending demonstrations like the one at the Pentagon [in 1967], or organizing efforts to help young people who had decided not to serve.[56]

Dershowitz also noted that the government hinted at additional conspiracy charges to penetrate what it viewed, in Dershowitz's words, as "a loosely knit, widespread and uncircumscribed conspiracy." In this context, Dershowitz noted, with apparent unease: "Another hint, this time not so subtle, about the scope of the conspiracy was dropped by the prosecutor when he described Noam Chomsky, professor of modern languages and linguistics at M.I.T., who was among the signers of 'A Call To Resist Illegitimate Authority,' as a person 'not sitting at the bar as a defendant' (impressive pause) '*today*.'"[57]

In September 1972, Dershowitz also wrote an influential op-ed piece for the *Boston Globe* titled "The Erosion of Our Rights," in which he defended the Bill of Rights and warned against the threat to it posed by the Nixon administration: "The American Bill of Rights, our most precious national resource, is in the process of being significantly eroded. The civil liberties of all Americans—the right to be free from unwarranted government intrusion, to speak critically of those in power, to be treated fairly and with due process—have been seriously curtailed over the past few years." Dershowitz continued at length: "The First Amendment's 'Right of the people to assemble and to petition' was emasculated when the Government indiscriminately rounded up more than 10,000 war protesters, most of whom, as the courts later held, were engaging in entirely legal behavior. Freedom of speech and the press has also been endangered by the Vice President's [Spiro Agnew's] thinly veiled threats against the broadcast media, whose licenses are regulated by the Federal Communication Commission. Most recently, the Vice President referred to authors of certain encyclopedia articles critical of the President as 'latter-day Goebbels of the radical left.'" In the same op-ed piece, Dershowitz accused the Nixon administration of "tak[ing] aim at the Fourth Amendment's protection against unreasonable searches and seizures," and for "audaciously claim[ing] to be exempt from the requirement that a court approved warrant be obtained before it may tap or bug conversations involving the national security; and it has defined national security in the most expansive way possible, to include American citizens engaged in what the Administration regards as radical activities." Dershowitz then noted that "in 1969 and 1970 alone, more than 40,000 days of tapping and bugging were conducted without court approval" and that "the number of innocent conversations illegally monitored in recent years is truly staggering." "The Fifth and Sixth Amendments," continued Dershowitz, "have fared no better." He wrote: "The privilege against self-incrimination and the right to counsel—the bulwarks of our adversary system of justice—may well become dead-letter if the Administration succeeds in its expressed goal of abrogating the rule under which illegally obtained evidence is excluded from trial, the only effective protection against unlawful police behavior." "The Eighth Amendment's right to reasonable bail has also been undercut by the Administration's preventive detention law, which authorizes the imprisonment of suspects not because of what they have done, but because of what it is predicted they might do at some future time," Dershowitz wrote, while adding that "the implications of preventive imprisonment based on future predictions are frightening to contemplate."

Dershowitz also protested that the Nixon administration, "more than any other in recent history, has adopted and encouraged the rhetoric of repression" as "the Vice President promiscuously lumps together for condemnation 'the whole damned zoo of dissenters, malcontents, radicals, incendiaries, and civil and uncivil disobedients.'" Dershowitz observed that "equating dissenters with incendiaries constitutes an unthinking and contagious attack on the very essence of the Bill of Rights."

Dershowitz then wrote a fitting summation: "Finally, and most important, there seems to be a mood of repression, of intolerance in the air. We, the American people, seem to have lost some of the vigilance that we have traditionally exercised in defense of sacred rights. It is as if we all believed that we have become permanent members of the majority whose rights will never need safeguarding, as if the Bill of Rights was designed, not to protect us, but to protect some vague group called 'them.' But 'we' are 'them.' If not today, then perhaps tomorrow. If not ourselves, then perhaps our children. We owe it to ourselves to see that our noble experiment with liberty, our Bill of Rights, is kept strong as we enter our third century of nationhood."[58] This op-ed piece in the *Boston Globe*, published in September 1972, perhaps as much as any single document that he has written, identified Dershowitz in the public eye as a spirited defender of constitutional rights and civil liberties.

Only eight days later, on the occasion of the new judicial term of the U.S. Supreme Court, an editorial in the *Boston Globe* cited the September 25 Dershowitz commentary on the Bill of Rights as follows: "[I]n the session that just opened yesterday, it will be the Supreme Court itself that will be on trial as the defender of fundamental liberties which rarely have been under such attack as now. As Professor Alan M. Dershowitz of the Harvard Law School stated on this page Sept. 25, 'the Bill of Rights is in greater danger today than it has been in decades.'"[59]

Three months later, in a 1,500-word editorial, the *Globe* published a more detailed reference to the September 25 op-ed piece by Dershowitz, referring to the original Dershowitz commentary four times.[60] The *Globe* began:

> How much do the people have a right to know? Merely to ask the question in the world's freest country is to answer it: Just about everything there is to know. But some people in government and elsewhere would not agree. And so, today, the public's right to be informed by a free press under the protection of the First Amendment is under the strongest attack in our nation's history. . . . Only last fall, Harvard Law School Prof. Alan Dershowitz documented in the Globe what he called the erosion of liberties guaranteed by five of the 10 Bill of Rights Amendments.[61]

The *Globe*, like Dershowitz, argued in defense of the Bill of Rights in response to a number of incidents, as the newspaper described them:

> • The Nixon administration had "rounded up 12,000 war protesters in the 1971 May Day peace demonstration in Washington." Although "the courts later held that almost all of them were engaged in entirely legal behavior . . . all were arrested and confined for up to 62 hours in a ball-park, in jam-packed police cells, and in the Coliseum on vague charges or none at all, and without legal counsel except for government and other attorneys who themselves were caught in the net" in violation of the First Amendment's "right of the people peaceably to assemble, and to petition

the government for a redress of grievances." The courts dismissed the arrests and detentions as "illegal, injudicious, and a charade."

• The Nixon administration "claimed to be exempt from a court warrant before it tapped or bugged conversations involving the national security" in violation of the Fourth Amendment's protections against "unreasonable searches and seizures." The *Globe* reported that "more than 40,000 days of tapping and bugging were conducted without court approval in 1969 and 1970 alone, said Dershowitz" in his September 1972 op-ed piece.

To describe its next two grievances against Nixon, the *Globe* editorial simply cited Dershowitz:

• "The Fifth and Sixth Amendments' protection against self-incrimination and for right to counsel and a fair trial could vanish, said Dershowitz, if the [Nixon] Administration succeeds in trying to abrogate the rule under which illegally obtained evidence is excluded from trial."

• "The Eighth Amendment's right to reasonable bail has been undercut, said Dershowitz, by the [Nixon] Administration's preventive detention law allowing imprisonment of suspects not because of what they have done, but because of what it is thought they might do. This year-old law, operative only in the District of Columbia, has been used only 20 times or so, but its implications of preventive imprisonment are frightening."

The *Globe* editorial also levied several complaints against the Nixon administration for its attempts to intimidate the press in response to press criticisms of the administration. This included requests to the television networks from the Nixon-appointed chair of the Federal Communications Commission to submit transcripts of the networks' commentaries on President Nixon to the FCC and "to make TV stations responsible" with proposed legislation that included this warning from the FCC chair: "Station managers and network officials who fail to act to correct imbalance or consistent bias in the networks—or who acquiesce by silence—can only be considered willing participants, to be held fully accountable . . . at license renewal time." This stance by the *Globe* on the Nixon administration's attacks against the press and the First Amendment also reflected the same criticism of the administration by Dershowitz in his September 1972 op-ed piece.[62]

A few years earlier, in 1969, two editorials in the *Boston Globe* and one in the *New York Times* cited Dershowitz as an authoritative opponent of preventive detention. In January, the *Globe* editorial reported with concern that "the Nixon administration is quietly studying the use of preventive detention as a means of dealing with the problem of crime committed by accused persons who have been released on bail pending trial." In opposing this measure, the *Globe* cited a 1951 U.S. Supreme Court case, *Stack v. Boyle*, which "lucidly set forth the rationale" behind the Eighth Amendment's bail clause: "This traditional right to freedom before conviction permits the unhampered preparation of a defense, and serves to prevent the infliction of punishment prior to conviction. . . . Unless this right to bail before trial is preserved, the presumption of innocence, secured only after centuries of struggle, would lose its meaning." The *Globe* also argued: "One of the practical difficulties [of revoking any right to bail] was recently pointed out by Prof. Alan M. Dershowitz of the Harvard Law School in testimony before the [U.S.] Senate Subcommittee on Constitutional Rights. He noted that there would be no sure way of knowing what percentage of defendants denied bail as bad risks would not have committed crimes if they had been released on bail."[63]

Two months later, in March 1969, a *New York Times* editorial, citing proposed changes to the code of criminal procedure for the state of New York, pointed out "some of its questionable, harsh sections," including "bail and detention." The proposed change in bail and detention "would permit a judge to consider whether an accused would be a danger to society if he were released pending trial on criminal charges—especially in cases of forcible rape and arson." The editorial noted that "Prof. Alan Dershowitz of Harvard Law School holds that the proposed criminal code would permit imprisonment without evidence," while also observing that "Prof. Abraham S. Goldstein of Yale Law School says that pretrial detention, once legitimated, is likely to develop a life of its own and would do 'irreparable harm to the presumption of innocence.'"[64]

And in August 1969, a *Boston Globe* editorial, in yet another condemnation of President Nixon's proposed preventive detention of "dangerous hardcore recidivists," began with this passage from *Alice in Wonderland*, where Alice learned from the Queen that "preventive detention is difficult to disparage effectively":

> "There's the King's Messenger (said the Queen). He's in prison now, being punished, and trial doesn't even begin till next Wednesday; and of course the crime comes last of all."
> "Suppose he never commits the crime?" asked Alice.
> "That would be all the better wouldn't it?" the Queen responded.
> Alice felt there was no denying that. "Of course it would be all the better," she said: "But it wouldn't be all the better his being punished."
> "You're wrong . . ." said the Queen. "Were you ever punished?"
> "Only for faults," said Alice.
> "And you were all the better for it, I know!" said the Queen triumphantly.
> Alice thought, "There's a mistake somewhere—"

The *Globe* observed: "Harvard Law School Prof. Alan M. Dershowitz, citing this colloquy on preventive detention in the *New York Review of Books* some time ago, pinpoints the wrongness of Mr. Nixon's proposal with compelling logic."[65]

That was then. Today, unfortunately, the record as presented in this volume shows that Dershowitz is not the advocate of human rights and civil liberties that he once was. Then, expressing his public views about the war with his signature attached to open letters and other such petitions, Dershowitz applied international law and human rights as critical criteria of U.S. foreign policy. Today, Dershowitz heatedly criticizes those who apply the same critical criteria to Israel's policies in the occupied Palestinian territories and the wider Middle East region. Then, Dershowitz referred to the Bill of Rights as "our most precious national resource," which guaranteed "the civil liberties of all Americans" and "the right to be free from unwarranted government intrusion" and "to be treated fairly and with due process." Today, Dershowitz is an advocate of a counterterrorist "jurisprudence of prevention and preemption" in the United States,[66] including a greatly diminished Bill of Rights and the similitudes of an authoritarian state, featuring preventive detention and torture at home, and the extrajudicial killing of suspected terrorists and preemptive and preventive wars abroad. Since these may be controversial assertions, it seems fair to permit Dershowitz to explain at some length in his own words.

In his 2006 manifesto of the counterterrorist preventive state—*Preemption: A Knife That Cuts Both Ways*, where he lays out the new thinking on terrorism, counterterrorism, human rights, and civil liberties—Dershowitz begins by introducing a number of hypothetical scenarios: "If reliable intelligence determined that a large-scale terrorist attack in your city were highly likely during the next few weeks, and it also pointed to a particular suspect, would you support the preventive detention of that suspect for a period of time—say, a month—until it could be determined whether he or she was, in fact, planning the attack?"; and, "What type and level of interrogation would you authorize to elicit the information necessary to prevent the attack?"; "If arrest were not feasible because the suspected terrorist was hiding in an enemy country, would you support his targeted assassination if that were the only way to stop the attack?"; "What if the attack could be prevented only by a military strike against a terrorist base in a foreign country?"; "What if a full-scale invasion were required?"[67] And so on. At the conclusion of this exercise, Dershowitz explained:

> The democratic world is experiencing a fundamental shift in its approach
> to controlling harmful conduct. We are moving away from our traditional
> reliance on deterrent and reactive approaches and toward more preventive

and proactive approaches. This shift has enormous implications for civil liberties, human rights, criminal justice, national security, foreign policy, and international law—implications that are not sufficiently considered. It is a conceptual shift in emphasis from a theory of deterrence to a theory of prevention, a shift that carries enormous implications for the actions a society may take to control dangerous human behavior, ranging from targeted killings of terrorists, to preemptive attacks against nuclear and other weapons of mass destruction, to preventive warfare . . . to prior restraints on dangerous or offensive speech, to the use of torture (or other extraordinary measures) as a means of gathering intelligence deemed necessary to prevent imminent acts of terrorism.

Although the seeds of this change were planted long ago and have blossomed gradually over the years, it was the terrorist attack against the United States on September 11, 2001, that expedited and, in the minds of many, legitimated this important development. Following that attack, the former attorney general John Ashcroft described the "number one priority" of the Justice Department as "prevention." The prevention of future crimes, especially terrorism, is now regarded as even "more important than prosecution" for past crimes, according to the Justice Department. In his confirmation hearings of January 5, 2005, Attorney General Alberto Gonzales reiterated that the administration's "top priority is to prevent terror attacks." The tactics that have been employed as part of this preventive approach include tighter border controls, profiling, preventive detention, the gathering of preventive intelligence through rough interrogations and more expansive surveillance, targeting of potential terrorists for assassination, preemptive attacks on terrorist bases, and full-scale preventive war.[68]

In a statement recognizing that many of these post–9/11 preemptive and preventive actions are or were illegal, Dershowitz wrote: "We are doing all this and more without a firm basis in law, jurisprudence, or morality, though there certainly are historical precedents—many questionable—for preventive actions."[69]

A few pages later, and now speaking specifically about preventive detention, Dershowitz continued:

Part of the reason for our neglect of the issues surrounding prevention is the mistaken assumption that any form of preventive detention would be alien to our traditions. Lord Justice Denning, one of the most prominent common law jurists of the twentieth century, purported to summarize the irreconcilability of preventive punishment with democratic principles: "It would be contrary to all principle for a man to be punished, not for what he has already done, but for what he may hereafter do." It may be contrary to all principle, but as we shall see, it is certainly not contrary to all practice.

The shift from responding to past events to preventing future harms is part of one of the most significant but unnoticed trends in the world today. It challenges our traditional reliance on a model of human behavior that presupposes a rational person capable of being deterred by the threat of punishment. The classic theory of deterrence postulates a calculating evildoer who can evaluate the cost-benefits of proposed actions and will act—and forebear from acting—on the basis of these calculations. . . . Among the most frightening sources of danger today are religious zealots whose actions are motivated as much by "otherworldly" costs and benefits as by the sorts of punishments and rewards that we are capable of threatening or offering. The paradigm is the suicide terrorist, such as the ones who attacked us on September 11. We have no morally acceptable way of deterring those willing to die for their cause, who are promised rewards in the world to come. . . . They are in some respects like "insane" criminals who believe that God or the devil told them to do it. Because they are not deterrable, the argument for taking preventive measures against them becomes compelling.[70]

About preemptive war, which Dershowitz notes is "limited to imminent threats," and preventive war, which has to do with "longer-range but relatively certain dangers,"[71] and after citing examples of descriptions of such wars from the Bible and *The Decline and Fall of the Roman Empire* by Edward Gibbon,[72] Dershowitz cited the perspectives of Machiavelli and Hugo Grotius, and gave some examples of modern state practice, all shining a flattering light on preemptive and preventive wars:

Not surprisingly, Machiavelli approved of the Roman approach to preemptive war: "The Romans did in such matters what all wise rulers ought to do. It is necessary not only to pay attention to immediate crises, but to foresee those that will come, and to make every effort to prevent them." He urged his prince to analogize military dangers to medical ones:

For if you see them coming well in advance, then you can easily take the appropriate action to remedy them, but if you wait until they are right on top of you, then the prescription will no longer take effect, because the disease is too far advanced. In this matter it is easy to cure, difficult to diagnose; but, after a while, if it has not been diagnosed and treated early, it becomes easy to diagnose and hard to cure. So, too, in politics, for if you foresee problems while they are off (which only a prudent man is able to do) they can easily be dealt with; but when, because you have failed to see them coming, you allow them to grow to the point that anyone can recognize them, then it is too late to do anything.

Machiavelli commended the Romans for always looking ahead and taking "action to remedy problems. . . . They never postponed action to avoid war, for they understood that you can not escape wars, and when you put them off only your opponents benefit."

Hugo Grotius, one of the founders of international law, argued that preemptive military action is justified whenever waiting would impose too high a price. He supported preventive measures designed "to kill him who is making ready to kill." Other leading lights of international law "recognized that states were not obligated to 'receive the first blow, or merely avoid and parry those aimed at [them]' but were rather entitled, at natural law, to engage in preventive war 'even though [an enemy] has not yet fully revealed his intentions. . . .'"[73] [Dershowitz continued by citing other proponents of preemptive and preventive war.[74]]

Although he observes at the beginning of *Preemption* that it was the terrorist attacks on 9/11 that had pushed the United States toward a more preemptive and preventive orientation,[75] the focus of Dershowitz's work shows that his interest in these issues seems to lie principally with constructing a framework legal defense of Israel's chronically illegal policies and transferring that framework to the United States for its adoption in both a domestic and foreign policy context. For example, in *Preemption*, Dershowitz writes:

Our [U.S.] military had carefully studied the actions of other nations, especially Israel, because it was one of the few modern democracies that had employed preemption successfully, particularly at the beginning of the Six-Day War in 1967, and had then employed prevention in its successful attack against the Iraqi nuclear reactor in 1981. Moreover, Israel had adopted preemption and prevention as important elements in its overall defense strategy.

Perhaps because of its small size, the nature of the threat posed by its surrounding neighbors, and its inability to secure the assistance of the United Nations, Israel, more than any other modern, democratic nation, has served as a laboratory for contemporary preventive and preemptive actions. Some have been widely approved by objective scholars, while others have been condemned. Many fall into intermediate categories. A review of some of Israel's anticipatory actions—the good along with the bad—will provide insights into the challenge of constructing a jurisprudence of prevention.[76]

Thus, Dershowitz developed his jurisprudence of terrorism prevention for the alleged benefit of the United States to a good extent from his perceptions of the legality and morality of Israeli policy. A major focus of this volume, then, is to assess Dershowitz's perceptions of the legality and morality of Israeli policy, and thereby evaluate the appropriateness of his legal and moral framework for adoption by the United States.

PART II
AGGRESSIVE WARFARE → TERRORISM

4

AGGRESSIVE WARFARE → TERRORISM → COUNTERTERRORISM → AUTHORITARIANISM

The thesis of this volume is that major *violations of international law*[1] by the United States and Israel against the Muslim world engender Muslim *terrorism* targeted at the United States and Israel, and that U.S. efforts to *counter terrorism* without ending its own violations of international law threaten to transform the United States into an *authoritarian* state. This idea can be expressed more economically as follows: Aggressive Warfare[2] → Terrorism → Counterterrorism → Authoritarianism. While Chomsky has asserted that violations of the human rights of Muslims engender terrorism targeted at the United States, Dershowitz has advanced a different theory of the Muslim terrorist, where such terrorists act in ahistorical spaces outside the realm of human reason and thus beyond the reach of the *deterrence-based* law-enforcement institutions of the Western world. Dershowitz has equated this notion to a "wild lion" theory of Muslim terrorism.[3]

To prevent Muslim terrorism, then, Dershowitz supports a *prevention-based* system of law enforcement—a "jurisprudence of prevention"[4]—which he has drawn for the most part from the Israeli model of counterterrorism and recommends for adoption by the United States. This highlights the obvious clash between Dershowitz's post–9/11 jurisprudence and the traditional view of civil liberties in the United States, as this volume will show.

While assigning virtually no relevance to the historical or personal experiences of Muslim communities, Dershowitz's ideological orientation is similar to that which exists in Israel, as described by *Ha'aretz* reporter Amira Hass: "For us, the Israelis, history always begins when the Palestinians hurt us, and then the pain is completely decontextualized."[5] Chomsky issued a similar assessment of the ideological orientation within the United States in his book *9-11*,[6] which was issued shortly after the terrorist attacks in New York and Washington on September 11, 2001. With respect to both U.S. and Israeli policy, Chomsky has examined numerous "contextual" (historical) events relevant to the Muslim point of view: Israel's annexation of East Jerusalem in 1967 and its military occupation of the West Bank and Gaza Strip since then;[7] the U.S. bombing of Iraq in 1991;[8] the U.S.-led economic sanctions against Iraq in the 1990s;[9] the 2001 U.S. invasion and occupation of Afghanistan;[10] the 2003 U.S. invasion and occupation of Iraq;[11] the numerous U.S.-supported Israeli uses of armed force in the Mideast region, including the various invasions, bombardments, and military occupations of Lebanon (in 1978, 1982, and 2006), the bombardment of Gaza in 2006 and the air-land invasion of Gaza of 2008–09;[12] the long-term "administrative detentions" of hundreds of Palestinians inside Israel; the U.S.-supported Israeli embargo of the Gaza Strip; the long-term indefinite detentions of suspected Muslim terrorists at Guantanamo Bay;[13] and the missile attacks with aerial drones on individuals in Afghanistan, Pakistan, and Yemen.[14] All of these U.S. or U.S.-supported actions have targeted Muslim populations and include the "excess deaths" of 500,000 Muslim children five years of age and younger due to the U.S.-led UN embargo of Iraq throughout the 1990s.[15] While Chomsky properly has not invoked these events to justify any acts of terrorism against American and Israeli civilians, it is disingenuous to imply, as Dershowitz does, that these actions by the United States and Israel would leave Muslims unaffected, with no motivation for violent retaliation and revenge.

Avram Noam Chomsky was born in Philadelphia in 1928, where he earned a PhD in linguistics from the University of Pennsylvania in 1955. As his MIT biography notes, Chomsky was a Junior Fellow of the Harvard University Society of Fellows (1951–1955) when he completed his doctoral dissertation in 1955, with "the major theoretical viewpoints" of it "appearing in the monograph *Syntactic Structures*, which was published in 1957," and which "formed part of a more extensive work, *The Logical Structure of Linguistic Theory*, circulated in mimeograph in 1955 and published in 1975."[16] In 1959, the journal *Language*, issued by the Linguistic Society of America, published Chomsky's "A Review of B. F. Skinner's *Verbal Behavior*."[17] About *Syntactic Structures* and Chomsky's critique of Skinner, *The Oxford Companion to Philosophy* observed: "Noam Chomsky, American linguist and philosopher whose pioneering work on language, *Syntactic Structures* (1957), and devastating 'Review of B. F. Skinner's *Verbal Behavior*' (1959), led to the cognitive revolution, and the demise of behaviorism, in psychology."[18]

As Chomsky's MIT biography also notes, he joined the faculty of the Massachusetts Institute of Technology in 1955, and in 1961 was appointed full professor in the Department of Modern Languages and Linguistics (now the Department of Linguistics and Philosophy). From 1966 to 1976 he held the Ferrari P. Ward Professorship of Modern Languages and Linguistics. In 1976 he was appointed Institute Professor—the highest honor that MIT awards to a member of its faculty.

From 1958 to 1959 Chomsky was in residence at the Institute for Advanced Study in Princeton, New Jersey. Chomsky delivered the John Locke Lectures at Oxford in 1969, the Bertrand Russell Memorial Lecture at Cambridge University in 1970, the Nehru Memorial Lecture in New Delhi in 1972, and the Huizinga Lecture in Leiden in 1977. Chomsky also has received honorary degrees from Harvard University, Columbia University, the University of Chicago, the University of Pennsylvania, Georgetown University, the University of Massachusetts, the University of Connecticut, Loyola University of Chicago, Amherst College, Swarthmore College, Bard College, McGill University, the University of Toronto, the University of Western Ontario, Cambridge University, the University of London, Delhi University, the University of Calcutta, the University of Buenos Aires, Universidad Nacional De Colombia, Universitat Rovira I Virgili, Tarragona (Spain), and Scuola Normale Superiore, Pisa (Italy). He is a Fellow of the American Academy of Arts and Sciences and the National Academy of Science, a recipient of the Distinguished Scientific Contribution Award of the American Psychological Association, the Kyoto Prize in Basic Sciences, the Helmholtz Medal, the Dorothy Eldridge Peacemaker Award, and the Ben Franklin Medal in Computer and Cognitive Science. Chomsky also has written and lectured widely on linguistics, philosophy, intellectual history, contemporary issues, international affairs, and U.S. foreign policy.[19] Concerning his publications in academic journals on linguistics alone, MIT lists 196 articles authored or coauthored by Chomsky.[20] Under the heading "Linguistic Books by Noam Chomsky," MIT lists thirty-three books.[21] Overall, Chomsky has authored and coauthored over one hundred books.[22]

In 1992, in an article titled "Chomsky Is Citation Champ," *MIT News* reported that scholarly references to Chomsky's work in the Arts and Humanities Citation Index between 1980 and 1992 "make him the most cited living person in that period and the eighth most cited person overall," just behind the Austrian psychoanalyst Sigmund Freud and just ahead of the German philosopher G.W.F. Hegel, with "the top ten cited sources during that period [being] Marx, Lenin, Shakespeare, Aristotle, the Bible, Plato, Freud, Chomsky, Hegel and Cicero." *MIT News* also reported that "from 1972 to 1992, Chomsky was cited 7,449 times in the Social Science Citation Index—likely the greatest number of times for a living person there as well," and that from 1974 to 1992 "he was cited 1,619 times in the Science Citation Index."[23]

Alan Morton Dershowitz was born in Brooklyn in 1938, where he graduated from Brooklyn College in 1959. Three years later, Dershowitz graduated first in his class from Yale Law School, where he was editor of the *Yale Law Journal*. After clerking for David Bazelon, chief judge of the United States Court of Appeals for the District of Columbia, and U.S. Supreme Court Justice Arthur Goldberg, Dershowitz was hired as an assistant professor by Harvard Law School in 1964, thereafter becoming full professor in 1967 at the age of twenty-eight, the youngest full professor in the history of the law school. He has held the Felix Frankfurter chair at Harvard since 1993.[24]

According to Dershowitz's Web site, he has taught courses in criminal law, psychiatry and law, constitutional litigation, civil liberties and violence, comparative criminal law, legal ethics, human rights, the Bible and justice, great trials, and neurobiology and the law. Dershowitz also has been awarded honorary degrees and medals from Yeshiva University, Syracuse University, Hebrew Union College, the University of Haifa, Monmouth College, Fitchburg College, and Brooklyn College. The Anti-Defamation League of B'nai B'rith presented him with the William O. Douglas First Amendment Award for his "compassionate eloquent leadership and persistent advocacy in the struggle for civil and human rights." The New York Criminal Bar Association honored Dershowitz for his "outstanding contribution as a scholar and dedicated defender of human rights." And the Lawyers' Club of San Francisco has honored him as a "Legend of the Law." Dershowitz also "has lectured throughout the country and around the world to more than a million people—from Carnegie Hall to the Kremlin." In 1979 he was awarded a Guggenheim Fellowship for his work in human rights. In 1981 he was invited to China to lecture and consult on their criminal code. He returned to China in 2001 to lecture to lawyers and law students. In 1987 he was named the John F. Kennedy-Fulbright Lecturer and toured New Zealand lecturing about the U.S. Bill of Rights. In 1988 he served as Visiting Professor of Law at the Hebrew University in Jerusalem and lectured in Israel on civil liberties during times of crisis. In 1990 he was invited to Moscow to lecture on human rights.[25]

Dershowitz has authored twenty-four nonfiction and three fiction books.[26] He also has authored or coauthored more than one hundred articles in magazines and journals,[27] including eleven in law journals.[28] He has written over one thousand opinion articles,[29] including these post–9/11 pieces: "Targeted Killing Vindicated" (about the killing of Osama bin Laden, 2011), "The Hypocrisy of 'Universal Jurisdiction'" (2009), "Targeted Killing Is Working, So Why Is the Press Not Reporting It" (2008), "The Geneva Conventions: Enabling Terror Through Rules of War" (2004), "Killing Terrorist Chieftains Is Legal" (2004), "Stop Winking at Torture and Codify It" (2004), "Rules of War Enable Terror" (2004), "The Straw Man Argument against Extra-Judicial Killings of Terrorist Leaders" (2004), "The Laws of War Weren't Written for This War" (2004), "Edward Said: The Palestinian Meir Kahane" (2003), "UN Sends Message That Terrorism Is OK" (2003), "Chomsky's Immoral Petition" (2002), "Is Torture of Terror Suspects Ever

Justified?" (2001), "Is There a Torturous Road to Justice?" (2001), "The Parallels between U.S. and Israel on Terror" (2001), and "Big Brother Where Art Thou? Rethinking Liberty in the Age of Terrorism" (2001).

By his own account, Dershowitz would like to see the United States transformed into a "preventive state"[30] with a reinvented jurisprudence that would facilitate counterterrorist methods that have been traditionally viewed as unconstitutional in the domestic context and violations of international law in the foreign policy setting. Although, obviously, the United States government needs to protect its citizens, cities, and infrastructure from terrorist attacks, Dershowitz's "preventive state" would likely increase the threat of terrorism while undermining the Bill of Rights. In a 2008 interview, Dershowitz spoke at length about his jurisprudence of the preventive state:

> My current life work has been to try to find the jurisprudence that constrains what I call the "preventive state." The state now is moving much more from reacting to violence—deterring people from committing violence by punishing those who've already done it—to a proactive, preemptive, preventive mode. Moving in. Stopping people from doing it. Preventive detention such as that which exists in Guantanamo and many other places around the world today. Preventive intelligence gathering. The use of cyberspace and picking up of conversations in space. The use of preventive interrogation, including torture. All of these things are part of one of the most important and yet unwritten about phenomena in the world. The preventive state. The state moving in early. Trying to anticipate. The state moving in against sexual predators. The state moving in against potential terrorists. And what I've been trying to do is construct a jurisprudence for that phenomenon.[31]

Although Dershowitz asserts here that his mission is to "constrain" what he depicts as the ineluctable momentum in the United States toward a preventive state, further reading demonstrates that Dershowitz in fact supports such a change, and that his intention "to construct a jurisprudence for" and to "regulate"[32] the preventive state are aspects of his overall efforts to see it formally legalized.

At the moment, Dershowitz recognizes that the contemporary frontiers of the preventive state—including preventive surveillance, preventive detention, preventive interrogations, preventive assassinations, and preventive wars, all of which are now employed or advocated by the United States (and Israel) to one degree or another—violate traditional American law; yet, Dershowitz is remarkably tolerant of these innately unconstitutional practices and writes about them mostly as an advocate of their legalization and regulation. This is evident in the same interview, where he continued at length:

> My large project, which I have been working on for probably—since 9/11 in the short term but almost all of my professional life in the long term—is this notion of the preventive state. That the Constitution, and our legal system, was built on the premise that we wait until people commit crimes, then we indict them, and prosecute them, give them all the due process safeguards, apply a standard of "better ten guilty go free than one innocent be wrongly convicted." We've worked on that jurisprudence for thousands of years. The Bible was based on that jurisprudence; Christian legal systems and theology [are] based on that system; Islamic and Anglo-American and Western [law], in general.
>
> But we're seeing a paradigm shift. We are now not able, it is thought, to wait until the crime is committed, particularly if the crime is a nuclear attack, a terrorist attack with biological weapons, with chemical weapons; sexual predators running rampant, drunken drivers killing people on the streets. All these potential dangers and harms have moved us ever closer so subtly, but very, very discernibly, toward the preventive state, where the state is empowered to move in before you've done any of these terrible things, and to try to stop you from doing them in advance.
>
> "An ounce of prevention is a worth a pound of cure." "A stitch in time saves nine." We all know the clichés. But how do you turn those clichés into a jurisprudence? Is it better for ten potential nuclear terrorists to go free than for one potential suspect to be detained for six months while we check out and see whether in fact he is a terrorist? The mantra of "better ten" doesn't really work.
>
> Can we hold people? And for how long can we hold them? And under what circumstances can we hold them because we strongly suspect that they are planning to do something terrible? If we can hold them, what can we do to them? Can we punish them? Can we coerce them? Can we make them provide information, real-time information, to help us prevent these terrible acts? If so, by what means? . . . Can we create profiles, whether they be based on ethnicity, race, and religion, or a combination of factors which include but aren't limited to these kinds of crude predictors? How good are we at predicting? How do we test the accuracy of our predictions? . . .
>
> The courts are going to have to come to grips with these issues, and they don't have a clue as to how to begin, because there is no on-the-ground jurisprudence that can deal with this developing phenomenon.
>
> Our legal system traditionally has been based on a theory of deterrence. You threaten punishment and if somebody does a criminal

act you punish them. You do something to them that they don't want to have happen to them. You put them in prison. You execute them, in extreme cases. The new paradigm of suicide terrorism makes our system of deterrence very hard to operate, especially coupled with individual guilt and individual responsibility. You could deter terrorism if you punish the families of the terrorist, but we can't do that because we believe in individual guilt. So the combination of the use of deterrence and the requirement of individual guilt makes it impossible for us to use the traditional legal methods and legal threats against suicide terrorists. That's why we need to move in preemptively. That's why we have to stop it from happening before it happens. . . .

So that's the problem. We haven't figured out a solution to that because our usual approach to the rule of law doesn't work. We need to create a new rule of law to govern the use of suicide terrorism.[33]

Although, by his own words, the preventive state clashes with enlightened Western legal traditions, Dershowitz gradually drops his nominally descriptive narrative of the preventive state and observes in his own right that "our usual approach to the rule of law doesn't work" with respect to suicide terrorism, and that "we need to create a new rule of law to govern the use of suicide terrorism."

In addition to the U.S. domestic setting, there is a substantial international dimension to Dershowitz's preventive state. Thus, in the same interview, and with respect to the suicide terrorist around whom he would like to construct a new jurisprudence of prevention for the United States, Dershowitz said:

Without trying to analogize humans to animals in any moral sense, when you have a person who will not fear death and will not stop from doing anything because of the threat of punishment, you really have to treat that person the way you would treat a wild tiger, or a wild lion. You don't reason with a lion. You don't try to deter a lion. You stop the lion by either building a cage between you and the lion or by disabling the lion or killing the lion. And that method has been adapted to the use against suicide terrorism.[34]

Dershowitz here is addressing the challenge of deterring a would-be suicide terrorist who is not deterrable by the deterrence-based jurisprudence of Western law, given that a suicide terrorist by definition would not survive to face any trial or punishment. The remedy, for Dershowitz—which he asserts has already "been adapted to the use against suicide terrorism," is to "cage" or "disable" or "kill" the suspected terrorist *prior* to the terrorist act—resembles Israel's policy toward the occupied Palestinian territories, including the Gaza Strip, where the human inhabitants are literally "caged" by a fence around the entire perimeter of the strip,[35] "disabled" by a brutal economic embargo,[36] and "killed" via Israel's policy of extrajudicial killings and repeated military invasions and incursions.[37] Dershowitz defends such measures by writing commentary such as "Terrorism Causes Occupation, Not Vice Versa"[38] and "The Palestinian Leadership Is Responsible for the Continuing Israeli Occupation of the West Bank."[39]

These views, like much of Dershowitz's commentary, are at odds with a nearly unanimous international consensus about the causes of anti-American and anti-Israel terrorism, including as presented in a 1987 UN General Assembly Resolution on "measures to prevent international terrorism," approved by a vote of 153 to 2 (the United States and Israel cast the two votes in dissent). The resolution asserted that "the underlying causes" of terrorism "lie in misery, frustration, grievance and despair and which cause some people to sacrifice human lives, including their own, in an attempt to effect radical changes."[40] Chomsky, in contrast to Dershowitz, supported the resolution and its findings, and rebuked the United States and Israel for opposing it.[41] The issue, then, of the causes of terrorism targeting the United States and Israel, and the policy remedies to prevent such terrorism, is a major source of disagreement between Chomsky and Dershowitz.

5

ON SEPTEMBER 29, 2000

The assertion by Alan Dershowitz, that the Bostonian "provocateurs" got what they deserved from the occupying forces of the British empire on the night of the Boston Massacre, would be little more than a minor nuisance to the revolutionary history of the United States if it hadn't foreshadowed the Harvard law professor's far more serious infidelity toward the great achievement of the American Revolution—the Bill of Rights. How did it come to pass that Dershowitz, who once described the Bill of Rights as "our most precious national resource," and who opposed the U.S. war in Vietnam, would devise a jurisprudence for a counterterrorist "preventive state" that would maximize the police, military, and surveillance powers of the United States?

The answer can be found to a good extent in Dershowitz's writings about the Israel-Palestine conflict—which has been the predominant focus of his work since the 9/11 terrorist attacks on the United States—and in his views in that context on state power and terrorism. Indeed, Dershowitz wrote his 2006 manifesto of the counterterrorist preventive state, *Preemption*, in his capacity as Israel's chief public defender in the United States. Dershowitz, in effect, touted that role himself with the prosecution/defense format of his 2003 book *The Case for Israel*, with Dershowitz pleading the defense case for Israel in response to the work of Noam Chomsky, Edward Said, and other critics of Israel. And the point of *Preemption* was to lay out his Israel-influenced jurisprudence for preventing terrorism and to recommend it for adoption by the United States and other Western democracies. However, the argument here is that Dershowitz's defense of Israel's Mideast policies, and the development of a jurisprudence of prevention derived largely from the counterterrorist practices of the Israeli government, should not be viewed as transferrable to the United States, given that the Dershowitz-made law derived from Israel clashes fundamentally with human rights abroad and long-standing American liberties at home. The purpose of this chapter is to present a case study of these claims by looking at how Dershowitz depicted the events that occurred before and after September 29, 2000, and how that depiction influences the terrorism-prevention jurisprudence that he seeks to apply to the United States.

Longtime U.S. presidential advisor Dennis Ross, in his 2004 book *The Missing Peace: The Inside Story of the Fight for Middle East Peace*, provides one of the most detailed accounts of events that began in earnest with the Camp David summit in July 2000—involving Israeli prime minister Ehud Barak, Palestinian chairman Yasser Arafat, and President Clinton—the failure of which led to the start a few months later of the Second Palestinian Intifada[1] on September 29, 2000. Ross's account of events is of special interest here, not only because he was the chief U.S. negotiator under the Clinton administration for the Israeli-Palestinian talks, but also because he is a major source in Dershowitz's own books and articles about the important events that occurred during those last several months of Bill Clinton's presidency.

One page before describing the events that led to the course-changing confrontation of September 28–29 at the Haram al-Sharif / Temple Mount in the Old City in East Jerusalem, Ross reported that he had personally lobbied Israeli and Palestinian government officials in Washington a few days earlier to continue the talks that had broken down during the Camp David summit in July. Ross noted that just before the negotiators arrived, "Arafat visited Barak at his home" in Israel and that "both sides reported that the meeting was very warm."[2] In his 2008 book *The Much Too Promised Land*, Aaron Miller, a U.S. negotiator at Camp David on Ross's team, reported that "in late September [2000], before the outbreak of the second intifada, [Barak] would have his best meeting with Arafat ever, and negotiations continued."[3] Ross also reported that Barak and Arafat "called President Clinton before concluding their evening, with Barak telling the President, 'I will be a better partner with the Chairman [Arafat] than even [former Israeli prime minister] Rabin.'" About the cordiality, Ross wrote that "it was in this seemingly hopeful setting that the negotiators arrived for three days of discussions" starting September 26, 2000. Ross also wrote that "little did I know that these three days [September 26–28] would mark probably the highest hopes for peace during my tenure—and that a descent into chaos and violence would soon follow."[4] Given these accounts, it is likely that neither Barak nor Arafat expected what was about to break out on September 29.

Indeed, looking back, Ross wrote: "At the time, there was one development that Palestinians say transformed everything: Ariel Sharon's visit to the Haram al-Sharif / Temple Mount. Sharon, the leader of the Likud opposition, visited the Temple Mount on September 28 with a large contingent of Israeli police providing security for him: both Likud Party politics and his desire to demonstrate that the Barak government could not surrender this sacred ground [in negotiations with the Palestinians] prompted his visit." Ross also revealed that on September 27, Saeb Erekat, a Palestinian negotiator, approached Ross during the negotiations in Washington with "a personal request from Arafat: Might I [Ross] be able to use [U.S.] influence to stop Sharon from going to the Haram Al-Sharif [Temple Mount] the next day?" Ross turned down Arafat's request, explaining: "I told Saeb that if we were to ask Sharon not to go, he would seize the U.S. request to make political hay with his right-wing base; he would castigate us and say he would not give in to pressure from any source—including the United States—on Israel's right to the Temple Mount."[5]

Thus, with Barak's acquiescence and no opposition from the United States, on September 28 Likud Party leader Sharon went to the Temple Mount in the Old City in the heart of Arab East Jerusalem, which Israel had annexed in 1967 immediately, and illegally, after its pivotal triumph in the Six-Day War.[6] The issue of which side rightfully claims sovereignty over the Old City and East Jerusalem is one of the most contentious issues of the Israel-Palestine conflict.

In an article with the headline "Sharon Touches a Nerve, and Jerusalem Explodes" and a dateline of September 28, the *New York Times'* Joel Greenberg reported the events at the Temple Mount pursuant to Sharon's visit: "Tightly guarded by an Israeli security cordon, Ariel Sharon, the right-wing Israeli opposition leader, led a group of Israeli legislators onto the bitterly contested Temple Mount today to assert Jewish claims there, setting off a stone-throwing clash that left several Palestinians and more than two dozen policemen injured. The violence spread later to the streets of East Jerusalem and to the West Bank town of Ramallah, where six Palestinians were reportedly hurt as Israeli soldiers fired rubber-coated bullets and protestors hurled rocks and bottles."[7]

On September 30 (with a September 29 dateline), the *Times* reported:

> Violence erupted in the sacred, contested center of Jerusalem's Old City today as stones and bullets interrupted a day of prayer for Muslims and Jews, turning it bloody. Four Palestinians were killed at Haram al-Sharif, known to Jews as Temple Mount, in a second day of rioting that began when Ariel Sharon, the rightist opposition leader, visited the Muslim compound on Thursday to assert Jewish claims to the site. Wearing full riot gear, Israeli police officers today stormed the Muslim area, where they rarely set foot, to disperse Palestinian youths who emerged from Friday prayer service to stone first a police post at the Moghrabi Gate and then Jewish worshippers at the Western Wall.[8]

On October 1 (September 30 dateline), the *Times* reported on the escalating violence: "Violent clashes between Palestinians and Israeli troops left at least 12 Palestinians dead and hundreds wounded in the third day of fierce fighting set off by the defiant visit on Thursday of a right-wing Israeli leader, Ariel Sharon, to the steps of the ancient mosques atop Jerusalem's Old City. . . .The Israeli military said tonight that seven Israeli soldiers had been lightly wounded by rocks in the disturbances today. At least 16 Palestinians have been killed and hundreds injured in the last three days."[9] Thus, up to this point, only Palestinians had been killed ("at least 16"), with no fatalities among Israelis.

On October 2 (October 1 dateline), the *Times* noted that "nine Palestinians were reported dead today, bringing the Arab death toll to 28 since Friday" (September 29). The *Times* also noted that "the riots claimed their first Israeli victim today, a border policeman fatally wounded during a gun battle that began when Palestinians surrounded Joseph's Tomb, a holy Jewish site, in Palestinian controlled Nablus."[10] In an article in the same edition, and in dramatic contrast to the optimism of September 26–28, the *Times*' Jane Perlez wrote about the implications of the Palestinian rioting and the harsh Israeli response:

> With the outbreak of the last four days of violence, the prospect that President Clinton can broker an end to the Israeli-Palestinian conflict before he leaves office has all but evaporated, diplomats and other experts said today. . . . Several experts pronounced the peace effort virtually dead, at least for the rest of Mr. Clinton's administration, largely because of the time it would take to reinvigorate a process that was already deadlocked over the future status of the Old City of Jerusalem, the very place that prompted the violence. In addition, the violence and the loss of trust it has generated may further undercut the peacemaking efforts of Prime Minister Ehud Barak of Israel, who was already in a weakened political position. And the clashes may also make it more difficult for the Palestinian leader, Yasir Arafat, to deliver the concessions that the administration has been looking for him to make.[11]

Thus, the prospects for a comprehensive peace agreement went from a day (September 26, 2000) that marked "probably the highest hopes for peace during my tenure" (Ross) to only a few days later, when the peace process "has all but evaporated" (Perlez) following Ariel Sharon's provocative visit to the Haram al-Sharif / Temple Mount on September 28, the stone-throwing Palestinian uprising on September 29 in response to Sharon's visit, and a post–September 29 casualty count of twenty-eight Palestinian fatalities and one Israeli soldier.

Indeed, the next day, October 3, the *Times* reported that "Prime Minister Ehud Barak of Israel said on Monday [October 2] that peace talks were now 'on the shelf' and Yasir Arafat called for an emergency Arab summit meeting as violence tore through Israel and the Palestinian territories for the fifth straight day."[12] Also on October 3, the *Times'* Deborah Sontag wrote about the purpose of Sharon's September 28 visit to the Temple Mount:

> What was Mr. Sharon's motive? Mr. Sharon maintained that it was just an ordinary visit by an Israeli to what Jews call Temple Mount, above the remains of the First and Second Temples—among the holiest sites of Islam, the holiest of Judaism. Many Israelis applauded him for this, whatever the consequences. Political experts [in Israel], however, widely speculated that Mr. Sharon was trying to steal the spotlight from Mr. [Benjamin] Netanyahu, his rival for leadership of the right wing, on the day after corruption charges against Mr. Netanyahu were dropped. Additionally and more significantly, Mr. Sharon, an old-time hard-liner, was seen to be making a deliberate nationalist statement, well aware of its potential both to hijack the peace efforts and to undermine Mr. Barak.[13]

Thus, at this key juncture in the peace negotiations, it was the Israeli domestic political situation, and the actions of Israeli political leaders, that accounted for the breakdown of negotiations, rather than any secret plan by Yasir Arafat, as Dershowitz has charged (see further on), to sabotage the negotiations by launching a terrorist campaign on September 29, 2000, against Israel.

With respect to Palestinian casualties, on October 4, the *Times'* William A. Orme Jr., upon interviewing Dr. Khaled Qurie, "the director of East Jerusalem's busiest hospital," reported the doctor's observation pertaining to "the high number of upper body injuries" that were sustained among the thirty-five Palestinians who had been admitted to Makassed Hospital on September 29 alone. Orme noted that "Israeli soldiers are taught to fire the coated ['rubber bullet'] projectiles from specially adapted M-16s from at least 100 feet away and only at the feet and legs." However, he reported: "But there are many documented instances of close-range shootings at eye level: since Friday [September 29] doctors at St. John's Eye Hospital in Jerusalem have treated 18 Palestinians who were shot in the eye with rubber projectiles." Most of the damaged eyes "were left sightless," said Michael Cook, the chief executive there. Orme then reported:

> Israel's critics, backed by the European Union, are calling for an international inquest into the casualties. At least 42 Palestinians have been killed in the clashes, including 13 children. And for the first time since peace talks led to the creation of the Palestinian Authority six years ago, Israelis have fired on civilians from helicopter gunships using armor-piercing missiles. To the dismay of Israeli officials, the United States has joined in the criticism. At the United Nations Security Council meeting in New York today, the United States provisionally agreed to a draft statement

condemning Israel for "the acts of provocation, the violence, and the excessive use of deadly force against Palestinian civilians in the past few days."[14]

On October 7, with the United States abstaining, the UN Security Council passed a resolution that "deplore[d] the provocation carried out at Al-Haram Al-Sharif [Temple Mount] in East Jerusalem on 28 September 2000, and the subsequent violence there and at other Holy Places, as well as in other areas throughout the territories occupied by Israel since 1967, resulting in over 80 Palestinian deaths and many other casualties." The resolution "condemn[ed] acts of violence, especially the excessive use of force against Palestinians, resulting in injury and loss of human life."[15]

To summarize events within the twelve-day period of September 26 to October 7: The lead U.S. negotiator, Dennis Ross, described an atmosphere of optimism among Israeli and Palestinian negotiators just prior to and during a three-day round of informal peace talks in Washington on September 26–28; Sharon's visit of September 28 to the Haram al-Sharif / Temple Mount was probably designed to be deliberately inflammatory and obstructive to the peace negotiations; the *New York Times* reported in its day-to-day coverage that Israel had employed nearly all of the deadly force on and immediately after September 29, with nearly all of the fatalities being Palestinian; and that the Israel-Palestine peace process under the auspices of the Clinton administration was seriously threatened as a direct consequence of this chain of events. While this narration of events would not seem to point toward a plot orchestrated by Palestinian leader Yasir Arafat to sabotage peace negotiations, or to the onset of Palestinian terrorism against Israeli civilians, that is how Dershowitz has unambiguously constructed these events in his books, newspaper articles, and public speeches since September 2000.

In probably his most influential book about the Israel-Palestine conflict, *The Case for Israel*, published in 2003, and while seamlessly welding the time framework of the Camp David summit in July 2000 to the Taba talks of January 2001, and thus opportunistically mashing together a highly differentiated sequence of events, Dershowitz observed in the introduction: "I decided to write this book after closely following the Camp David–Taba peace negotiations of 2000–2001, then watching as so many people throughout the world turned viciously against Israel when the negotiations failed and the Palestinians turned once again to terrorism." Similarly, and also in the introduction, Dershowitz wrote that in response to "Barak's generous offer [in July 2000], Arafat decided to make his counteroffer in the form of suicide bombings and escalating violence," and that "the [Palestinian] excuse for the escalation of suicide bombings was Ariel Sharon's visit to the Temple

Mount."[16] Although these statements apparently have no factual basis, such statements are a staple in Dershowitz's books and articles about this juncture in Israel-Palestine relations.

Dershowitz then explained why the world "turned against Israel" after the failed peace negotiations and the start of the Palestinian Intifada:

> The answer comes in two parts. The first is rather obvious: Arafat played the tried-and-true terrorism card that had worked for him so many times over his long and tortuous career as a terrorist diplomat. By targeting Israel's civilians—children on school buses, pregnant women in shopping malls, teenagers at a discotheque, families at a Passover Seder, university students in a cafeteria—Arafat knew he could get Israel to overreact, first by electing a more hawkish prime minister to replace the dovish Ehud Barak, then by provoking the [Israeli] military to take actions that would inevitably result in the deaths of Palestinian civilians.[17]

In his sequel *The Case for Peace: How the Arab-Israeli Conflict Can Be Resolved*, published in 2005, Dershowitz repeated the claim that Arafat had ordered a terrorist campaign following the failure of the peace negotiations: "A leadership willing to use violence rather than settle for 95 percent of the loaf [the West Bank] is not a leadership really interested in peace. This was demonstrated by Yasser Arafat at Camp David and Taba in 2000 and 2001."[18] Dershowitz repeated the same claim elsewhere in his book, including "after Israel made momentous concessions at Camp David and Taba and Arafat rejected those concessions," Arafat "opened the floodgates of suicide terrorism."[19]

All of this follows his 2002 assessment in *Why Terrorism Works: Understanding the Threat, Responding to the Challenge*:

> In light of the success of terrorism as a tactic, it should come as no surprise that Arafat would once again play the terrorism card after walking away from the Camp David negotiations in 2000, when Israeli prime minister Ehud Barak's government, with the support of the Clinton administration, had offered the Palestinians nearly everything they were seeking. Rather than trying to negotiate some additional concessions—or compromising their maximalist claims—the Palestinians reverted to the terrorist tactics that had brought them so far already. These included the renewal of the intifada of the late 1980s—only this time featuring much more deadly violence against Israeli civilians than before.[20]

Although Dershowitz repeats this rendition of events ad nauseam in his published writings, as far as I can tell there is no discernible factual basis for it in the documentary record.

Even more to the point is the detailed chronology of post–September 28 deadly fire by Israelis and Palestinians. Recall that Dershowitz wrote that "by targeting Israel's civilians [with terrorism] . . . Arafat knew he could get Israel to overreact, first by electing a more hawkish prime minister to replace the dovish Ehud Barak, then by provoking the military to take actions that would inevitably result in the deaths of Palestinian civilians." However, the election to which Dershowitz refers—in which the right-wing Ariel Sharon became Israel's prime minister by defeating Ehud Barak—took place on February 6, 2001.[21] Yet the first Palestinian terrorist attack inside Israel during this period did not occur until October 28, 2001, according to a document titled "Major Terrorist Attacks in Israel" issued by the U.S.-based Anti-Defamation League.[22] The ADL's chronology of terrorist attacks inside Israel following the events of September 28–29, 2000 is corroborated by numerous reports by the major human rights organizations and the United Nations—none of which support Dershowitz's claim that it was the Palestinians who initiated lethal violence after Sharon's visit to the Temple Mount on September 28, 2000.

In its first public statement on the events of September 28–29, 2000, an Amnesty International press release dated October 2 stated:

> Amnesty International condemned indiscriminate killings of civilians following four days of clashes in Israel and the Occupied Territories which have left at least 35 Palestinian civilians dead and hundreds of others injured. "The dead civilians, among them young children, include those uninvolved in the conflict and seeking safety," the human rights organization said. "The loss of civilian life is devastating and this is compounded by the fact that many appear to have been killed or injured as a result of the use of excessive or indiscriminate force." "Israeli security forces appear to have used indiscriminate lethal force on many occasions when their lives were not in danger," Amnesty International said. "We have been saying for years that Israel is killing civilians unlawfully by firing at them during demonstrations and riots."[23]

One week later, on October 9, Amnesty issued another press release, this one about the findings of a three-person delegation that the human rights organization had sent to investigate the circumstances of the killings:[24]

> "Since 29 September, Israeli security forces have frequently used excessive force on demonstrators when lives were not in immediate danger," Amnesty International said today. In preliminary conclusions from Amnesty International's delegation in Israel and the Occupied Territories the human rights organization reiterated its condemnation of the exces-

sive use of force by law enforcement officials. "In many cases the Israel Defence Forces (IDF), the Israel Police and the Border Police have apparently breached their own internal regulations on the use of force, as well as international human rights standards on the use of force and firearms," Amnesty International said. More than 80 people, including children, nearly all of them Palestinians from the Occupied Territories and Israel, have died since clashes began on 29 September 2000 between Israeli security forces and Palestinian demonstrators all over the West Bank and the Gaza Strip, as well as in Israel.[25]

In a report issued in October 2000, and following a fact-finding investigation that it conducted into the unlawful use of force in Israel, the West Bank, and the Gaza Strip, Human Rights Watch issued the following assessment:

[Human Rights Watch] found a pattern of repeated Israeli use of excessive lethal force during clashes between its security forces and Palestinian demonstrators in situations where demonstrators were unarmed and posed no threat of death or serious injury to the security forces or to others. In cases that Human Rights Watch investigated where gunfire by Palestinian security forces or armed protestors was a factor, use of lethal force by the Israel Defense Forces (IDF) was indiscriminate and not directed at the source of the threat, in violation of international law enforcement standards. In Israel, the West Bank, and the Gaza Strip, the IDF regularly used rubber bullets and plastic-coated metal bullets as well as live ammunition in an excessive or indiscriminate manner. A particularly egregious example of such unlawful fire is the IDF's use of medium-caliber bullets against unarmed demonstrators in the West Bank and Gaza Strip, and in some instances, such as the Netzarim Junction in the Gaza Strip, against medical personnel. These military weapons, which inflict massive trauma when striking flesh, are normally used to penetrate concrete and are not appropriate for crowd control.[26]

In a report issued on December 31, 2000, Defence for Children International, a Switzerland-based independent NGO founded in 1979, the International Year of the Child,[27] published a detailed list, reproduced here, of the names of Palestinian children "who were killed as a direct result of Israeli military and settler presence in the Occupied Palestinian Territories" from September 29 to December 31, 2000.[28]

FULL INFORMATION: CHILDREN KILLED

DATE	NAME	AGE	RESIDENCE	CAUSE OF DEATH
30 September	Mohammad Jamal Mohammad al-Dura	11	al-Breij/Gaza	Live bullet to multiple places
30 September	Nizar Mohammad Eida	16	Deir Ammar/Ramallah	Live bullet to chest
30 September	Khaled Adli Insooh al-Bazyan	15	Nablus	Exploding bullet to head
1 October	Samir Sidqi Tabanja	12	Nablus	Live bullet to chest
1 October	Sarah 'Abdel Atheem ' Abdel Haq	18 mos.	Talfit/Nablus	Live bullet to head. *Killed by Israeli Settlers.*
1 October	Hussam Bakhit	17	Balatta Refugee Camp/ Nablus	Live bullet to head
1 October	Iyad Ahmad Salim al-Khoshashee	16	Nablus	Live bullet to multiple places. *Iyad's body was found Sunday in the hills surrounding Nablus, but he is believed to have died on Saturday.*
1 October	Sami Fathi Mohammad al-Taramsi	16	Sheikh Radwan/Gaza	Live bullet to chest
1 October	Mohammad Nabeel Hamed Daoud	14	al-Bireh/Ramallah	Live bullet to head
2 October	Wa'el Tayseer Mohammad Qatawi	16	Balatta Refugee Camp/ Nablus	Live bullet to eye
2 October	Muslih Hussein Ibrahim Jarad	17	Deir Balah/Gaza *Killed in Um al-Fahim*	Live bullet to chest
2 October	'Aseel Hassan 'Assalih	17	'Arrabeh al-Batouf/ Upper Galilee	Live bullet to neck
3 October	Hussam Ismail al-Hamshari	16	Tulkarem	Exploding bullet to head
3 October	Ammar Khalil al-Rafa'i	17	al-Maghazi/Gaza	Hit by missile in the head
4 October	Mohammad Zayed Yousef Abu 'Assi	13	Bani Sahla/Gaza	Live bullet to chest
6 October	Saleh Issa Yousef al-Raiyati	17	Rafah/Gaza	Live bullet to head
6 October	Majdi Samir Maslamani	15	Beit Hanina/Jerusalem	Exploding bullet to head
6 October	Mohammad Khaled Tammam	17	Tulkarem	Live bullet to chest
8 October	Yousef Diab Yousef Khalaf	17	al-Breij/Gaza	Died from injuries sustained on 2 October, shrapnel to head.
11 October	Karam Omar Ibrahim Qannan	17	Khan Younis Refugee Camp/Gaza	Rubber-coated steel bullet to chest
11 October	Sami Hassan Salim al-Balduna	17	Tulkarem Refugee Camp	Live bullet to chest
12 October	Sami Fathi Abu Jezr	12	Rafah/Gaza	Died from injuries sustained on 11 October, Live bullet to head
16 October	Mo'ayyad Osaama al-Jawareesh	14	Aida Refugee Camp/ Bethlehem	Rubber-coated steel bullet to head
20 October	Mohammad 'Adil Abu Tahoun	15	Tulkarem	Live bullet to multiple places
20 October	Samir Talal 'Oweisi	16	Qalqiliya	Live bullet to chest
20 October	'Alaa Bassam Beni Nimra	16	Salfit	Live bullet to chest
21 October	Omar Ismail al-Abheisi	15	Deir Balah/Gaza	Exploding bullet to chest
21 October	Majed Ibrahim Hawamda	15	Ramallah	Exploding bullet to head
22 October	Wa'el Mahmoud Mohammad Imad	13	Jabaliya Refugee Camp/ Gaza	Live bullet to head
22 October	Salah al-Din Fawzi Nejmi	16	al-Maghazi Camp/Gaza	Live bullet to chest
23 October	Ashraf Habayab	15	Askar Refugee Camp/ Nablus	Exploding bullet to head. *Died from injuries sustained 16 October.*
24 October	Iyad Osaama Tahir Sha'ath	12	Khan Younis/Gaza	Live bullet to head. *Died from injuries sustained 21 October.*
24 October	Nidal Mohammad Zuhudi al-Dubeiki	16	Hai al-Darraj/Gaza	Exploding bullet to abdomen

Date	Name	Age	Location	Cause
26 October	'Alaa Mohammad Mahfouth	14	Arroub Refugee Camp /Hebron	Live bullet to head. *Died from injuries sustained on 6 October.*
27 October	Bashir Salah Musa Shelwit	16	Qalqiliya	Live bullet to chest
29 October	Husni Ibrahim Najjar	16	Rafah/Gaza Strip	Live bullet to head
31 October	Shadi Awad Nimir Odeh	17	Hai Zaitun/Gaza Strip	Live bullet to head
1 November	Ahmad Suleiman Abu Tayeh	17	Shatti Refugee Camp/Gaza	Live bullets and exploding bullets to multiple places
1 November	Mohammad Ibrahim Hajaaj	14	Sheja'aya/Gaza	Live bullet to head
1 November	Ibrahim Riziq Mohammad Omar	14	Shatti Refugee Camp/Gaza	Live bullet to chest
2 November	Khaled Mohammad Ahmad Riziq	17	Hizma/Jerusalem	Live bullet to multiple places
2 November	Yazen Mohammad Issa al-Khalaiqa	14	al-Shiyoukh/Hebron *Killed in Bethlehem*	Live bullet to back
4 November	Rami Ahmad Abdel Fatah	15	Hizma/Jerusalem	Exploding bullet to multiple places
4 November	Hind Nidal Jameel Abu Quweider	23 days old	Hebron	Tear gas inhalation
5 November	Maher Mohammad al-Sa'idi	15	al-Breij/Gaza	Live bullet to head
6 November	Wajdi al-Lam al-Hattab	15	Tulkarem	Exploding bullet to chest
6 November	Mohammad Nawwaf al-Ta'aban	17	Deir Balah/Gaza	Live bullet to chest
7 November	Ahmad Amin al-Khufash	6	Marda/Salfit	Run over by Israeli settler
8 November	Ibrahim Fouad al-Qassas	15	Khan Younis/Gaza	Live bullet to eye. *Died from injuries sustained on 5 November.*
8 November	Faris Fa'iq Odeh	15	Hai Zaitun/Gaza	Live bullet to head
8 November	Mohammad Misbah Abu Ghali	16	Khan Younis Refugee Camp/Gaza	Live bullet to chest
8 November	Ra'ed Abdel Hamid Daoud	14	Heras/Salfit	Exploding bullet to multiple places
9 November	Mahmoud Kamel Khalil Sharab	17	Khan Younis/Gaza	Live bullet to back
10 November	Osaama Mazen Saleem 'Azouqah	14	Jenin	Live bullet to chest
10 November	Osaama Samir al-Jerjawee	17	Hai al-Daraj/Gaza	Live bullet to chest
11 November	Musa Ibrahim al-Dibs	14	Jabalia Camp/Gaza	Live bullet to chest
12 November	Mohammad Nafiz Abu Naji	16	Sheikh Radwan/Gaza	Live bullet to chest
13 November	Yahya Naif Abu Shemaali	17	Khan Younis/Gaza	Live bullet to chest
14 November	Saber Khamis Brash	15	Al 'Amari Camp/Ramallah	Live bullet to chest
14 November	Mohammad Khatir Al 'Ajli	13	Hai Sheju'a/Gaza	Exploding bullet to head
15 November	Ibrahim Abdel Raouf Jaidi	15	Qalqiliya	Live bullet to chest
15 November	Jadua Munia Mohammad Abu Kupashe	16	al-Samua/Hebron	Live bullets to multiple places
15 November	Ahmad Samir Basel	17	Tel al-Howwa/Gaza	Live bullet to chest
15 November	Mohammad Nasser Mohammad al-Sharafe	17	Nasser/Gaza	Live bullet to head
15 November	Jihad Suheil Abu Shahma	12	Khan Younis/Gaza	Live bullet to head
15 November	Ahmad Said Ahmad Sha'aban	16	Jalama/Jenin	Exploding bullet to abdomen
16 November	Samir Mohammad Hassan al-Khudour	17	al-Fawwar Refugee Camp/Hebron	Exploding bullet to chest
17 November	Rami Imad Yassin	17	Zeitun/Gaza	Live bullet to chest
17 November	Mohammad Abdel Jalil Mohammad Abu Rayyan	16	Halhoul/Hebron	Live bullet to head
19 November	Abdel Rahman Ziad Dahshan	14	Sabra/Gaza	Live bullet to chest
20 November	Ibrahim Hassan Ahmad Uthman	17	Tel al-Sultan/Gaza	Live bullet to chest

Date	Name	Age	Residence	Injury
21 November	Yasser Taleb Mohammad Tebatitti	16	Tulkarem. *Killed while on vacation. Family lives in Saudi Arabia.*	Live bullet to chest
22 November	Ibrahim Hussein al-Muqannan	14	Khan Younis/Gaza Strip	Live bullet to head. *Died from injuries sustained on 20 November.*
23 November	Maram Imad Ahmad Saleh Hassouneh	3	Jalazone Refugee Camp/ Ramallah	Tear gas inhalation
24 November	Aysar Mohammad Sadiq Hassis	15	Jenin	Exploding bullet to eye
24 November	Majdi Ali Abed	15	Sheju'a/Gaza Strip	Live bullet to head. *Died from injuries sustained on 17 November.*
26 November	Ziad Ghaleb Zaid Selmi	17	Habla/Qalqiliya	Live bullets to multiple places.
26 November	Mahdi Qassem Jaber	16	Habla/Qalqiliya	Live bullets to multiple places.
28 November	Karam Fathi al-Kurd	14	Khan Younis/Gaza Strip	Live bullet to head. *Died from injuries sustained on 23 November.*
29 November	Mohammad Abdullah al-Mashharawi	14	Gaza	Live bullet to head. *Died from injuries sustained on 26 November.*
30 November	Walid Mohammad Ahmad Hamida	17	Teku'a/Bethlehem	Live bullet to chest
30 November	Shadi Ahmad Hassan Zghoul	16	Hussan/Bethlehem	Run over by Israeli settler
1 December	Mohammed Salih Mohammad al-Arjah	12	Rafah/Gaza Strip	Live bullet to head
5 December	Ramzi Adil Mohammed Bayatni	15	Abu Qash/Ramallah	Live bullet to eye
8 December	Mohammad Abdullah Mohammad Yahya	16	Kufr Rai/Jenin	Hit by missile
8 December	Alaa Abdelatif Mohammad Abu Jaber	17	al-Maghayeer/Jenin	Hit by missile
8 December	Ammar Samir al-Mashni	17	Beit Or al-Tahta/Ramallah	Live bullet to head
8 December	Mu'ataz Azmi Ismail Talakh	16	Dheishe Refugee Camp/ Bethlehem	Live bullet to head
9 December	Salim Mohammad Hamaideh	12	Rafah/Gaza	Live bullet to head
11 December	Ahmad Ali Hassan Qawasmeh	15	Hebron	Live bullet to head
20 December	Hani Yusef al-Sufi	14	Rafah/Gaza	Shrapnel to head
22 December	Arafat Mohammad Ali al-Jabarin	17	Sa'ir/Hebron	Live bullet to head
31 December	Mo'ath Ahmad Abu Hedwan	12	Hebron	Shrapnel to head

CLINICALLY DEAD
The following Palestinian children have been declared clinically dead.

DATE	NAME	AGE	RESIDENCE	INJURY
30 September	Khaled Hameed	17	Rafah/Gaza	Live bullet to head
30 September	Mohammad Nawaf Abu Owemer	13	Deir Balah/Gaza	Live bullet to head
30 September	Mohammad Sami al-Hummos	14	Rafah/Gaza	Live bullet to head
5 November	Ghazaleh Joudet Jaradat	14	Sa'ir/Hebron	Rubber-coated steel bullet to head
11 November	Hamad Jamal al-Faraa	13	Khan Younis/Gaza Strip	Live bullet to head

CHILDREN DEATHS AS A RESULT OF THE ISRAELI IMPOSED CLOSURE

DATE	NAME	AGE	RESIDENCE	CAUSE
13 October	Alaa Osaama Hamdan	10	Assawiya/Nablus	Died from a severe lung infection after Israeli soldiers prohibited her father from passing through a checkpoint to transport her to a hospital

This compilation of fatalities is corroborated by other human rights organizations. In a report that was issued in March 2001, Giorgio Giacomelli, the UN's Special Rapporteur to the Commission on Human Rights, wrote: "From 29 September to end of February 2001, Israeli settlers and soldiers killed approximately 145 Palestinian children under 18, of whom at least 59 were under 15 years of age. An overwhelming 72 percent of child deaths have resulted from gunshot wounds in the upper body (head and chest), which may indicate a 'shoot-to-kill' policy."[29] Also in March 2001, the United Nations Commission on Human Rights, in a report authored by John Dugard of South Africa, Richard Falk of the United States, and Kamal Hossain of Bangladesh, following a visit to the occupied Palestinian territories and Israel on February 10–18, 2001, and citing "conservative estimates," reported that from September 29, 2000, to February 21, 2001, "84 Palestinian children under the age of 17 years have been killed and some 5,000 injured; 1 Israeli child has been killed and 15 injured." Overall, the authors of the report found that, since the beginning of the Palestinian Intifada on September 29, 2000, "311 Palestinians (civilians and security forces) have been killed by Israeli security forces and civilians in the OPT [Occupied Palestinian Territories]," and that "47 Israelis (civilians and security forces) have been killed by Palestinian civilians and security forces," while "11,575 Palestinians and 466 Israelis have been injured."[30]

One could continue to quote likewise from such reports, with similar results, including those issued a year or more after the start of the Palestinian uprising. For example, in October 2001, John Dugard, then the Special Rapporteur to the UN Commission on Human Rights in the Occupied Palestinian Territories, issued an assessment of the violence following the events of September 28–29, 2000: "The first few months of the second intifada were characterized by violent clashes between Palestinian protestors, whose weapons were stones and Molotov cocktails, and the Israel Defense Force. Most deaths and injuries were the result of gunfire from the Israel Defense Forces."[31]

In summary, there is no discernible basis to support the assertions by Dershowitz that when the peace negotiations in 2000 failed, "the Palestinians turned once again to terrorism," or, more specifically, that Arafat had targeted Israeli civilians with terrorism in order to "get Israel to overreact, first by electing a more hawkish prime minister" (Ariel Sharon), "then by provoking the [Israeli] military to take actions that would inevitably result in the deaths of Palestinian civilians."[32]

That the Palestinians had not resorted to lethal violence against Israeli civilians either on September 29, 2000, or for many months afterward, undermines only one count of Dershowitz's two-count indictment of Yasser Arafat and the Palestinians. Recall Dershowitz's claim that "after Israel made momentous concessions at Camp David and Taba . . . Arafat rejected those concesssions."[33] To assess the credibility of this claim, one must review the details of what was presented to the Palestinians (a) at Camp David, Maryland, in July 2000; (b) at Washington, DC, September 26–28, 2000; (c) at the White House on December 23, 2000; and (d) at the Egyptian resort city of Taba on the northern coast of the Gulf of Aqaba in late January 2001.

Camp David, July 11–25, 2000. While a number of commentators have written about the proposals that were tabled at the Camp David summit attended by Israeli prime minister Ehud Barak and President Bill Clinton,[34] Dershowitz relies heavily on Dennis Ross and his book *The Missing Peace*. For example, in *The Case for Israel*, Dershowitz wrote, again resorting to ambiguous and nonspecific assertions, in this case concerning "Barak's offer" and "Israel's offer":

> Virtually everyone who played any role in the Camp David–Taba peace process now places the entire blame for its failure on Arafat's decision to turn down Barak's offer. President Clinton, who was furious at Arafat and has called him a liar, has blamed the failure completely on Arafat. Dennis Ross, who was the chief U.S. negotiator, has said that Arafat was unwilling to accept any peace proposal, because for Arafat "to end the conflict is to end himself." The best proof of Ross's point is that Arafat did not even offer a counterproposal to Israel's offer. He simply rejected it and ordered preparation for renewed terrorism.[35]

Since Dershowitz cites Ross as his most authoritative source about what happened at Camp David in July 2000, it seems appropriate to quickly review how Ross himself represented what the Israelis and Americans presented to the Palestinians as a final-status peace agreement.[36]

On July 15, Day 5 of the Camp David summit, Barak presented his opening proposals, including a map of the West Bank that, according to Ross, "showed three different colors—brown for the Palestinian state, orange for the areas the Israelis would annex, and red for transitional areas," which depicted a 14 percent Israeli annexation of the West Bank, including "orange areas in the Jordan Valley and in the corridor from Jerusalem to Jericho," thus depicting a corridor of Israel-annexed Palestinian land not only along the east border of the West Bank, but another corridor of Israel-annexed land that severed the bottom third of the West Bank from the top two-thirds.[37] At Camp David, according to Ross, Barak later proposed Israeli annexation of 10.5 percent of the West Bank, leaving 89.5 percent to the Palestinians (Day 6),[38] Israeli annexation of 11.3 percent of the West Bank, leaving 88.7 percent to the Palestinians (Day 7),[39] and Israeli annexation reportedly of 9 percent of the West Bank (with a 1 percent swap of unspecified Israeli territory), leaving a net 92 percent of the West Bank to the Palestinians (Day 8).[40] This is very different from what Dershowitz described in his nonspecific claims about "Barak's offer" and "Israel's offer."

Furthermore, it is curiously unclear in Ross's book whether Israel ever withdrew its proposal to dissect the West Bank—with a west-to-east corridor of Israel-annexed West Bank land from Jerusalem to Jericho, connected to the north-south corridor of Israel-annexed land along the Jordan River—since Ross cited the proposed Jerusalem-to-Jericho corridor in his Day 5 account of the Camp David negotiations, without revisiting the status of that detail again in his book.

Washington, DC, September 26–28, 2000. After the breakdown of negotiations at Camp David in July 2000, the chief negotiators met two months later in Washington. One question at issue during this round of meetings was whether the Clinton administration would present a comprehensive peace plan to the Israeli and Palestinian delegations at some point. (The administration formally presented no such plan at Camp David in July.) Although Ross told the negotiators that it was up to the president to decide whether he would issue such a proposal, Ross nevertheless gave each side "a sense of [the U.S.] direction on each issue":

> On borders, I [Ross] said our proposal would be less than 9 percent [Israeli] annexation discussed at Camp David, but would be closer to that 9 percent [annexation] than to the 2 percent [annexation] the Palestinians had countered with at that time; on [territorial] swaps, I said we would offer more than at Camp David but the swap would neither be equal to the Israeli annexation nor large; on security, I told each [delegation] that the Dahlan [Palestinian negotiator] approach was serious, but the [Israeli] right of reentry [of military forces into the newly created Palestinian state] in clearly defined emergencies was important; on refugees, I said there would be no right of return [of Palestinian refugees] to Israel.[41]

The White House, December 23, 2000. In December, President Clinton and his advisers had decided to present a set of "ideas" or "parameters" for a comprehensive Israeli-Palestinian peace. Clinton declined to present his parameters in writing, and no publicly issued official draft exists of what the president put forward. Rather, Clinton recited the parameters verbally at the White House to the Israeli and Palestinian delegations. In *The Missing Peace*, Ross itemized the Clinton parameters as follows:

> President Clinton proceeded to present his ideas. What follows is the essence of his presentation. On territory, there would be a range of 4 to 6 percent [Israeli] annexation in the West Bank to accommodate 80 percent of the Israeli settlers in three settler blocs. In partial compensation [to the Palestinians] for the annexation [of Palestinian land], there would be a range of 1 to 3 percent swap of territory provided to the Palestinians, and nonterritorial compensation could include the creation of a permanent safe passage between the West Bank and Gaza. President Clinton

emphasized that in drawing the borders, we would insist on contiguity of territory for the Palestinian state and on minimizing the number of Palestinians absorbed into the areas the Israelis annexed.

On security, the key would lie in an international presence that could be withdrawn only by mutual consent; it would monitor the implementation of the agreement. This security force would gradually take the place of the Israel Defense Forces, which would remain in the Jordan Valley for a period of up to six years. Israel would also retain three early-warning sites in the West Bank with a Palestinian liaison presence for as long as Israel deemed necessary. The Palestinian state would be nonmilitarized, with a strong Palestinian security force for internal security and with the international force providing border security and deterrence. Palestinians would have sovereignty over their airspace but would have to accommodate Israeli training and operational needs. And the IDF could redeploy to the Jordan River in the event of an external threat, constituting a "national state of emergency" in Israel.

On refugees, the solution had to be consistent with the two-state approach. The formulation on "right of return" had to "make clear that there is no specific right of return to Israeli [*sic*] itself" while not negating "the aspiration of the Palestinian people to return to the area." With this in mind, two alternative formulations were proposed: both sides recognize the right of Palestinian refugees to return to historic Palestine, or alternatively both sides recognize the right of Palestinian refugees to return to their homeland.

Five possible homes for Palestinian refugees were identified: the state of Palestine; areas in Israel being transferred to Palestine in a land swap; rehabilitation in a host country; resettlement in a third country (like the United States, Canada, Australia, Great Britain, etc.); and admission to Israel. The right of return would pertain only to the first two homes— meaning the new state of Palestine. Admission into Israel would be Israel's sovereign decision. Priority should be given to the refugee population in Lebanon, and it would be agreed that this basic approach would constitute implementation of UN General Assembly resolution 194.[42]

Thus, according to Ross's summary of the Clinton parameters, the United States had offered the Palestinians the following: (a) a state that would permit Israel to annex—that is, incorporate into Israel's territorial and legal dominion—4 to 6 percent of West Bank territory for the benefit of 80 percent of Israel's West Bank settlers, with "a range of 1 to 3 percent swap" of Israeli territory in return; (b) three "early warning" Israeli military facilities located permanently in the West Bank; (c) a "nonmilitarized" Palestinian state that would be required to allow Israeli military forces to enter West Bank territory during "emergencies" declared by Israel at its discretion; and (d) Palestinian sovereignty over Palestinian airspace that nevertheless would have to accommodate Israeli military "training" and "operational" needs.

Clinton also presented his parameters to both parties as nonnegotiable. Yet, it appears that Israel was permitted to modify the Clinton parameters, which already were favorably disposed toward it, by "accepting" the parameters with "twenty pages of reservations," as Jimmy Carter reported.[43] On this count, Ross wrote: "On the twenty-seventh [of December], Barak convened his security cabinet in Jerusalem and they voted to accept the Clinton ideas with reservations. But the reservations were within the parameters, not outside them."[44] Ross provided no additional details. However, as Jeremy Pressman observed in a detailed review of Ross's book in *Boston Review*: "Barak had the Israeli cabinet approve the Clinton plan and then, in a separate time and place, presented Clinton with its own list of reservations," and "in January 2001 Barak publicly rejected the Clinton plan's call for Palestinian sovereignty over the Haram al-Sharif, the Noble Sanctuary."[45]

Yet, when Arafat sought "clarifications" about the Clinton parameters, as one might imagine in the absence of a formal written draft and, for example, about Palestinian "sovereignty" over its airspace and borders that nevertheless must accede to Israel's "security needs" inside the West Bank, Ross wrote: "Arafat was never good at facing moments of truth. They tended by definition to close doors, to foreclose options. Now, especially with the end of the conflict as part of the President's ideas, he was on the spot. Almost immediately he looked for ways to avoid an early decision. He wanted clarifications." Or, as Ross also reported: "Arafat was not up for peacemaking" due to "his rejection of the most basic elements of the Israeli security needs, and his dismissal of our refugee formula."[46] In his book, Ross's account of the negotiations essentially ends with his account of the Clinton parameters of late December 2000, after which he devoted only one brief paragraph to the Taba round in January 2001.[47]

Apart from Ross, Dershowitz also relied to a good extent on an article published in March 2003 in the *New Yorker* titled "The Prince: How the Saudi Ambassador Became Washington's Indispensable Operator," by Elsa Walsh. However, while citing the December 2000 Clinton parameters and Bandar's talk with Arafat on January 2, Walsh provided few details concerning the actual negotiations and seemed at times to be ill-informed about their most fundamental aspects. For example, she wrote:

> Clinton, who continued to apply his considerable energy to finding a Middle East solution, came to believe, in December of 2000, that he had finally found a formula for peace; he asked once more for Bandar's help. Bandar's first reaction was not to get involved; the Syrian summit had

failed, and talks between Barak and Arafat at Camp David, in July, had collapsed. But when Dennis Ross showed Bandar the President's talking papers Bandar recognized that in its newest iteration the peace plan was a remarkable development. It gave Arafat almost everything he wanted, including the return of about ninety-seven per cent of the land of the occupied territories; all of Jerusalem except the Jewish and Armenian quarters, with Jews preserving the right to worship at the Temple Mount; and a thirty-billion-dollar compensation fund.[48]

However, as Ross reported, President Clinton offered the Palestinians not 97 percent per se "of the land of the occupied territories," as Walsh reported, but 94 to 96 percent, with a swap of unspecified land from Israel of 1 to 3 percent. Also, the president did not offer the Palestinians "all of Jerusalem except the Jewish and Armenian quarters," at least as far as sovereignty was concerned; rather, Clinton's offer to Arafat was Palestinian sovereignty of the Arab quarter in the Old City, which is a one-square-kilometer section of East Jerusalem[49]—the total area of East Jerusalem overall is seventy square kilometers.[50]

Furthermore, Walsh's narrative is of interest for another reason. In *The Case for Israel*, Dershowitz spoke of "Prince Bandar, who played a central beyond-the-scenes [*sic*] role in the peace negotiations."[51] Yet, in her *New Yorker* article, Walsh detailed no input from Bandar on the content of the negotiations; she wrote that Bandar had not been involved in the peace negotiations prior to Ross approaching him about the Clinton parameters of December 2000 and there is no evidence of Bandar's involvement with Clinton officials beyond his receipt of that single briefing from Ross.[52] The portrait painted in the *New Yorker* is not of Bandar being an insider to the negotiations, but of Bandar agreeing to do a last-minute favor for the American administration by picking Arafat up at the airport on January 2. Despite these limitations, Dershowitz cited the *New Yorker* article by Elsa Walsh as a key source[53] in *The Case for Israel* to support his claims that Arafat had rejected Barak's generous parameters (when the parameters in fact were Clinton's) and to assert a crucial role for Bandar "behind-the-scenes" in the negotiations (when Bandar's role was minor). Thus, Dershowitz wrote: "In a remarkable series of interviews conducted by Elsa Walsh for the *New Yorker*, Prince Bandar of Saudi Arabia has publicly disclosed his behind-the-scenes role in the peace process and what he told Arafat. Bandar's disclosures go well beyond anything previously revealed by an inside source to the negotiations and provide the best available evidence of how Arafat plays the terrorism card to shift public opinion not only in the Arab and Muslim worlds but in the world at large."[54]

Taba, January 21–27, 2001. Nearly three weeks after Arafat's meeting with President Clinton on January 2, 2001—and after Ross rejected Arafat's request for clarifications—bilateral negotiations between Israeli and Palestinian negotiators were conducted at Taba on January 21–27. As to the question of which side ended these negotiations, one might turn to what a couple of genuine insiders to the peace talks—Israeli journalist Akiva Eldar and Israeli negotiator Yossi Beilin, who was present at Taba—have written about this question. In his introduction to the "Moratinos Document," which is a first hand summary of the Taba negotiations by the European Union's representative to the Taba talks, and which was published for the first time in *Ha'aretz* in February 2002, Eldar reported what Beilen had told him about the Taba negotiations: "Beilen stressed that the Taba talks were not halted because they hit a crisis, but rather because of the Israeli election" on February 6, 2001.[55] In his 2004 book about the peace process, Beilin himself wrote: "The talks at Taba were stopped on Saturday night, January 27 [2001], because Shlomo Ben-Ami [chief Israeli negotiator] and Abu Ala [chief Palestinian negotiator] agreed that it would be difficult to reach further breakthroughs at that juncture. It was resolved that the talks would continue in a more limited framework over the next two days, ahead of a possible summit meeting between Barak and Arafat in Sweden on the thirtieth [of January]. . . . But a series of events prevented the summit."[56]

With respect to those events, Beilin wrote about Arafat's reaction to the lethal Israeli response (detailed earlier) to the Palestinian Intifada that had begun on September 29, 2000: "And then on Sunday [January 28, 2001], Shimon Peres and Yasser Arafat appeared before a large audience at Davos [Switzerland], and after Peres's speech, Arafat issued a poisonous attack on the Israeli government. He accused Israel of using non-conventional weapons and deliberate economic suffocation, in language reminiscent of the pre-Oslo Arafat." According to Beilin, and due to Arafat's speech, "the irreversible impression had been created that Arafat was not prepared for a reconciliatory summit meeting." Beilin wrote that "Barak was stunned by [Arafat's] speech and the tone with which it was presented." Arafat then "attempted to correct himself, and expressed his desire to reach an agreement, but this could not soften the harsh impression he had made." Barak "said that he would not meet with Arafat in light of the Davos speech, but later decided not to close the door on the summit." After no summit invitation had been issued by the Swedish government, and after three Israeli settlers were killed in the West Bank by Palestinians around that time, "Barak announced that there would be no summit meeting with Arafat."[57] Thus, Barak—not Arafat—cancelled the summit and terminated the peace process. Days later, Ariel Sharon defeated Barak in the Israeli election of February 6.

While Dershowitz may be the most prolific U.S. proponent of the view that Arafat rejected peace at Camp David in July 2000 and resorted instead to terrorism on September 29, 2000, he is not its only advocate. For example, in his 2009 polemic *One State, Two States: Resolving the Israel/Palestine Conflict*, Israeli historian Benny

Morris dramatically interpreted the failure of the peace negotiations in 2000 as a rejection by the Palestinians of a two-state solution to the conflict:

> Had the Palestinian national movement really abandoned its one-state goal? As with 1937 and 1947, the year 2000 represented a milestone in the Palestinian approach to a solution to the conflict. But, in a sense, it was a more defining milestone than its predecessors. For in 1937 and 1947, in rejecting the two-state solutions proposed, respectively, by the Peel Commission and the UN General Assembly, the Palestinian Arabs had merely been expressing their consistently held and publicized attitude toward a resolution of the conflict; only a one-state solution, a Palestinian Arab state with a miniscule, disempowered Jewish minority, was acceptable. In rejecting the two-state solution offered, in two versions, in 2000, they were also—so it seemed—reneging on a process and on a commitment they had made, and repeated, in the course of the 1990s. And whereas in 1937 and 1947 they had rejected merely a two-state vision, a possibility, as it were, in 2000 they were also rejecting a reality, denying the legitimacy and right to life of an existing state [Israel], subverting a principle on which the international order rests.[58]

In the United States, Ethan Bronner, then the Middle East editor of the *New York Times*, in his November 2003 review of *The Case for Israel*, assimilated Dershowitz's core claim by writing, "in 2000, when Israel offered Yasir Arafat more than 90 percent of the occupied West Bank and Gaza Strip for a Palestinian state, his rejection was accompanied by a terrorist war that shows no sign of stopping."[59]

But not everyone in the United States and Israel shares these views. On the one-year anniversary of the collapse of the July 2000 Camp David summit, *New York Times* reporter Deborah Sontag wrote a lengthy review of the failed negotiations, which included the following assessment:

> In the tumble of the all-consuming violence, much has not been revealed or examined. Rather, a potent, simplistic narrative has taken hold in Israel and to some extent in the United States. It says: Mr. Barak offered Mr. Arafat the moon at Camp David last summer. Mr. Arafat turned it down, and then "pushed the button" and chose the path of violence. . . . But many diplomats and officials believe that the dynamic was far more complex and that Mr. Arafat does not bear sole responsibility for the breakdown of the peace effort. . . . Mr. Barak did not offer Mr. Arafat the moon at Camp David. He broke Israeli taboos against any discussion of dividing Jerusalem, and he sketched out an offer that was politically courageous, especially for an Israeli leader with a faltering coalition. But it was a proposal that the Palestinians did not believe would leave them with a

viable state. And although Mr. Barak said no Israeli leader could go further, he himself improved considerably on his Camp David proposal six months later [at Taba]. "It is a terrible myth that Arafat and only Arafat caused this catastrophic failure," Terje Roed-Larsen, the United Nations special envoy [to the Palestinian territories], said in an interview. "All three parties made mistakes, and in such complex negotiations, everyone is bound to. But no one is solely to blame. . . ." Despite reports to the contrary in Israel, however, Mr. Arafat never turned down "97 percent of the West Bank" at Taba, as many Israelis hold. The negotiations were suspended by Israel because elections were imminent and "the pressure of Israeli public opinion against the talks could not be resisted," said Shlomo Ben-Ami, who was Israel's foreign minister at the time.[60]

Nearly a year after this article in the *Times* was published, a Benny Morris interview with Ehud Barak appeared in the *New York Review of Books* in June 2002, which began with Morris describing a phone call that was placed the year before to Barak by former president Clinton: "The call from Bill Clinton came hours after the publication in the *New York Times* of Deborah Sontag's 'revisionist' article on the Israeli-Palestinian peace process." Barak took the call while swimming in a cove in Sardinia. Clinton said (according to Barak, via Morris): "What the hell is this? Why is [Sontag] turning the mistakes we [the U.S. and Israel] made into the essence? The true story of Camp David was that for the first time in the history of the conflict the American President put on the table a proposal, based on U.N. Security Council resolutions 242 and 338, very close to the Palestinian demands, and Arafat refused even to accept it as a basis for negotiations, walked out of the room, and deliberately turned to terrorism. That's the real story—all the rest is gossip."[61] As Morris noted, "Clinton was speaking of the two-week-long July 2000 Camp David conference that he had organized and mediated and its failure."[62]

While quoting Barak referring to those who challenged the Clinton-Barak rendition of the negotiations as "revisionists," Morris wrote: "Regarding the core of the Israeli-American proposals, the 'revisionists' have charged that Israel offered the Palestinians not a continuous state but a collection of 'bantustans' or 'cantons.' 'This is one of the most embarrassing lies to have emerged from Camp David,' says Barak." Morris then quoted Barak as follows: "I ask myself why is [Arafat] lying. To put it simply, any proposal that offers 92 percent of the West Bank cannot, almost by definition, break up the territory into noncontiguous cantons. The West Bank and the Gaza Strip are separate, but that cannot be helped."[63] (Note that Barak apparently was referring to his final offer at Camp David of 92 percent of the West Bank to the Palestinians.)

Finally, in response to Benny Morris's interview with Ehud Barak in June 2002, Robert Malley, who in July 2000 was director for Near Eastern Affairs in Clinton's

National Security Council and a U.S. negotiator with Dennis Ross at Camp David,[64] and Hussein Agha, a Palestinian negotiator at Camp David,[65] disagreed with the Barak-Morris explanation of why the 2000 peace negotiations failed. They wrote, also in the *New York Review*:

> Barak's assessment that the talks failed because Yasser Arafat cannot make peace with Israel and that his answer to Israel's unprecedented offer was to resort to terrorist violence has become central to the argument that Israel is in a fight for its survival against those who deny its very right to exist. So much of what is said and done today derives from and is justified by that crude appraisal. . . . The one-sided account that was set in motion in the wake of Camp David has had devastating effects—on Israeli public opinion as well as on U.S. foreign policy. That was clear enough a year ago; it has become far clearer since. Rectifying it does not mean, to quote Barak, engaging in "Palestinian propaganda." Rather, it means taking a close look at what actually happened.[66]

One of the things that happened during the discussions among U.S. negotiators between the Camp David summit in July and the presentation of the Clinton parameters in December, as reported by Dennis Ross in *The Missing Peace*, was a conversation between Ross and his aides, including Robert Malley and Aaron Miller. Ross wrote:

> Our internal discussions were heated. Indeed, I would often say that if outside observers saw our discussions, they could easily conclude that we disliked each other. They would have been dead wrong. Our passion for the issue—the desire for peace—was an extraordinary unifier. It was a bond that we shared. However, we also felt the responsibility that came with putting an American proposal on the table. Suddenly our judgments about what would work also came into conflict with what we thought was right or just or fair. Aaron [Miller] was also arguing for a just and fair proposal. I was not against a fair proposal. But I felt the very concept of "fairness" was, by definition, subjective. Similarly, both Rob [Malley] and Gamal [Helal] believed that the Palestinians were entitled to 100 percent of the [Gaza and West Bank] territory. Swaps should thus be equal. They believed this was a Palestinian right. Aaron tended to agree with them not on the basis of right, but on the basis that every other Arab negotiating partner had gotten 100 percent. Why should the Palestinians be different? I disagreed. I was focused not on reconciling rights but on addressing needs.[67]

While foregoing any actual examination of Palestinian rights under international law, and declining to explain why Israel's political "needs" might trump Palestinian territorial rights, Ross noted: "I felt that that the Israelis needed 6 to 7 percent of the [Palestinian West Bank] territory for both security and political purposes," while also observing one paragraph later: "I felt strongly about a 6 to 7 percent [Israeli] annexation [of Palestinian territory], and I was not prepared to lower the ceiling. Nor was I prepared to introduce the idea of an equivalent [land] swap."[68] In fact, at no time throughout the 2000 peace negotiations, under the tutelage of Bill Clinton and Dennis Ross, did the United States or Israel acknowledge that the Fourth Geneva Convention renders the Israeli settlements in East Jerusalem and the West Bank illegal and that Israel had no right to retain any of its settlements (see chapter 6 in this volume), or that the Palestinians at a minimum had a right to a one-to-one territorial swap as a fair measure of compensation for any Israel-annexed Palestinian land.

While former Israeli prime minister Ehud Barak referred to those who found fault with the official edition of facts as "revisionists," Dershowitz was less restrained while referring to the same group of commentators as "enemies of Israel." Thus, how did Israel's "enemies"— Noam Chomsky, Richard Falk, Edward Said, and Norman Finkelstein, identified as such in Dershowitz's 2008 book *The Case against Israel's Enemies*—describe the events of 2000? Here are a few brief samples, all of which more accurately reflect the facts than what Dershowitz has written about the negotiations.

In *Failed States: The Abuse of Power and the Assault on Democracy*, published in 2006, Chomsky wrote:

> In the real world, the Camp David proposals could not possibly be accepted by any Palestinian leader (including [Mahmoud] Abbas, who rejected them). That is evident from a look at the maps that were easily available from standard sources, though apparently are nowhere to be found in the U.S. mainstream. In the most careful analysis, Ron Pundak and Shaul Arieli conclude that Barak's opening offer left Israel in control of 13 percent of the West Bank . . . though Barak's final offer reduced it to 12 percent. The most authoritative map, which Pundak provided in another analysis, reveals that the U.S.-Israeli proposal established three cantons in the remnants of the West Bank left to the Palestinians. The three are formed by the Israeli salients [corridors] extending from Israel well into the West Bank. . . . The effect is largely to separate the southern and central [West Bank] cantons from the northern one. Along with other significant expansion, the proposals effectively cut off the major Palestinian towns (Bethlehem, Ramallah, Nablus) from one another. And all Palestinian fragments are largely separated from the small sector of

East Jerusalem that is the center of Palestinian commercial, cultural, religious, and political life and institutions.[69]

In a 2003 volume *Unlocking the Middle East: The Writings of Richard Falk*, the Princeton professor of international law wrote:

> It has been endlessly repeated, without any demonstration, that the Israelis under Prime Minister Ehud Barak made a generous offer at Camp David in the summer of 2000. It is then alleged that Arafat rejected an offer he should have accepted and resumed armed struggle. Further, it has been alleged that Arafat's rejection was tantamount to saying that the struggle was not about establishing a Palestinian state but about ending the existence of the Jewish state. It was this one-sided assessment, alongside others, that led to [Ariel] Sharon's election, which meant that Israel would henceforth be represented by a man with a long record of uncompromising brutality toward Palestinians and a disregard of their legitimate claims for self-determination.[70]

Writing about the September 28, 2000 visit by Likud leader Ariel Sharon to the Haram al-Sharif / Temple Mount and the start of the Second Palestinian Intifada, Edward Said wrote this analysis in his 2001 volume *The End of the Peace Process: Oslo and After*:

> Misreported and flawed from the start, the Oslo peace process has entered its terminal phase of violent confrontation, disproportionately massive Israeli repression, widespread Palestinian rebellion and great loss of life, mainly Palestinian. . . . Labor and Likud leaders alike make no secret of the fact that Oslo was designed to segregate the Palestinians in non-contiguous, economically unviable enclaves, surrounded by Israeli-controlled borders, with settlements and settlement roads punctuating and essentially violating the territories' integrity. Expropriations and house demolitions proceeded inexorably through the Rabin, Peres, Netanyahu, and Barak administrations, along with the expansion and multiplication of settlements, military occupation continuing and every tiny step taken toward Palestinian sovereignty—including agreements to withdraw in miniscule, agreed-upon phases—stymied, delayed, canceled at Israel's will.[71]

In his 2005 book *Beyond Chutzpah*, which scrutinized in detail numerous factually problematic claims by Dershowitz, including those relating to the 2000 peace negotiations and the start of the Second Palestinian Intifada,[72] Finkelstein wrote: "During the early weeks of the second intifada (beginning in late September 2000), the ratio of Palestinians to Israelis killed was 20:1, with the overwhelming majority of Palestinians 'killed in demonstrations in circumstances when the lives of the [Israeli] security services were not in danger' (Amnesty International)."[73] Furthermore, in a lengthy review of Dennis Ross's book *The Missing Peace*, with a focus at one point on the matter of Ross's subordination of established Palestinian rights to Israel's domestic political needs, Finkelstein wrote: "It is not immediately obvious why a standard of rights reached by broad international consensus and codified in international law is more 'subjective' than a standard of needs on which there is neither consensus nor codification. . . . What is most peculiar about Ross's argument is his apparent belief that his personal adjudication is less arbitrary than reference to a consensual body of laws."[74]

According to the Anti-Defamation League, the Palestinian terrorist attacks that killed and injured civilians inside Israel began on October 28, 2001—not on September 29, 2000—and continued as follows:

- *October 28, 2001*: "Two Palestinian gunmen killed four Israeli women at a crowded bus stop in the city of Hadera."
- *November 27, 2001*: "Two Palestinian gunmen opened fire on a crowd of people near the central bus station in the city of Afula, killing two people."
- *November 29, 2001*: "A suicide bombing of a bus on its way from Nazareth to Hadera killed three people."
- *December 1, 2001*: "A double suicide bombing at the Ben-Yehuda pedestrian mall in Jerusalem at 11:30 PM on a Saturday night killed 11 people, aged 12–21, and injured 188 people."
- *December 2, 2001*: "A suicide bombing on a No. 16 Egged bus in Haifa killed 15 people and injured about 40 people."
- *December 12, 2001*: "Palestinian gunmen attacked a No. 189 Dan bus and several passenger cars near the entrance to the settlement of Emmanuel, killing 10 people and injuring about 30 people."
- *January 17, 2002*: "A Palestinian gunman burst into a bat mitzvah celebration in a banquet hall in Hadera, opening fire on the 180 guests with an M-16 assault rifle, killing 6 people and injuring 35 people."
- *January 22, 2002*: "A Palestinian terrorist opened fire with an M-16 assault rifle near a bus stop in downtown Jerusalem, killing two women and injuring about 40 others."
- *January 25, 2002*: "A suicide bombing outside a cafe on a pedestrian mall in Tel Aviv injured 25 people."
- *January 27, 2002*: "A suicide bombing in the center of Jerusalem killed one person and wounded more than 150."

- *February 8, 2002:* "A 25-year-old Israeli woman was stabbed to death by four Palestinians, ages 14–16, while strolling with her boyfriend in the Peace Forest, below the Sherover Promenade in Jerusalem's Armon Hanatziv neighborhood."[75]

These terrorist attacks initiated a long line of Palestinian terrorist attacks against Israel, most of which targeted and killed Israeli civilians, violated international humanitarian law and human rights law, and were deplorable and criminal acts. If the policy objectives of the United States and Israel are to prevent such terrorist acts, one should note that the long sequence of terrorist attacks on Israeli civilians in this instance began more than a year after the onset of the Second Palestinian Intifada on September 29, 2000, and thus well after Israeli security forces had killed hundreds of Palestinians, including many Palestinian children, while injuring many thousands more, including those who were severely injured and permanently disabled. Furthermore, these lethal Israeli attacks on Palestinians not only violated humanitarian law and the human rights of the Palestinians who were killed and injured, they followed peace talks at which both the United States and Israel ignored Palestinian territorial rights under international law, as Dennis Ross, the chief U.S. negotiator, clearly concedes.

On the basis, therefore, of the sequence of events detailed previously, this chapter functions as a case study to support the argument in this volume that aggressive warfare by the United States and Israel generates anti-American and anti-Israel terrorism, and that a plausible theory to reduce the threat of such terrorism would be for the United States and Israel to comply with *existing* international law with respect to Muslim populations. This chapter also shows that Dershowitz is an unreliable reporter of facts, and that his jurisprudence of terrorism prevention for the United States—which is grounded in misleading representations of the causes of Muslim terrorism and would probably lead to an increased threat of terrorism against the United States and increasingly intrusive counterterrorism measures—threatens the Bill of Rights.

6

THE FOURTH GENEVA CONVENTION

If you have never heard of the Fourth Geneva Convention of 1949 and thus do not know what Article 49, paragraph 6, of the convention says, or which UN member states and which institutions do or do not recognize the applicability of the convention to Israel's occupation of Palestinian territory, then it would not be possible to understand a core aspect of that conflict as it has existed since June 1967. Nor would it be possible to assess the simple fairness of the American and Israeli proposals at Camp David in July 2000, and throughout the rest of that year, which featured the retention of large Israeli settlement blocs in the Palestinian West Bank, in addition, obviously, to the Palestinian land on which the settlements were built. And if you have been reading only Alan Dershowitz's writings about the Israel-Palestine conflict over the past several years, you would know very little about the Fourth Geneva Convention and what it says.

In fact, one way to assess the validity of the work of Noam Chomsky and Alan Dershowitz is to be acquainted with their respective positions on the applicability of the Fourth Geneva Convention to the Israel-Palestine conflict overall and to the Israeli settlements in particular. Chomsky, consistent with a nearly unanimous international consensus, holds that the convention is legally applicable to Israel's occupation of the Palestinian territories. Dershowitz, on the other hand, ignores the Fourth Geneva Convention. In this regard, there isn't much difference between Dershowitz's writings and the mainstream U.S. sources that he often credits to support his public defense of Israel's policies, since the Fourth Geneva Convention also is not mentioned in *The Missing Peace* (2004) by Dennis Ross, *Madam Secretary* (2005) by Madeleine Albright, U.S. Secretary of State under President Clinton and during the 2000 Israel-Palestine negotiations, and *My Life* (2005) by Bill Clinton.

To begin, and very briefly, the Fourth Geneva Convention is the modern foundation of international humanitarian law, which consists of the rules of armed conflict seeking to protect people not taking part in hostilities.[1] During World War II, "the law of Geneva," as embodied in the three Geneva Conventions in force at the time, applied only to military personnel who were no longer taking part in the fighting. These included the wounded and sick members of the armed forces (Geneva I), the wounded, sick, and shipwrecked members of the armed forces at sea (Geneva II), and prisoners of war (Geneva III).[2] However, when the war led to the killing of 50–70 million civilians worldwide, the international community established the Fourth Geneva Convention (1949) for the protection of civilians in two settings: armed conflict and military occupation.[3]

A key prohibition of the Fourth Geneva Convention, which is especially relevant to the Israeli military occupation of the Palestinian territories, is expressed in Article 49(6), which states: "The Occupying Power shall not deport or transfer parts of its own civilian population into the territory it occupies."[4] This provision would appear to outlaw all Israeli settlements in the occupied territories, including the big Israeli settlement blocs in the West Bank, given that the settlements are the product of the transfer of parts of Israel's population into Israel-occupied Palestinian territory. Since Israel's settlements are a key obstacle to a comprehensive Israel-Palestine peace agreement—and implicate questions pertaining to borders and the territorial contiguity of the West Bank in a Palestinian state—the issue of the legal status of the settlements is crucial. And, on this point, virtually every UN member state (except the United States and Israel), and every authoritative third-party legal assessment, has concluded that the Fourth Geneva Convention is legally applicable to the Israeli occupation and that the convention outlaws Israel's settlements in the West Bank, including in East Jerusalem. The long-standing established fact of the nearly unanimous international consensus about the Fourth Geneva Convention outlawing the Israeli settlements may explain why the convention is not mentioned by Dershowitz in his published works or in the memoirs of the principal U.S. participants in the 2000 peace negotiations.

A summary of the international consensus on the applicability of the Fourth Geneva Convention to the Israel-Palestine conflict is presented in this chapter, featuring the positions of the UN Security Council, the UN General Assembly, and the International Court of Justice, in addition to the major human rights organizations that have addressed this question: the Geneva-based International Committee of the Red Cross, the London-based Amnesty International, the New York-based Human Rights Watch, and the Israel-based B'Tselem.

The UN Security Council on the Fourth Geneva Convention. In a resolution issued in September 1969, the UN Security Council called upon "Israel scrupulously to observe the provisions of the Geneva Conventions and international law governing military occupation."[5] In March 1979, the Security Council stated that

Israel's settlements on occupied Arab territory had "no legal validity" and affirmed "once again" that the Fourth Geneva Convention "is applicable to the Arab territories occupied by Israel since 1967, including Jerusalem."[6] In December 1992, the Security Council "reaffirm[ed] the applicability of the Fourth Geneva Convention of 12 August 1949 to all the Palestinian territories occupied by Israel since 1967, including Jerusalem."[7] And in March 1994, the Security Council again "affirmed the applicability of the Fourth Geneva Convention of 12 August 1949 to the territories occupied by Israel in June 1967."[8]

The UN General Assembly on the Fourth Geneva Convention. From 1970 to 1998, in a series of resolutions that were supported by the vast majority of UN member states (the lone member states in dissent being Israel and the United States), the General Assembly declared that the Fourth Geneva Convention of 1949 was applicable to Israel's occupation of the Palestinian territories. The resolutions also declared that Israel's annexation of East Jerusalem, in addition to its settlements in the West Bank and Gaza, violated the convention.

In a resolution issued in 1970, the General Assembly called on Israel "to comply" with its legal obligations under the Fourth Geneva Convention.[9] A 1971 resolution called on Israel "to comply fully" with the convention.[10] The United States and Israel voted against both resolutions.[11] In a 1972 resolution, the General Assembly specifically linked Israel's obligations under the Fourth Geneva Convention, which Israel ratified in 1951, to its annexation and settlement policies at the time. The United States and Israel voted against this resolution as well.[12]

In 1973, UN member states voted unanimously to affirm that the Fourth Geneva Convention applies to the Arab territories occupied by Israel since 1967, and "call[ed] upon Israeli occupation authorities to respect and comply with the provisions of that Convention." The General Assembly vote supporting the resolution was 120 to 0 with five abstentions; the United States voted for the resolution while Israel abstained.[13] In a similar General Assembly resolution in 1974, the vote was 121 to 0 with seven abstentions; the U.S. favored the resolution with Israel abstaining.[14] In 1975, the vote on the same issue was 112 to 2 with seven abstentions; the United States and Israel issued the only votes in opposition.[15] And in 1976, the vote was 134 to 0 with two abstentions—Israel and Haiti.[16]

Beginning in 1977, and following the watershed electoral victory of the right-wing Likud Party, which included Menachem Begin as prime minister, Israel would vote against every subsequent General Assembly resolution affirming the applicability of the Fourth Geneva Convention to the Israeli occupation of the Arab territories, and in each such vote up to 1994—a period of eighteen years— Israel was the only UN member state to do so. However, in 1994 and 1995, the Clinton administration joined Israel in denying the applicability of the Fourth Geneva Convention to the Israel-occupied Arab territories. The vote count at the

UN General Assembly from 1977 through 1995 affirming the applicability of the convention is presented as follows:

1977: 131 to 1 (Israel opposed) with seven abstentions;
1978: 140 to 1 (Israel) with one abstention;
1979: 139 to 1 (Israel) with one abstention;
1980: 141 to 1 (Israel) with one abstention;
1981: 142 to 1 (Israel) with three abstentions;
1982: 134 to 1 (Israel) with one abstention;
1983: 146 to 1 (Israel) with one abstention;
1984: 140 to 1 (Israel) with three abstentions;
1985: 137 to 1 (Israel) with six abstentions;
1986: 145 to 1 (Israel) with six abstentions;
1987: 142 to 1 (Israel) with eight abstentions;
1988: 148 to 1 (Israel) with four abstentions;
1989: 149 to 1 (Israel) with two abstentions;
1990: 145 to 1 (Israel) with one abstention;
1991: 153 to 1 (Israel) with three abstentions;
1992: 141 to 1 (Israel) with four abstentions;
1993: 152 to 1 (Israel) with six abstentions;
1994: 155 to 3 (U.S., Israel, and Gambia) with five abstentions;
1995: 147 to 2 (U.S. and Israel) with four abstentions.[17]

Beginning in 1996, the General Assembly began issuing short, stand-alone resolutions focused exclusively on reaffirming the applicability of the Fourth Geneva Convention to the Israel-occupied territories. In each vote in each of these years, the United States (under presidents Bill Clinton, George W. Bush, and Barack Obama) voted against the international consensus by denying the applicability of the convention to the occupation. The vote tallies follow:

1996: 156 to 2 (U.S. and Israel opposed) with three abstentions;
1997: 156 to 2 (U.S. and Israel) with three abstentions;
1998: 155 to 2 (U.S. and Israel) with two abstentions;
1999: 154 to 2 (U.S. and Israel) with one abstention;
2000: 152 to 2 (U.S. and Israel) with two abstentions;
2001: 152 to 2 (U.S. and Israel) with two abstentions;
2002: 155 to 6 (U.S., Israel, Marshall Islands, Micronesia, Nauru, Palau) with three abstentions;
2003: 164 to 6 (U.S., Israel, Marshall Islands, Micronesia, Nauru, Palau) with four abstentions;
2004: 160 to 7 (U.S., Israel, Grenada, Marshall Islands, Mauritania, Mi-

cronesia, Palau) with eleven abstentions;

2005: 158 to 6 (U.S., Israel, Grenada, Marshall Islands, Micronesia, Palau) with seven abstentions;

2006: 165 to 7 (U.S., Israel, Marshall Islands, Micronesia, Nauru, Palau, Tuvalu) with ten abstentions;

2007: 169 to 6 (U.S., Israel, Marshall Islands, Micronesia, Nauru, Palau) with three abstentions;

2008: 173 to 6 (U.S., Israel, Marshall Islands, Micronesia, Nauru, Palau) with one abstention;

2009: 168 to 6 (U.S., Israel, Marshall Islands, Micronesia, Nauru, Palau) with four abstentions;

2010: 169 to 6 (U.S., Israel, Marshall Islands, Micronesia, Nauru, Palau) with two abstentions.[18]

Furthermore, in December 2010, the United States and Israel voted against a General Assembly resolution which, upon affirming once again the applicability of the Fourth Geneva Convention, also "reaffirm[ed] that the Israeli settlements in the Palestinian territory, including East Jerusalem, and in the occupied Syrian Golan, are illegal and an obstacle to peace and economic and social development."[19]

Similar resolutions citing the illegal status of Israel's settlements under the Fourth Geneva Convention were issued by the General Assembly from 1996 to 2009, which the United States and Israel opposed in each instance as follows, including with the usual votes from the Pacific island-states and later the right-wing government of Australian prime minister John Howard:

1996: 152 to 2 (U.S. and Israel opposed) with six abstentions;

1997: 149 to 2 (U.S. and Israel) with seven abstentions;

1998: 150 to 3 (U.S., Israel, Micronesia) with two abstentions;

1999: 149 to 3 (U.S., Israel, Micronesia) with three abstentions;

2000: 152 to 4 (U.S., Israel, Marshall Islands, Micronesia) with no abstentions;

2001: 145 to 4 (U.S., Israel, Marshall Islands, Micronesia) with three abstentions;

2002: 154 to 6 (U.S., Israel, Marshall Islands, Micronesia, Nauru, Palau) with three abstentions;

2003: 156 to 6 (U.S., Israel, Marshall Islands, Micronesia, Nauru, Palau) with thirteen abstentions;

2004: 155 to 8 (U.S., Israel, Australia, Grenada, Marshall Islands, Micronesia, Nauru, Palau) with fifteen abstentions;

2005: 153 to 7 (U.S., Israel, Australia, Grenada, Marshall Islands, Micronesia, Palau) with ten abstentions;

2006: 162 to 8 (U.S., Israel, Australia, Marshall Islands, Micronesia,

Nauru, Palau, Tuvalu) with ten abstentions;

2007: 165 to 7 (U.S., Israel, Australia, Marshall Islands, Micronesia, Nauru, Palau) with five abstentions;

2008: 171 to 6 (U.S., Israel, Marshall Islands, Micronesia, Nauru, Palau) with two abstentions;

2009: 167 to 7 (U.S., Israel, Marshall Islands, Micronesia, Nauru, Palau, Panama) with three abstentions.[20]

As the votes on these resolutions indicate, and despite an overwhelming consensus among member states at the United Nations, the U.S. and Israel have refused to affirm either that the Fourth Geneva Convention applies to Israel's occupation or that the convention outlaws the Israeli settlements. And given that the United States under President Clinton voted against the applicability of the Fourth Geneva Convention to the Israeli occupation, it seems unlikely that he would have acted as an honest broker between the Israelis and Palestinians at the Camp David summit in July 2000 by applying Israel's legal obligations to the convention as part of the substantive negotiations with the Palestinians.

The International Court of Justice (ICJ) on the Fourth Geneva Convention. In its 2004 advisory opinion on the "Legal Consequences of the Construction of a Wall in the Occupied Palestinian Territory," the International Court of Justice, which is the judicial arm of the United Nations, legally settled the issue of the applicability of the Fourth Geneva Convention to the Israel-occupied territories. By a 14 to 1 majority (with the U.S. judge in dissent), and about the core issue before the court, it concluded that "the construction of the wall being built by Israel, the occupying Power, in the Occupied Palestinian Territory, including in and around East Jerusalem, and its associated régime, are contrary to international law."[21] Relatedly, the court also ruled on aspects of the Fourth Geneva Convention as it pertains to Israel's occupation, including as follows:

- "In view of the foregoing, the Court considers that the Fourth Geneva Convention is applicable in the Palestinian territories which before the 1967 conflict lay to the east of the Green Line and which, during that conflict, were occupied by Israel, there being no need for any enquiry into the precise prior status of those territories."[22]
- "The information provided to the Court shows that, since 1977, Israel has conducted a policy and developed practices involving the establishment of settlements in the Occupied Palestinian Territory, contrary to the terms of Article 49, paragraph 6, of the Fourth Geneva Convention which provides: 'The Occupying Power shall not deport or transfer parts of its own civilian population into the territory it occupies.' The Security Council has taken the view that such policy and practices 'have no legal validity' and constitute

a 'flagrant violation' of the Convention. The Court concludes that the Israeli settlements in the Occupied Palestinian Territory (including East Jerusalem) have been established in breach of international law."[23]

Even the U.S. judge, Thomas Buergenthal, who was the lone dissenting vote in five of the court's seven decisions,[24] agreed with the other fourteen judges that the Fourth Geneva Convention applies to the Israeli occupation. On this point, Buergenthal concluded "that Article 49, paragraph 6, which provides that 'the Occupying Power shall not deport or transfer parts of its own civilian population into the territory it occupies,' applies to the Israeli settlements in the West Bank, and that they violate Article 49, paragraph 6."[25]

The International Committee of the Red Cross (ICRC) on the Fourth Geneva Convention. In addition to the ICJ and the great majority of UN member states, the four major human rights organizations with institutional or organizational mandates requiring them to oversee the implementation of international humanitarian law, including the Fourth Geneva Convention, all recognize the applicability of the convention to Israel's occupation, as well as the illegal status of Israel's settlements. On December 5, 2001, the ICRC, which officially administers the Geneva Conventions, reaffirmed its long-standing view: "In accordance with a number of resolutions adopted by the United Nations General Assembly and Security Council and by the International Conference of the Red Cross and Red Crescent, which reflect the view of the international community, the ICRC has always affirmed the de jure applicability of the Fourth Geneva Convention to the territories occupied since 1967 by the State of Israel, including East Jerusalem." The ICRC stated further: "In the course of its activities in the territories occupied by Israel, the ICRC has repeatedly noted breaches of various provisions of international humanitarian law, such as the transfer by Israel of parts of its population into the occupied territories. . . . In particular, the ICRC has expressed growing concern about the consequences in humanitarian terms of the establishment of Israeli settlements in the occupied territories, in violation of the Fourth Geneva Convention."[26]

Amnesty International on the Fourth Geneva Convention. Amnesty International also recognizes the applicability of the Fourth Geneva Convention to the Israeli occupation. In a press release issued on December 4, 2001, just prior to the ICRC's official statement of December 5, Amnesty International "welcomed the reaffirmation of the principles of the Fourth Geneva Convention" to the occupied Palestinian territories by its high contracting parties (states that have ratified the convention), and urged the parties to "now agree on concrete measures to ensure respect for the Convention and prevent further deterioration of the human rights situation in the Occupied Territories."[27] In response to a February 2011 U.S. veto of a UN Security Council resolution condemning Israel's settlements, Amnesty responded as follows:

Israel's policy of settling its civilians on occupied land violates the Fourth Geneva Convention, and is considered a war crime according to the statute of the International Criminal Court. Israel's settlement policy is also inherently discriminatory and results in continuing violations of the rights to adequate housing, water and livelihoods for Palestinians in the occupied West Bank, as Amnesty International has repeatedly documented. Reported US government attempts to pressure the Palestinian Authority not to bring this resolution to a vote at the UN Security Council, including threats to cut US aid, are also troubling. If the Obama administration is serious about promoting a lasting, just resolution to the Israeli-Palestinian conflict, it should fully back the international consensus against Israel's illegal settlements and the human rights violations that result from them.[28]

Human Rights Watch on the Fourth Geneva Convention. Like Amnesty International, Human Rights Watch recognizes the applicability of the Fourth Geneva Convention to the Israeli occupation, including as stated in a 2001 report (parentheses in original): "Two legal regimes are directly relevant to Israel's obligations in the Occupied West Bank and the Gaza Strip. The first legal regime is that of International Humanitarian Law (particularly the Fourth Geneva Convention), which applies to situations of belligerent occupation as well as situations where hostilities rise to the level of international armed conflict."[29] In a report issued one year later, Human Rights Watch stated: "The Palestinian civilian inhabitants of the occupied West Bank and Gaza Strip are 'Protected Persons' under the Fourth Geneva Convention. They are entitled to extensive protections under the laws of war."[30] In February 2011, Human Rights Watch responded to the U.S. veto of the UN effort to condemn Israel's settlements: "The US veto of a proposed United Nations Security Council Resolution calling upon Israel to end illegal policies that promote settlements in the occupied West Bank, including East Jerusalem, undermines enforcement of international law. . . . The Fourth Geneva Convention of 1949 explicitly prohibits an occupying power from transferring its civilian population into occupied territory. Notwithstanding this ban, almost half-a-million Jewish Israelis with Israeli government support have moved into settlements it has constructed in the Occupied Palestinian Territories, and formally annexed occupied territory in East Jerusalem, a move not recognized by any other government in the world."[31]

B'Tselem on the Fourth Geneva Convention. In a section on "International Humanitarian Law" on its Web site, B'Tselem states that "the Fourth Geneva Convention deals with the protection of civilians during war or under occupation, and therefore relates to Israel's actions in the Occupied Territories."[32] In a section on "Land Expropriation and Settlements," B'Tselem states (parentheses in original): "The establishment of settlements in the West Bank violates international humanitarian law which establishes principles that apply during war and occupation. . . . The Fourth Geneva Convention prohibits an occupying power from transferring citizens from its own territory to the occupied territory (Article 49). . . . The establishment of settlements results in the violation of the rights of Palestinians as enshrined in international human rights law. Among other violations, the settlements infringe the right to self-determination, equality, property, an adequate standard of living, and freedom of movement."[33]

Noam Chomsky on the Fourth Geneva Convention. Consistent with the international consensus, Chomsky recognizes that the Fourth Geneva Convention applies to the Israeli occupation and outlaws the Israeli settlements. In a recent book, Chomsky wrote: "It is useful to bear in mind that Israel understood at once that its settlement projects in the occupied territories, and anything related to them, are illegal. Israel's top legal authority on international law, Theodor Meron, a distinguished international lawyer and a leading figure in international tribunals, informed the government in September 1967 'that civilian settlement in the administered [Palestinian] territories contravenes the explicit provisions of the Fourth Geneva Convention,' the core of international humanitarian law."[34]

Two relatively recent books by Israeli scholars on the history of the settlements—Chomsky has cited both,[35] while Dershowitz has ignored them— concur with the international consensus on the applicability of the Fourth Geneva Convention. In his 2006 book *The Accidental Empire: Israel and the Birth of the Settlements, 1967–1977*, Gershom Gorenberg reproduced the memorandum by Theodor Meron cited by Chomsky:

> Jerusalem, 13 Elul, 5727
> September 18, 1967
>
> Top Secret
>
> To: Mr. Yafeh, Political Secretary of the Prime Minister
> From: Legal Counsel of the Foreign Ministry
> Re: Settlement in the Administered Territories
>
> As per your request . . . I hereby provide you a copy of my memorandum of September 14, 1967, which I presented to the Foreign Minister. My conclusion is that civilian settlements in the administered territories contravene the explicit provisions of the Fourth Geneva Convention.
>
> Sincerely,
> T. Meron

About Meron and the legal memorandum, Gorenberg wrote:

> As legal counsel to the Foreign Ministry, Meron was the Israeli government's authority on international law. He had achieved that position at a remarkably young age and with an even more remarkable biography. Born in Poland in 1930, he had spent four years of his youth in the Nazi labor camp at Czestochowa. For the entire war, "from age 9 to 15, I did not go to school at all," he told a *New York Times* interviewer decades later. "There were tremendous gaps in my education. It gave me a great hunger for learning, and I dreamed one day I could go to school." After reaching Palestine as a teenager he voraciously made up for lost time—earning a law degree at Hebrew University, then a doctorate at Harvard, then studying international law at Cambridge. The boy who received his first education in war crimes as a victim was on his way to becoming one of the world's most prominent experts on the limits that nations put on the conduct of war. . . .
>
> The key provision in international law that stood in the way of settlement, Meron wrote, was the Fourth Geneva Convention on protection of civilians in time of war, adopted in 1949, which stated that an "Occupying Power shall not deport or transfer parts of its own civilian population into the territory it occupies." The authoritative commentary, he added, stated: "This clause . . . is intended to prevent a practice adopted during the Second World War by certain Powers, which transferred portions of their own population to occupied territory for political and racial reasons or in order, as they claimed, to colonize these territories." Writing those words, Meron knew all too vividly who the "certain Powers" had been.[36]

In the second major book on the history of the Israeli settlements, *Lords of the Land: The War Over Israel's Settlements in the Occupied Territories, 1967–2007*, Israeli historian Idith Zertal and Israeli journalist Akiva Eldar cited not only the legal status of the Israeli settlements, but also the impact of the settlements on the human rights of Palestinians:

> Throughout the years of occupation, and under the auspices of the Israeli legal system, the steadily tightening Israeli rule had been in far-reaching breach of international conventions and particularly the Fourth Geneva Convention. Israel has tried, successfully, to enjoy the best of several worlds that do not reconcile with one another legally. It has maintained a regime in the territories based on a military commander's authority and power in an occupied territory. However, it has not taken upon itself the limitations and prohibitions that obligate an occupying state, like the prohibition on transferring population from that state into the occupied territory, or the prohibition on confiscating private property. . . .

The Jewish settlement, at God's command and at the government's will, has thus caused continuing and extensive damage to the basic human rights of the Palestinians who live in the territories, among them the rights to personal liberty, freedom of movement, and property; it has also thwarted any possibility for the realization of the collective rights of those who lived in the territory before the intrusion of the Israeli forces, such as the right to national self-determination, including statehood. The entrenchment of more than a quarter of a million Jews in the Palestinian territories (and close to twice that if one counts East Jerusalem), and the making of the well-being and security of the Jewish settlers Israel's top priority, created a situation of critical separation, persecution, and discrimination. The state has given minimal protection and legal aid to the Palestinian inhabitants in the face of fanaticism and violence from Jewish settlers and the discriminatory attitudes of authorities such as the army and the police.[37]

In addition to citing Meron and Gorenberg, Chomsky has also observed that the Bush administration, in December 2001, boycotted the Switzerland-sponsored conference in Geneva of the high contracting parties to the Fourth Geneva Convention, which "specifically declared the U.S.-funded Israeli settlements to be illegal."[38]

Alan Dershowitz on the Fourth Geneva Convention. In contrast to Chomsky, and despite writing prolifically about the Israel-Palestine conflict in books as well as in newspapers and Web commentary, Dershowitz in essence has ignored the international consensus on the applicability of the Fourth Geneva Convention to the Israeli occupation, as well as the established legal fact that the convention outlaws the Israeli settlements in Palestinian territory. From 2002 to 2008, Dershowitz published five books, all widely reviewed, that were wholly or largely about the Israel-Palestine conflict: *Why Terrorism Works: Understanding the Threat, Responding to the Challenge* (2002); *The Case for Israel* (2003); *The Case for Peace: How the Arab-Israeli Conflict Can Be Resolved* (2005); *Preemption: A Knife That Cuts Both Ways* (2006); and *The Case against Israel's Enemies: Exposing Jimmy Carter and Others Who Stand in the Way of Peace* (2008). Despite the core relevance of the Fourth Geneva Convention to the Israeli occupation, including with respect to the Israeli settlements, Dershowitz barely mentions the convention, if at all, in these books.

In *Why Terrorism Works*, there is no reference to the "Fourth Geneva Convention" in the index, and a search in Google Books shows a single reference by Dershowitz to "the Geneva Convention" in an endnote to chapter 5. The index also lists a reference to what Dershowitz refers to as the "Geneva Accords," which appears in a paragraph in his book about whether "the international law of war" is a serviceable legal context for Israel and the United States in their war against terrorism. In that paragraph, Dershowitz notes that "traditional wars were fought by combatants in uniform, representing nations with return addresses and accountability." He continues: "The current terrorist wars are different. The terrorists are themselves 'civilians,' their targets are civilians, they hide among civilians, and they are supported and financed by civilians. They exploit the traditional international law of war, especially the *Geneva Accords*, to their advantage and place those who seek to protect their civilian populations on the defensive [emphasis added]."[39] While the accuracy of Dershowitz's claims pertaining to the alleged unfairness of the laws of war to states like the United States and Israel is disputed in this volume, it is sufficient to note for now that there are no "Geneva Accords" in international humanitarian law, as Dershowitz wrote. He continued: "Since these terrorists ignore the law of war, they are free to target civilians with impunity. If they are captured, they demand 'prisoner of war' status. If the nations they target try to defend themselves by going after terrorists hiding among civilians, the terrorists inevitably complain that these nations are violating the *Geneva Accords* by endangering 'civilians.' It is a win-win situation for the terrorists and a lose-lose situation for the victims—because of the inadequacy of current law [emphasis added]."[40]

Once again, Dershowitz cites something called the "Geneva Accords" while referring to international humanitarian law, when no such instrument of humanitarian law exists by that designation. Thus, in the context of his expert complaint, being a professor of law at Harvard, that international humanitarian law is inherently unfair to the United States and Israel, and upon neglecting to mention the Fourth Geneva Convention, let alone as to whether it applies to the Israeli occupation and settlements, Dershowitz misspeaks (not once but twice) by invoking nonexistent "Geneva Accords" in humanitarian law that he claims are "exploited" by terrorists.[41]

Notwithstanding these bungled references to "Geneva Accords," Dershowitz's first major book on the Israel-Palestine conflict, *Why Terrorism Works*, contained no actual references to the Fourth Geneva Convention, despite arguing in that book that international humanitarian law, of which the Fourth Geneva Convention is the core body of law, favors the terrorists against the United States and Israel, and therefore must be changed to better accommodate those two states.

His next book, *The Case for Israel*, contains a single reference to the "Fourth Geneva Convention," which appears in the context of a petition by faculty and students at MIT and Harvard University "to divest from Israel, and from US companies that sell arms to Israel, until these conditions are met." The petitioners then listed their four "conditions" with which the two universities must be "in compliance," the third of which was stated in its entirety as follows (parentheses in original): "In compliance with the Fourth Geneva Convention ('The occupying power shall not deport or transfer parts of its own civilian population into territories it occupies'; Article 49, paragraph 6), Israel ceases building new settlements, and vacates existing settlements, in the Occupied Territories."[42] While referring to this demand and the others, Dershowitz mentions the Fourth Geneva Convention in *The Case for Israel* once as follows: "The [divestment] petition demands that Israel comply with UN Resolution 242, the UN Committee against Torture 2001 Report, the Fourth Geneva Convention, and UN Resolution 194 with respect to the rights of refugees. Apparently, most of the signatories of this petition, which included 130 Harvard and MIT faculty members at last count, are unaware of the fact that Israel has *already* complied with or has offered to comply with each of these conditions."[43] Without noting that Israel has refused for decades to recognize the applicability of the Fourth Geneva Convention to its occupation of the Palestinian territories, that it does not acknowledge publicly the illegal status of its settlements under the convention and that Israel obviously has not dismantled its settlements, and without footnoting his claims that both the state of Israel and "a significant number of the settlers have now expressed a willingness to leave their homes in exchange for peace," Dershowitz blamed the Palestinians for the ongoing existence of the Israeli settlements: "But the Palestinians have refused to accept peace offers made by the Israeli government. Many moderate Palestinians agree that Arafat's rejection of the peace offer made at Camp David and at Taba was a tactical mistake and that the resumption of terrorism against Israel is morally indefensible."[44] This is yet another application of Dershowitz's faulty representations about the negotiations at Camp David in July 2000, and it is the sole context under which Dershowitz claimed that Israel has already complied, or has offered to comply, with the Fourth Geneva Convention with respect to its settlements.

In the three remaining books—*The Case for Peace* (2005), *Preemption* (2006), and *The Case against Israel's Enemies* (2008)—Dershowitz never mentions the Fourth Geneva Convention by name. In *The Case for Peace*, Dershowitz alludes to the ICRC conference on the Fourth Geneva Convention by referring untidily to "the reconvening of the Geneva Convention on December 5, 2001."[45] This reference also appeared in a section titled "Overcoming the Hatred Barriers to Peace," and in a paragraph that began: "UN hate [against Israel] has actually accelerated in recent years."[46] Dershowitz wrote no other words of his own concerning the December 2001 conference in Geneva on the Fourth Geneva Convention and thus declined to mention that the conference was called to reaffirm the applicability of the convention to an Israeli occupation that, at the time, was in its fourth decade.

While not commenting himself, Dershowitz instead invoked the words of Irwin Cotler, former attorney general of Canada, who described the December 2001 ICRC conference as "a prime example of discriminatory treatment" against Israel. Cotler continued, referring to the ICRC conference as "government-sanctioned hate speech" against Israel:

Fifty-two years after its adoption in 1949, the contracting parties of the Geneva Convention met again in Geneva to put Israel in the dock for violating the convention. Until that time, not one country in the international community was ever brought before the contracting parties of the Geneva Convention—not Cambodia with regard to genocide, not the Balkan states with regard to ethnic cleansing, not Rwanda with regard to genocide, not Sudan or Sierra Leone with regard to the killings fields in those countries. When politics overruns the law, the result is prejudice to the Geneva Convention and to the *universality of its principles.* *Regrettably*, in the Middle East, and particularly with regard to the Israeli-Palestinian conflict, this government-sanctioned hate speech has not been given the importance it deserves. It is this state-sanctioned culture of incitement that is the most proximate cause of violence and terror. The assault on terrorism should, in fact, begin with efforts to end this state-sanctioned incitement.[47] (Emphasis added.)

In quoting Cotler, Dershowitz declined the use of ellipses to mark the points in Cotler's original text that Dershowitz omitted. Indeed, after "the universality of its principles" and before "Regrettably" in Dershowitz's reproduction—which is where Dershowitz should have inserted ellipses—Cotler likened the December 2001 conference in Geneva to the "state-sanctioned culture of hate" of the Nazis, as follows:

What are the lessons to be learned? The first lesson is the danger of a state-sanctioned culture of hate. We learned from World War II and the genocide of European Jewry that the Holocaust did not come about simply as a result of the industry of death and the technology of terror of the Nazis, but rather because of the ideology—indeed pathology—of hate. This demonizing of the other, this teaching of contempt, is where it all begins. As the Supreme Court of Canada put it in validating anti-hate legislation in Canada, "The Holocaust did not begin in the gas chambers; it began with words." In fact, some 50 years later those lessons remained unlearned and the tragedies were repeated, because both in Bosnia and in Rwanda it was government-sanctioned hate speech that led to ethnic cleansing.[48]

By not contributing any words of his own, Dershowitz simply let Cotler's remarks stand, though he prudently omitted Cotler's analogy to the ICRC's conference on the applicability of the Fourth Geneva Convention to the Israeli occupation to the hatred of Jews by the Nazis.

Furthermore, any concerns about genocide or ethnic cleansing, as in Cambodia, the Balkans, and Rwanda, as Cotler invoked them, would likely fall primarily under the legal authority internationally of the Genocide Convention of 1948. Nor did the United Nations forego the investigation and prosecution of war crimes committed in the former Yugoslavia and Rwanda, having established the United Nations International Criminal Tribunal for the former Yugoslavia,[49] and the International Criminal Tribunal for Rwanda.[50] In addition, the international effort to establish an international criminal tribunal for Cambodia was met for years with significant political resistance within Cambodia.[51] In contrast, there has been no UN tribunal on Israeli war crimes in the occupied Palestinian territories. Thus, it seems that Cotler was mistaken when he complained that the United Nations and the contracting parties to the Fourth Geneva Convention were engaged in discriminatory conduct and "government-sanctioned hate speech" against Israel upon convening a conference merely to reaffirm the applicability of the convention to four decades of Israel's occupation of the Palestinian territories.

The status of the Fourth Geneva Convention, as it applies to Israel's occupation of the Palestinian territories, is presented here not only as an introduction to an important issue that is central to the Israel-Palestine conflict, but also to make the point that the conflict is viewed from the perspective of the United States in an isolated and provincial manner. Furthermore, the focus on humanitarian law and human rights as applied to the conflict is not mere legalism; it is a guide to Israel's U.S.-supported violations of Palestinian rights. This "rejectionism" of settled law (to quote Chomsky[52]) is as extreme as the rejection of settled science by climate change denialists, who also are headquartered in the United States.

Also evident is the extent to which Dershowitz mishandles the facts and law. As we proceed, and as the mishandling multiplies, one may wonder whether Dershowitz's standards of analysis are indeed that poor, or whether they are beholden exclusively to the defense of Israel's conduct, regardless of the consequences to humanitarian law, human rights, and democratic debate. Considering Dershowitz's position of defense attorney and his role as Israel's chief public defender in the United States, it is helpful to review, in an attempt to discern an analytical standard, how Dershowitz describes the institutional role of a defense lawyer, and where he might draw the intellectual and ethical lines in his public defense of Israel.

In his 2001 book *Letters to a Young Lawyer*, Dershowitz wrote, "inevitably, all advice is, at least in part, autobiographical."[53] Dershowitz's advice may have been particularly autobiographical when he wrote the following thoughts about what constitutes "doing good" within his profession: "So you want to do good. Don't we all? But when you become a lawyer, you have to define good differently than you did before. As a lawyer, you're someone else's representative. You're acting on their behalf. You're their spokesperson. You may not like the term, but you're their mouthpiece. You are they, only you are better educated and more articulate. So doing good means doing good specifically for your client, not for the world at large, and certainly not for yourself."[54] This statement prompts the following questions: Upon acting as Israel's foremost public defender in the United States, has Dershowitz carried over the ethics of his profession (as he sees them) to his role as a public intellectual, and is he therefore guided in his defense of Israel's conduct by the narrow standard of what is good defense lawyering?

In addition to his take on "doing good," what are Dershowitz's views about "truth" and "justice"? In *Letters to a Young Lawyer*, Dershowitz continued: "The defense attorney comes close to being a pure one-sided advocate for his generally guilty client. His job—when his client is guilty—is to prevent, by all lawful and ethical means, the 'whole truth' from coming out. He is not concerned about 'justice' for the general public or about the rights of victims. He is supposed to try to get his guilty client the best possible deal, preferably an acquittal."[55] The evident methods and values that underlie Dershowitz's published work on the Israel-Palestine conflict bear some resemblance to the advice that he gives to young lawyers. For example, we might ask in the context of such advice: In those five books about the Israel-Palestine conflict, did Dershowitz fail to mention the Fourth Geneva Convention, and that it applies to Israel's occupation and outlaws the Israeli settlements, because he is ignorant of those facts? Or is it far more likely that Dershowitz neglected to put those references into play because they inexorably point to the "guilt" of his "client"—the state of Israel? Being a "one-sided advocate for his generally guilty client," Dershowitz likely decided not to disclose these facts about the Fourth Geneva Convention and its legal effects on Israel's policies in the occupied Palestinian territories.

PART III
DERSHOWITZ'S CASE LAW

7

JIMMY CARTER AND APARTHEID

Like other Americans in 2008, I followed the campaign to elect a new president after eight years of George W. Bush and Dick Cheney, which, in addition to reading the newspapers and watching the televised debates, included viewing the Democratic National Convention in August. On the first day of the convention, I watched with interest the odd one-minute appearance by Jimmy and Rosalynn Carter, with the lyrics of "Georgia on My Mind" by Ray Charles the only words that would emanate to the arena and TV audience while the former president was on stage. Having been limited to hand-waving by the time he had left the stage, it seemed possible that the party's presidential nominee, Barack Obama, had acquiesced to the critics of Carter's book *Palestine Peace Not Apartheid*, which was published in November 2006 and debated for many months afterward. I not only viewed what seemed like the public humiliation of the founder of the Carter Center as an insult and a bad omen for an Obama presidency, including with respect to the Israel-Palestine conflict, but I had an uncomfortable sense about whose views in particular had prevailed over Carter's within the Obama campaign.

Sure enough, ten days after Obama was elected on November 4, Shalom TV, a cable TV network in the United States, reported that "Harvard Law professor Alan Dershowitz revealed that he was among those who convinced Barack Obama to keep Jimmy Carter from addressing the Democratic National Convention." The cable network quoted Dershowitz in its exclusive interview as follows: "I pushed him very hard to make that decision. Barack Obama had to make a choice between his Jewish supporters and his anti-Israel supporters like Jimmy Carter, and he did not choose Jimmy Carter. And that was an embarrassment for Jimmy Carter and a show of disrespect. And I'm very glad he made that decision. It was a good decision, a wise decision, a moral decision."[1]

That the Obama campaign would value the advice and influence of Alan Dershowitz over Jimmy Carter's was disturbing, though not altogether surprising, given the manner in which Carter's book was treated in the United States, the instrumental role that Dershowitz played in a loud crescendo of inaccurate and misleading statements about the book, and the precedent set by major news organizations in promoting the Dershowitzian rebuttal. If there was any surprise in witnessing Obama's abandonment of Carter at the convention, and thereafter reading that Dershowitz had played a role in that decision, it was that Obama, upon rejecting Carter, had in effect ratified not only the substance of Dershowitz's claims against Carter, which was bad enough, but also the manner in which Dershowitz pressed those claims to the public.

One memorable example was an interview, again on Shalom TV, on March 3, 2008—five months before the Democratic convention—when Dershowitz issued the following statement in the context of discussing Carter's book: "Whatever the reason or reasons for Jimmy Carter's descent into the gutter of bigotry, history will not judge him kindly. Jimmy Carter has literally become such an anti-Israel bigot that there's a kind of special place in hell reserved for somebody like that."[2] Having read Carter's book and witnessed this video and other such comments by Dershowitz by summer 2008, I somewhat surrealistically experienced the applause of Carter's brief appearance at the Democratic convention as a salute to a successful smear campaign of a former president that had little basis in fact.

It is clear that the most aggravating aspect of *Palestine Peace Not Apartheid* among Carter's critics was his use of the word "apartheid" in the book's title. Writing in the *Guardian*, Michael Kinsley, for example, commented: "It's not clear what he means by using the loaded word, 'apartheid,' since the book makes no attempt to explain it, but the only reasonable interpretation is that Carter is comparing Israel to the former white racist government of South Africa."[3] Like other such criticisms of Carter's book, this statement was not accurate, since Carter had likened the conditions in the Israel-occupied Palestinian West Bank, and not Israel itself, to South Africa's former apartheid regime. This was clear in Carter's book, as he wrote, for example, while referring to the Israel-built separation wall (barrier) between the state of Israel and the Palestinian West Bank: "Israeli leaders have embarked on a series of unilateral decisions, bypassing both Washington and the Palestinians. Their presumption is that an encircling barrier will finally resolve the Palestinian problem. Utilizing their political and military dominance, they are imposing a system of partial withdrawal, encapsulation, and apartheid on the Muslim and Christian citizens of the occupied territories. The driving purpose for the forced separation of the two peoples is unlike that in South Africa— not racism, but the acquisition of land." Carter continued: "There has been a remarkably effective effort to isolate [Israeli] settlers from Palestinians, so that a Jewish family can commute from Jerusalem to their highly subsidized home deep in the West Bank on roads from which others are excluded, without ever coming in contact with any facet of Arab life."[4] Elsewhere, again referring only to the West Bank and not to conditions within Israel itself, Carter invoked "a system of apartheid, with two peoples occupying the same land but completely separated from each other, with Israelis totally dominant and suppressing violence by depriving Palestinians of their basic human rights."[5] Thus, unlike what Kinsley wrote, Carter did not compare Israel itself to the South African apartheid system. Misrepresenting the context in which Carter applied "apartheid" permitted critics to denounce Carter without having to respond in a substantive sense to the actual Israel-imposed conditions in the occupied territories that Carter cited in his book as resembling the apartheid system of South Africa. Dershowitz perhaps was the most high-profile critic who accused Carter in this manner.

In November 2006, the month in which Carter's book was published in the United States, and in his own first published comments about it, Dershowitz wrote: "[Carter's] bias against Israel shows by his selection of the book's title, *Palestine Peace Not Apartheid.* The suggestion that without peace Israel is an apartheid state analogous to South Africa is simply wrong."[6] As noted previously, Carter did not compare the state of Israel to South Africa; he compared Israel's occupation of Palestinian territory to conditions in apartheid South Africa. The great convenience here is that Dershowitz can attack Carter with indignation for unfairly comparing Israel to apartheid South Africa, while Dershowitz options himself out of having to address the occupation-related conditions in the West Bank.

Furthermore, one month after his book was published, Carter met with leaders of the Board of Rabbis of Greater Phoenix. Following that meeting, Carter posted "A Letter to Jewish Citizens of America" on the Web site of the Carter Center. In the letter, Carter wrote: "The chairman of the group [of Phoenix rabbis], Rabbi Andrew Straus, then suggested that I make clear to all American Jews that my use of 'apartheid' does not apply to circumstances within Israel, that I acknowledge the deep concerns of Israelis about the threat of terrorism and other acts of violence from some Palestinians, and that the majority of Israelis sincerely want a peaceful existence with their neighbors." In his posted letter, Carter then wrote, "The purpose of this letter is to reiterate these points."[7] The date of the letter, December 2006, is significant, since nearly two years later, in his 2008 book *The Case against Israel's Enemies: Exposing Jimmy Carter and Others Who Stand in the Way of Peace*, Dershowitz repeated his claim as follows that Carter had applied "apartheid" to Israel: "Israel's most dangerous enemies are those who wield the power—political, academic, religious, and military—to challenge Israel's continued existence as a Jewish, democratic, multiethnic, and multicultural state. These include Western political leaders, led by former president Jimmy Carter, who would delegitimize Israel as an apartheid regime subject to the same fate as white South Africa."[8]

Furthermore, Carter never issued any challenges to "Israel's continued existence," as Dershowitz claimed. To the contrary, in his book, Carter presented his "three most basic principles" of an Israel-Palestine peace treaty:

1. Israel's right to exist within recognized borders—and to live in peace— must be accepted by Palestinians and all other neighbors;
2. The killing of noncombatants in Israel, Palestine, and Lebanon by bombs, missile attacks, assassinations, or other acts of violence cannot be condoned; and
3. Palestinians must live in peace and dignity in their own land as specified by international law unless modified by good-faith negotiations with Israel.[9]

And in his December 2006 letter after the meeting in Phoenix, Carter reiterated his commitment to peace within the framework of a recognized state of Israel: "When asked [by the Phoenix rabbis] my proposals for peace in the Middle East, I summarized by calling for Hamas members and all other Palestinians to renounce violence and adopt the same commitment made by the Arab nations in 2002: the full recognition of Israel's right to exist in peace within its legally recognized 1967 borders (to be modified by mutual agreement by land swaps)."[10] The fact is that Carter did not liken conditions within Israel to apartheid South Africa, nor did he challenge Israel's continued existence, as Dershowitz falsely claimed on both counts.

Dershowitz also criticized Carter for failing to provide support for a charge that Carter never made. For example, Dershowitz wrote: "Carter, despite the title of his book, offered no shred of evidence to prove that Israel practices apartheid."[11] If Dershowitz means by this statement that Carter provided no evidence that Israel practices apartheid inside Israel, he is correct that Carter provided no such evidence, inasmuch as Carter made no such charge. Also, as Dershowitz correctly pointed out, Carter barely mentions the word "apartheid" in his book: "Search through the pages carefully, and you will find the word apartheid mentioned only three times. Carter does not even define what the term means."[12] Dershowitz's complaint here is accurate—the word "apartheid" appears only three times in Carter's book (pp. 30, 189, 215)—and Carter provides no definition *per se* of the term. However, in his third mention of the word, Carter described well enough what he meant by "apartheid" as follows: "A system of apartheid, with two peoples occupying the same land but completely separated from each other, with Israelis totally dominant and suppressing violence by depriving Palestinians of their basic human rights."[13] In my view, and given the title of his book, Carter could have done more to explain his use of "apartheid" and how it applies to the Israel-occupied Palestinian territories, since that was his actual application of the term. However, given the scarce number of appearances of "apartheid" in Carter's book, there were few opportunities to misconstrue Carter's actual use of the term, and thus to claim, inaccurately as Dershowitz did, that Carter had applied the word to conditions within Israel itself.[14]

John Dugard is probably the most qualified person in the world to speak to the issue of an Israel-imposed system of apartheid in the West Bank. As a South African professor of international law, he has written extensively about, and in opposition to, South African apartheid. His books include *Human Rights and the South African Legal Order* (1978), *The Last Years of Apartheid* (1992), and *International Law: A South African Perspective* (2006). Beginning in 2001 he was appointed by the UN Human Rights Commission (later renamed the Human Rights Council) as special rapporteur on human rights in the occupied Palestinian territories and issued several reports in that capacity. There are few if any legal scholars who have had this amount of access to both the South African system of apartheid and Israel's occupation of the West Bank. Dugard is thus uniquely qualified to assess whether the two-tier legal and political system that is imposed on the Palestinians in the West Bank by the state of Israel legitimately can be called an apartheid-like system of segregation.

Dugard in fact made several references to "apartheid" in a 2007 report and suggested that the question of apartheid in the West Bank be submitted to the International Court of Justice for a definitive opinion: "The international community has identified three regimes as inimical to human rights—colonialism, apartheid and foreign occupation. Israel is clearly in military occupation of the OPT [Occupied Palestinian Territory]. At the same time elements of the occupation constitute forms of colonialism and of apartheid, which are contrary to international law. What are the legal consequences of a regime of prolonged occupation with features of colonialism and apartheid for the occupied people, the occupying Power and third States? It is suggested that this question might appropriately be put to the International Court of Justice for a further advisory opinion."[15] Note here that Dugard is asserting "features of colonialism and of apartheid" in the Israel-occupied Palestinian territories, not inside Israel itself. Dugard then emphasized the unique nature of the Israeli occupation: "The Occupied Palestinian Territory is the only instance of a developing country that is denied the right of self-determination and oppressed by a Western-affiliated State. The apparent failure of Western States to take steps to bring such a situation to an end places the future of the international protection of human rights in jeopardy as developing nations begin to question the commitment of Western

States to human rights."[16] This statement to some degree responds to a frequent complaint by Dershowitz that Western critics of Israel are "bigoted" due to a focus on Israel's human rights violations as opposed to the violations of other states, such as Sudan and Somalia; that is, that the Israeli occupation, which features "elements of colonialism and of apartheid," is a Western-supported phenomenon, and in particular a U.S.-supported one.

Having noted in a preliminary sense the apartheid-like conditions in the Palestinian territories, Dugard suggested that the 1966 International Convention on the Elimination of All Forms of Racial Discrimination, and the 1973 International Convention on the Suppression and Punishment of the Crime of Apartheid, may apply to Israel's occupation of the West Bank. Noting that "Israel vehemently denies the application of these Conventions to its laws and practices in the Occupied Palestinian Territory," Dugard nevertheless wrote that "it is difficult to resist the conclusion that many of Israel's laws and practices violate the 1966 Convention on the Elimination of All Forms of Racial Discrimination." Dugard continued:

> Israelis are entitled to enter the closed zone between the [Israel-constructed] Wall and the Green Line [the internationally recognized border between Israel and the West Bank] without permits while Palestinians require permits to enter the closed zone; house demolitions in the [Israel-occupied] West Bank and East Jerusalem are carried out in a manner that discriminates against Palestinians; throughout the West Bank, and particularly in Hebron, [Israeli] settlers are given preferential treatment over Palestinians in respect of movement (major roads are reserved exclusively for settlers), building rights and army protection; and the laws governing family reunification unashamedly discriminate against Palestinians.[17]

Dugard wrote that he was "less certain" that Israel was in violation of the Apartheid Convention in the occupied territories. However, upon referring to policies and conduct prohibited by the convention, Dugard noted that "the IDF [Israel Defense Forces] inflicts serious bodily and mental harm on Palestinians, both in Gaza and the West Bank; over 700 Palestinians are held without trial; prisoners are subjected to inhuman and degrading treatment; and Palestinians throughout the OPT are denied freedom of movement." Citing language from the Apartheid Convention, Dugard continued: "Can it seriously be denied that the purpose of such actions is to establish and maintain domination by one racial group (Jews) over another racial group (Palestinians) and systematically oppressing them?" Dugard then observed: "Israel denies that this is its intention or purpose. But such an intention or purpose may be inferred from the actions described in this report."[18]

In the 2007 report, Dugard also approached the issue of apartheid in the occupied Palestinian territories as follows:

Israel's practices and policies in the OPT are frequently likened to those of apartheid South Africa (see, for example, Jimmy Carter, *Palestine: Peace Not Apartheid*, 2006). On the face of it, occupation and apartheid are two very different regimes. Occupation is not intended to be a long-term oppressive regime but an interim measure that maintains law and order in a territory following an armed conflict and pending a peace settlement. Apartheid is a system of institutionalized racial discrimination that the white minority in South Africa employed to maintain power over the black majority. It was characterized by the denial of political rights to blacks, the fragmentation of the country into white areas and black areas (called Bantustans) and by the imposition on blacks of restrictive measures designed to achieve white superiority, racial separation and white security. Freedom of movement was restricted by the "pass system" which sought to restrict the entry of blacks into the cities. Apartheid was enforced by a brutal security apparatus in which torture played a significant role.

Though he professed an absence of absolute certainty, Dugard concluded by observing that "although the two regimes are different, Israel's laws and practices in the OPT certainly resemble aspects of apartheid . . . and probably fall within the scope of the 1973 International Convention on the Suppression and Punishment of the Crime of Apartheid."[19]

Another prominent South African, Desmond Tutu, also views the conditions in the occupied Palestinian territories as resembling apartheid in South Africa. Tutu supported investment boycotts and street demonstrations against the South African apartheid regime and in the mid-1990s led the Truth and Reconciliation Commission on South African Apartheid. It is therefore noteworthy that in April 2002, BBC News reported: "South African Archbishop Desmond Tutu has accused Israel of practicing apartheid in its policies towards the Palestinians. The Nobel peace laureate said he was 'very deeply distressed' by a visit to the Holy Land, adding that 'it reminded me so much of what happened to us black people in South Africa.'" Tutu observed that he saw "the humiliation of the Palestinians at checkpoints and roadblocks, suffering like us when young white police officers prevented us from moving about."[20] Two months later, in an article in the *Nation* titled "Against Israeli Apartheid," Tutu described "parallels" in the West Bank "to the struggle against apartheid" in South Africa:

> Yesterday's South African township dwellers can tell you about today's life in the occupied [Palestinian] territories. To travel only blocks in his own [Palestinian] homeland, a grandfather waits on the whim of a teenage soldier. More than an emergency is needed to get to a hospital; less than

a crime earns a trip to jail. The lucky ones have a permit to leave their squalor to work in Israel's cities, but their luck runs out when security closes all checkpoints, paralyzing an entire people. The indignities, dependence and anger are all too familiar. Many South Africans are beginning to recognize the parallels to what we went through.[21]

Indeed, a year earlier, in October 2001, South Africans of Jewish descent issued a "Declaration of Conscience" about the Israel-Palestine conflict, which stated: "We assert that the fundamental causes of the current conflict are Israel's suppression of the Palestinian struggle for national self-determination and its continued occupation of Palestinian lands. We do not dispute that certain sectors of the Palestinian population have resorted to terror and we condemn killings of innocent civilians from whatever quarter. Yet this is not the root cause of the problem." The declaration continued: "In light of the suffering that we Jews have experienced ourselves, especially in the past century, we object to the ruthless security measures employed by the Israeli government against Palestinians. . . . We take note of the fact-finding report by members of South Africa's Parliament who visited the Middle East in July 2001. The report observes 'it becomes difficult, particularly from a South African perspective, not to draw parallels with the oppression experienced by Palestinians under the hand of Israel and the oppression experienced in South Africa under apartheid rule.'" The declaration was authored by Ronnie Kasrils, South African Minister of Water Affairs and Forestry, and Max Ozinsky, a member of the Western Cape Legislature, and endorsed by 290 prominent South Africans of Jewish descent.[22]

Seven years later, in July 2008, the *Independent* reported that a twenty-three-member delegation of human rights lawyers from South Africa, which included several Jewish South Africans, visited the West Bank to assess the living conditions there. As the *Independent* reported: "Veterans of the anti-apartheid struggle said last night that the restrictions endured by Palestinians in the Israeli-occupied territories were in some respects worse than that imposed on the black majority under white rule in South Africa." About the West Bank, a former deputy health minister of South Africa, Nozizwe Madlala-Routledge, stated: "Even with the system of permits, even with the limits of movement to South Africa, we never had as much restriction on movement as I see for the people here." At the same time, Dennis Davis, a South African high court judge and a Jewish member of the delegation, said that comparisons between the Israel-occupied Palestinian territories and South African apartheid were "very unhelpful," although Davis also reported that "the level of social control I've seen here, separate roads, different number plates [for Palestinian and Israeli cars] may well be more cynically pernicious than what we have ever had."[23]

In May 2009, a South African research organization, the Research Council (HSRC), issued a report—"Occupation. Apartheid? A Re-assessment of Israel's Practices in the Occupie Territories under International Law"—which set out to examine wheth of Israel's long occupation of the Palestinian territories amount to colonia apartheid. HSRC was established in 1968 by an act of the South A. Parliament to conduct social science research in the public interest and serves the national social science council for South Africa.[24] The report's editor was Virginia Tilley, a South African scholar of the Middle East, and its six principal contributors and eight consultants were academics and human rights officials from South Africa, the United Kingdom, Israel, and the West Bank.[25] A "Background Note" to the report stated: "Over a period of 15 months, the team of scholars engaged in extensive research, discussion, and rounds of lively debate through seven drafts. The result is the consensus represented in this report." The report's executive summary was presented in May 2009 at the Law School of the School of Oriental and African Studies at the University of London. Absent an advisory opinion from the International Court of Justice, the HSRC report on the question of colonialism and apartheid in the Israel-occupied territories is the most scholarly and rigorous assessment available to date and, as such, merits the extensive review presented here.

The genesis of the HSRC report (hereinafter the "Tilley report"), as it noted, "was the suggestion made in January 2007 by Professor John Dugard, in his capacity as UN Special Rapporteur on the human rights situation in the occupied Palestinian territories, that Israel's military occupation displays elements of colonialism and apartheid."[26] The Tilley report then asserted, upon summarizing its conclusions, that "elements of the occupation constitute forms of colonialism and apartheid, which are contrary to international law." Like Jimmy Carter, the report's authors also made it clear that the scope of their study was "whether Israel's practices in the OPT amount to colonialism or apartheid under international law," and not "Israel's practices inside the Green Line (1949 Armistice Line)," except "where they illuminate Israeli policies in the OPT." Thus, the Tilley report did not make claims about elements of colonialism or apartheid inside Israel itself and confined its conclusions to the Israel-occupied Palestinian territories.

In examining whether Israel's laws and practices in the occupied territories contain aspects of "colonialism," the Tilley report sought first to define what it meant by the term. It thus reported "although international law provides no single decisive definition of colonialism, the terms of the [UN's] Declaration on Colonialism indicate that a situation may be classified as colonial when the acts of a State have the cumulative outcome that it annexes or otherwise unlawfully retains control over territory and thus aims permanently to deny its indigenous population the exercise of its right to self-determination." The report continued:

Human Sciences
Colonialism,
Palestinian
elements
ism and
ican

awful in themselves, taken together make it evident
has assumed such a colonial character."[27]

five elements that the report identified, it is relevant
on Colonialism" is a shorthand reference to the 1960
ration on the Granting of Independence to Colonial
h defines the essential character of colonialism as
lien subjugation, domination and exploitation." The
rights under international law, including "the right
"all peoples" may "freely determine their political
freely pursue their economic, social, and cultural development." The
declaration also stipulates that "all armed action or repressive measures of all kinds
directed against dependent peoples shall cease in order to enable them to exercise
peacefully and freely their right to complete independence, and the integrity of
their national territory shall be respected." The resolution was passed unanimously
in 1960 by eighty-nine states, with nine countries abstaining, including the United
States, the United Kingdom, France, Spain, Portugal, Belgium, Australia, and
apartheid South Africa.[28] Having identified the Declaration on Colonialism as its
principal reference, the Tilley report identified the five colonialist elements of
Israel's occupation.

Violating the Territorial Integrity of Occupied Territory. "Israel's annexation [in
1967] of East Jerusalem is manifestly an act based on colonial intent. It is unlawful
in itself, as annexation breaches the principle underpinning the law of occupation:
that occupation is only a temporary situation that does not vest sovereignty in the
Occupying Power. Annexation also breaches the legal prohibition on the acquisition of territory through the threat or use of force. This prohibition has peremptory
[absolute, conclusive, incontrovertible[29]] status, as it is a corollary of the prohibition
on the use of force in international relations enshrined in Article 2(4) of the UN
Charter. Israel's acquisition of territory in the West Bank also starkly illustrates this
intent: the construction of Jewish-only settlements within contiguous blocs of land
that Palestinians cannot enter; a connecting road system between the settlements
and the settlements and cities within the Green Line, the use of which is denied to
Palestinians; and a Wall that separates Jewish and Palestinian populations while
also dividing Palestinian communities from each other, with passage between
Palestinian areas controlled by Israel. By thus partitioning contiguous blocs of
Palestinian areas into cantons, Israel has violated the territorial integrity of the OPT
in violation of the Declaration on Colonialism."[30]

*Depriving the Population of Occupied Territory of the Capacity for Self-
Governance.* "The physical control exercised over [the OPT] is complemented by
the administration that Israel exercises over the OPT, which prevents its protected
population [the Palestinian inhabitants] from freely exercising political authority
over that territory. This determination is unaffected by the conclusion of the Oslo

Accords and the creation of the Palestinian National Authority and Legislative Council. The devolution of power to these institutions has been only partial, and Israel retains ultimate control. By preventing the free expression of the Palestinian population's political will, Israel has violated that population's right to self-determination."[31]

Integrating the Economy of Occupied Territory into That of the Occupant. "The law of self-determination further requires a State in belligerent occupation of foreign territory to keep that territory separate from its own, in order to prevent its annexation, and also to keep their economies separate. Israel has subordinated the economy of the OPT to its own, depriving the population under occupation of the capacity to govern its economic affairs. In particular, the creation of a customs union between Israel and the OPT is a measure of prohibited annexation.[32] By virtue of the structural economic measures it has imposed on the OPT, Israel has violated the Palestinian population's right of economic self-determination and its duties as an Occupying Power."[33]

Breaching the Principle of Permanent Sovereignty over Natural Resources in Relation to the Occupied Territory. "The economic dimension of self-determination is also expressed in the right of permanent sovereignty over natural resources, which entitles a people to dispose freely of the natural wealth and resources found within the limits of its national jurisdiction. Israel's settlement policy and the construction of the bypass road network and the Wall have deprived the Palestinian population of the control and development of an estimated 38 percent of West Bank land. It has also implemented a water management and allocation system that favors Israel and Jewish settlers in the OPT to the detriment of the Palestinian population. Not only is this practice contrary to the lawful use of natural resources in time of occupation, which is limited to the needs of the occupying army, but it is also contrary to international water law as the allocation employed is both unjust and inequitable. . . . Thus, by its treatment of the natural resources of the OPT, Israel has further breached the economic dimensions of self-determination, as expressed in the right of permanent sovereignty over natural resources."[34]

Denying the Population of Occupied Territory the Right Freely to Express, Develop, and Practice Its Culture. "Self-determination also has a cultural component: a people entitled to exercise the right of self-determination have the right to develop and practice its culture. Israeli practices privilege the language and cultural referents of the occupier, while materially hampering the cultural development and expression of the Palestinian population. This last issue renders Israel's denial of the right to self-determination in the OPT comprehensive."[35]

In similar fashion, the Tilley report set out to assess whether Israel's policies in the occupied territories amount to a system of apartheid. It noted that the

1965 International Convention on the Elimination of All Forms of Racial Discrimination "prohibits the practice of apartheid as a particularly egregious form of discrimination, but it does not define the practice with precision." It also noted that the Apartheid Convention and the Rome Statute of the International Criminal Court "further elaborate the definition of apartheid" and "criminalize certain apartheid-related acts." The Apartheid Convention indeed criminalizes "inhuman acts committed for the purpose of establishing and maintaining domination by one racial group of persons over any other racial group of persons and systematically oppressing them." Likewise, the Rome Statute criminalizes inhuman acts "committed in the context of, and to maintain, an institutional regime of systematic oppression and domination by one racial group over any other racial group." The Tilley report commented that both the Apartheid Convention and the Rome Statute "focus on the *systematic, institutionalized,* and *oppressive* character of the discrimination involved and the purpose of domination that is entailed" (emphasis in original) and that the systematic and institutionalized oppressive character "distinguishes the practice of apartheid from other forms of prohibited discrimination." The Tilley report also observed that the prohibition of apartheid "has assumed the status of customary international law and, further, is established as a peremptory norm which entails obligations owed to the international community as a whole."[36]

A key assessment in the Tilley report was whether "the groups involved" in the Israel-Palestine context "can be understood as 'racial groups.'" In seeking to resolve this question, the report's authors examined how racial discrimination is defined in the UN's International Convention on the Elimination of All Forms of Racial Discrimination and in the jurisprudence of the International Criminal Tribunals for Rwanda and the former Yugoslavia, which concluded that "no scientific or impartial method exists for determining whether any group is a racial group and that the question rests on local perceptions." The Tilley report found "that 'Jewish' and 'Palestinian' identities are socially constructed in the OPT as groups distinguished by ancestry or descent as well as nationality, ethnicity, and religion," and "on this basis, the study concludes that Israeli Jews and Palestinian Arabs can be considered 'racial groups' for the purposes of the definition of apartheid in international law." Accordingly, the Tilley report stated, by way of conclusion: "By examining Israel's practices in the light of Article 2 of the Apartheid Convention, this study concludes that Israel has introduced a system of apartheid in the OPT."[37]

In reaching that conclusion, the authors of the Tilley report also conducted a comparative analysis between South African apartheid practices and the Israel-imposed conditions in the occupied territories. In doing so, the authors noted: "Certainly differences are evident between apartheid as it was applied in

South Africa and Israel's policies and practices in the OPT. Nevertheless, the two systems can be defined by similar dominant features."[38] In defining these features, the Tilley report described the "three pillars" of South African apartheid and compared the laws and policies that characterized each pillar to a corresponding set of Israeli practices in the occupied Palestinian territories. As the report indicated: "Israel's practices in the OPT can be defined by the same three 'pillars' of apartheid."[39]

The first pillar of South African apartheid cited in the Tilley report was a formal demarcation of the population into racial groups in accordance with the 1950 Population Registration Act, in addition to the superior rights, privileges, and services rendered to the white racial group in South Africa through the Bantu Building Workers Act of 1951, and the Bantu Education Act and the Separate Amenities Act enacted in 1953. These laws "consolidated earlier discriminatory laws into a pervasive system of institutionalized racial discrimination, which prevented the enjoyment of basic human rights by non-white South Africans based on their racial identity."

The corresponding first pillar in the Israel-occupied Palestinian territories, according to the Tilley report, "derives from Israeli laws and policies that establish Jewish identity for purposes of law and afford a preferential legal status and material benefits to Jews over non–Jews." The report found that this "institution-alized system . . . privileges Jewish settlers and discriminates against Palestinians on the basis of the inferior status afforded to non-Jews by Israel. At the root of this system are Israel's citizenship laws, whereby group identity is the primary factor in determining questions involving the acquisition of Israeli citizenship." The Tilley report then itemized the Israeli laws and their effects:

> The 1950 Law of Return defines who is a Jew for purposes of the law and allows every Jew to immigrate to Israel or the OPT. The 1952 Citizenship Law then grants automatic citizenship to people who immigrate under the Law of Return, while erecting insurmountable obstacles to citizenship for Palestinian refugees. Israeli law conveying special standing to Jewish identity is then applied extraterritorially to extend preferential legal status and material privileges to Jewish settlers in the OPT and thus discriminate against Palestinians. . . . The 2003 Citizenship and Entry into Israel Law banning Palestinian family unification is a further example of legislation that confers benefits to Jews over Palestinians and illustrates the adverse impact of having the status of Palestinian Arab.[40]

The Tilley report authors then commented that "the disparity in how the two groups are treated by Israel is highlighted through the application of a harsher set of laws and different courts for Palestinians in the OPT than for Jewish settlers, as well as through the restrictions imposed [in the OPT] by the permit and ID systems."

The second pillar of apartheid in South Africa "was to segregate the population into different geographic areas, which were allocated by law to different racial groups, and restrict passage by members of any group into the area allocated to other groups, thus preventing any contact between groups that might ultimately compromise white supremacy." The South African laws that facilitated these conditions were identified in the Tilley report as "the Group Areas Act of 1950 and the Pass Laws—which included the Native Laws Amendment Act of 1952 and the Natives (Abolition of Passes and Co-ordination of Documents) Act of 1952—as well as the Natives (Urban Areas) Amendment Act of 1955, the Bantu (Urban Areas) Consolidation Act of 1945 and the Coloured Persons Communal Reserves Act of 1961." This forced separation of racial groups "constituted the basis for the policy labeled 'grand apartheid' by its South African architects, which provided for the establishment of 'Homelands' or 'Bantustans' into which denationalized black South Africans were transferred and forced to reside."

The corresponding second pillar of conditions in the occupied Palestinian territories is reflected in Israel's policy of "fragment[ing] the OPT for the purposes of segregation and domination." The Tilley report continued:

> This policy is evidenced by Israel's extensive appropriation of Palestinian land, which continues to shrink the territorial space available to Palestinians; the hermetic closure and isolation of the Gaza Strip from the rest of the OPT; the deliberate severing of East Jerusalem from the rest of the West Bank; and the appropriation and construction policies serving to carve up the West Bank into an intricate and well-serviced network of connected settlements for Jewish-Israelis and an archipelago of besieged and non-contiguous enclaves for Palestinians. That these measures are intended to segregate the population along racial lines in violation of Article 2(d) of the Apartheid Convention is clear from the visible web of walls, separate roads, and checkpoints, and the invisible web of permit and ID systems, which combine to ensure that Palestinians remain confined to the reserves designated for them while Israeli Jews are prohibited from entering those reserves but enjoy freedom of movement throughout the rest of the Palestinian territory.

With respect to these conditions, the Tilley report noted that "much as the same restrictions functioned in apartheid South Africa, the policy of geographic fragmentation has the effect of crushing Palestinian socio-economic life, securing Palestinian vulnerability to Israeli economic dominance, and of enforcing a rigid segregation of Palestinian and Jewish populations."[41]

The third pillar of South African apartheid was "a matrix of draconian 'security' laws and policies that were employed to suppress any opposition to the [apartheid] regime and reinforce the system of racial domination, by providing for administrative detention, torture, censorship, banning, and assassination."[42] As assessed in the Tilley report, the corresponding "third pillar upon which Israel's system of apartheid in the OPT rests is its 'security' laws and policies." These include, as itemized in the report, "the extrajudicial killing, torture and cruel, inhuman or degrading treatment and arbitrary arrest and imprisonment of Palestinians, as described under the rubric of Article 2(a) of the Apartheid Convention." The report observed that "these policies are State-sanctioned, often approved by the Israeli judicial system, and supported by an oppressive code of military laws and a system of improperly constituted military courts."

Finally, the Tilley report issued this clarification: "This study does not contend that Israel's claims about security are by definition lacking in merit, but rather that Israel's invocation of 'security' to validate severe policies and disproportionate practices toward the Palestinians is operating principally to validate suppression of Palestinian opposition to a system of domination by one racial group over another."[43]

Though the executive summary and the larger report from the South African Human Sciences Research Council was issued in 2009, and thus after much of Dershowitz's criticism of Jimmy Carter's use of "apartheid" in *Palestine Peace Not Apartheid*, the value of the Tilley report is the scholarly and legal rigor of its assessment of the Israel-imposed apartheid-like conditions in the occupied Palestinian territories. To my knowledge, it is the most authoritative and pains-taking response to the question of whether Israel's occupation of the Palestinian territories amounts to a colonial and apartheid regime as characterized in both instances under international law.

In addition to numerous South African commentators who have likened the conditions in the Israel-occupied Palestinian West Bank to apartheid South Africa, many Israeli, British, and U.S. critics have as well. For example, the Israeli human rights organization B'Tselem, in a report issued in May 2002, stated: "Israel has created in the Occupied Territories a regime of separation based on discrimination, applying two separate systems of law in the same area and basing the rights of individuals on their nationality. This regime is the only one of its kind in the world, and is reminiscent of distasteful regimes from the past, such as the Apartheid regime in South Africa."[44] Two years later, in August 2004, and in a report on Israel's vast network of roads in the West Bank, which permits Israelis to use the roads while prohibiting Palestinians, B'Tselem reported: "The roads regime, which is based on separation through discrimination, bears clear similarities to the racist apartheid regime that existed in South Africa until 1994. An individual's national origin determines their right to use various roads."[45]

Writing in April 2004 about Israel's planned unilateral disengagement from the Gaza Strip, pursuant to which in August 2005 Israel withdrew its settlers and military personnel, in addition to removing a few Israeli settlements from the northern West Bank, journalist Akiva Eldar, Israel's leading diplomatic correspondent, wrote in an opinion piece for *Ha'aretz* titled "Creating a Bantustan in Gaza": "South Africa will be very interested in the Israeli disengagement plan published yesterday. The political, military, and economic aspects of the plan for the Gaza Strip and the [settler] enclave in the northern West Bank are amazingly similar to the homelands, one of the last inventions of the white minority in South Africa to perpetuate its rule over the black majority. The black and colored people that were concentrated in 10 isolated enclaves had limited autonomy, but their economic well-being depended on the good will of the white government."[46] Ten days later in the *Guardian*, in a piece titled "Bantustan Plan for an Apartheid Israel," former deputy mayor of Jerusalem Meron Benvenisti wrote about the Israeli disengagement plan: "The Bantustan model for Gaza, as depicted in the disengagement plan, is a model that Sharon plans to copy on the West Bank. His announcement that he will not start to disengage before construction of the fence is completed along a route that will include all settlement blocs (in keeping with Binyamin Netanyahu's demand), underscores the continuity of the Bantustan concept. The fence creates three Bantustans on the West Bank—Jenin-Nablus, Bethlehem-Hebron, and Ramallah. This is the real link between the Gaza and West Bank plans."[47]

In an interview in 2005 with Amy Goodman for *Democracy Now!*, the Israeli journalist Amira Hass discussed her longtime reporting from the Palestinian territories under Israel's occupation, including her characterization of the Israeli occupation as a form of apartheid, as follows:

> *Goodman*: Amira Hass, you have said there has been a form of apartheid for 33 years, talking about Israel and the Occupied Territories, and the Oslo Accords did nothing to change that. . . . Can you talk about what you mean by an apartheid-like system?
>
> *Hass*: An apartheid-like system is when we are talking about two peoples who live in the same territory, between the sea and the river, the Mediterranean and the River of Jordan, two peoples. And there are two sets of laws which apply to each separate people. There are two—there are privileges and rights for the one people, for the Israeli people . . . and there are restrictions and decrees and military laws which apply to the other people, to the Palestinians. The Palestinians, as a people, are divided into subgroups, something which is reminiscent also of South Africa under apartheid rule. . . . And then you have one government, which is elected, which actually decides about the future of both peoples, the scope of development of both peoples, but it is being elected only by one people.

For me, this is a form of apartheid, of demographic separation which is meant to improve the conditions and the well-being and the future of one people on the account of the other.[48]

Another Israeli journalist, Danny Rubenstein, stated in August 2007 that "Israel today was an apartheid state with four different Palestinian groups: those in Gaza, East Jerusalem, the West Bank and Israeli Palestinians, each of which had a different status."[49] A year later, Yossi Sarid, another prominent Israeli journalist, in commentary for *Ha'aretz* titled "Yes, It Is Apartheid," responded with satire to the virulent tone of Carter's critics:

> Let's let old Carter be, so he may let sleeping warriors lie; he will not be back. The contents of his words, however, should not be ignored. "Apartheid," he said, "apartheid"—a dark, scary word coined by Afrikaners and meaning segregation, racial segregation.
>
> What does he want from us, that evil man: What do we have to do with apartheid? Does a separation fence constitute separation? Do separate roads for Jewish settlers and Palestinians really separate? Are Palestinian enclaves between Jewish settlements Bantustans?
>
> There is no hint of similarity between South Africa and Israel, and only a sick mind could draw such shadowy connections between them. Roadblocks and inspections at every turn; licenses and permits for every little matter; the arbitrary seizure of land; special privileges in water use; cheap, hard labor; forming and uniting families by bureaucratic whim— none of these are apartheid, in any way. They are an incontrovertible security necessity, period.
>
> The white Afrikaners, too, had reasons for their segregation policy; they, too, felt threatened—a great evil was at their door, and they were frightened, out to defend themselves. Unfortunately, however, all good reasons for apartheid are bad reasons; apartheid always has a reason, and it never has a justification. And what acts like apartheid, is run like apartheid, and harasses like apartheid, is not a duck—it is apartheid.[50]

Similarly, a former education minister of Israel, Shulamit Aloni, recipient of both the Israel Prize and the Emil Grunzweig Human Rights Award from the Association for Civil Rights in Israel, wrote in response to the attacks on Carter and his book:

> The U.S. Jewish Establishment's onslaught on former President Jimmy Carter is based on him daring to tell the truth which is known to all: through its army, the government of Israel practices a brutal form of Apartheid in the territory it occupies. Its army has turned every Palestinian village and town into a fenced-in, or blocked-in, detention

camp. All this is done in order to keep an eye on the population's move-ments and to make its life difficult. Israel even imposes a curfew whenever the settlers, who have illegally usurped the Palestinians' land, celebrate their holidays or conduct their parades.

If that were not enough, the generals commanding the region frequently issue further orders, regulations, instructions and rules (let us not forget, they are the lords of the land). By now they have requisitioned further lands for the purpose of constructing "Jewish only" roads. Wonderful roads, wide roads, well-paved roads, brightly lit at night—all that on stolen land. When a Palestinian drives on such a road, his vehicle is confiscated and he is sent on his way.[51]

While misrepresenting Carter's apartheid claim—implying or stating outright that Carter applied it to Israel rather than to the Israel-occupied Palestinian territories—Dershowitz ignored these persuasive assessments of the Israel-imposed apartheid system in the occupied territories.

Having given an appearance of soundly trouncing Carter's use of "apartheid" while never actually addressing the substantive context in which Carter used the term, Dershowitz also spent a fair amount of time in *The Case against Israel's Enemies* recounting a series of anecdotes involving himself and Carter, including during the former president's appearance at Brandeis University, where, according to Dershowitz, "some hard-left professors" at the school had invited Carter to speak, and where "most of the students remained" to see his response to Carter, although "some from the hard-left walked out on my talk."[52] Following the Brandeis event, according to Dershowitz, "Carter's tone became more shrill and his substantive accusations against Israel became more one-sided, even bigoted."[53] Two pages later, Dershowitz wrote that because the slaughter in Darfur is being conducted with the support of Arab governments, "the hard left that Carter has come to represent has refused to condemn it as genocide."[54] About the Carter v. Dershowitz debate controversy that Carter's invitation to speak at Brandeis engendered, Dershowitz wrote that Carter had "simply lied" about whether Dershowitz had challenged him to a debate, that the *Boston Globe* "makes it clear that [Carter] was lying," and that Carter's alleged lying about the debates "was part of a pattern of lying" by Carter.[55]

These attacks by Dershowitz against Carter's use of "apartheid," and against his integrity as a commentator on issues of great public concern, are representative of Dershowitz's successful tactic of branding Israel's legitimate critics with defamatory epithets, including in this case characterizations of Carter's book as "bigoted" and filled with "lies," and taunting Carter in the idiom of authoritarianism as a "hard-leftist" and "enemy" of Israel. Dershowitz's book *The Case against Israel's*

Enemies: Exposing Jimmy Carter and Others Who Stand in the Way of Peace is in fact a Nixonesque catalog of enemies; literally an enemies list of prominent critics of Israel's policies. The two lists—the one by Nixon and by Dershowitz—even share a common lexicon that abhors "liberals," "leftists," "haters," and "enemies."

While composing Nixon's enemies list, White House counsel Charles Colson described Bernard Feld, an MIT physicist and proponent of nuclear-arms reduction, as a recipient of "heavy far left funding." He described journalist Daniel Schorr as "a real media enemy," columnist Mary McGrory as the author of "daily hate Nixon articles," and actor Paul Newman as a supporter of "radic-lib causes."[56] The enemies list compiled by Dershowitz in *The Case against Israel's Enemies*, which features a former U.S. president, prominent academics, and world-renowned human rights organizations, is presented in an equally malicious manner. About John J. Mearsheimer, the R. Wendell Harrison Distinguished Service Professor of Political Science at the University of Chicago, and Stephen M. Walt, the Robert and Renee Belfer Professor of International Affairs at the John F. Kennedy School of Government at Harvard University, who together authored *The Israel Lobby and U.S. Foreign Policy* (2007), Dershowitz wrote, "they are hate-mongers who have given up on scholarly debate and the democratic process in order to become rock-star heroes of anti-Israel extremists."[57] Because Amnesty International and Human Rights Watch issued reports that were critical of Israel's conduct in the Gaza Strip and Lebanon in summer 2006, Dershowitz referred to them as "so-called human rights groups" and described their reports as "bigotry—pure and simple."[58]

Dershowitz also cited "Amnesty International's predisposition to blame everything on Israel," claimed that "Amnesty International just can't seem to help itself when it comes to blaming Israel for the evils of the world," and described Amnesty as "a once reputable organization that has destroyed its own credibility by repeatedly applying a double standard to Israel."[59] Dershowitz also wrote that "Human Rights Watch (HRW) was even more biased in its reporting of the facts on the ground" during the Israel-Lebanon war in summer 2006[60] and commented as follows: "HRW no longer deserves the support of real human rights advocates. Nor should its so-called reporting be credited by objective news organizations. The same must be said about Amnesty International."[61] Dershowitz then claimed that the "biased" and "bigoted" human rights organizations "side with the terrorists": "The so-called human rights organizations that constantly side with the terrorists are actually guilty of encouraging the tactic of using human shields and firing rockets from civilian neighborhoods. The terrorists themselves acknowledge that they are counting on these biased organizations to make their case for them, and the organizations are succeeding. That's why terrorists persist in this doubly criminal tactic and civilians continue to be killed. And that is why Israel did not win a more decisive victory in its battle against Hezbollah in the summer of

2006."[62] And should the analogy to Nixon's enemies list seem exaggerated, consider Dershowitz's remarks again from his 2001 book *Letters to a Young Lawyer*. While advising the young lawyers to "Have a Good Enemies' List"—the title of chapter 3 in that book—Dershowitz wrote: "Your mother told you it's important to have the right friends. But it's equally important to have the right enemies. Pick your enemies as carefully as your friends. A really good enemies' list is often a sure sign of a courageous and moral person. The world is full of evil people and it is important to stand up to evil."[63]

Using Dershowitz's own standard for identifying the moral makeup of a person as judged by his enemies' list, what can we presume about Dershowitz when his own such list features Jimmy Carter (founder of the superb Carter Center), Noam Chomsky (one of the world's most important intellectuals of the twentieth century), Edward Said (one of the great public intellectuals of the twentieth century), Richard Falk (one of the most important international law scholars of the twentieth century), South African Anglican Archbishop Desmond Tutu (recipient of the Nobel Peace Prize in 1984 and the Albert Schweitzer Prize for Humanitarianism in 1987), and Amnesty International and Human Rights Watch (the two most important human rights organizations in the world). While one can easily imagine these same names making the enemies' list of the Latin American military dictatorships of Pinochet and Somoza, it is simply stunning that a law professor from Harvard, who is supposed to be a civil libertarian, would compose such a list, publish it, and thereby defame such persons in a manner that resembles the hatred toward liberal intellectuals and human rights organizations that have marked the most vicious right-wing governments of the twentieth century. For example, one of the definitive scholarly accounts of the dictatorial regime of Augusto Pinochet in Chile is titled *A Nation of Enemies*.[64] Also, in 1977, U.S. journalist Jack Anderson reported:

> Nicaragua's big banana, Anastasio Somoza, has picked up one tactic from his friend Richard Nixon. The Nicaraguan dictator has compiled his own private enemies list. Sources who have had secret access to the list say it contains the names of individuals and organizations in the United States whom Somoza regards as 'potential enemies to the government of Nicaragua.' Among his imagined adversaries are such prominent senators as Ted Kennedy, D–Mass., Hubert Humphrey, D–Minn., Frank Church, D–Idaho, and George McGovern, D–S.D. Somoza also has enemies in the House, including Reps. John Conyers, D–Mich., Don Fraser, D–Minn., and Ed Koch, D–N.Y. The eminent Father Theodore Hesburgh, president of Notre Dame University, is listed.[65]

Like the enemies list of Dershowitz, Somoza's list was composed almost entirely of political liberals and leftists. Also recall that the hallmark speech of Senator

Joseph McCarthy, delivered in 1950, is known as the "Enemies from Within" speech,[66] as Dershowitz no doubt is aware.

Referring to Rabbi Michael Lerner, editor of *Tikkun*, Dershowitz resorted to the default Nixon's-list assault, calling Lerner a "hard-left academic."[67] This is a common designation of "evil" for Dershowitz, who also wrote that Archbishop Tutu "has joined anti-Israel extremists in likening Israel to apartheid South Africa."[68] As he did with Jimmy Carter's use of "apartheid," Dershowitz misrepresented how Tutu applied the term.

About Pope Benedict XVI, another "enemy" of Israel, Dershowitz wrote:

> In 2005, Pope Benedict XVI condemned terrorist attacks against civilians in Great Britain, Egypt, Iraq, and Turkey. In a pregnant omission—very pregnant, in light of the Vatican's long history of silence in the face of attacks against Jews—the pope omitted any mention of the country that has suffered the largest number of terrorist attacks against civilians since 9/11, namely, Israel.[69]

Note that Dershowitz criticizes Pope Benedict not because of anything that the pope actually said in this instance; his criticism is that the pope *did not* say anything about Israel, which, according to Dershowitz, "has suffered the largest number of terrorist attacks against civilians since 9/11." But how should the pope handle the situation in the manner in which Dershowitz would like, when Israel has killed nearly six times the number of Palestinian civilians? According to B'Tselem, from September 29, 2000 to January 31, 2011, Palestinians have killed 1,085 Israelis, while Israelis have killed 6,383 Palestinians. These Palestinian fatalities include 1,315 Palestinian children (ages seventeen and younger), which is a higher number of fatalities than all Israelis killed for the same period.[70] B'Tselem's statistics on Israeli-Palestinian casualties closely track the statistics reported by Amnesty International and Human Rights Watch. This means that, according to Dershowitz's own logic, the pope should have mentioned the killing of Palestinian civilians and children before mentioning the killing of Israeli civilians and children.

Another of Dershowitz's practices is that while he regularly invokes "anti-Semitism" and "anti-Israel bigotry" when attacking Israel's "enemies," he denies calling Israel's critics anti-Semites and argues that claims to the contrary are fabricated. In his introduction to *The Case against Israel's Enemies*, Dershowitz wrote: "The claim that critics of Israel are branded anti-Semites is a straw man and a fabrication of Israel's enemies who seek to play the victim card."[71] Dershowitz made the same claim elsewhere in the same book, while referring to Carter, Mearsheimer, and Walt: "Ironically, they have attempted to hide from scrutiny by labeling their critics intolerant, using the same ad hominem attacks that they claim they are victims of. They refer to me, for example, as being 'often quick to brand Israel's critics as anti-Semites,' without offering a shred of proof."[72]

There is in fact more than a shred of evidence that Dershowitz and other prominent Jewish-Americans do what Carter, Mearsheimer, and Walt have claimed. In 2007, Abraham Foxman, national director of the Anti-Defamation League, published a book titled *The Deadliest Lies: The Israel Lobby and the Myth of Jewish Control* as a response to the Mearsheimer and Walt article, "The Israel Lobby," published in 2006 in the *London Review of Books*. Foxman's book was published to coincide with the publication of the follow-up book by Mearsheimer and Walt, *The Israel Lobby and U.S. Foreign Policy*. In his book, Foxman wrote "anti-Semitism," "anti-Semitic," "anti-Semite," "bigotry," "bigoted," or "bigot" about seventy times, including over twenty times in the introduction alone.[73] Yet, despite this immersion into "anti-Semitism" and anti-Israel "bigotry" as a direct response to Mearsheimer and Walt, Foxman, like Dershowitz, denied, as follows, in the same book that he labels legitimate critics of Israel as "anti-Semites" and anti-Israel "bigots": "It's an accusation I deny. Are there some overly sensitive Jews who are excessively prone to seeing anti-Semitism where none really exists? There probably are. But I don't agree that this charge applies to me, to the Anti-Defamation League, or to the great majority of Jewish leaders and Jewish organizations with which I'm acquainted. We know the difference between criticism of Israel and anti-Semitism, and we are careful to respect that difference."[74] This being the case, why write a book in direct response to Mearsheimer and Walt that is immersed in references to anti-Semitism and anti-Israel bigotry? Either Foxman should have argued outright with evidence that Mearsheimer and Walt are anti-Semitic, or he should have declined to infuse his book with a multitude of references to anti-Semitism and anti-Jewish bigotry as the highly suggestive characterization of the work of Mearsheimer and Walt.

Similarly, while Dershowitz denies resorting to charges that Israel's most prominent critics are anti-Semites, *The Case against Israel's Enemies*, published in 2008, contains about 140 references to "anti-Semitism," "anti-Semitic," "anti-Semite," "bigot," "bigoted," or "bigotry."[75] His 2005 book, *The Case for Peace*, has about 110 such references.[76] And his 2003 book, *The Case for Israel*, includes about eighty such references.[77]

In *The Case against Israel's Enemies*, and about Jimmy Carter, Dershowitz wrote: "Initially, I defended Carter against accusations of anti-Semitism" with respect to Carter's book;[78] the implication being that the *initial* assessment was a mistake. Dershowitz then wrote in an article in the *Jerusalem Post*, titled "Has Carter Crossed the Line," about Carter's public statements issued after the publication of his book, that "Carter has gone well beyond what he says in his book and may have crossed the line into bigotry."[79] And referring to John Dugard and Richard Falk, Dershowitz wrote: "Carter's book has given aid and comfort to such bigots"— that is, to Dugard and Falk.[80]

In his chapter titled "The Case against Mearsheimer and Walt," Dershowitz wrote that the two professors "acknowledge some of the concerns that critics of their essay have raised about anti-Semitism, declaring, 'Let us be clear: we categorically reject all of these anti-Semitic claims'";[81] later, in the same chapter, Dershowitz denounced "the incantation of boilerplate disclaimers against anti-Semitism" by Mearsheimer and Walt.[82] Dershowitz also argued that Mearsheimer and Walt "write behind a façade of erudition that purports to reject anti-Semitism but copies its classic archetype."[83] And in the concluding paragraph of his chapter on Mearsheimer and Walt, Dershowitz called them "hate mongers" who sought "to become rock-star heroes of anti-Israel extremists," and he observed, "perhaps this is not anti-Semitism but misanthropy."[84] Thus, after Dershowitz denied "that critics of Israel are branded anti-Semites" and offered that such claims are a "straw man and a fabrication of Israel's enemies who seek to play the victim card,"[85] he proceeded to tar Carter, Mearsheimer, and Walt with inferences and innuendo of anti-Semitism. Now, in perhaps the starkest literal sense, none of this means that he ever actually called anyone an anti-Semite.

Furthermore, upon writing in *The Case against Israel's Enemies* about the British University and College Union (BUCU) boycott of Israeli educators and academic institutions, Dershowitz explained how he and others wrote an op-ed piece for the *Times* of London, "in which we demonstrated parallels between this boycott and previous anti-Jewish boycotts that were undoubtedly motivated by anti-Semitism."[86] The signed authors of the op-ed piece, which included Dershowitz, then "turned to the motive underlying the [boycott] campaign" and asked, "To be blunt, is it anti-Semitic?"[87] While the issue motivating the boycott was Israel's forty-year occupation of Palestinian territory, and the attendant and systemic violations of Palestinian rights, Dershowitz and his coauthors argued that "in supporting a boycott they have put themselves in anti-Semitism's camp," and that the boycotter's motivation was "the desire to destroy Jews."[88]

Likewise, and still writing in *The Case against Israel's Enemies*, Dershowitz condemned a U.S. Presbyterian divestment initiative targeting multinational corporations that sell goods and services that support the Israeli occupation. About the Presbyterian initiative, the Israel-based Committee against House Demolitions (ICAHD) reported: "ICAHD supports the initiative of the Presbyterian Church of the US to divest in 'multinational corporations that provide products or services to . . . the Israeli police or military to support and maintain the occupation, . . . that have established facilities or operations on occupied land, . . . that provide services or products for the establishment, expansion or maintenance of Israeli settlements, . . . that provide products or services to Israeli or Palestinian organizations/groups that support or facilitate violent acts against innocent civilians, . . . that provide products or services that support or facilitate the construction of the Separation Barrier.'"[89] While mentioning none of these details, Dershowitz simply referred to "the Presbyterians in their malevolent divestment campaign."[90] Omitting such details makes it easier for Dershowitz to argue, as he did in this instance, that "the Presbyterian [divestment] resolution is so anti-Israel in its rhetoric and so ignorant of the realities on the ground that it can only be explained by the kind of bigotry that the Presbyterian Church itself condemned in 1987, when it acknowledged its long history of anti-Semitism and 'never again to participate in, to contribute to, or (insofar as we are able) to allow the persecution or denigration of Jews.'"[91] Dershowitz added that "unless the [Presbyterian] church rescinds this immoral, sinful, and biased attack on the Jewish state, it will once again be 'participating in' and 'contributing to' bigotry and the encouragement of terrorism."[92]

Based on Dershowitz's expert assessment of anti-Israel bigotry within the ranks of the Presbyterian Church and its alleged "encouragement of terrorism," shouldn't the FBI launch an investigation and initiate surveillance of the church's leaders and rank and file? Likewise, should the FBI similarly investigate the American novelist Alice Walker, after Dershowitz charged that "Walker participated in unlawful efforts to break Israel's entirely lawful military blockade of the Gaza Strip" and thus "she has provided material support for terrorism, in violation of the law of the United States and several other countries"?[93]

Apart from the fact that the Israeli embargo on all 1.5 million inhabitants of Gaza is a form of collective punishment and is therefore "a flagrant violation of international law,"[94] and that Walker's participation in a protest to end the illegal blockade was a humanitarian act, since "rather than targeting armed groups, the blockade mainly hits the most vulnerable, such as children (who make up more than half of the population in Gaza), the elderly, the sick and the Gaza Strip's large refugee population,"[95] Dershowitz's charge that Walker "ha[d] provided material support for terrorism" is a mere hint of the degree to which the Harvard law school professor has become an "enemy" (to use his own language) of political dissent in the United States when it involves criticism of Israel's policies.

8

RICHARD FALK AND SELF-DEFENSE

One certain feature of authoritarian states is the detention and imprisonment of intellectuals. The United States hasn't detained any prominent U.S. intellectuals for political reasons in recent years, but Israel has, and it has done so without protest by the United States. Not only are these the very same American intellectuals whom Dershowitz has identified as "enemies of Israel," but the state of Israel detained these individuals with Dershowitz's silence or publicly issued support.

On December 15, 2008, the *New York Times* reported that "Israeli authorities on Monday expelled Richard Falk, a United Nations investigator of human rights in the Palestinian territories, saying he was unwelcome because of what the government has regarded as his hostile position toward Israel." The *Times* reported that Falk "was held at the [Ben Gurion] airport and placed on the first available flight back to Geneva, his point of departure," and that Falk "has long been criticized in Israel for what many Israelis say are unfair and unpalatable views."[1]

In an article that he wrote for the *Guardian* a few days later, Falk elaborated on the circumstances of his detention:

> I was separated [at the airport] from my two UN companions who were allowed to enter Israel and taken to the airport detention facility a mile or so away. I was required to put all my bags and cell phone in a room and taken to a locked tiny room that smelled of urine and filth. It contained five other detainees and was an unwelcome invitation to claustrophobia. I spent the next 15 hours or so confined, which amounted to a cram course on the miseries of prison life. . . . Of course, my disappointment and harsh confinement were trivial matters, not by themselves worthy of notice, given the sorts of serious hardships that millions around the world daily endure. Their importance is largely symbolic. I am an individual who had done

nothing wrong beyond express strong disapproval of policies of a sovereign state. More importantly, the obvious intention was to humble me as a UN representative and thereby send a message of defiance to the United Nations.[2]

By December 2008, Falk was not the only American professor who had been detained by Israeli authorities. Seven months earlier, in May 2008, the Israeli newspaper *Haaretz* reported that "the Shin Bet security service detained and deported an American Jewish professor who is a prominent critic of the Israeli occupation when he landed at Ben Gurion International Airport." *Haaretz* reported that "Professor Norman Finkelstein was interrogated for several hours and held in an airport cell before being put on a plane back to Amsterdam, his point of departure," and was told that "he could not return to Israel for 10 years." The Shin Bet told the newspaper that Finkelstein was not permitted to enter Israel "because of suspicions involving hostile elements in Lebanon," and because he "did not give a full accounting to interrogators with regard to these suspicions." However, after leaving Israel, and in an email and phone conversations with *Haaretz*, Finkelstein responded: "I did my best to provide absolutely candid and comprehensive answers to all the questions put to me. I am confident that I have nothing to hide. Apart from my political views, and the supporting scholarship, there isn't much more to say for myself: alas, no suicide missions or secret rendezvous with terrorist organizations. I've always supported a two-state solution based on the 1967 borders." Finkelstein then told *Haaretz*, "I'm not an enemy of Israel."[3]

Two years after the detention in Israel of Falk and Finkelstein, Noam Chomsky was detained by Israeli authorities at the Allenby Bridge on the border of the West Bank and the state of Jordan, as *Haaretz* reported: "Professor Noam Chomsky, an American linguist and left-wing activist, was denied entry into Israel on Sunday [May 16, 2010], for reasons that were not immediately clear." *Haaretz* noted that "Chomsky is a professor at the Massachusetts Institute of Technology and is considered among the foremost academics in the world," and that Chomsky's Israeli interrogators "had told him he had written things that the Israeli government did not like."[4] On the same day, the *New York Times* reported that Chomsky, "who had been invited to speak about American foreign and domestic policy by the philosophy department at the Palestinian university in Ramallah," was "interrogated for several hours before being told that he would not be allowed to cross into occupied Palestinian territory."[5] According to Assaf Kfoury, a professor of computer science at Boston University, Noam Chomsky's daughter, Aviva Chomsky, an intellectual and author in her own right,[6] also was denied entry into the West Bank.[7] The next day, the *Boston Globe* reported that Noam Chomsky "believed he was being singled out for his criticism of Israel." Chomsky said that Israeli authorities "are carrying out an action of a kind that I've never heard of before, except in totalitarian states."[8]

The *Globe* also cited the statement about Chomsky's detention by the Association for Civil Rights in Israel (ACRI): "A democratic state, which considers freedom of expression a guiding principle, does not close itself off to criticism or uncomfortable notions and does not refuse entry to visitors whose views it does not accept, but rather deals with them through public discourse."[9] The *Globe* thus reproduced the ACRI statement nearly in its entirety, for some reason omitting the first sentence, which read: "The decision to prevent an individual from expressing his or her views by denying entry is characteristic of a totalitarian regime."[10] The same day, the *Jerusalem Post* reported that, "according to the Association of Civil Rights in Israel, left-wingers are denied entrance to Israel on a regular basis."[11]

As if to illustrate the point, four months later, in September 2010, the *Jerusalem Post* reported: "Nobel Peace Prize winner and pro-Palestinian activist Mairead Maguire was refused entry into Israel on Tuesday [September 28], and was detained in the airport ahead of deportation. Maguire will reportedly be appealing the decision, and will therefore remain in custody until a court date is set."[12] And regular readers of the English-language Israeli press may also have noticed a report titled "Shin Bet Deports Spain's Most Famous Clown Upon Arrival in Israel," which was published by *Ha'aretz* about a week before Chomsky's detention: "Ivan Prado, the most famous clown in Spain, did not expect to be put on a return flight back to Madrid soon after arriving at Ben-Gurion International Airport late last month, after spending six hours with officials from the Shin Bet security service and the Interior Ministry. Foreign Ministry officials, meanwhile, say the incident caused grave damage to Israel's image in Spain." *Ha'aretz* reported that after Prado returned to Madrid, "he launched a media campaign denouncing Israel and comparing the situation of Palestinians in the West Bank with Jews in Poland," and that Shin Bet later "issued a statement to *Ha'aretz* lacking specific details about the reasons behind the decision" to detain and expel Prado.[13]

Falk, Finkelstein, and Chomsky were detained and expelled without having committed any crimes, and without being charged with any crimes. The arrests and detentions of these three prominent American academics were ordered by Israeli authorities as a response to their political views. This being the case, the detentions and expulsions may have violated the Universal Declaration of Human Rights, which gives everyone "the right to freedom of opinion and expression . . . without interference and to seek, receive and impart information and ideas through any media and regardless of frontiers" (Article 19). The declaration also stipulates that "no one shall be subjected to arbitrary arrest, detention or exile" (Article 9).[14] Under the circumstances, it seems that the arrest and detention of these U.S. academics were purely punitive, given their political views, and designed also to inhibit the imparting of information and ideas that the state of Israel found objectionable.

While writing nothing to my knowledge that deplored the detention in Israel of his academic colleagues and fellow Americans, Dershowitz instead wrote a column for publication in Israel that rebuked and berated Falk. Posted two days after Falk's description of his detention in the *Guardian*, Dershowitz wrote in the *Jerusalem Post* that "one can certainly understand why the Jewish state would refuse to cooperate with a [UN] rapporteur [Falk] whose objectivity has been compromised by his bigotry." Astonishingly, Dershowitz somehow managed to forego any mention of the fact of Falk's detention and reported only that Israel had merely "refused to cooperate" with Falk. Thus, Dershowitz wrote an article for publication in a foreign country for the purpose of justifying the detention in that same foreign country of an American academic colleague for his alleged lack of "objectivity." And, for good measure, Dershowitz added the charge of "bigotry" to Falk's offense against that country. Presumably, Dershowitz—an apparent advocate of preventive detention in the United States (see chapter 11 in this volume)—views allegations of a "lack of objectivity" in one's political views, and allegations of anti-Jewish "bigotry" (never mind that Falk is Jewish), as sufficient grounds for detention. Furthermore, while providing supporting material to help justify Israel's detention of Falk, and somehow without irony, Dershowitz claimed to support the principle of free speech, even as it had just been violated by Israel with his support: "Bigots and crackpots are free to set up soapboxes anywhere they choose, and everyone is free to accept or reject their ideas in the market-place."[15] Yet, Dershowitz said nothing that was critical of Israel for its deprivation of Falk's liberty on speech grounds, and all of his criticism was directed at Falk.

In his same piece in the *Jerusalem Post*, Dershowitz liberally assigned the words "bigot," "bigotry," and "crackpot" to Falk and his views. Dershowitz also compared Falk to David Duke and Iran's Mahmoud Ahmadinejad while implying that Falk is a Holocaust-denier.[16] Dershowitz wrote: "It has become conventional for anti-Israel extremists to compare the Jewish state of Israel to the Nazi government that came close to murdering all the Jews of Europe. That is why this false comparison is the province of anti-Semites, assorted nuts of the hard right and the hard left, and haters such as Richard Falk."[17] Keep in mind that Dershowitz wrote all of this in the immediate aftermath of Israel's detention and expulsion of Falk on the basis of Falk's political views.

Before proceeding, and for the record, here is what Falk wrote in full in 2007, which prompted Dershowitz to call Falk a "bigot" and a "hater" in the immediate context of Falk's detention in 2008 by Israel:

> There is little doubt that the Nazi Holocaust was as close to unconditional evil as has been revealed throughout the entire bloody history of the

human species. Its massiveness, unconcealed genocidal intent, and reliance on the mentality and instruments of modernity give its enactment in the death camps of Europe a special status in our moral imagination. This special status is exhibited in the continuing presentation of its gruesome realities through film, books, and a variety of cultural artifacts more than six decades after the events in question ceased. The permanent memory of the Holocaust is also kept alive by the existence of several notable museums devoted exclusively to the depiction of the horrors that took place during the period of Nazi rule in Germany.

Against this background, it is especially painful for me, as an American Jew, to feel compelled to portray the ongoing and intensifying abuse of the Palestinian people by Israel through a reliance on such an inflammatory metaphor as "holocaust." The word is derived from the Greek *holos* (meaning "completely") and *kaustos* (meaning "burnt"), and was used in ancient Greece to refer to the complete burning of a sacrificial offering to a divinity. Because such a background implies a religious undertaking, there is some inclination in Jewish literature to prefer the Hebrew word "Shoah" that can be translated roughly as "calamity," and was the name given to the 1985 epic nine-hour narration of the Nazi experience by the French filmmaker, Claude Lanzmann. The Germans themselves were more antiseptic in their designation, officially naming their undertaking as the "Final Solution of the Jewish Question." The label is, of course, inaccurate as a variety of non-Jewish identities were also targets of this genocidal assault, including the Roma and Sinti ("gypsies"), Jehovah Witnesses, gays, disabled persons, political opponents.

Is it an irresponsible overstatement to associate the treatment of Palestinians with this criminalized Nazi record of collective atrocity? I think not. The recent developments in Gaza are especially disturbing because they express so vividly a deliberate intention on the part of Israel and its allies to subject an entire human community to life-endangering conditions of utmost cruelty. The suggestion that this pattern of conduct is a holocaust-in-the-making represents a rather desperate appeal to the governments of the world and to international public opinion to act urgently to prevent these current genocidal tendencies from culminating in a collective tragedy. If ever the ethos of "a responsibility to protect," recently adopted by the UN Security Council as the basis of "humanitarian intervention" is applicable, it would be to act now to start protecting the people of Gaza from further pain and suffering. But it would be unrealistic to expect the UN to do anything in the face of this crisis, given the pattern of US support for Israel and taking into account the extent to which European governments have lent their weight to recent illicit efforts to crush Hamas as a Palestinian political force.[18]

For one thing, this is hardly holocaust denialism. For another, Falk's reluctant tone and tenor, here and elsewhere, is in no way comparable to the relentlessly offensive tone and content of the written and spoken commentary of Alan Dershowitz. In any event, regardless of Falk's views, and whatever historical analogies he may have drawn to Israel's occupation of the Palestinian territories, it is highly objectionable that Dershowitz would invoke this or any other remnant of the writings of a leading American intellectual and UN representative while seeking to validate that person's detention and expulsion by the state of Israel.

Another aspect of Dershowitz's public gesture of support for Israel's detention of Falk was his argument, in the same article in the *Jerusalem Post*, that "Falk ignored the Hamas rockets directed against Israeli citizens and the suicide bombs employed by Palestinian terrorists to blow up school buses, discos and religious ceremonies," and that "any comparison between Israeli efforts to defend its citizens from terrorism on the one hand, and the Nazi Holocaust on the other hand, is obscene and ignorant." Dershowitz continued: "Even if one believes that the Israeli military has overreacted to terrorist provocations, there is surely a difference between military actions taken in self defense, and the systematic policy of the Nazis to murder every Jewish man, woman, and child living in Europe."[19] Although it is disturbing that Dershowitz would write an article seemingly to justify the detention of Richard Falk by invoking the Holocaust, I will leave Dershowitz's references to the Holocaust aside at this point to focus on his claim that Israel acts in self-defense as a matter of policy when it resorts to the use of force against Palestinians, beginning with his reference to "Hamas rockets directed against Israeli civilians," while declining to observe that Israel has fired thousands more, and far more powerful, rockets (artillery shells) into Gaza. In a report issued in June 2007, one year before Dershowitz sought to discredit Falk after he was detained by Israel, Human Rights Watch reported that "Palestinian armed groups fired about 2,700 Qassam-type rockets from September 2005 through May 2007" into Israel.[20] In the same report, however, Human Rights Watch noted that Israel had fired many more rockets into the Gaza Strip during the same period: "From September 2005, when the IDF withdrew from the Gaza Strip, through May 2007, Israel fired more than 14,600 artillery shells in the Gaza Strip, primarily in the north, killing 59 Palestinians and injuring 270," with Palestinian fatalities being "primarily if not exclusively civilians," including seventeen children under the age of sixteen. Palestinian rockets for the same period killed four Israelis, all civilians, while injuring seventy-five Israeli civilians and nine soldiers.[21] These figures do not include the incident of November 8, 2006, when "IDF shelling in Beit Hanoun [in Gaza] killed or mortally wounded 23 Palestinians and wounded at least 40 more, all civilians."[22] This one incident alone killed more Palestinians than all Israelis killed by Qassam-type rockets since 2001.

In addition to Israel reportedly firing over fourteen thousand artillery shells into the Gaza Strip during the twenty-one-month period examined by Human Rights Watch, these shells are many times more powerful than the Qassam-type rockets fired from Gaza into Israel. The most common artillery shell used by Israel's twenty-eight-ton howitzer cannons are the M170 155mm high-explosive artillery shells, described by Human Rights Watch as "extremely deadly weapons," with a lethal radius of 50 to 150 meters and a casualty radius of 100 to 300 meters.[23]

While neither Israel nor the groups in Gaza who fire the Qassam-type rockets into Israel have a right under international law to target civilians or fire indiscriminately, including as "reprisals" to rocket fire from the other side, applying Dershowitz's interpretation of international law would yield a right of "self-defense" to both sides to exchange retaliatory rocket fire in perpetuity; however, to make matters even worse, Dershowitz grants this nonexistent right only to Israel. The fact is that neither side has any such right of "self-defense" under international law to launch rockets indiscriminately, or directly at civilian targets, as reprisals to rockets launched at them.

It also happens, ironically with respect to Dershowitz's perpetual claims of Israeli self-defense, that Richard Falk, not Dershowitz, is one of the world's leading experts concerning the use of force by states under the UN Charter—including the resort to force as "self-defense"—a fact which Dershowitz omitted from his published biography of Falk as a "bigot" and "hater" on the occasion of Falk's detention by Israel. Indeed, Falk's expertise about a key rule of international law— a rule that Dershowitz invokes with great frequency and imprecision—spans five decades, beginning with his opposition to the U.S. war in Vietnam.

In 1954, at the northern Vietnamese city of Dien Bien Phu, the Viet Minh forces of Ho Chi Minh defeated France's Far East Expeditionary Corps, ending the colonial occupation of Vietnam that had begun in the late nineteenth century. About this key event in the history of Vietnam, Stanley Karnow wrote: "On the afternoon of May 7, 1954, the Vietminh's red flag went up over the French command bunker at Dienbienphu. The next morning in Geneva, nine delegations assembled around a horseshoe-shaped table at the old League of Nations building to open their discussions of the Indochina problem."[24] Two months later, the signing ceremony of the Geneva Accords on July 21, 1954, marked the official end of the French colonial war in Vietnam, during which, from 1946 to 1954, more than 300,000 Vietnamese were killed, with nearly a billion dollars a year from the United States in support of the French effort.[25]

The Geneva Accords of 1954 consisted of three agreements on the cessation of hostilities, one each for Vietnam, Laos, and Cambodia, in addition to a "Final Declaration of the Geneva Conference" that "takes note of the agreements ending hostilities in Cambodia, Laos, and Vietnam and organiz[es] international control and the supervision of the provisions of the agreements."[26] The Final Declaration was signed by France, the United Kingdom, the Soviet Union, and the People's Republic of China; the United States, fatefully, did not sign.

Referring to the 1954 Geneva Accords a little more than a decade later, the Lawyers Committee on American Policy Towards Vietnam, chaired by Richard Falk, assessed the legal status of the accords as follows: "While the Charter of the United Nations, as the most comprehensive basis of world legal order, is of course applicable to the Vietnam situation, the particular situation in Vietnam is grounded by a series of compacts, namely, the Geneva Accords of 1954. Under a general principle of international law, special compacts prevail over general rules, insofar as they do not violate them in letter or spirit. The Geneva Accords, carefully designed to restore peace to a war-torn area, fulfill the highest aim of the Charter."[27]

In July 1954—four years after Senator Joseph McCarthy claimed in a speech from Wheeling, West Virginia, that he held a list of dozens of communists working at the U.S. State Department,[28] and one month after McCarthy's televised hearings, where he alleged that communists had infiltrated the CIA[29]—a *New York Times* editorial supported the American rejection of the Geneva Accords because the treaty would "turn over more than half of [Vietnam's] 22 million people to Communist rule."[30] However, the Pentagon Papers, a secret history that in part reviewed U.S. policy toward Indochina during and immediately following World War II, revealed "the fact that Ho [Chi Minh] was acknowledged to be a genuine nationalist, as well as a communist, who was intent on maintaining his independence from the Soviet Union and China."[31]

Following its rejection of the Final Declaration of the Geneva Conference, the United States proceeded systematically to violate the terms of the Geneva Accords on Vietnam. While "both the French [to the south] and the Vietnam People's Republic [to the north] properly withdrew to their respective sides of the 17th parallel" as the legally required prelude to unification elections, "the refusal of South Vietnam, with United States backing, to hold the elections for unification, violated the provisions of the Geneva Accords that had made them acceptable to the Viet Minh."[32] South Vietnam's refusal to participate in the unification elections—which would have been won by Ho Chi Minh with "possibly 80 percent" of the popular vote according to President Dwight Eisenhower[33]—contributed to the establishment of the armed insurgency of the National Front for the Liberation of Vietnam (called "Viet Cong" in the United States) and to the eventual full-blown, overt U.S. military involvement in Vietnam.

In an official government memorandum dated March 4, 1966, and titled "The Legality of United States Participation in the Defense of Vietnam," President Johnson's State Department set out to justify the U.S. military intervention in Vietnam, and started a debate in the United States about the U.S. resort to force as "self-defense" under the UN Charter. In bold type, the State Department emphatically presented its key claims:

- **The United States and South Vietnam Have the Right under International Law to Participate in the Collective Defense of South Vietnam against Armed Attack;**
- **South Vietnam Is Being Subjected to Armed Attack by Communist North Vietnam;**
- **International Law Recognizes the Right of Individual and Collective Self-Defense against Armed Attack.**[34]

In response to the State Department's memorandum, a number of prominent U.S. international law scholars and foreign policy intellectuals, including Quincy Wright (University of Chicago), Hans Morgenthau (University of Chicago), Stanley Hoffmann (Harvard University), and Richard Falk (Princeton University)—a total of twelve altogether[35]—formed the Lawyers Committee on American Policy Towards Vietnam. The Lawyers Committee advanced two principal points in response to the State Department memorandum, the first of which is: "(a) The military intervention by the United States in Vietnam violates the Charter of the United Nations; the intervention is not justified by the right of collective self-defense."[36] Citing UN Charter Article 2, paragraph 4,[37] the Lawyers Committee wrote: "One of the abiding Principles of the Charter of the United Nations is the obligation of its Members to eliminate the *use* of force, and even the *threat* of force, in international relations. . . . The State Department Memorandum interprets Article 2(4) with curious superficiality. Calling this Principle 'an important limitation on the use of force,' the memorandum creates a misleading impression. It is not a 'limitation' but the keystone of modern international law. Threat or use of force are not 'limited'; in principle they are outlawed."[38] The lawyers continued: "The Charter acknowledges that, for the very purpose of maintaining peace, various measures, and ultimately force, may be required. It confers the competence to use force upon the [UN] Security Council, thus making force the instrument of the world community and not of individual states." And: "The essential meaning of this rule of international law is that no country shall decide for itself whether to use force—and, especially, whether to wage war through an intervention in a foreign conflict."[39] At all times after July 1954 the United States "decided for itself" whether to wage war against Vietnam; at no time was the U.S. military intervention in Vietnam authorized by the UN Security Council. The second point is: "(b) The Charter permits collective self-defense only in case of an 'armed attack.' The existence of an 'armed attack' is not established by the [State Department] Memorandum."[40]

Responding also to the State Department's claim that the United States possesses an "inherent" right to self-defense in Vietnam, the lawyers wrote:

[UN Charter] Article 51 constitutes, as has been emphasized by many international lawyers, the single exception to the keystone principle of the Charter and contemporary world order—that is, the prohibition of unilateral use or threat of force. It is an accepted canon of construction that if a treaty grants an exception to a basic rule, such exception must be interpreted restrictively. . . . Seizing upon the reference in the United Nations Charter to the right of self-defense as "inherent" (that is, allegedly outside and independent of the Charter), the State Department argues in favor of a doctrine of self-defense that did not exist even before the Charter and which, if accepted, would establish a unilateral right of military intervention and confer a competence upon nation-states to wage wars that might have the greatest consequences for the world.[41]

Explaining further, the lawyers wrote: "The right of self-defense under the Charter arises only if an 'armed attack' has occurred. The language of Article 51 is unequivocal on this point. The term 'armed attack' has an established meaning in international law. It was deliberately employed in the Charter to reduce drastically the discretion of states to determine for themselves the scope of permissible self-defense both with regard to claims of individual and collective self-defense."

Describing a key formulation concerning the charter's prohibition of the use and threat of force, and the single exception of self-defense, the lawyers explained:

Individual self-defense and, *a fortiori*, collective self-defense, is not a lawful response to the commission of action unilaterally described as "indirect aggression," but only in the event that the victim state experiences an "armed attack," that is, if military forces cross an international boundary in visible, massive and sustained form. The objective of Article 51 was to confine the discretion of a state to claim self-defense to those instances "when the necessity for action" is "instant, overwhelming, and leaving no choice of means, and no moment for deliberation." In explaining Article 51, legal authorities usually invoke the classical definition of self-defense given by Secretary of State Daniel Webster in *The Caroline*. Mr. Webster's description of the permissible basis for self-defense was relied upon in the Nuremberg Judgment in the case against major German war criminals.[42]

Thus, as the lawyers argued, the State Department's own description in its legal memorandum of the alleged "armed attack" by North Vietnam against South Vietnam—that it "is not as easily fixed by date and hour as in the case of traditional warfare"—undermined its own case that the U.S. military intervention in Vietnam was an act of collective self-defense in response to an "armed attack" as the concept is defined under international law.

Furthermore, the Lawyers Committee argued that the United States began its overt war actions against North Vietnam not in self-defense but as armed "reprisal," that "this reprisal was unlawful," and that "reprisals involving the use of force are illegal."[43] About the legal status of armed reprisals, the lawyers observed that "in the present system of world order, injured states may take actions short of violence, but a general consensus prohibits the use of force in reprisal, in view of the categorical provisions [prohibiting the resort to force] of the United Nations Charter." As a study by the Royal Institute of International Affairs (London) concluded: "It is now generally considered that reprisals involving the use of force are illegal."[44] And in the wake of British raids against Yemen in response to Yemen's attacks on the British Protectorate of Aden in 1964, the UN Security Council condemned reprisals "as incompatible with the purposes and principles of the United Nations." In the preceding debate, U.S. Ambassador Adlai Stevenson "emphasized United States disapproval of 'retaliatory raids, wherever they occur and by whomever they are committed.'"[45]

Thus—and referring back to Dershowitz's claim that Israel has a right of self-defense under international law to retaliate unilaterally and at its own discretion with military force against Qassam rockets fired from the Gaza Strip—Dershowitz confuses Israel's right of self-defense in response to an armed attack (should such an armed attack actually occur) with Israel's illegal military reprisals in response to the Qassam rockets. Furthermore, the legal logic of the prohibition against the threat and use of force would prohibit both Israel and any governing authorities in Gaza from launching missiles as reprisals to any previous launch by the other side, thus preventing a cycle of violence. In contrast, and as things now stand, under Dershowitz's view of international law, when Israel launches its rockets, it's "self-defense"; when the Palestinians do it, it's "terrorism."

This double standard, which he applies throughout his writings, is indicative of the flaws of Dershowitz's "jurisprudence" on the Israel-Palestine conflict and the so-called war on terrorism. Indeed, in his five books on the Israel-Palestine conflict: *Why Terrorism Works* (2002), *The Case for Israel* (2003), *The Case for Peace* (2005), *Preemption* (2006), and *The Case against Israel's Enemies* (2008)— where Dershowitz frequently cites "self-defense" under international law to justify a multitude of Israeli uses of force, he fails to mention (a) UN Charter Article 2(4), which prohibits the use and threat of force by states; (b) that the prohibition against force is the cardinal rule of the charter and a peremptory norm of international law, that is, an absolute and incontrovertible rule; and (c) that the right of self-defense by states is the lone, highly circumscribed exception to the prohibition against force. In many cases, Dershowitz simply asserts that a given

Israeli military action is "self-defense"—end of story. In short, Dershowitz habitually invokes the exception to the rule (self-defense) without citing the rule itself (the prohibition against force).

For example, a week after Dershowitz wrote a column in the *Jerusalem Post* (December 21, 2008) to defend Israel's detention and expulsion of Falk, Israel launched its air-land invasion of the Gaza Strip (December 27). On January 4, Dershowitz wrote: "Israel's military actions in Gaza are entirely justified under international law, and Israel should be commended for its act of self-defense against international terrorism. Article 51 of the United Nations Charter reserves to every nation the right to engage in self-defense against armed attacks." Here, as is his practice, Dershowitz cites UN Charter Article 51 (the self-defense exception) without elaboration and without mentioning UN Charter Article 2(4) (the prohibition against force.) He concluded that Israel's bombardment of Gaza was both "lawful and commendable."[46] Likewise, in a column in the *Jerusalem Post* on January 13, Dershowitz wrote:

> Every Hamas rocket attack against Israeli civilians—and there have been more than 6,500 of them since Israel ended its occupation of Gaza [in September 2005]—is an armed attack against Israel under Article 51 of the United Nations Charter, which authorizes member nations to respond militarily to armed attacks against it. Under international law, Israel is entitled to do whatever it takes militarily to stop Hamas rockets from targeting its civilians. . . . In fact, under international law, Israel has the right to declare all-out war against the Hamas-controlled government of Gaza. In an all-out war, there would be no obligation to provide humanitarian assistance, electricity or any other services to an enemy who had started the war by an armed attack.[47]

Here, and repeatedly, Dershowitz writes as if Hamas is the only rocket-launching party. And he makes almost no attempt to define the term "armed attack" under international law. To quote Richard Falk and his cohort of legal scholars from 1967, Dershowitz thus argues here "in favor of a doctrine of self-defense which, if accepted, would establish a unilateral right of military intervention" in response to virtually any military provocation.

Perhaps most tellingly, Dershowitz's column in the *Jerusalem Post* of January 13, which articulated a de facto doctrine of Israeli unilateralism, ignored and thus did not respond to the statement published on January 11 in the *Times* (London) by twenty-seven leading international law scholars, including Ian Brownlie and Richard Falk. The lawyers' statement, which contradicts the legal claims by Dershowitz as applied to Israel's bombardment and invasion of Gaza, was published as follows in its entirety:

Israel has sought to justify its military atta[...]
amounts to an act of "self-defence" as reco[...]
Nations Charter. We categorically reject thi[...]
tacks on Israel by Hamas deplorable as they a[...]
and effect amount to an armed attack entitlin[...]
fence. Under international law, self-defence is a[...]
subject to the customary rules of proportionality[...]
of almost 800 Palestinians, mostly civilians, and n[...]
accompanied by the destruction of schools, mosc[...]
pounds and government buildings, which Israel [...]
protect under the Fourth Geneva Convention, is r[...] ...nsurate to
the deaths caused by Hamas rocket fire.

For 18 months Israel had imposed an unlawful blockade on the coastal strip that brought Gazan society to the brink of collapse. In the three years after Israel's redeployment from Gaza [in September 2005], 11 Israelis were killed by rocket fire. And yet in 2005–2008, according to the UN, the Israeli army killed about 1,200 Palestinians in Gaza, including 222 children. Throughout this time the Gaza Strip remained occupied territory under international law because Israel maintained effective control over it.

Israel's actions amount to aggression, not self-defence, not least because its assault on Gaza was unnecessary. Israel could have agreed to renew the truce with Hamas. Instead it killed 225 Palestinians on the first day of its attack. As things stand, its invasion and bombardment of Gaza amounts to collective punishment of Gaza's 1.5m inhabitants contrary to international humanitarian and human rights law. In addition, the blockade of humanitarian relief, the destruction of civilian infrastructure, and preventing access to basic necessities such as food and fuel, are prima facie war crimes.

We condemn the firing of rockets by Hamas into Israel and suicide bombings which are also contrary to international humanitarian law and are war crimes. Israel has a right to take reasonable and proportionate means to protect its civilian population from such attacks. However, the manner and scale of its operations in Gaza amount to an act of aggression and is contrary to international law, notwithstanding the rocket attacks by Hamas.[48]

The first signature (among the nonalphabetized signatures) to appear below this published statement belonged to the eminent British legal scholar Ian Brownlie, author of the most authoritative text on the legality of the use of force, *International Law and the Use of Force by States*, published by Oxford University

ing also the signature of Falk, who chaired the 1967 study *...tional Law*, and who edited the three-volume *The Vietnam ...tional Law*, which was sponsored by the American Society of ... Law,[50] it is difficult to fathom how Dershowitz's column of January ... argued that Israel's air-land invasion of the Gaza Strip was "self defense," ... so comfortably ignore the Brownlie-Falk statement of January 11, which authoritatively presented a legal opinion totally at odds with the one that Dershowitz sketched two days later.

While it is clear that the indiscriminate firing of Qassam and Qassam-like rockets by Palestinian militants into mostly civilian areas of southern Israel are violations of international humanitarian law and, as such, are deplorable and criminal acts, it is also clear that the preponderance of military power is owned and exercised by Israel. The underlying circumstances surrounding the Palestinian capture of Israeli soldier Gilad Shalit on June 25, 2006—that is, Israel's military conduct leading up to June 25 and the number of Palestinian prisoners in Israeli prisons up to that date—illustrate the point.

As I have already reported, from September 2005 through May 2007, Israel fired approximately 14,600 artillery shells into the Gaza Strip, while Palestinian armed groups fired about 2,700 Qassam-type rockets into Israel.[51] About midway through this period, on June 9, 2006—a little more than two weeks before the capture of Shalit—Israel fired several 155mm howitzer shells onto a beach in Beit Lahiya in northern Gaza. A few days later, on June 12, Amnesty International issued a statement "calling on Israel to end immediately its reckless shelling and air strikes against the Gaza Strip, which have killed and injured scores of unarmed Palestinians, including several women and children, in recent months." Amnesty continued:

> In the latest such attack on the afternoon of 9 June 2006, seven members of the same Palestinian family were killed and ten other civilians were in-jured when Israeli forces fired several artillery shells at a beach in the North of the Gaza Strip. The beach was crowded with Palestinian families enjoying the first weekend of the school holidays. Ali Issa Ghalia, his wife Raissa and their five children—a one-year-old son and four daughters aged two, four, 15 and 17—were killed and other members of their family, including two children, were injured when an Israeli shell landed where they were sitting.

Amnesty observed that "the seven members of the Ghalia family were the most recent among a growing number of victims of increasingly frequent and dis-proportionate Israeli attacks against the Gaza Strip."[52]

Likewise, on June 21, in response to the ongoing Israeli shelling and air attacks on the Gaza Strip, Amnesty "called for the establishment of an international investigation to examine the circumstances in which scores of Palestinians have been killed by Israeli forces in the Gaza Strip in recent months." The Amnesty statement continued: "Since the beginning of this year [2006] Israeli forces have killed some 150 Palestinians—many of them unarmed—including more than 25 children. About half of the victims were killed in the Gaza Strip. To date none of these cases have been adequately investigated." Amnesty also noted that "since the end of March 2006" up to the date of its June 2006 report—a period of a little more than two months—"the Israeli army has launched close to 6,000 artillery shells and more than 80 air strikes against densely populated areas in the Gaza Strip," and that "such disproportionate attacks have killed dozens of Palestinians, including several women and children." Parallel to those artillery shells launched by Israel from March to June 2006, Amnesty reported that "Palestinian armed groups have launched hundreds of 'qassam' rockets at Israel, injuring several Israelis."[53]

On June 25, four days after Amnesty International issued its report, Palestinian militants crossed the border from Gaza into southern Israel and captured Corporal Gilad Shalit, at the time a nineteen-year-old Israeli soldier. About this incident, Amnesty reported: "Amnesty International calls on the Palestinian armed groups who are holding hostage a 19-year-old Israeli soldier, Corporal Gilad Shalit, not to harm him and to release him promptly," and the groups "are demanding the release of Palestinian women and children detained by Israel in exchange for information about the hostage."[54] About the women and children detained in Israel, the *New York Times* reported on June 27, two days after Shalit was captured, that "there are 95 Palestinian women and 313 Palestinians under 18 in Israeli jails, of a prison population [inside Israel] of about 9,000 Palestinians."[55] Israel rejected the Palestinian demand to exchange Shalit for all Palestinian women and children in detention in Israel.[56]

Rather than seek a nonmilitary remedy to the capture of the Israeli soldier, on June 28 Israel launched a highly destructive ground invasion and aerial bombardment of the Gaza Strip, as the *New York Times* reported: "Israel sent troops into southern Gaza and its planes attacked three bridges and a power station early Wednesday [June 28], in an effort to prevent militants from moving a wounded Israeli soldier they abducted Sunday, Israeli Army officials said. Israeli troops and tanks began to move in force in an effort to rescue the soldier, Cpl. Gilad Shalit, 19, who is believed to be held there."[57]

About the June 28 Israeli bombardment and invasion, Amnesty International reported on June 30: "The deliberate destruction of the Gaza Strip's only electricity power station, water networks, bridges, roads and other infrastructure is a violation of the Fourth Geneva Convention and has major and long-term humanitarian consequences for the 1.5 million inhabitants of the Gaza Strip."[58]

B'Tselem called the Israeli bombing "an act of vengeance" in response to the capture of Shalit, while also reporting:

> In the early morning hours of 28 June 2006, following the abduction of Cpl. Gilad Shalit, the Israeli Air Force attacked the only electrical power plant operating in the Gaza Strip. . . . As a result of the lack of electricity, the level of medical services provided by clinics and hospitals has declined significantly; most of the urban population receive only two or three hours of water a day; the sewage system is on the verge of collapse; many inhabitants' mobility has been severely restricted as a result of non-functioning elevators; and the lack of refrigeration has exposed many to the danger of food-poisoning. Small businesses reliant on a regular power supply have been badly affected. The hardship involved in living without a steady flow of electricity is exacerbated by the deep economic crisis afflicting the Gaza Strip. . . . Aiming attacks at civilian objects is forbidden under International Humanitarian Law and is considered a war crime. The power plant bombed by Israel is a purely civilian object and bombing it did nothing to impede the ability of Palestinian organizations to fire rockets into Israeli territory.[59]

Human Rights Watch agreed: "Israel's destruction of Gaza's only electrical plant needlessly punishes the civilian population and has created the potential for a serious humanitarian crisis."[60]

B'Tselem also described an additional dimension of the collective punishment, in response to the capture of Shalit, ordered by the Israeli government:

> During its operation in the Gaza Strip following the abduction of Cpl. Gilad Shalit, Israeli air force jets have carried out low-altitude sorties over the Gaza Strip in which they intentionally cause powerful sonic booms. The air force has used sonic booms a number of times since the completion of the Gaza disengagement plan. In the present operation, the air force has caused three or four sonic-boom sorties a night. The sole purpose of these sorties is to prevent the residents from sleeping and to create an ongoing sense of fear and anxiety. Regarding the sonic booms, Prime Minister Ehud Olmert said that "thousands of residents in southern Israel live in fear and discomfort, so I gave instructions that nobody will sleep at night in the meantime in Gaza." The clear intention of the practice is to pressure the Palestinian Authority and the armed Palestinian organizations by harming the entire civilian population.

B'Tselem then described some of the effects of the Israeli action: "Children, in particular, suffer from the sonic booms. In the past, the Gaza Community Mental Health Center reported that the supersonic sorties caused fear among many children, which led to a loss of concentration, loss of appetite, bedwetting, and other disorders. The Center also reported that sonic booms caused headaches, stomach aches, shortness of breath, and other physical effects that appeared among both children and adults. Sonic booms also cause property damage, primarily shattered windows." B'Tselem also indicated that the use of sonic booms in this fashion violates Article 33 of the Fourth Geneva Convention, which states that "collective penalties and likewise all measures of intimidation or of terrorism are prohibited" and that "reprisals against protected persons [under the Fourth Geneva Convention] and their property are prohibited."[61]

Furthermore, on June 29, *Ha'aretz* reported: "Israel Defense Forces troops launched early Thursday a major arrest operation against Hamas officials. Israel Radio reported that a total of 62 Hamas men were arrested in overnight raids, including eight [government] ministers and 20 lawmakers."[62] On July 1, the Associated Press reported that "Israeli aircraft fired missiles at the Palestinian prime minister's office, setting the building on fire."[63] On July 4, the Associated Press reported that "Switzerland said that Israel has been violating international law in its Gaza offensive by heavy destruction and endangering civilians in acts of collective punishment banned under the Geneva Conventions on the conduct of warfare."[64]

Given these accounts, it is apparent that by initiating the aerial bombing and ground invasion of the Gaza Strip in June 2006, Israel violated the UN Charter's prohibition against the use of force (Article 2, paragraph 4), that the capture of the Israeli soldier, Gilad Shalit, did not constitute an "armed attack" against Israel, and that Israel engaged in the bombardment and invasion of Gaza without UN Security Council authorization. Israel's military actions in Gaza also violated the Fourth Geneva Convention by its "extreme measures" (Ehud Olmert) and "deliberate attacks" (Amnesty International) against Gaza's civilians and civilian infrastructure.

On July 12, 2006, in the midst of the Israeli bombardment and invasion of Gaza, and at about 9 AM Israel time, Hezbollah militants attacked Israeli military positions in northern Israel, killing three Israeli soldiers and capturing two. The purpose of the raid was to capture IDF personnel to exchange for Lebanese prisoners in Israel. The Hezbollah raid was a provocative and deplorable incident; however, it was also clearly limited, did not threaten the state of Israel, and was not an "armed attack" as defined under international law. Nor did Israel have authorization from the UN Security Council to bomb or invade Lebanon in response. Nevertheless, only hours after the initial Hezbollah incursion, Israel retaliated with a massive air strike and ground invasion of Lebanon. This response violated international law on at least four counts: (a) it violated UN Charter

Article 2(4), which prohibits the threat and use of force by states; (b) Israel's armed reprisals were illegal, given the broad prohibition against the use of force in international affairs; (c) the massively disproportionate scale of the Israeli reprisals, relative to the original Hezbollah incursion, violated international humanitarian law; and (d) Israel's failure to distinguish between civilian and military targets in its air strikes and artillery fire also violated international humanitarian law.

Indeed, news outlets throughout the night of July 12, and into the early morning hours of July 13, reported as follows the Israeli reprisal actions—all of which preceded the first Hezbollah firing on July 13 of missiles into Israel's northern cities:

- The "IDF responded to the [Hezbollah] attacks from Lebanon with heavy artillery and tank fire"; "IDF artillery was pounding the fringes of the [Lebanese] villages of Aita el-Shaab, Ramieh and Yaroun in the hills east of the coastal border port of Naqoura"; "Israeli jets struck roads, bridges and Hezbollah guerrilla positions in southern Lebanon"; "Two Lebanese civilians were killed and a Lebanese soldier was wounded in the IAF air strike on the coastal Qasmiyeh bridge in the south of [Lebanon]." ("Hezbollah Kidnaps 2 IDF Soldiers during Clashes on Israeli-Lebanon Border," *Ha'aretz*, July 12, 2006)
- "Israeli war planes and gunboats struck a Palestinian guerrilla base 10 miles south of Beirut late Wednesday [July 12], Lebanese security officials said, in the closest raid to the Lebanese capital since fighting erupted in southern Lebanon after guerrillas captured two Israeli soldiers"; This attack "comes after Israeli warplanes pounded more than 30 targets in southern Lebanon and Israel leaders promised Lebanon a painful response for the capture of the soldiers." ("Israelis Attack Just 10 Miles from Beirut," Associated Press, July 12, 2006)
- "The Israeli Air Force on Wednesday night [July 12] struck at least 40 targets in different places across Lebanon, including bridges and infrastructures along the Litani and Wazzani rivers." ("Nahariya: Woman Killed in Katyusha Attack," *Ynet*, July 13, 2006)
- Referring to the Israeli bombing of Lebanon on the night of July 12, the Associated Press reported: "[Israeli] Air Force Gen. Amir Eshel said the [bombing] campaign was likely Israel's largest ever in Lebanon 'if you measure it in number of targets hit in one night, the complexity of the strikes.'" ("Israel Claims Hundreds of Hits in Lebanon," Associated Press, July 13, 2006)

In response to these events and the nearly simultaneous Israeli military campaign in Gaza in June/July, 2006, Dershowitz sought to defend the bombing of civilians and civilian infrastructure in both Gaza and Lebanon by redefining the legal and moral status of the persons detained and bombed by Israel. Thus, in a *Huffington Post* column on July 14, and with respect to the Palestinian women and children and Lebanese men held in prisons in Israel, he wrote: "Anti-Israel zealots are insisting that the kidnapping by Hamas and Hezbollah of Israeli soldiers is the moral and legal equivalent of Israel's confinement of Palestinian and Hezbollah terrorists, and that accordingly a 'prisoner exchange' is being appropriately demanded by the terrorists who crossed over into Israeli territory to kidnap the soldiers. Nothing could be further from the truth. Every single prisoner held by Israel has judicial review available to him or her and some have won release. Every one of them has access to Red Cross visitation, can communicate with family, and has a known whereabout."[65] Dershowitz cited no sources while making these assertions.

With respect to the detention of Palestinians, and in contrast to Dershowitz's claims, B'Tselem described Israel's long-standing practice: "Over the years, Israel has administratively detained thousands of Palestinians for prolonged periods of time, without prosecuting them, without informing them of the charges against them, and without allowing them or their attorneys to study the evidence, making a mockery of the protections specified in Israeli and international law to protect the right to liberty and due process, the right of defendants to state their case, and the presumption of innocence." B'Tselem reported that for the period 2005–2007—the same period within which Dershowitz made the aforementioned claims on July 14, 2006—Israel administratively detained or imprisoned "about 750" Palestinians per year under these conditions. Furthermore, B'Tselem reported: "Administrative detention is detention without charge or trial that is authorized by administrative order rather than by judicial decree. Under international law, it is allowed under certain circumstances. However, because of the serious injury to due-process rights inherent in this measure and the obvious danger of its abuse, international law has placed rigid restrictions on its application. . . . Israel's use of administrative detention blatantly violates these restrictions."

And with additional special relevance to Dershowitz's claims about the legal propriety of Israel's imprisonment of Palestinian and Lebanese persons, B'Tselem reported that in 2002 Israel passed "The Internment of Unlawful Combatants Law," about which the human rights organization observed: "Originally, the law was intended to enable the holding of Lebanese citizens who were being held in Israel at the time as 'bargaining chips' for the return of [Israeli] captives and bodies. Now, Israel uses the law to detain Palestinian residents of the Gaza Strip without trial."[66] And only two months after Dershowitz claimed in *Huffington Post* that Israel detained and imprisoned Palestinians in a manner that was consistent with international law, B'Tselem reported that "almost 9,000 Palestinians are being held in prisons inside Israel in violation of international humanitarian law."[67]

Dershowitz also wrote in the same commentary on *Huffington Post* on July 14: "Moreover, the prisoners being held by Israel are terrorists—that is, unlawful combatants. Many are murderers who have been convicted and sentenced in accordance with due process. The 'women' and 'children' are guilty of having murdered or attempted to murder innocent babies and other non-combatants."[68] Dershowitz cited no source to support his claim that the Palestinian women and children detained in Israel had murdered Israeli babies and other civilians.

Finally, a B'Tselem report issued in July 2011 provided an alternative explanation for the Israeli imprisonment of Palestinian children: "93 percent of all [Palestinian] minors convicted of stone throwing were given jail sentences." According to B'Tselem, from 2005 to 2010, a total of 835 Palestinian children—including 34 twelve- to thirteen-year-olds, 255 fourteen- to fifteen-year-olds, and 546 sixteen- to seventeen-year-olds—were prosecuted in Israel for stone-throwing, of which 93 percent (776) were given jail sentences in Israel of four months to a year.[69]

According to Amnesty International and Lebanon's Higher Relief Council, during the 34 days of the Israeli bombing and shelling of Lebanon—from July 12 to August 14, 2006—Israel killed more than 1,000 Lebanese civilians, including 300 children, and destroyed 15,000 Lebanese homes, 900 commercial structures (including farms and factories), 400 miles of roads, 80 bridges, Lebanon's international airport, and displaced over 900,000 Lebanese civilians;[70] 43 Israeli civilians reportedly were killed, mainly by Hezbollah rockets fired indiscriminately on Israel's northern cities.[71]

This amount of death and destruction in Lebanon was the product not only of an Israeli resort to force in violation of UN Charter Article 2(4), but also of the "hasty" and "impulsive" decision to bomb Lebanon, according to the report of the Israeli government's Winograd Commission, which investigated the decision-making process of Prime Minister Ehud Olmert and his top officials in the context of their decision to bomb and invade Lebanon without delay in response to the Hezbollah provocation of July 12. The five-person commission of inquiry, chaired by Eliyahu Winograd, a retired Israeli judge, harshly criticized Olmert for his decision to resort to "an immediate, intensive military strike." It was in response to this "intensive military strike" on July 12 by Israel that Hezbollah launched rockets against Israel's northern cities, as the commission observed: "The [Israeli] decision to respond with an immediate, intensive military strike was not based on a detailed, comprehensive and authorized military plan, based on careful study of the complex characteristics of the Lebanon arena. . . . A meticulous examination of these characteristics would have revealed the following . . . an Israeli military strike would inevitably lead to missiles fired at the Israeli civilian north."[72]

About Olmert's decision to attack Lebanon within hours of the Hezbollah raid, the commission also asserted: "The Prime Minister made up his mind hastily, despite the fact that no detailed military plan was submitted to him and without asking for one." About Israel's defense minister, Amir Peretz, who also hastily concurred with the use of force, the commission concluded: "The Minister of Defense did not have knowledge or experience in military, political or governmental matters. He also did not have good knowledge of the basic principles of using military force to achieve political goals. Despite these serious gaps, he made his decisions during this period without systematic consultations with experienced political and professional experts, including outside the security establishment." And about the chief of staff at the time, Dan Halutz, Israel's top military commander, the commission decided: "The army and the COS [chief of staff] were not prepared for the event of the abduction despite recurring alerts. When the abduction happened, he responded impulsively."[73]

It is quite clear, therefore, that the Hezbollah military incursion of July 12 was not an armed attack against Israel requiring an immediate military response, that the UN Security Council had not authorized the Israeli bombing and invasion of Lebanon, and that the Israel-based Winograd Commission found that the Olmert government indeed had acted hastily and impulsively by deciding to bomb and invade Lebanon as an immediate response to the Hezbollah incursion. In short, the Israeli bombing of Lebanon in July/August 2006, like Israel's bombing of the Gaza Strip in June/July 2006 and December/January 2008–2009, were hardly legitimate acts of self-defense under the UN Charter, as Dershowitz asserted.

9

RICHARD GOLDSTONE AND WAR CRIMES

On September 15, 2009, an eminent South African jurist and authority on international law, Richard Goldstone, with three other international law experts, issued their 575-page "Report of the United Nations Fact Finding Mission on the Gaza Conflict"—that is, on Israel's air-land invasion of the Gaza Strip in December 2008 to January 2009. Dershowitz responded as follows two days later in the *Jerusalem Post*: "Richard Goldstone—the primary author of a one-sided United Nations attack on Israeli actions during the Gaza war—has now become a full-fledged member of the international bash-Israel chorus. His name will forever be linked in infamy with such distorters of history and truth as Noam Chomsky, Norman Finkelstein and Jimmy Carter. The so-called report commissioned by the notorious United Nations Human Rights Council and issued under his name is so filled with lies, distortions and blood libels that it could have been drafted by Hamas extremists. Wait—in effect, it was!"[1]

How was the Goldstone report in effect drafted by Hamas extremists? Dershowitz explains in the next sentence: "One member of [Goldstone's] group is an Hamas lackey who before being appointed as an 'objective' judge had already reached the conclusion—without conducting any investigation or hearing any evidence—that Israel's military actions 'amount to aggression, not self-defense' and that 'the manner and scale of its operation in Gaza amount to an act of aggression and is contrary to international law.'"[2]

In making these charges, Dershowitz identified neither the Goldstone-commission member by name, nor the source of the allegedly incriminating statement, which had marked the member, according to Dershowitz, as a "Hamas extremist" and "Hamas lackey." However, given the text quoted by Dershowitz, it is clear that the Goldstone commission member to which Dershowitz referred was Christine Chinkin, a professor of international law at the London School of Economics, and the words that he attributed to her were from the published statement of January 11, 2009, in the the *Times* of London, which was signed by twenty-seven eminent international law scholars, including Ian Brownlie, Richard Falk, and . . . Christine Chinkin.[3] It is indeed the very same statement, published on January 11, 2009, to which I alluded in the previous chapter that authoritatively rejected Israel's claim that its air-land invasion of Gaza in 2008–2009 was initiated in self-defense. It is also the same statement that Dershowitz ignored in his *Jerusalem Post* column of January 13, wherein he supported Israel's claim of self-defense—an endorsement that Dershowitz asserted without citing a single legal source and without even attempting to reconcile the prohibition against the use and threat of force under international law with the Israeli military assault on Gaza. Rather, Dershowitz only dealt with the Brownlie-Falk-Chinkin statement of January 11, and even then without specifically citing it, in an attempt to discredit Richard Goldstone and a distinguished member of the four-person Goldstone mission. And Dershowitz did this despite the total absence of any connection whatsoever between the published Brownlie-Falk-Chinkin statement in the *Times* with Hamas.

While also asserting that Chinkin had signed the Brownlie-Falk statement "without conducting any investigation or hearing any evidence," Dershowitz appeared to be making a principled argument that neither the illegality, nor the legality, of the Israeli invasion of late December 2008 could have been determined by January 11, 2009, given the absence at the time of a formal investigation that weighed the available facts and the applicable law. Yet, on January 4, 2009—a week before the Brownlie statement of January 11 in the *Times* (signed also by Falk and Chinkin)—Dershowitz posted a column on the Internet edition of the *Jerusalem Post*, titled "Israel's Actions Are Lawful and Commendable," wherein he wrote: "Israel's military actions in Gaza are entirely justified under international law, and Israel should be commended for its act of self-defense against international terrorism."[4] Thus, Dershowitz pleaded a legal case in support of Israel's actions a full week prior to the publication of the Brownlie-Falk-Chinkin statement and before any formal investigation.

Furthermore, the *prima facie* case against Israel with respect to the legality of its aerial bombardment and land invasion of Gaza was clear enough from the outset: (a) there was no UN Security Council authorization for the Israeli use of force; (b) there was no "armed attack" against Israel from the Gaza Strip that would have enabled Israel to resort to force legally in self-defense; and (c) there is no military capability in Gaza to engage Israel in an "armed attack," as that term is defined under international law, given the absence of a Gazan army, navy, and air force.

Christine Chinkin was one member of the four-person Goldstone mission who investigated the events associated with the Israeli air-land invasion of Gaza of

2008–2009. Another was Colonel Desmond Travers, a former officer in Ireland's defense forces and member of the Board of Directors of the Institute for International Criminal Investigations. About Travers, Dershowitz posted a column in February 2010 on *Huffington Post* titled "An Anti-Israel Extremist Seeks Revenge through Goldstone Report." Dershowitz wrote: "When Irish Colonel Travers eagerly accepted an appointment to the Goldstone Commission, he was hell-bent on revenge against Israel based on paranoid fantasies and hard left anti-Israel propaganda. He actually believed, as he put it in a recent interview, that 'so many Irish soldiers had been killed by Israelis [with] a significant number who were taken out deliberately and shot (in South Lebanon).' This is of course complete and utter fantasy, but it was obviously part of Colonel Travers bigoted reality."[5] Thus, in addition to charging Christine Chinkin with being a Hamas lackey, Dershowitz introduced a second member of the four-member Goldstone mission as an anti-Israel bigot. Here is the fuller statement by Travers from which Dershowitz classified him as such (parentheses in original):

> The strangest thing, I think, if you go back and look at Ireland's history and its dealings about the Middle East, is that there was a traditional feeling of being sympathetic to Israel and we were very, very proud in the 1980s and 90s that the president of Israel [Chaim Herzog] was from Ireland. When he was interviewed he spoke with a strong Irish accent. A lovely man, a very nice man. But anyway, because so many Irish soldiers had been killed by Israelis (some too by Palestinians and/or their Lebanese cohorts), with a significant number who were taken out and deliberately shot (in South Lebanon), slowly but surely, the body-bag phenomenon came into effect, and suddenly Ireland is now perceived as almost entirely pro-Palestinian.[6]

Given this statement, and its tone and context, Travers said nothing that could be construed as bigoted. And while Travers did indeed state that Irish peacekeepers were deliberately shot by Israelis, he also said in the same sentence "some too [were shot] by Palestinians and/or their Lebanese cohorts," which Dershowitz omitted.

In addition, much of the general substance of what Travers said appeared to be accurate. From the Israeli invasion of Lebanon in 1978 to the Israeli withdrawal in 2000, Irish UN peacekeeping battalions had been stationed continuously in southern Lebanon. Irish commandant Dan Harvey, who headed Irish peacekeeping in Lebanon in 1984–1985, reported in his 2001 book *Peacekeepers: Irish Soldiers in the Lebanon*: "The Israeli army did not want impartial European troops watching their behavior, monitoring their movements and trying to establish the sovereignty of the Lebanese government in an area in which the Israeli army wanted their own [Lebanese Christian] militias to hold sway. Thus firing on Irish troops became a nightly occurrence." Harvey also wrote that in the course of "forty-seven successive Irish battalions over twenty-three years" of peacekeeping in southern Lebanon, "forty-seven Irish soldiers had died." Harvey's book also contains personal and reported accounts of military intimidation of both Lebanese civilians and Irish peacekeepers by Israeli forces and the Israel-funded right-wing Christian militias in southern Lebanon,[7] also referred to as the South Lebanon Army, and which Robert Fisk described as "a murderous collection of Phalangist gunmen, renegade soldiers from the national [Lebanese] army and square yards of land south of Hasbaya."[8]

Furthermore, the *New York Times* reported in March 1989: "The peacekeeping forces contingent of 600 Irish soldiers has repeatedly come under attack from the South Lebanon Army, mainly because the Irish are deployed between Israeli positions and those of Muslim militias trying to drive the Israelis out. An Irish soldier was shot dead by soldiers of the South Lebanon Army last month. Israeli and South Lebanon Army patrols often cross into the peace force's sector in pursuit of guerrillas and sometimes clash with the peacekeeping troops."[9] In January 1987, the *Los Angeles Times* reported: "An Israeli tank fired on a village in southern Lebanon and killed an Irish U.N. soldier, officials said Sunday. The U.N. commander protested to Israel, and Ireland said it will reconsider its peacekeeping role. A spokesman for the U.N. Interim Force in Lebanon—UNIFIL—said the Irish contingent had fired flares to warn the Israelis to stop firing on the village of Braachit six miles north of the border Saturday night, but the Israelis persisted, killing Cpl. Dermot McLoughlin, 33, and severely damaging the U.N. position."[10]

In his 2002 book, *Pity the Nation: The Abduction of Lebanon*, Fisk provides accounts of "Yassir Arafat's radical opponents within the PLO initially show[ing] no inclination to accept the UN's presence in southern Lebanon,"[11] while also reporting that most of the military resistance came from the Israelis and the Israel-supported Lebanese Christian militia forces of Major Saad Haddad,[12] with Fisk concluding that "it was the Israelis who destroyed any opportunity the UN might have had of fulfilling its mandate" in southern Lebanon.[13] The bottom line being that there was no basis for Dershowitz to claim that Desmond Travers, an Irish member of the four-person Goldstone mission to Gaza, was seeking "revenge" against Israel and is an anti-Israel "bigot."

In addition to Chinkin and Travers, and Goldstone himself, the fourth member of the four-person Goldstone mission was Hina Jilani, Advocate of the Supreme Court of Pakistan and former member of the International Commission of Inquiry on Darfur.[14] About Jilani, Dershowitz wrote: "Hina Jilani had also condemned Israel before her appointment to the [Goldstone] group, and then said that it would be 'very cruel to not give credence to voices' of the victims, apparently without regard to whether they were telling the truth." Dershowitz then wrote that Jilani, like her fellow members of the Goldstone commission, had "pre-judged the evidence" and "came to their jobs with agendas and biases" against Israel.[15] Upon accusing Jilani in this fashion, however, Dershowitz misrepresented the precise meaning of the words that he attributed in quotation marks to her. This is what Jilani actually said in an interview with Haroon Siddiqui of the *Toronto Star*: "Of [Mahmoud] Abbas's initial decision to shelve the [Goldstone] report, Jilani said: 'I think it was a very ill-considered move on his part. I've been in Gaza. I've met the victims, as I've met the victims from southern Israel of rocket attacks from Hamas and other groups. And I know what the victims' expectations are. I think it'd be very cruel to not give credence to their voices.'"[16]

It is clear here that Jilani was referring to both Gazan and Israeli victims. Dershowitz implied, however, that Jilani advocated giving voices only to the victims of military attack in Gaza, which in any event experienced the overwhelming preponderance of suffering and casualties.

Having attacked the three other members of the Goldstone mission with gross misrepresentations of their professional and personal character, Dershowitz targeted Goldstone himself with the most prolonged and vicious treatment, referring to Goldstone, a South African Jew, as a "knave"[17] and "traitor to the Jewish people"[18] after the September 2009 release of the Goldstone report. In a column in the *Jerusalem Post* titled "Legitimating Bigotry: The Legacy of Richard Goldstone," Dershowitz attacked Goldstone's career as a judge in South Africa:

> Richard Goldstone, author of the notorious Goldstone report, did not become a South African judge in the post-apartheid Mandela Era, as the *New York Times* and other media have erroneously reported. He accepted a judgeship during the worst days of Apartheid and helped legitimate one of the most racist regimes in the world by granting the imprimatur of the rule of law to some of the most undemocratic and discriminatory decrees.
>
> Goldstone was—quite literally—a hanging judge. He imposed and affirmed death sentences for more than two dozen blacks under circumstances where whites would almost certainly have escaped the noose. And he affirmed sentences of physical torture—euphemistically called flogging—for other blacks. He also enforced miscegenation [marriage between persons of different races] and other racist laws with nary a word of criticism or dissent. He was an important part of the machinery of death, torture and racial subjugation that characterized Apartheid South Africa. His robe and gavel lent an air of legitimacy to an entirely illegitimate and barbaric regime.

It is no surprise that Goldstone kept this part of his life secret from academic colleagues, friends and the general public. I recall him at the lunch and dinner tables in Cambridge describing himself as a heroic part of the struggle against Apartheid. Now it turns out he was the ugly face of Apartheid, covering its sins and crimes with a judicial robe. How differently we would have looked at him if we knew that he had climbed the judicial ladder on whipped backs and hanged bodies.[19]

For one thing, there is no dark secret about when Goldstone became a judge in South Africa, as Dershowitz suggests. The very first sentence in Goldstone's 2000 book, published by Yale University Press, states: "Perhaps the most difficult professional decision of my career was whether to accept the invitation to become a judge in the Transvaal High Court [in apartheid South Africa] in 1980. I was forty-one years old and involved in a successful commercial practice at the Johannesburg bar. . . . Suffice it to say that I decided to accept the invitation and assume the comparatively cloistered existence that is generally associated with judicial office."[20] The year 1980 in South Africa, when Goldstone first became a judge, was clearly within the apartheid era, with the beginning of negotiations to end apartheid a full decade in the future.

Furthermore, since Dershowitz himself cited no sources to support his charges that Goldstone had "helped legitimate one of the most racist regimes in the world" and "granted the imprimatur of the rule of law to some of the most undemocratic and discriminatory decrees," we must assume that Dershowitz, writing at the time on May 9, 2010, based these comments on a May 6, 2010 report in the online Israeli newspaper *Ynet*, which reported that Goldstone, while sitting as judge in the South African appellate court during the 1980s and 1990s, "sentenced dozens of blacks mercilessly to their death." The *Ynet* report continued: "Yedioth Ahronoth's [*Ynet's*] findings show that Goldstone sentenced at least 28 black defendants to death. Most of them were found guilty of murder and sought to appeal the verdict. In those days, he actually made sure he showed his support for the execution policy, writing in one verdict that it reflects society's demands that a price be paid for crimes it rightfully views as frightening."[21]

Although *Ynet* reportedly contacted Goldstone for a response, the article in which these charges were made included no quoted comments from him. However, in its own response to the *Ynet* piece, *Ha'aretz* did quote Goldstone: "The law at the time stated that when there were aggravating circumstances, the death penalty was obligatory. The regrets I have now are the same that I had at the time. I have not changed my position on this. It was unpleasant to be involved in capital punishment—then and now. And I've always been against the death penalty. But when I accepted the position to the bench I had to honor the oath of office."[22] Indeed, the same *Ynet* article reported that "only in 1995 when Nelson Mandela took power was the South African constitution amended and the death penalty abolished."[23] Thus, while calling Goldstone "quite literally a hanging judge" as a way of discrediting the Goldstone report, Dershowitz left out these mitigating details. However one might view Goldstone's explanation in giving death sentences, Dershowitz clearly omitted important details from both *Ynet* and *Ha'aretz* about the circumstances under which the death sentences were handed down.

Upon asserting without references that Goldstone "was an important part of the machinery of death, torture and racial subjugation that characterized Apartheid South Africa," Dershowitz omitted other relevant details about Goldstone, including a key commission and investigation in apartheid South Africa in 1990, the circumstances of which, as reported by the *Los Angeles Times*, bear some resemblance to the circumstances under which the Goldstone report on Israel and Gaza was issued: "In a scathing report released Saturday, an independent judicial inquiry into the police slayings of five black protesters in Sebokeng last March concludes that at least 30 [South African government] officers opened fire on a crowd without legal justification. The investigation, chaired by Justice Richard J. Goldstone, recommended that the attorney general consider filing criminal charges against the police officers 'who shot live ammunition into the crowd.'" The *Los Angeles Times* reported that Goldstone's inquiry was "one of the strongest indictments of South Africa's police ever made by a government-appointed investigator."[24] Nor did Dershowitz mention a *Los Angeles Times* article in April 2009, in which South African lawyer Mervyn Smith, a former president of the South African Jewish Board of Deputies, called Goldstone "a person of impeccable integrity."[25] And Dershowitz failed to cite a review in the *American Journal of International Law* of Goldstone's 2000 book, *For Humanity: Reflections of a War Crimes Investigator*, in which William A. Schabas, director of the Irish Center for Human Rights at the National University of Ireland in Galway, wrote that "Goldstone played a significant role in the dismantling of apartheid."[26]

Upon defending Israel's air-land invasion of the Gaza Strip of 2008–2009 as "self-defense," Dershowitz also did not detail events preceding the invasion that invalidated his claim of "self-defense" beyond what I've already reported. On June 18, 2008—six months before the invasion—Israel and Hamas agreed to a six-month cease-fire, the terms of which featured a cessation of Qassam-type rocket fire into southern Israel, an easing of Israel's economic blockade of the Gaza Strip and its 1.5 million inhabitants, and negotiations on the release of the Israeli soldier Gilad Shalit.[27] A mere sixteen days later, on July 4, Amnesty International reported an Israeli tightening of the economic blockade, which was a major violation of the cease-fire: "A humanitarian crisis is engulfing Gaza" due to "the tightening of the Israeli blockade," which left the Palestinians in Gaza "surviving, but only just."

While Shalit was the only Israeli held by Hamas, Amnesty reported that "some 8,500 Palestinians are detained in Israeli jails," including nine hundred from the Gaza Strip, "all of whom have been denied visits by their families since June 2007."[28]

On August 14, a month later, Amnesty reported that "some 400 Palestinian students may lose their university places and scholarships" in the Middle East, Europe, Canada, and the United States "unless the Israeli authorities allow them to leave the Gaza Strip before the new academic year."[29] On August 22, Amnesty reported that "critically ill patients are still being denied permission to leave Gaza for treatment abroad," that "hundreds" had been so affected, and that "dozens of patients have died in recent months following delays to, or denials of, permits to leave Gaza" for medical treatment.[30] On August 27, Amnesty reported that "with Gaza locked down and cut off from the outside world by a stifling Israeli blockade, 46 peace activists from the world over set sail for Gaza on August 22 to, in their words, 'break the siege that Israel has imposed on the civilian population of Gaza.'" Amnesty noted that "with the ceasefire holding, the suffering in Gaza has fallen off the international news agenda." On August 29, Amnesty reported that "Israeli authorities are still denying scores of critically ill patients the authorization they need to leave Gaza for medical treatment that is unavailable in Gaza."[31]

On October 16, Amnesty identified six children—ages five months to six years of age—who suffer from serious heart conditions and who needed urgent surgery that could not be done in Gaza. Amnesty reported that "the children were due to be operated on by a team of British heart specialists at Makassad Hospital in East Jerusalem," but the children "were not able to leave the Gaza Strip because the Israeli authorities refused permissions to their mothers/grandmothers to leave Gaza to accompany them."[32]

On November 5, in an article titled "Israeli Strike Is First in Gaza since Start of Cease-Fire," the *New York Times* reported that Israel had broken the June cease-fire, in addition to its continuation of the blockade, with a cross-border land raid and airstrike on Gaza. The next day, Reuters reported that "Hamas fired dozens of rockets at Israel from the Gaza Strip on Wednesday after Israeli forces killed at least five Palestinian militants in an eruption of violence that disrupted a four-month-old truce."[33] About the broken cease-fire, Amnesty International reported that "the killing of six Palestinian militants in Gaza by Israeli forces in a ground incursion and air strikes on 4 November was followed by a barrage of dozens of Palestinian rockets on nearby towns and villages in the south of Israel."[34]

On November 14, Amnesty reported that "the Israeli army has completely blocked the delivery of urgently needed humanitarian aid and medical supplies to the Gaza Strip for more than a week," which, as Amnesty noted, "made an already dire humanitarian situation markedly worse," observing further that the blockade "is nothing short of collective punishment on Gaza's civilian population and it must stop immediately." Amnesty reported that "the breakdown last week of a four-and-a-half-month ceasefire between Israeli forces and Palestinian militants in Gaza has generated a renewed wave of violence," including "a barrage of Palestinian rockets on nearby Israeli towns and villages." Amnesty also reported that eleven Palestinians and no Israelis had been killed since the Israeli military raid of November 4.[35]

On November 24, Andrea Becker, head of Medical Aid for Palestinians, in an article in the Guardian titled "The Slow Death of Gaza," wrote that "the collective punishment of Gaza's civilian population is illegal, but international law was tossed aside long ago."[36] On December 5, Amnesty International reported that "the Israeli blockade of the Gaza Strip is having ever more serious consequences on its population," and that "the blockade has become tighter than ever since the break-down of a five-and-a-half-month ceasefire between Israeli forces and Palestinian militants on 5 November."[37] On December 15, Chris Hedges, former *New York Times* Middle East correspondent, wrote: "Israel's siege of Gaza, largely unseen by the outside world because of Jerusalem's refusal to allow humanitarian aid workers, reporters and photographers access to Gaza, rivals the most egregious crimes carried out at the height of apartheid by the South African regime. It comes close to the horrors visited on Sarajevo by the Bosnian Serbs. It has disturbing echoes of the Nazi ghettos of Lodz and Warsaw."[38]

In an article published in *Foreign Policy in Focus*, the online journal of the Washington, D.C.-based Institute for Policy Studies, Steve Niva wrote that "there was a genuine lull in rocket and mortar fire between June 19 and November 4, due to Hamas compliance and only sporadically violated by a small number of launchings carried out by rival Fatah and Islamic Jihad militants, largely in defiance of Hamas." Niva observed that during the cease-fire, "Israeli civilians living near Gaza [in southern Israel] experienced an almost unprecedented degree of security" with "no Israeli casualties."[39] Amnesty International concurred, observing in November: "The ceasefire has brought enormous improvements in the quality of life in Sderot [in southern Israel] and other Israeli villages near Gaza, where before the ceasefire residents lived in fear of the next Palestinian rocket strike. However, nearby in the Gaza Strip the Israeli blockade remains in place and the population has so far seen few dividends from the ceasefire."[40] Writing in the *London Review of Books* on January 1, 2009, in the midst of the Israeli bombardment of Gaza, Sara Roy observed that "Israel's siege of Gaza began on 5 November, the day after an Israeli attack inside the strip, no doubt designed finally to undermine the truce between Israel and Hamas established last June. Although both sides had violated the agreement before, this [Israeli] incursion [on November 4] was on a different scale. Hamas responded by firing [Qassam-type] rockets into Israel and the violence has not abated since then."[41] Commenting as if she were responding directly to Dershowitz, who wrote on January 13, 2009, that "under international law, Israel is entitled to do whatever it takes militarily to stop Hamas rockets from targeting its civilians,"[42] Amira Hass wrote in *Ha'aretz* a day later that "history did not begin with the Qassam rockets, but for us, the Israelis, history always begins when the Palestinians hurt us, and then the pain is completely decontextualized."[43]

The contextual record shows that Israel was the chief transgressor of the six-month June 2008 cease-fire by its tightening of the economic blockade and its military raids on Gaza on November 4.[44] In addition, no Gazan entity engaged in an "armed attack" against Israel, nor did the UN Security Council authorize the Israeli use of force against Gaza. In short, there was no factual or legal basis for Dershowitz to claim that the Israeli air-land invasion of Gaza of December 2008 to January 2009 was initiated in "self-defense." Indeed, as both the Brownlie-Falk-Chinkin statement and the Goldstone report concluded, Israel's invasion of Gaza was an illegal use of force and a war crime.[45]

Once the Israeli invasion was under way, and in addition to his claim of Israeli "self-defense" in seeking to justify at the outset the Israeli use of force, Dershowitz wrote also in support of the tactics of the Israeli military. Thus, on January 16, 2009—two days before Israel began withdrawing its forces—Dershowitz wrote an op-ed piece for the *Miami Herald*, in which he claimed: "The war in Gaza is as pure a conflict between good and evil as I have experienced,"[46] with the good side being Israel. Once again, Dershowitz's extremist claims cannot stand up to the facts.

Israel began bombing the Gaza Strip on Saturday, December 27, 2008. On that day, Reuters reported that "Israeli warplanes and combat helicopters pounded the Hamas-ruled Gaza Strip, killing at least 155 people in the bloodiest day for Palestinians in more than 20 years of conflict."[47] The next day, December 28, Amnesty International reported that "some 280 Palestinians and one Israeli civilian" had been killed in the first day of the Israeli campaign, and that "this is the highest level of Palestinian fatalities and casualties in four decades of Israeli occupation of the West Bank and Gaza Strip."[48] On December 29, the *Guardian* reported that the Palestinian "death toll" was "above 300" with "another 600 people injured." Also on December 29, Norman Solomon, founder of the Institute for Public Accuracy, commented as follows about the Israeli bombing and the Palestinian casualties: "Even if you set aside the magnitude of Israel's violations of the Geneva Conventions and the long terrible history of its methodical collective punishment of 1.5 million Palestinians in Gaza, consider the vastly disproportionate carnage in the [Gaza] conflict. 'An eye for an eye makes the whole world blind,' Gandhi said. What about a hundred eyes for an eye?"[49]

On the same day, Robert Fisk, the veteran Middle East reporter for the British newspaper the *Independent*, speaking of the ratio of Palestinian-to-Israeli casualties, wrote: "By last night, the exchange rate stood at 296 Palestinians dead for one dead Israeli. Back in 2006, it was 10 Lebanese dead for one Israeli dead. This weekend was the most inflationary exchange rate in a single day."[50] Also on December 29, the U.S. National Lawyers Guild issued a press release in which it "condemn[ed] Israel's massive bombardment of the Gaza Strip which has left over 300 dead and 1,400 wounded, with the tolls mounting." Significantly, the Lawyers Guild also stated: "Israel claims that the attack is in response to Palestinian rocket fire, which caused no recent Israeli deaths and few injuries. However, Israel's 'rolling bombardment' and impending ground invasion is grossly disproportionate in light of the minimal damage caused by Palestinian rockets."[51]

On December 30, B'Tselem reported that 383 Palestinians had been killed and over 1,000 injured since December 27 and, due to "hundreds of rockets" fired into southern Israel from the Gaza Strip "in the past weeks," three Israeli civilians and one Israeli soldier had been killed. B'Tselem observed: "The media and the human rights organizations also report that the humanitarian crisis in the Gaza Strip has reached an unprecedented level of severity. Hospitals are incapable of dealing with the sheer number of patients, and the electricity, water and sewage systems are barely functioning."[52]

While one could continue to highlight similar reports from the news media and human rights groups, which criticized in principle the violations of the laws of war on both sides while detailing the far more extensive destruction caused by Israel's superior military forces, I will cite only a few other such reports while comparing them to Dershowitz's comments during the same period. For example, on January 15, while underscoring the fact that one-third of the Palestinians killed and injured by the Israelis in Gaza were children, *Haaretz* columnist Gideon Levy wrote:

> The fighting in Gaza is "war deluxe." Compared with previous wars, it is child's play—[Israeli] pilots bombing unimpeded as if on practice runs, tank and artillery soldiers shelling houses and civilians from their armored vehicles, combat engineering troops destroying entire streets in their ominous protected vehicles without facing serious opposition. A large, broad army is fighting against a helpless population and a weak, ragged organization that has fled the conflict zones and is barely putting up a fight. All this must be said openly, before we begin exulting in our heroism and victory.
>
> This war is also child's play because of its victims. About a third of those killed in Gaza have been children—311 according to the Palestinian Health Ministry, 270 according to the B'Tselem human rights group— out of the 1,000 total killed as of Wednesday [January 14]. Around 1,550 of the 4,500 wounded have also been children according to figures from

the UN, which says the number of children killed has tripled since the ground operation began. This is too large a proportion by any humanitarian or ethical standard.[53]

The next day, January 16, Dershowitz published his op-ed piece in the *Miami Herald*[54] that bore his claim that Israel was waging a "pure" military campaign in Gaza, which to that point had killed 300 children and wounded another 1,550 children in less than three weeks. Compare Dershowitz's column to a January 16 column by Gideon Levy in *Ha'aretz* titled "Someone Must Stop Israel's Rampant Madness in Gaza."[55]

On January 22, in its review of the Israeli invasion of Gaza, and referring to the tactics of the Israeli military, an editorial in *Ha'aretz* commented gravely as follows: "In the aftermath of the war. . . . the questions are plentiful and troubling: the mass killing of civilians, among them 300 children and 100 women; the shooting at medical crews; the use of illegal munitions against a civilian population, including white phosphorus shells; the prevention of the evacuation of wounded; bombing and shelling of schools, hospitals, supply convoys and a UN facility. These questions cannot remain unanswered. The suspicion that Israel committed war crimes in Gaza is liable to cause it great damage."[56]

Dershowitz's approval of the Israeli application of force in the Gaza Strip can be compared to other such reports and commentary, including one by Chris Hedges on December 30: "Ehud Barak, Israel's defense minister, said Israel is engaged in a 'war to the bitter end' against Hamas in Gaza. A war? Israel uses sophisticated attack jets and naval vessels to bomb densely crowded refugee camps and slums, to attack a population that has no air force, no air defense, no navy, no heavy weapons, no artillery units, no mechanized armor, no command and control, no army, and calls it a war. It is not a war. It is murder." Commenting about the implications of U.S. support of Israel's conduct, Hedges also wrote: "Can anyone who is following the Israeli air attacks on Gaza—the buildings blown to rubble, the children killed on their way to school, the long rows of mutilated corpses, the wailing mothers and wives, the crowds of terrified Palestinians not knowing where to flee, the hospitals so overburdened and out of supplies they cannot treat the wounded, and our studied, callous indifference to this widespread human suffering—wonder why we are hated?"[57]

Similarly, and also on December 30, Richard Falk wrote that "the Israeli airstrikes on the Gaza Strip represent severe and massive violations of international humanitarian law as defined in the Geneva Conventions, both in regard to the obligations of an Occupying Power and in the requirements of the laws of war." Falk listed a few such violations: "Collective punishment: The entire 1.5 million people who live in the crowded Gaza Strip are being punished for the actions of a few militants. Targeting civilians: The airstrikes were aimed at civilian areas in one of the most crowded stretches of land in the world, certainly the most densely populated area of the Middle East. Disproportionate military response: The airstrikes have not only destroyed every police and security office of Gaza's elected government, but have killed and injured hundreds of civilians."[58] Once again in contrast, on January 2, Dershowitz published an op-ed piece in the *Wall Street Journal* titled "Israel's Policy Is Perfectly 'Proportionate,'" wherein he wrote: "Israel's actions in Gaza are justified under international law, and Israel should be commended for its self-defense against terrorism."[59]

One might also note that Dershowitz's analysis throughout the Israeli military campaign in Gaza was consistent with the published statements of the major Jewish American organizations. For example, on December 31, the American Israel Public Affairs Committee (AIPAC) urged the United States to "stand firmly with Israel as it strives to defend itself."[60] And the Anti-Defamation League asserted that "Israel's actions were taken in self-defense, a right given to every nation."[61]

In addition to issuing misleading claims about Israeli "self-defense," Dershowitz also sought to give legal support to the Israeli invasion by citing the "moral authority" of democracies under international law. Thus, Dershowitz wrote: "The only limitation international law places on a democracy is that its actions must satisfy the principle of proportionality."[62] However, the UN Charter, which applies to all UN member states, makes no distinction in foreign affairs between the conduct of democratic states and nondemocratic states. Nor is the conduct of a democratic state privileged under international humanitarian law in the manner suggested by Dershowitz. Rather than present a polished legal brief that one might expect from a professor of law at Harvard, Dershowitz defended a barbaric application of military power simply by asserting the "pure," "good," and "moral" absolutism of Israel's motives and conduct.

When Israel's military forces pulled out of the Gaza Strip on January 18, 2009, news agencies and human rights groups, with post-invasion boots on the ground, began to investigate, and subsequently issued reports that also contradicted Dershowitz's claim that the Israeli invasion was "pure," "good," "moral," and "proportionate." These reports issued by news agencies and human rights organizations also were consistent with what the Goldstone report found with respect to its own factual and legal findings, again, all in conflict with Dershowitz. For example, following a lengthy inquiry, in September 2009—the same month in which the Goldstone report was released to the public—B'Tselem published data on Israel's invasion of Gaza, and reported that "Israeli security forces killed 1,387 Palestinians during the operation," of which 773 "did not take part in host   ."
B'Tselem also listed the number of "minors killed who did not take p

hostilities," reporting that 320 Palestinian children under the age of eighteen were killed, including 119 under the age of eleven, sixty of which were five years old and younger. B'Tselem also itemized the fatal Israeli casualties: "During [Operation Cast Lead], Palestinians killed nine Israelis, as follows: Three civilians, who were killed by Qassam and Grad rocket fire [and] six members of the [Israeli] security forces; in addition, four soldiers were killed by friendly fire."[63] This means that twenty times the number of Palestinian children five years of age and younger were killed (sixty) than all Israeli civilians killed (three). With these casualty figures in mind, it is enlightening to review briefly the reports by news agencies and human rights groups in the months following the Israeli air-land invasion that were consistent with the factual and legal findings of the Goldstone report, and which contradict Dershowitz's claims that Israel's air-land invasion of 2008–2009 was a morally "pure" campaign.

February 2009

February 9. A few weeks after Israel withdrew from Gaza, the National Lawyers Guild issued a forty-one-page report, which stated:

> During its 22 day offensive, Israeli forces killed more than 1,400 Palestinians, including at least 288 children, and injured over 5,300, of which at least 1,606 were children. The majority of those killed were civilians. Two weeks after Israel declared a unilateral ceasefire, a National Lawyers Guild Delegation of seven attorneys and one law student traveled to Gaza to investigate the circumstances that led to the massive Palestinian casualties, and to determine what, if any, violations of international law occurred, and whether U.S. domestic law was violated as a consequence. The Delegation found more than ample evidence to establish a *prima facie* case that the Israeli military committed significant violations of international law in Gaza from December 27, 2008, to January 18, 2009.[64]

February 23. Citing Amnesty International, the *Guardian* reported that "detailed evidence has emerged of Israel's extensive use of US-made weaponry during its war in Gaza last month, including white phosphorus artillery shells, 500 lb. bombs, and Hellfire missiles." Amnesty reported that "the Israeli military had used white phosphorus in densely populated civilian areas, which it said was an indiscriminate form of attack and a war crime."[65]

March 2009

March 5. Citing Human Rights Watch, *Ha'aretz* reported that "the Israeli army unlawfully fired white phosphorus shells over densely populated areas of the Gaza

Strip during its recent military offensive, needlessly killing and injuring civilians. . . . Human Rights Watch researchers found spent shells, canister liners, and dozens of burnt felt wedges containing white phosphorus on city streets, apartment roofs, residential courtyards and at a United Nations school." *Ha'aretz* also reported that "Israel has accused Hamas of putting civilians at risk by using them as 'human shields' and by drawing Israeli forces into densely populated areas," and that "Human Rights Watch said it found no evidence of Hamas using 'human shields' in the cases it documented in the report."[66]

March 16. Amnesty International reported that "a 16-strong group of the world's most experienced investigators and judges have today called for a full international investigation into alleged abuses of international law during the recent Gaza conflict." Amnesty reported: "The call is made in an open letter to the United Nations Secretary-General Ban Ki-moon as well as all members of the UN Security Council. . . . The signatories—who have led investigations of crimes committed in former Yugoslavia, Kosovo, Darfur, Rwanda, Sierra Leone, South Africa, East Timor, Lebanon and Peru—say that they have been 'shocked to the core' by events in Gaza."[67]

March 24. The *Guardian* reported that it "has compiled detailed evidence of alleged war crimes committed by Israel during the 23-day offensive in the Gaza Strip earlier this year, involving the use of Palestinian children as human shields and the targeting of medics and hospitals." The newspaper observed that its month-long investigation "also obtained evidence of civilians being hit by fire from unmanned drone aircraft said to be so accurate that their operators can tell the colour of the clothes worn by a target." The *Guardian's* findings included the following: "Medics and ambulance drivers said they were targeted when they tried to tend to the wounded; sixteen were killed. According to the World Health Organization, more than half of Gaza's 27 hospitals and 44 clinics were destroyed by Israeli bombs"; "A medical human rights group said there was 'certainty' that Israel violated international humanitarian law during the war, with attacks on medics, damage to medical buildings, indiscriminate attacks on civilians and delays in medical treatment for the injured. 'We have noticed a stark decline in IDF morals concerning the Palestinian population of Gaza, which in reality amounts to contempt for Palestinian lives,' said Dani Filc, chairman of Physicians for Human Rights in Israel"; "An IDF squad leader is quoted in the daily newspaper *Ha'aretz* as saying his soldiers interpreted the rules [of engagement] to mean 'we shall kill everyone there [in the center of Gaza]. Everyone there is a terrorist.'"[68] In a companion piece to the *Guardian* investigation, which was conducted by Clancy Chassay and Julian Borger, a newspaper editorial observed that "it is difficult to imagine how anyone watching Clancy Chassay's three short films on Israel's devastating attack on Gaza could deny that Israel has a clear case to answer on commission of war crimes."[69] The *Guardian's* report included Chassay's three films.[70]

March 25. Human Rights Watch, in a report titled "Rain of Fire: Israel's Unlawful Use of White Phosphorus in Gaza," issued these findings: "This report documents Israel's extensive use of white phosphorus munitions during its 22-day military operation in Gaza, from December 27, 2008 to January 18, 2009, named Operation Cast Lead," including "in the air over populated areas, killing and injuring civilians, and damaging civilian structures, including a school, a market, a humanitarian aid warehouse and a hospital." The report noted: "The unlawful use of white phosphorus was neither incidental nor accidental."[71] The report also included a film documenting the real-time use by Israel of white phosphorus munitions in a civilian area.[72]

April 2009

April 6. Two medical organizations—Physicians for Human Rights in Israel and the Palestinian Medical Relief Society—issued a ninety-two-page report based on their fact-finding mission in Gaza about the Israeli invasion in December 27, 2008–January 18, 2009. After detailing fatalities and injuries, the report concluded:

> The underlying meaning of the attack on the Gaza Strip, or at least its final consequence, appears to be one of creating terror without mercy to anyone. . . . It appears that the wide range of attacks with sophisticated weaponry was predominantly focused on terrorising the population. The attack caused an enormous amount of infrastructural damage and destruction, displacing a large volume of the population to other areas. An estimated 21,000 homes were destroyed or badly damaged and the total number of people being displaced from their original home is estimated over 50,000. . . . The patterns of injuries, many of which were apparently caused by anti-personnel weapons, are characterized by a high proportion of maiming and amputations, which will cause lifelong disabilities for many. . . . There is absolutely no doubt that the number of medical institutions, such as hospitals and mobile clinics, were specifically targeted including a large number of ambulances. . . . The attack had an enormously distressing effect on the population of children and it appears that children were disproportionately affected by the attack.[73]

May 2009

May 5. The *Guardian* reported that a United Nations inquiry, with a narrow mandate of investigating attacks exclusively on eight UN installations in Gaza and one UN convoy, "accused the Israeli military of 'negligence or recklessness' in its conduct of the January war in Gaza and said the [UN] should press claims for reparations and damage." Among the inquiry's findings: "Israel had fired several 120mm mortar rounds in the 'immediate vicinity' of a UN boys' preparatory school in Jabaliya that was being used as a shelter for hundreds of Palestinians who had fled their homes to escape the fighting, killing 30 to 40 Palestinians. Although Israel at the time said Hamas had fired mortars from within the school, the inquiry found this as not true"; "An Israeli air strike hit the UN Asma elementary school in Gaza City, where hundreds more Palestinians were sheltering, killing three young men who had been walking to the bathroom in the school compound"; "Israeli soldiers fired at a UN convoy, damaging one of the vehicles in Ezbet Abed Rabou"; "The UN's main headquarters in Gaza was badly damaged when it was hit by several Israeli artillery shells, including some containing white phosphorus. The shelling continued despite warnings from the UN to the Israeli military"; "Israeli 155mm artillery loaded with white phosphorus exploded early in the morning above the UN Beit Lahiya elementary school, where nearly 2,000 Palestinians were sheltering from the fighting. Two children, aged five and seven, were killed inside a classroom and their mother and cousin were seriously injured by shards of shell casings."[74]

June 2009

June 1. Ha'aretz reported: "A United Nations team headed by a veteran war crimes prosecutor has begun its probe into possible war crimes by Israel and Hamas militants during Operation Cast Lead. The team entered Gaza via Egypt Monday without having secured Israel's cooperation. . . . The probe is headed by Richard Goldstone, a respected South African judge."[75] On the same day, the *Jerusalem Post* reported that "[Israeli] Defense Minister Ehud Barak said on Monday that Israel would not cooperate with a United Nations probe into alleged war crimes by both the IDF and Hamas during Operation Cast Lead earlier this year. . . . Barak told reporters he thought investigators would not be objective. Therefore, he said, 'I don't think Israel has to, or will, cooperate with this investigation.'"[76]

July 2009

July 2. Agence France Presse reported that "Amnesty [International] accused Israeli forces on Thursday of war crimes in Gaza, saying they used children as human shields and conducted wanton attacks on civilians, in a report rejected as 'unbalanced' by Israel. The London-based human rights group also accused Hamas of war crimes, but said it found no evidence to support Israeli claims that Gaza's Islamist rulers used civilians as human shields during Israel's massive 22-day offensive."[77] In its lengthy report, Amnesty summarized its major findings as follows:

• Hundreds of civilians were killed in attacks carried out using high-precision weapons—air-delivered bombs and missiles, and tank shells. Others, including women and children, were shot at short range when posing no threat to the lives of the Israeli soldiers. Aerial bombardments launched from Israeli F-16 combat aircraft targeted and destroyed civilian homes without warning, killing and injuring scores of their inhabitants, often while they slept. Children playing on the roofs of their homes or in the street and other civilians going about their daily business, as well as medical staff attending the wounded, were killed in broad daylight by Hellfire and other highly accurate missiles launched from helicopters and unmanned aerial vehicles (UAVs), or drones, and by precision projectiles fired from tanks. Disturbing questions remain unanswered as to why such high-precision weapons, whose operators can see even small details of their targets and which can accurately strike even fast moving vehicles, killed so many children and other civilians.

• Scores of civilians were also killed and injured by less precise weapons, such as artillery shells and mortars, and flechette tank shells, which can be accurately aimed but which disperse thousands of deadly metal darts at great velocity over a large area. White phosphorus, a highly incendiary substance, was repeatedly fired indiscriminately over densely populated residential areas, killing and wounding civilians and destroying civilian property. . . . Artillery in general and white phosphorus shells in particular should never be used in populated areas. Yet in Gaza Israeli forces repeatedly fired them into densely populated residential areas, knowing that such imprecise weapons would kill and injure civilians. Such attacks were indiscriminate and as such unlawful under international law.

• Thousands of civilian homes, businesses and public buildings were destroyed. In some areas entire neighbourhoods were flattened and livestock killed. Much of the destruction was wanton and deliberate, and was carried out in a manner and circumstances which indicated that it could not be justified on grounds of military necessity. Rather, it was often the result of reckless and indiscriminate attacks, which were seemingly tolerated or even directly sanctioned up the chain of command, and which at times appeared intended to collectively punish local residents for the actions of armed groups.

• Throughout Operation Cast Lead Israeli forces frequently obstructed access to medical care and humanitarian aid for those wounded and trapped. They prevented ambulances and medical staff from attending to the wounded and transporting them to hospital and in several cases targeted ambulance and rescue crews and others who were trying to evacuate the wounded. As a result people who could have been saved died and others endured needless suffering and a worsening of their injuries. Children, women and elderly people were among those trapped and refused access to medical care and/or passage out of areas which had been taken over by Israeli forces. Medical and humanitarian vehicles and facilities were also destroyed or damaged as a result of both targeted and indiscriminate Israeli attacks.

• In several cases Israeli soldiers also used civilians, including children, as "human shields," endangering their lives by forcing them to remain in or near houses which they took over and used as military positions. Some were forced to carry out dangerous tasks such as inspecting properties or objects suspected of being booby-trapped. Soldiers also took positions and launched attacks from and around inhabited houses, exposing local residents to the danger of attacks or of being caught in the crossfire.

• Randomly placed telephone calls with recorded warning messages, radio broadcasts and leaflets dropped by the Israeli army all over Gaza telling people to leave their homes and neighbourhoods caused widespread panic but offered little protection. In some areas residents were trapped in their homes, hearing the Israeli army broadcasts warning people to leave but unable to do so because Israeli forces in the area were not allowing any movement and therefore anyone who went out risked coming under fire. Others who fled their homes were killed or injured when UN schools and other places where they had sought shelter came under Israeli attack.[78]

Agence France Presse also reported that the Israeli military issued a statement, in which it claimed that "the slant of [Amnesty International's] report indicates that the organisation succumbed to the manipulations of the Hamas terror organisation."[79]

September 2009

September 28. An investigation conducted by the European human rights organization Defence for Children International–Palestine Section (DCI) reported that "at least 353 children were killed and a further 860 injured" in the twenty-two days of Israel's Operation Cast Lead in the Gaza Strip, including "66 of these children [who] died after Israeli forces obstructed medical access and 116 killed by missiles launched by unmanned aircraft (drones)," which "fire precision missiles and have the ability to distinguish clearly between children and adults." DCI reported that Israel's air-land invasion of 2008–2009 was an "intensification" of previous attacks on Gaza, including Israel's Operation Summer Rains (June–September 2006) and Operation Autumn Clouds (November 2006), when over four hundred Palestinians and eighty-five children were killed, and Operation Warm Winter (February 2008), which killed thirty-three children in five days.[80]

In its 115-page report, DCI also reported detailed case studies of the impact on Gazan children, including "Killing and Maiming of Children and Obstructed Medical Access to Injured Children," "Human Shields," "Attacks on Schools and the Right to Education," "Destruction of Civilian Homes," "Destruction of Water and Sanitation Infrastructure," and "Children Arrested and Detained in the West Bank during Operation Cast Lead." DCI reported that most of the Palestinian children in Gaza who are arrested and detained by Israeli security forces are charged with stone-throwing, with these arrests and detentions involving a "high level of physical abuse against child detainees." "Once arrested," the report continued, "children are tried and prosecuted under conditions which violate fundamental international legal standards," with the children detainees "invariably denied access to a lawyer until the end of the interrogation process, and they are often forced to make a confession under duress."

Referring to the damage and destruction of water and sanitation infrastructure in Gaza, DCI reported: "During the 23-day military offensive, Israeli forces damaged 19,000 metres of pipes, several vital water tanks and 38 wells; 74 wells were totally destroyed. Sewage infrastructure was also the target of attacks." Due to these Israeli attacks, "500,000 Palestinians, including around 250,000 children, completely lost access to running water." DCI reported further that due to the Israeli attacks on sewage systems, "sewage flowed in the water system in a number of areas" throughout Gaza, contaminating local water supplies.

DCI also reported that "at least 26 children were killed while near schools, on their way to or from schools, or while sheltering in schools, and at least 922 registered schoolchildren were injured, approximately 732 of whom sustained some form of long-term disability as a consequence of the offensive."

In addition to similar reports by B'Tselem and Amnesty International, DCI reported several incidents in which children were used as human shields by the Israeli military, including an incident when five Palestinian children, ages twelve to seventeen, "were detained in a trench for several days as soldiers carried out attacks around it, shooting over the heads of the children." Another reported incident involved a seventeen-year-old Palestinian, who "was forced to accompany [Israeli] soldiers deploying through his neighbourhood" and "forced to crawl in front of the soldiers" while being "handcuffed, blindfolded and beaten several times during his ordeal." Another incident involved a nine-year-old Palestinian boy who "was ordered at gunpoint to open bags and suitcases suspected of being booby-trapped," and who "was grabbed by the hair, slapped and slammed against a wall."[81]

The reports summarized here—an editorial in *Ha'aretz*, an investigation by the *Guardian*, a published statement by twenty-seven international law scholars, including Ian Brownlie and Richard Falk, and fact-finding assessments by Amnesty International, Human Rights Watch, Physicians for Human Rights in Israel, and the Palestine Section of Defense for Children International—accused Israel of committing war crimes in Gaza, or, in the case of *Ha'aretz*, expressed concerns that it might have committed such crimes. This was the consensus view within the human rights community in which Richard Goldstone and his three colleagues—Christine Chinkin, Desmond Travers, and Hina Jilani—issued the results of their fact-finding mission on the Israeli invasion of Gaza, which independently arrived at similar conclusions. Furthermore, it is likely that most people who have actually read the 575-page document, and who were familiar with the international fact-finding reports and the consensus therein reached, would agree with Falk that the Goldstone report was a relatively "ordinary text" about an "extraordinary event," and that, as Falk wrote, "the conclusions of the Goldstone Report were mainly confirmatory of prior reports that were already sufficiently authoritative to convey an impression to world public opinion that Israel's attacks at the end of 2008 on Gaza involved the widespread commission of war crimes."[82]

The main findings of the Goldstone report indeed were quite consistent with the findings of the news organizations and human rights groups cited earlier. For example, under the heading "Deliberate Attacks against the Civilian Population," the Goldstone report observed: "The [four-member Goldstone] Mission investigated eleven incidents in which Israeli forces launched direct attacks against civilians with lethal outcome. . . . The first two incidents are attacks against houses in the Samouni neighbourhood south of Gaza City, including the shelling of a house in which Palestinian civilians had been forced to assemble by the Israeli forces." Other incidents "concern the shooting of civilians while they were trying to leave their homes to walk to a safer place, waving white flags and, in some cases, following an injunction from the Israeli forces to do so." The report noted that "in the majority of these incidents, the consequences of the Israeli attacks against civilians were aggravated by their subsequent refusal to allow the evacuation of the wounded or to permit access to ambulances."[83] The Goldstone report described numerous other such incidents of the deliberate killing of Palestinian civilians.[84]

The Goldstone report also gave evidence of Israel's "attacks on the foundations of civilian life in Gaza," including "destruction of industrial infrastructure, food production, water installations, sewage treatment and housing," of "the use of Palestinian civilians as human shields," and of "the deprivation of liberty" of Gazans detained during the Israeli operation:[85] The evidence presented by the Goldstone report included the following:

• At the beginning of the [Israeli military] operations, the Al Bader flour mill was the only flour mill in the Gaza Strip still operating. The flour mill was hit by a series of air strikes on 9 January 2009 after several false warnings had been issued on previous days. The [Goldstone] Mission finds that its destruction had no military justification. The nature of the strikes, in particular the precise targeting of crucial machinery, suggests that the intention was to disable the factory in terms of its productive capacity. From the facts it ascertained, the Mission finds that there has been a violation of the grave breaches provisions of the Fourth Geneva Convention. Unlawful and wanton destruction which is not justified by military necessity amounts to a war crime. The Mission also finds that the destruction of the mill was carried out for the purposes of denying sustenance to the civilian population, which is a violation of customary international law and may constitute a war crime. The strike on the flour mill further constitutes a violation of human rights provisions regarding the right to adequate food and means of sustenance.

• The chicken farms of Mr. Sameh Sawafeary in the Zeitoun neighbourhood south of Gaza City reportedly supplied over 10 per cent of the Gaza egg market. Armoured bulldozers of the Israeli forces systematically flattened the chicken coops, killing all 31,000 chickens inside, and destroyed the plant and material necessary for the business. The Mission concludes that this was a deliberate act of wanton destruction not justified by any military necessity and draws the same legal conclusions as in the case of the destruction of the flour mill.

• Israeli forces also carried out a strike against a wall of one of the raw sewage lagoons of the Gaza Waste Water Treatment Plant, which caused the outflow of more than 200,000 cubic metres of raw sewage into neighbouring farmland. The circumstances of the strike on the lagoon suggest that it was deliberate and premeditated. The Namar Wells complex in Jabaliya consisted of two water wells, pumping machines, a generator, fuel storage, a reservoir chlorination unit, buildings and related equipment. All were destroyed by multiple air strikes on the first day of the Israeli aerial attack. The Mission considers it unlikely that a target the size of the Namar Wells could have been hit by multiple strikes in error. It found no grounds to suggest that there was any military advantage to be had by hitting the wells and noted that there was no suggestion that Palestinian armed groups had used the wells for any purpose. Considering that the right to drinking water is part of the right to adequate food, the Mission makes the same legal findings as in the case of the Al Bader flour mill.

• During its visits to the Gaza Strip, the Mission witnessed the extent of the destruction of residential housing caused by air strikes, mortar and artillery shelling, missile strikes, the operation of bulldozers and demolition charges. In some cases, residential neighbourhoods were subjected to air-launched bombing and to intensive shelling apparently in the context of the advance of Israeli ground forces. In other cases, the facts gathered by the Mission strongly suggest that the destruction of housing was carried out in the absence of any link to combat engagements with Palestinian armed groups or any other effective contribution to military action. Combining the results of its own fact finding on the ground with UNOSAT imagery and the published testimonies of Israeli soldiers, the Mission concludes that, in addition to the extensive destruction of housing for so-called "operational necessity" during their advance, the Israeli forces engaged in another wave of systematic destruction of civilian buildings during the last three days of their presence in Gaza, aware of the imminence of withdrawal. The conduct of the Israeli forces in this respect violated the principle of distinction between civilian and military objects and amounted to the grave breach of "extensive destruction . . . of property, not justified by military necessity and carried out unlawfully and wantonly." Israeli forces further violated the right to adequate housing of the families concerned.

• The attacks on industrial facilities, food production and water infrastructure investigated by the Mission are part of a broader pattern of destruction, which includes the destruction of the only cement packaging plant in Gaza (the Atta Abu Jubbah plant), the Abu Eida factories for ready-mix concrete, further chicken farms and the Al Wadia Group's foods and drinks factories. The facts ascertained by the Mission indicate that there was a deliberate and systematic policy on the part of the Israeli armed forces to target industrial sites and water installations.[86]

Given these findings, and many others not included here, the Goldstone mission, toward the end of its report, concluded:

• "From the facts gathered, the Mission found that the following grave breaches of the Fourth Geneva Convention were committed by Israeli forces in Gaza: wilful killing, torture or inhuman treatment, wilfully causing great suffering or serious injury to body or health, and extensive destruction of property, not justified by military necessity and carried out unlawfully and wantonly"; "As grave breaches these acts give rise to individual criminal responsibility" under the Rome Statute of the International Criminal Court.[87]

• "The Mission further considers that the series of acts that deprive Palestinians in the Gaza Strip of their means of subsistence, employment, housing and water, that deny their freedom of movement and their right to leave and enter their own country, that limit their rights to access a court of law and an effective remedy, could lead a competent court to find that the crime of persecution, a crime against humanity, has been committed."[88]

• "The Mission considers that the serious violations of International Humanitarian Law recounted in this report fall within the subject-matter jurisdiction of the International Criminal Court. . . . The Mission is persuaded that, in the light of the long-standing nature of the conflict, the frequent and consistent allegations of violations of international humanitarian law against all parties, the apparent increase in intensity of such violations in the recent military operations, and the regrettable possibility of a return to further violence, meaningful and practical steps to end impunity for such violations would offer an effective way to deter such violations recurring in the future. The Mission is of the view that the prosecution of persons responsible for serious violations of international humanitarian law would contribute to ending such violations, to the protection of civilians and to the restoration and maintenance of peace."[89]

• "The Mission recommends that States Parties to the Geneva Conventions of 1949 start criminal investigations in national courts, using universal jurisdiction, where there is sufficient evidence of the commission of grave breaches of the Geneva Conventions of 1949. Where so warranted following investigation, alleged perpetrators should be arrested and prosecuted in accordance with internationally recognised standards of justice."[90]

The Goldstone report's conclusions that Israeli government officials and military personnel had deliberately committed war crimes, along with militants in Gaza who had fired rockets indiscriminately into southern Israel,[91] and that individuals responsible for planning and committing such crimes should be criminally prosecuted, outraged a number of Israeli and Jewish commentators who then sought to discredit Goldstone and the report bearing his name. Nearly all such critics of the Goldstone report declined to address the factual and legal substance of the report in any significant sense. For example, it is important to reiterate that the Goldstone report was issued publicly on September 15, 2009, and thus after nearly all of the reports by news agencies and human rights organizations cited earlier were issued (the exception being the September 28 report by Amnesty International). Thus, in contrast not only to the Goldstone report, but to these reports as well, Dershowitz wrote on September 22: "There are many things wrong with the Goldstone report, which accuses Israel of deliberately targeting civilians in order to punish the people of Gaza. First, its primary conclusions are entirely false as a matter of demonstrable fact." Yet, Dershowitz did not "demonstrate" how this was so. "Second," he wrote, "it defames one of the most moral military forces in the world, along with one of the most responsive legal systems and one of the freest nations in the world when it comes to dissent." This statement did not speak directly to the content of the Goldstone report with respect to its findings on the facts and law that, if accurate, would certainly undermine Dershowitz's moral claims on behalf of Israel's military. "Third," Dershowitz continued, "it destroys the credibility of 'international human rights' and proves that this honorable concept has been hijacked for political purposes directed primarily against one nation—Israel."[92] To the contrary: the "credibility" of the Goldstone report was supported by nearly every major news organization and human rights group that similarly investigated the details of the Israeli invasion. Nor did Dershowitz detail how the Goldstone report might have defamed the concept of international human rights.

Other critics of the Goldstone report issued similar complaints. For example, Israel's ambassador to the United States, Michael Oren, repeated the claims of his government that it did its "utmost to avoid inflicting civilian casualties." The manner in which Oren pressed this claim, in the *Boston Globe* on September 24, 2009, and his criticism of the Goldstone report, is worth noting. With the United States standing in for Israel, and the Taliban for Hamas, Oren began his defense of Israel's invasion of Gaza, and his condemnation of the Goldstone report, with this analogy:

> [A]n international organization notorious for its one-sided condemnations of America launches an investigation into U.S. "war crimes." The inquiry is held under Taliban auspices, and Taliban commanders—disguised as civilians—are interviewed. Inexorably, the organization finds America guilty of mounting a pre-meditated campaign to inflict the maximum amount of civilian deaths and of failing to try those responsible. The final report calls for punitive actions against the United States for its "crimes against humanity." If true, this scenario would mark an unparalleled victory for terror and deal a crippling blow to any democracy trying to defend itself. Yet, this is precisely the catastrophe created by a UN report [the Goldstone report] on Israeli military actions against Hamas in Gaza last January.

Thus, within the framework of his analogy, Oren is claiming here that the Palestinian civilians interviewed by the authors of the Goldstone report in Gaza were "Hamas commanders" disguised as Gazan civilians, and that the Hamas commanders, having posed and testified as Gazan civilians, set into motion the wrong-headed conclusions that were reported by the Goldstone mission.[93]

Writing in the *Wall Street Journal* one day later (September 25), in an op-ed piece titled "At the U.N., Terrorism Pays," Israel's defense minister, Ehud Barak, who noted that he was "outraged" by the Goldstone report's accusations of Israeli war crimes, wrote: "It is the duty of every nation to defend itself. This is a basic obligation that all responsible governments owe their citizens. Israel is no different. After enduring eight years of ongoing rocket fire—in which 12,000 missiles were launched against our cities, and after all diplomatic efforts to stop this barrage failed—it was my duty as defense minister to do something about it. It's as simple and self-evident as the right to self-defense."[94] A former Israeli defense minister, Moshe Arens, in a piece for *Ha'aretz* titled "A License to Kill," wrote eleven days later (October 6) that the Goldstone report "is in effect a license to kill—for Hamas, for Hezbollah, and for terrorists all over the world."[95] For his part, Dershowitz also wrote: "Civilian deaths are inevitable in a conflict of this kind, but the accusation that they are part of a deliberate Israeli plan or policy defies reality and is wrong as a matter of fact."[96] However, not only were the findings of the Goldstone report consistent with those of the press outlets and human rights organizations that likewise reported on the Israeli air-land invasion of Gaza in 2008–2009, but they also were consistent with what was reported about the Israeli military tactics used in its air-land invasion of Lebanon two years earlier in summer 2006, which Dershowitz also defended, in part by attacking Amnesty International and Human Rights Watch just as he would attack Goldstone three years later.

On July 31, 2006, in the early afternoon, Dershowitz posted an article on *Huffington Post* in which he argued that the Israeli bombing of a three-story residential building in the town of Qana in southern Lebanon, where at least twenty-eight civilians were killed, including sixteen children, was in fact the work of Hezbollah, a Lebanese political party and militant group. In his article, titled "Hezbollah's Triumph: Israeli Rockets Hits [*sic*] Lebanese Children," Dershowitz wrote: "Sunday [July 30] was a day of great triumph for Hezbollah. Its tactics had worked. By launching rockets at Israeli civilians within yards of a building filled with refugees, Hezbollah had induced Israel to make a terrible mistake. Its defensive rocket had missed the Hezbollah launchers and hit the civilian building. That was Hezbollah's plan all along. As Israelis wept in grief over the deaths of the Lebanese children, Hezbollah leaders celebrated its [*sic*] propaganda victory."[97] Dershowitz also wrote:

> Israel produced evidence proving that it [the Israeli bombing of the residential building in Qana] was largely Hezbollah's fault. Hezbollah was using Lebanese children as involuntary human shields—surely a

war crime. Hezbollah was preventing civilians—who had been repeatedly warned by Israel to leave the battle zone—from moving out of harm's way. Hezbollah sympathizers were shown on TV defiantly tearing up the Israeli leaflets, as if to say "we're staying." Hezbollah had refused to build bomb shelters for ordinary civilians—only for their own leaders. Hezbollah knew (and Israel didn't) that children were in the so-called safe house. That is why it deliberately used the safe house as a shield behind which to five [sic] rockets at Israel. Hezbollah used its rocket launchers as "bait" to induce Israel to fire at them in order to increase the chances that Israel's rocket would misfire and hit the "safe house." It was a perfect plan. Leaders of Hezbollah knew it could count on the international community to finish its dirty work by condemning Israel, rather than Hezbollah for the deaths caused deliberately by Hezbollah.[98]

Dershowitz thus asserted that Hezbollah had engineered the Israeli bombing of the residential building in Qana by firing rockets at Israel from nearby the building, and in this manner used the building as "bait" to lure the Israelis into killing Lebanese civilians, including many children. Dershowitz himself provided no sources, beyond a lone reference to "Israel" as his source. Meanwhile, the *New York Times*, in the early morning of July 31, prominently covered the Qana bombing in its print edition on the front page, and reported that "Israel said the Qana raid was aimed at Hezbollah fighters firing rockets into Israel from the area," an assertion attributed to Israel's prime minister at the time, Ehud Olmert, and the Israeli army.[99] Thus, Dershowitz's highly detailed quick-response scenario of July 31 appeared to rely on statements issued by the Israeli government, which Dershowitz repeated as certain facts.

However, two days later, on August 2, Human Rights Watch issued the findings of its preliminary investigation:

The Israeli government initially claimed that the military targeted the house [in Qana] because Hezbollah fighters had fired rockets from the area. Human Rights Watch researchers who visited Qana on July 31, the day after the attack, did not find any destroyed military equipment in or near the home. Similarly, none of the dozens of international journalists, rescue workers and international observers who visited Qana on July 30 and 31 reported seeing any evidence of Hezbollah military presence in or around the home. Rescue workers recovered no bodies of apparent Hezbollah fighters from inside or near the building.

The IDF [Israel Defense Forces] subsequently changed its story, with one of Israel's top military correspondents reporting on August 1 that "It now appears that the military had no information on rockets launched from the site of the building, or the presence of Hezbollah men at the time."[100]

It thus appears that Dershowitz's claims about Hezbollah "baiting" the Israeli military to bomb a residential building in southern Lebanon packed with Lebanese civilians, including many children, simply reflected without question the unverified statements of the Israeli government in the immediate aftermath of the bombing.

Dershowitz ended his article on *Huffington Post* of July 31 by asserting: "The sad truth is that the Israelis care more about the lives of innocent Lebanese children than Hezbollah does."[101] This statement is reminiscent of one by U.S. secretary of state Madeleine Albright, as quoted by Joy Gordon in her 2010 book, *Invisible War: The United States and the Iraq Sanctions*, about the U.S.-led economic embargo against Iraq throughout the 1990s. Gordon wrote: "It was the consistent policy of all three U.S. administrations, from 1990 to 2003, to inflict the most extreme economic damage possible on Iraq. This was true even though each administration insisted that it was committed to the well-being of the Iraqi population. Secretary of State Madeleine Albright once said, 'I care more about the children of Iraq than Saddam Hussein does.' But the truth was that in implementing the policy on sanctions, the human damage was never a factor in U.S. policy, except insofar as it presented a political liability for U.S. administrations."[102]

A week after his July 31 commentary for *Huffington Post*, Dershowitz wrote an encore column titled "Lebanon Is Not a Victim," wherein he referred to Lebanese civilians killed by Israel as "civilians," with quotation marks, as he also did with Arab "eyewitnesses" to the bombing in Lebanon. Dershowitz's preferred references to Lebanon's civilians were "collaborators" and "facilitators," since, as his logic dictated, a majority of Lebanese had voted for the Lebanese government in power at that time, which in turn supported Hezbollah. Dershowitz also argued that the hundreds of Lebanese children who were killed and wounded by the Israeli military were the victims of their own parents, who, as he implied, used them as human shields in their homes when they were bombed by Israel. Here is what Dershowitz wrote, again without the use of references:

> It is virtually impossible to distinguish the Hezbollah dead from the truly civilian dead, just as it is virtually impossible to distinguish the Hezbollah living from the civilian living, especially in the south [of Lebanon]. The "civilian" death figures reported by the Lebanese authorities include large numbers of Hezbollah fighters, collaborators, facilitators and active supporters. They also include civilians who were warned to leave, but chose to remain, sometimes with their children, to serve as human

shields. The deaths of these "civilians" are the responsibility of Hezbollah and the Lebanese government, which has done little to protect its civilians.

Lebanon has chosen sides. . . . When a nation chooses sides in a war, especially when it chooses the side of terrorism, its civilians pay a price for that choice. This has been true of every war. We must stop viewing Lebanon as a victim and begin to see it as a collaborator with terrorism.[103]

Dershowitz issued these assertions on August 7, 2006, and therefore only a few days after Human Rights Watch issued a report on August 3 titled "Fatal Strikes: Israel's Indiscriminate Attacks against Civilians in Lebanon," which noted:

To date, the chief cause of civilian deaths from the Israeli campaign is targeted strikes on civilian homes in villages of Lebanon's South. There has also been large-scale destruction of civilian apartment buildings in southern Beirut, though most of the residents of those buildings had evacuated prior to the attacks. According to the Lebanese Ministry of Social Affairs, the IDF destroyed or damaged up to 5,000 civilian homes in air strikes during the first two weeks of the war. As demonstrated by the case studies below, Israel has caused large-scale civilian casualties by striking civilian homes, with no apparent military objective either inside the home or in the vicinity. In some cases, warplanes returned to strike again while residents and neighbors had gathered around the house to remove the dead and assist the wounded.[104]

The report by Human Rights Watch on August 3 strongly suggested that Dershowitz's efforts of August 7 to blame the Lebanese government and the Lebanese civilians themselves for the deaths and injuries of Lebanon's civilians at the hands of the Israeli military were not only highly improper and inaccurate, but that the Israeli bombing of the three-story residential building in Qana on July 30 was hardly an anomalous event, but consistent with the pattern of Israel's bombardment and missile attacks on thousands of other civilian homes in Lebanon.

While he was seeking to clear the Israeli government of any legal culpability for war crimes in Lebanon, Dershowitz never mentioned the Israeli attack of July 15 on the civilian car caravan from Marwaheen, a village near the city of Tyre in southern Lebanon. In a news story published that day titled "Children Die in Convoy Attack as Israel Widens Lebanon Assault," the *Guardian* reported that "Israel steeply escalated its military campaign against Hizbollah in Lebanon yesterday with a series of air strikes that left more than 35 civilians dead, including a single strike on a convoy of families fleeing the fighting in a village near Tyre in the south of the country that killed more than 20 people, most of them children."[105] The next day, July 16, in a front-page story, the *New York Times* described the Israeli attack on the Marwaheen civilian convoy as "the deadliest single attack in the past four days of fighting."[106]

On July 20, Robert Fisk wrote from the scene for the *Independent* about the Israeli bombing of the car caravan from Marwaheen:

> How soon must we use the words "war crime"? How many children must be scattered in the rubble of Israeli air attacks before we reject the obscene phrase "collateral damage" and start talking about prosecution for crimes against humanity? The child whose dead body lies like a rag doll beside the cars which were supposedly taking her and her family to safety is a symbol of the latest Lebanon war; she was hurled from the vehicle in which she and her family were traveling in southern Lebanon as they fled their village—on Israel's own instructions. Because her parents were apparently killed in the same Israeli air attack, her name is still unknown. Not an unknown warrior, but an unknown child.

Fisk continued:

> The story of her death, however, is well documented. On Saturday, the inhabitants of the tiny border village of Marwaheen were ordered by Israeli troops—apparently using a bullhorn—to leave their homes by 6 PM Marwaheen lies closest to the spot where Hizbollah guerrillas broke through the frontier wire a week ago to capture two Israeli soldiers and kill three others, the attack which provoked this latest cruel war in Lebanon. The villagers obeyed the Israeli orders and initially appealed to local UN troops of the Ghanaian battalion for protection.
>
> But the Ghanaian soldiers, obeying guidelines set down by the UN's headquarters in New York in 1996, refused to permit the Lebanese civilians to enter their base. By terrible irony, the UN's rules had been drawn up after their soldiers gave protection to civilians during an Israeli bombardment of southern Lebanon in 1996 in which 106 Lebanese, more than half of them children, were slaughtered when the Israelis shelled the UN compound at Qana, in which they had been given sanctuary.
>
> So the people of Marwaheen set off for the north in a convoy of cars which only minutes later, close to the village of Tel Harfa, were attacked by an Israeli F-16 fighter-bomber. It bombed all the cars and killed at least 20 of the civilians travelling in them, many of them women and children. Twelve people were burnt alive in their vehicles but others, including the child who lies like a rag doll near the charred civilian convoy, whose photograph was taken—at great risk—by an

Associated Press photographer, Nasser Nasser, were blown clear of the cars by the blast of the bombs and fell into fields and a valley near the scene of the attack. There has been no apology or expression of regret from Israel for these deaths.[107]

This information about the Israeli attack on the car caravan from Marwaheen, as reported by the *Guardian* (July 15), the *New York Times* (July 16), and the *Independent* (July 20), was published well before Dershowitz's July 31 and August 7 columns for *Huffington Post*, in which he strongly implied that Lebanon's "civilians" (his quotation marks) were legitimate military targets of the Israel Defense Forces.

Two months later, Fisk traveled to Marwaheen and the surrounding area and wrote a second account in September for the *Independent*. As Fisk makes clear, the Israeli bombing of the Marwaheen car caravan on July 15, 2006 was almost certainly a war crime:

> In antiquity, Pliny [the Roman naturalist] wrote of the cliffs of Bayada. The chalk runs down to the Mediterranean in an almost Dover-like cascade of white rock, and the view from the top—just below the little Lebanese village of Chama'a—is breathtaking. To the south lies the United Nations headquarters and the Israeli frontier, to the north the city of Tyre, its long promontory built by Alexander the Great, lunging out into the green-blue sea. A winding, poorly-made road runs down to the shore below Chama'a and for some reason—perhaps because he had caught sight of the Israeli warship off the coast—58-year-old Ali Kemal Abdullah took a right turn above the Mediterranean on the morning of 15 July. In the open-topped pick-up behind him, Ali had packed 27 Lebanese refugees, most of them children. Twenty-three of them were to die within the next 15 minutes.
>
> The tragedy of these poor young people and of their desperate attempts to survive their repeated machine-gunning from the air is as well-known in Lebanon as it is already forgotten abroad. War crimes are easy to talk about when they have been committed in Rwanda or Bosnia; less so in Lebanon, especially when the Israelis are involved. But all the evidence suggests that what happened on this blissfully lovely coastline two and a half months ago was a crime against humanity, one that is impossible to justify on any military grounds since the dead and wounded were fleeing their homes on the express orders of the Israelis themselves.[108]

Just as the Israeli bombing of the house in Qana was no anomaly, the Israeli attacks on the civilian car caravan out of Marwaheen wasn't either, as Human Rights

Watch reported a year later in September 2007:

> Among the deadly attacks on civilians trying to flee the conflict are the killing of 23 civilians, including 14 children and seven women, fleeing from Marwahin on July 15; the killing of six and wounding of eight civilians fleeing from 'Aitaroun on July 19; the killing of three and wounding of 14 civilians fleeing from al-Tiri on July 23; the killing of 2 and wounding of four civilians fleeing from Mansouri on July 23; the wounding of nine civilians fleeing from Mansouri on July 23; the wounding of six ambulance drivers and three passengers in Qana on July 23; the killing of one civilian on a motorcycle on his way to buy food and medicines on July 24; the killing of seven civilians fleeing from Marja'youn on August 11; and the killing of seven and wounding of six civilians in the Beka' Valley on August 14. In all these cases, there is no evidence of a Hezbollah military presence that would justify the attacks.[109]

In a report issued in August 2006, Amnesty International similarly reported:

> Between 12 July and 14 August, a major military confrontation took place between Hizbullah and Israel, following the capture of two Israeli soldiers, and the killing of others, by Hizbullah in a raid across the border between Israel and Lebanon. Israel conducted attacks throughout Lebanon from land, sea and air, killing some 1,000 civilians. Hizbullah launched thousands of rockets on northern Israel, killing some 40 civilians. Hundreds of thousands of civilians in Israel and Lebanon were displaced. . . .
>
> During more than four weeks of ground and aerial bombardment of Lebanon by the Israeli armed forces, the country's infrastructure suffered destruction on a catastrophic scale. Israeli forces pounded buildings into the ground, reducing entire neighbourhoods to rubble and turning villages and towns into ghost towns, as their inhabitants fled the bombardments. Main roads, bridges and petrol stations were blown to bits. Entire families were killed in air strikes on their homes or in their vehicles while fleeing the aerial assaults on their villages. Scores lay buried beneath the rubble of their houses for weeks, as the Red Cross and other rescue workers were prevented from accessing the areas by continuing Israeli strikes. The hundreds of thousands of Lebanese who fled the bombardment now face the danger of unexploded munitions as they head home. . . .
>
> The Lebanese government estimates that 31 "vital points" (such as airports, ports, water and sewage treatment plants, electrical facilities) have been completely or partially destroyed, as have around 80 bridges and 94 roads. More than 25 fuel stations and around 900 commercial enterprises were hit. The number of residential properties, offices and shops

completely destroyed exceeds 30,000. Two government hospitals—in Bint Jbeil and in Meis al-Jebel—were completely destroyed in Israeli attacks and three others were seriously damaged.[110]

Amnesty also reported: "Israeli government spokespeople have insisted that they were targeting Hizbullah positions and support facilities, and that damage to civilian infrastructure was incidental or resulted from Hizbullah using the civilian population as a 'human shield.' However, the pattern and scope of the attacks, as well as the number of civilian casualties and the amount of damage sustained, makes the justification ring hollow. The evidence strongly suggests that the extensive destruction of public works, power systems, civilian homes and industry was deliberate and an integral part of the military strategy, rather than 'collateral damage'—incidental damage to civilians or civilian property resulting from targeting military objectives."[111]

Shortly after the thirty-four-day armed conflict between Israel and Hezbollah had ended on August 14, Dershowitz condemned both Human Rights Watch and Amnesty International for their coverage. On August 21 Dershowitz accused Human Rights Watch of "cook[ing] the books about facts, cheat[ing] on interviews, and put[ting] out pre-determined conclusions that are driven more by their ideology than by evidence." "These are serious accusations," Dershowitz wrote, "and they are demonstrably true."[112]

   Indeed, Dershowitz's featured allegation against Human Rights Watch was that it refused to accuse Hezbollah of using human shields in Lebanon. Dershowitz presented this claim as follows:

> [Dershowitz:] Consider the highly publicized "conclusion" reached by Human Rights Watch about the recent war in Lebanon between Hezbollah and Israel. This is their conclusion, allegedly reached after extensive "investigations" on the ground:
> [Quoting Human Rights Watch:] "Human Rights Watch found no cases in which Hezbollah deliberately used civilians as shields to protect them from retaliatory IDF attack."
> [Dershowitz:] After investigating a handful of cases, Human Rights Watch found that in "none of the cases of civilian deaths documented in this report [Qana, Srifa, Tyre, and southern Beirut] is there evidence to suggest that Hezbollah forces or weapons were in or near the area that the IDF targeted during or just prior to the attack." No cases! None! Not one![113]

Upon locating the Dershowitz-quoted sentences from the Human Rights Watch report of August 3, "Fatal Strikes: Israel's Indiscriminate Attacks against Civilians in Lebanon," it seems that Dershowitz quoted from that report in a misleading manner. To illustrate, here is what Human Rights Watch actually reported in full on August 3 (with Dershowitz quoting only the words in bold):

> **Human Rights Watch found no cases in which Hezbollah deliberately used civilians as shields to protect them from retaliatory IDF attack.** Hezbollah occasionally did store weapons in or near civilian homes and fighters placed rocket launchers within populated areas or near U.N. observers, which are serious violations of the laws of war because they violate the duty to take all feasible precautions to avoid civilian casualties. However, those cases do not justify the IDF's extensive use of indiscriminate force which has cost so many civilian lives. **In none of the cases of civilian deaths documented in this report is there evidence to suggest that Hezbollah forces or weapons were in or near the area that the IDF targeted during or just prior to the attack.**[114]

For his part, Dershowitz reproduced only the first and fourth sentences (in bold type), and omitted mentioning the second and third sentences (in regular type). Although he must have read that Human Rights Watch had indeed found that "Hezbollah occasionally did store weapons in or near civilian homes and fighters placed rocket launchers within populated areas or near U.N. observers," Dershowitz nevertheless accused Human Rights Watch of reporting that it found no such incidents, and theatrically misled his readers by claiming that the human rights group had found "No cases! None! Not one!"[115]

On August 29, Dershowitz condemned Amnesty International in a similar fashion in another article for *Huffington Post* titled "Amnesty International's Biased Definition of War Crimes: Whatever Israel Does to Defend Its Citizens." Amnesty's offense in what Dershowitz called "its race to the bottom" with Human Rights Watch was its August 22 report, "Lebanon: Deliberate Destruction or Collateral Damage? Israeli Attacks on Civilian Infrastructure." About this report, Dershowitz wrote: "There are two problems with the Amnesty report and conclusion. First, Amnesty is wrong about the law."[116] Yet, Dershowitz mentions no source of international law—or any law—at any point in his August 29 piece for *Huffington Post*. Dershowitz then absolved Israel of committing any crimes in Lebanon: "Israel committed no war crimes by attacking parts of the civilian infrastructure of Lebanon."[117] Thus, upon clearing Israel of war crimes in Lebanon without referring to any law, Dershowitz declined to cite the Rome Statute of the International Criminal Court, which defines "war crimes" exactly as Israel's military activities in Lebanon were described and documented by Amnesty International in its report of August 22: "Article 8: War Crimes. . . . 2. For the purpose of this Statute, "war crimes" means. . . .(b) (v) Attacking or bombarding, by whatever means, towns, villages, dwellings or buildings which are undefended and which are not military objectives."[118] Yet, in his response to Amnesty International of August 29, Dershowitz claimed that Israel had practiced "restraint" in its bombing of Lebanon, and that Amnesty had engaged in "bigotry, pure and simple," by accusing Israel of war crimes in Lebanon.[119]

PART IV
FROM THE BILL OF RIGHTS
TO AUTHORITARIANISM

country has comprehensively reduced civil liberties in the name of an expanded security state. The most recent example of this was the National Defense Authorization Act, signed Dec. 31, which allows for the indefinite detention of citizens. At what point does the reduction of individual rights in our country change how we define ourselves?

Accordingly, Turley wrote that "the list of powers acquired by the U.S. government since 9/11 puts us in rather troubling company," as he pointed out in detail:

- *Assassinations of U.S. citizens*: "President Obama has claimed, as President George W. Bush did before him, the right to order the killing of any citizen considered a terrorist or an abettor of terrorism. Last year, he approved the killing of U.S. citizen Anwar al-Awlaqi and another citizen under this claimed inherent authority. Last month, administration officials affirmed that power, stating that the president can order the assassination of any citizen whom he considers allied with terrorists."
- *Indefinite detention*: "Under the law signed last month, terrorism suspects are to be held by the military; the president also has the authority to indefinitely detain citizens accused of terrorism. While the administration claims that this provision only codified existing law, experts widely contest this view, and the administration has opposed efforts to challenge such authority in federal courts. The government continues to claim the right to strip citizens of legal protections based on its sole discretion."
- *Arbitrary justice*: "The president now decides whether a person will receive a trial in the federal courts or in a military tribunal, a system that has been ridiculed around the world for lacking basic due process protections. Bush claimed this authority in 2001, and Obama has continued the practice."
- *Warrantless searches*: "The president may now order warrantless surveillance, including a new capability to force companies and organizations to turn over information on citizens' finances, communications and associations. Bush acquired this sweeping power under the Patriot Act in 2001, and in 2011, Obama extended the power, including searches of everything from business documents to library records. The government can use 'national security letters' to demand, without probable cause, that organizations turn over information on citizens—and order them not to reveal the disclosure to the affected party."
- *Secret evidence*: "The government now routinely uses secret evidence to detain individuals and employs secret evidence in federal and military courts. It also forces the dismissal of cases against the United States by simply filing declarations that the cases would make the government

reveal classified information that would harm national security—a claim made in a variety of privacy lawsuits and largely accepted by federal judges without question. Even legal opinions, cited as the basis for the government's actions under the Bush and Obama administrations, have been classified. This allows the government to claim secret legal arguments to support secret proceedings using secret evidence. In addition, some cases never make it to court at all. The federal courts routinely deny constitutional challenges to policies and programs under a narrow definition of standing to bring a case."

• *War crimes*: "The world clamored for prosecutions of those responsible for waterboarding terrorism suspects during the Bush administration, but the Obama administration said in 2009 that it would not allow CIA employees to be investigated or prosecuted for such actions. This gutted not just treaty obligations but the Nuremberg principles of international law. When courts in countries such as Spain moved to investigate Bush officials for war crimes, the Obama administration reportedly urged foreign officials not to allow such cases to proceed, despite the fact that the United States has long claimed the same authority with regard to alleged war criminals in other countries."

• *Secret court*: "The government has increased its use of the secret Foreign Intelligence Surveillance Court, which has expanded its secret warrants to include individuals deemed to be aiding or abetting hostile foreign governments or organizations. In 2011, Obama renewed these powers, including allowing secret searches of individuals who are not part of an identifiable terrorist group. The administration has asserted the right to ignore congressional limits on such surveillance."

• *Immunity from judicial review*: "Like the Bush administration, the Obama administration has successfully pushed for immunity for companies that assist in warrantless surveillance of citizens, blocking the ability of citizens to challenge the violation of privacy."

• *Continual monitoring of citizens*: "The Obama administration has successfully defended its claim that it can use GPS devices to monitor every move of targeted citizens without securing any court order or review."

• *Extraordinary renditions*: "The government now has the ability to transfer both citizens and noncitizens to another country under a system known as extraordinary rendition, which has been denounced as using other countries, such as Syria, Saudi Arabia, Egypt and Pakistan, to torture suspects. The Obama administration says it is not continuing the abuses of this practice under Bush, but it insists on the unfettered right to order such transfers—including the possible transfer of U.S. citizens."

Turley also noted that "these new laws have come with an infusion of money into an expanded security system on the state and federal levels, including more public surveillance cameras, tens of thousands of security personnel and a massive expansion of a terrorist-chasing bureaucracy." He then observed: "An authoritarian nation is defined not just by the use of authoritarian powers, but by the ability to use them. If a president can take away your freedom or your life on his own authority, all rights become little more than a discretionary grant subject to executive will."[7]

Likewise, Bill Quigley, associate director of the Center for Constitutional Rights, in an article in December 2011 titled "Twenty Examples of the Obama Administration Assault on Domestic Civil Liberties," wrote: "The Obama administration has affirmed, continued and expanded almost all of the draconian domestic civil liberties intrusions pioneered under the Bush administration. Here are twenty examples of serious assaults on the domestic rights to freedom of speech, freedom of assembly, freedom of association, the right to privacy, the right to a fair trial, freedom of religion, and freedom of conscience that have occurred since the Obama administration has assumed power." Quigley then itemized the infringements, including:

> • *Patriot Act*: "On May 27, 2011, President Obama, over widespread bipartisan objections, approved a Congressional four year extension of controversial parts of the Patriot Act that were set to expire. In March of 2010, Obama signed a similar extension of the Patriot Act for one year. These provisions allow the government, with permission from a special secret court, to seize records without the owner's knowledge, conduct secret surveillance of suspicious people who have no known ties to terrorist groups and to obtain secret roving wiretaps on people."
> • *Criminalization of dissent and militarization of the police*: "Anyone who has gone to a peace or justice protest in recent years has seen it—local police have been turned into SWAT teams, and SWAT teams into heavily armored military. Officer Friendly or even Officer Unfriendly has given way to police uniformed like soldiers with SWAT shields, shin guards, heavy vests, military helmets, visors, and vastly increased firepower. Protest police sport ninja turtle–like outfits and are accompanied by helicopters, special tanks, and even sound blasting vehicles first used in Iraq. Wireless fingerprint scanners first used by troops in Iraq are now being utilized by local police departments to check motorists. Facial recognition software introduced in war zones is now being used in Arizona and other jurisdictions. Drones just like the ones used in Kosovo, Iraq and Afghanistan are being used along the Mexican and Canadian borders. These activities continue to expand under the Obama administration."

- *Wiretaps*: "Wiretaps for oral, electronic or wire communications, approved by federal and state courts, are at an all-time high. Wiretaps in year 2010 were up 34% from 2009, according to the Administrative Office of the US Courts."
- *Top Secret America*: "In July 2010, the *Washington Post* released 'Top Secret America,' a series of articles detailing the results of a two year investigation into the rapidly expanding world of homeland security, intelligence and counter-terrorism. It found 1,271 government organizations and 1,931 private companies work on counterterrorism, homeland security and intelligence at about 10,000 locations across the US. Every single day, the National Security Agency intercepts and stores more than 1.7 billion emails, phone calls and other types of communications."
- *Other domestic spying*: "There are at least 72 fusion centers across the US which collect local domestic police information and merge it into multi-jurisdictional intelligence centers, according to a recent report by the ACLU. These centers share information from federal, state and local law enforcement and some private companies to secretly spy on Americans. These all continue to grow and flourish under the Obama administration."
- *Material support*: "The Obama administration successfully asked the US Supreme Court not to apply the First Amendment and to allow the government to criminalize humanitarian aid and legal activities of people providing advice or support to foreign organizations which are listed on the government list as terrorist organizations. The material support law can now be read to penalize people who provide humanitarian aid or human rights advocacy. The Obama administration Solicitor General argued to the court 'when you help Hezbollah build homes, you are also helping Hezbollah build bombs.' The Court agreed with the Obama argument that national security trumps free speech in these circumstances."
- *Punishing whistleblowers*: "The Obama administration has prosecuted five whistleblowers under the Espionage Act, more than all the other administrations in [U.S.] history put together. They charged a National Security Agency advisor with ten felonies under the Espionage Act for telling the press that government eavesdroppers were wasting hundreds of millions of dollars on misguided and failed projects. After their case collapsed, the government, which was chastised by the federal judge as engaging in unconscionable conduct, allowed him to plead to a misdemeanor and walk. The administration has also prosecuted former members of the CIA, the State Department, and the FBI. They even tried to subpoena a journalist and one of the lawyers for the whistleblowers."

Quigley also asserted that these instances, and the several others that he reported, "documented a sustained assault on domestic civil liberties in the United States under the Obama administration."[8]

Four months later, Quigley wrote "Thirteen Ways Government Tracks Us" and listed the ways, including the ones enumerated as follows:

- *One*: "The National Security Agency (NSA) collects hundreds of millions of emails, texts and phone calls every day and has the ability to collect and sift through billions more. Wired just reported NSA is building an immense new data center which will intercept, analyze and store even more electronic communications from satellites and cables across the nation and the world. Though NSA is not supposed to focus on US citizens, it does."
- *Two*: "The Federal Bureau of Investigation (FBI) National Security Branch Analysis Center (NSAC) has more than 1.5 billion government and private sector records about US citizens collected from commercial databases, government information, and criminal probes."
- *Three*: "The American Civil Liberties Union and the *New York Times* recently reported that cell phones of private individuals in the US are being tracked without warrants by state and local law enforcement all across the country. With more than 300 million cell phones in the US connected to more than 200,000 cell phone towers, cell phone tracking software can pinpoint the location of a phone and document the places the cell phone user visits over the course of a day, week, month or longer."
- *Four*: "More than 62 million people in the US have their fingerprints on file with the FBI, state and local governments. This system, called the Integrated Automated Fingerprint Identification System (IAFIS), shares information with 43 states and 5 federal agencies. This system conducts more than 168,000 checks each day."
- *Five*: "Over 126 million people have their fingerprints, photographs and biographical information accessible on the US Department of Homeland Security Automated Biometric Identification System (IDENT). This system conducts about 250,000 biometric transactions each day. The goal of this system is to provide information for national security, law enforcement, immigration, intelligence and other Homeland Security Functions. . . ."
- *Thirteen*: "The FBI admits it has about 3,000 GPS tracking devices on cars of unsuspecting people in the US right now, even after the US Supreme Court decision authorizing these only after a warrant for probable cause has been issued."

In his summary, Quigley wrote: "The technology for tracking and identifying people is exploding as is the government appetite for it. . . . The advanced technology of the war on terrorism, combined with deferential courts and legislators, have endangered both the right to privacy and the right of people to be free from government snooping and tracking."[9]

In a concurring opinion, in May 2012, Ralph Nader, who is a lawyer, wrote:

> The rule of law is rapidly breaking down at the top levels of our government. As officers of the court, we have sworn to "support the Constitution," which clearly implies an affirmative commitment on our part. Take the administrations of George W. Bush and Barack Obama. The conservative American Bar Association sent three white papers to President Bush describing his continual unconstitutional policies. Then and now civil liberties groups and a few law professors, such as the stalwart David Cole of Georgetown University and Jonathan Turley of George Washington University, have distinguished themselves in calling out both presidents for such violations and the necessity for enforcing the rule of law. Sadly, the bulk of our profession, as individuals and through their bar associations, has remained quietly on the sidelines. They have turned away from their role as "first-responders" to protect the Constitution from its official violators.[10]

In contrast to the likes of Cole, Turley, Quigley, and Nader, in addition to Jameel Jaffer of the American Civil Liberties Union,[11] Michael Ratner of the Center for Constitutional Rights,[12] and Marjorie Cohn of the National Lawyers Guild and the Thomas Jefferson School of Law,[13] Alan Dershowitz is not only silent in response to the contemporary assault on civil liberties, he is a leading academic proponent of what Jonathan Turley appropriately refers to as the turn toward "authoritarianism" in the United States in response to 9/11 (see chapter 11 in this volume).

Furthermore, it was Noam Chomsky, not Alan Dershowitz, who joined a lawsuit as a plaintiff against the federal government over the 2011 National Defense Authorization Act (NDAA), two paragraphs of which give the president the authority to indefinitely detain American citizens without a trial. About the act, Chris Hedges, who initiated the legal action against the government, wrote in April 2012: "This act, signed into law by President Barack Obama last Dec. 31, puts into the hands of people with no discernible understanding of legitimate dissent the power to use the military to deny due process to all deemed to be terrorists, or terrorist sympathizers, and hold them indefinitely in military detention."[14] In May 2012, as the *Common Dreams* Web site reported:

> A federal judge in New York on Wednesday ruled in favor of a group of civilian activists and journalists and struck down highly controversial

"indefinite detention" and "material support" provisions of the National Defense Authorization Act, enacted by Congress and signed into law by President Obama last December. In their suit, the plaintiffs stated they could be detained "indefinitely" for their constitutionally protected activities. Citing the "vagueness" of certain language in the bill, U.S. District Judge Katherine Forrest—who was appointed to the court by Obama—agreed, and said the law could have a "chilling impact on First Amendment rights" for journalists, activists, and potentially all US citizens. . . . The ruling came as part of a lawsuit brought by seven plaintiffs—Chris Hedges, Dan Ellsberg, Noam Chomsky, Birgitta Jonsdottir, Alexa O'Brien, Kai Wargall, and Jennifer Bolen—alleging that the NDAA violates "both their free speech and associational rights guaranteed by the First Amendment as well as due process rights guaranteed by the Fifth Amendment of the United States Constitution."[15]

In addition, it is Chomsky, not Dershowitz, who has asserted a viable alternative to the war on terrorism that would be far more likely to reduce the threat of terrorism against the United States, and thereby ease the assault on civil liberties.

Shortly after President Barack Obama announced in December 2009 that he had authorized sending additional U.S. troops to Afghanistan in an escalation of that war, Chomsky gave his advice about how to diminish the threat of terrorism from that region if not by waging a ground and air war in Afghanistan and a drone war in Pakistan. Upon citing Nir Rosen, a fellow at New York University's Center on Law and Security who has covered Afghanistan for several years, Chomsky said: "If you want to stop Muslims killing you, stop killing them."[16] In his original comments, Rosen said: "Be perceived as a fair player in the Middle East and the Muslim world. Stop killing Muslims, and Muslims will not want to kill you. It's really very easy."[17] This is quite contrary to Dershowitz's counterterrorism recommendations, which feature the liberal killing and maiming of Muslims in what he refers to as "preventive" and "preemptive" wars and wars in "self-defense," in addition to extrajudicial targeted killings, all of which are not only legally and morally objectionable but almost certainly increase the threat of terrorism against the United States.

Meanwhile, there is substantial support for the implementation of the policy guidance of Chomsky and Rosen on reducing the threat of terrorism, which includes a report issued internally in September 2004 by the Pentagon's Defense Science Board and posted on the Web site of the department of defense two months later. In a summary titled "Terror War Seen Hurting U.S. in Muslim World," the Associated Press included some excerpts:

The U.S. invasions of Afghanistan and Iraq have created a shared anti-Americanism among otherwise-divided Muslim extremists and raised the stature of the radicals in the eyes of ordinary Muslims, a Pentagon advisory panel says. . . . At the root of the problem, the report says, is a fundamental misunderstanding of why Muslims are hostile toward the United States. "They hate our policies," not our freedom, it said. The report cites a "pervasive atmosphere of hostility" toward the American government that has intensified since the terrorist attacks of Sept. 11, 2001, and the U.S. response to them. "The dramatic narrative since 9/11 has essentially borne out the entire radical Islamist bill of particulars" against the United States, the report said. "American actions and the flow of events have elevated the authority of the Jihadi insurgents and tended to ratify their legitimacy among Muslims."

"In other words," as the board concluded, "Americans have become the enemy" of the Muslim world.[18] In a similar sense, *The 9/11 Commission Report* observed in October 2004 that "American foreign policy is part of the message [to the Muslim world]. America's policy choices have consequences. Right or wrong, it is simply a fact that American policy regarding the Israeli-Palestinian conflict and American actions in Iraq are dominant staples of popular commentary across the Arab and Muslim world."[19]

Two years later, in September 2006, the *New York Times* reported that "a stark assessment of terrorism trends by American intelligence agencies has found that the American invasion and occupation of Iraq has helped spawn a new generation of Islamic radicalism and that the overall terrorist threat has grown since the Sept. 11 attacks." Mark Mazzetti of the *Times* observed that the classified U.S. National Intelligence Estimate, upon which his report was based, is "the most authoritative document that the intelligence community produces on a specific national security issue" and, in this instance, was "the first formal appraisal of global terrorism by United States intelligence agencies since the Iraq war began, and represents a consensus view of the 16 disparate spy services inside government." The intelligence estimate, titled "Indicators of the Spread of the Global Jihadist Movement," asserted that "Islamic terrorism, rather than being in retreat, has metastasized and spread across the globe" and cited "the Iraq war as a reason for the diffusion of jihad ideology."[20]

Beyond these official assessments, there have been numerous privately issued appraisals that the Bush administration's "war on terrorism," featuring the 2001 invasion of Afghanistan and the 2003 invasion of Iraq, had enhanced the threat of terrorism against the United States and its allies. In November 2003, a former head of Mossad, Major General Danny Yatom, said that "the presence of Western forces in Iraq has presented the opportunity for a holy war by Islamists in a country [Israel] surrounded by Muslim neighbors," and accused the United States and Britain of a "lack of foresight over the Iraq invasion."[21] In April 2004, then Egyptian president Hosni Mubarak said that "today there is hatred of the Americans like never before in the region" following the invasion of Iraq.[22] In October 2004, Agence France Presse reported that Hans Blix, the former chief UN arms inspector in Iraq, said that "if this [invasion of Iraq] was meant to be a signal to terrorists to stop their activities, it has failed miserably, it has stimulated terrorism."[23] In May 2004, the London-based International Institute for Strategic Studies reported that "the U.S.-led war on Iraq, far from countering terrorism, has helped revitalize the Al-Qaeda terror network," pointing to "devastating blasts in Morocco, Saudi Arabia and Turkey in 2003 and 2004 as further evidence that anti-US sentiment had soared since the Iraq war."[24] In March 2005 in Madrid, on the occasion of the one-year anniversary of the Madrid terrorist train bombings on March 11, 2004, scholars and experts convened to advise European governments about how to avoid such attacks in the future, and "where several delegates pointed to the dangers of the 'war on terror' led by the United States." Mark Juergensmeyer, director of international studies at the University of California at Santa Barbara, said that the U.S. military's detention of Muslims as "prisoners of war" at Guantanamo Bay had exacerbated the threat of terrorism. "We have the Guantanamo effect," Juergensmeyer said, that is, "dealing with terrorism in such a way that it has an incubator effect." Arguing that the U.S. government should behave in a "counterintuitive way," he said that "military strikes in the aftermath of a terrorist attack were meant to appease voters," but "they often played into the hands of extremists by helping them recruit more followers." Speaking in agreement, Jerrold Post, professor of psychiatry and international affairs at George Washington University, said that "most strong counter terror attacks are for assuring domestic voters that something is being done, but there is usually an increase in terrorism afterwards." Louise Richardson, dean of the Radcliffe Institute at Harvard University, said she opposed the U.S. invasion of Iraq "precisely because I feared that it would have this effect" of increasing terrorism. Richardson commented that "the U.S. government has done a lot of things in response to terrorism that it may regret." George Soros, a speaker at the Madrid conference, said: "In Iraq, there are more people wanting to kill Americans than there were before. These people didn't think like that before the Americans arrived and did what they did." In a statement that resembles the Chomsky-Rosen assessment of the causes of terrorism against the United States, Soros said: "The attitude of creating innocent victims creates terrorists. It's as simple as that."[25]

Even shortly after the terrorist attacks on the United States on 9/11, it was clear among many analysts that invading Afghanistan and Iraq in response was morally indefensible. On September 30, 2001, Chalmers Johnson wrote in the *Los Angeles Times*: "No political cause can justify the killing on Sept. 11 of thousands of innocent people in New York, Washington and Pennsylvania. But neither would our killing innocent people in retaliation be justifiable."[26] In November 2001, Chandra Muzaffar, a Muslim peace activist based in Kuala Lumpur, in an op-ed piece in the *International Herald Tribune* titled "Decent People Reject Terrorism and U.S. Bombing at the Same Time," wrote: "A dangerous idea is gaining currency in the U.S. administration and among a significant segment of the American public: If a person does not support the U.S.-led bombing, it means that he or she backs Osama bin Laden and the Qaida network. . . . Yet many honest people condemn the carnage of Sept. 11 and are determined to see terrorism eliminated, while being genuinely pained by the bombing of Afghanistan. Such people in America and many other countries are deeply concerned at the deaths of many Afghan civilians who are no less innocent than the Sept. 11 victims."[27]

In December 2001, the *Tribune* published the results of a poll it conducted with the Pew Research Center of "elite opinion" in twenty-four countries, which found "significant splits" between Americans and non-Americans about U.S. foreign policy. "Most significantly," the Tribune noted, "a majority of non-Americans see U.S. policies as a principal cause of the Sept. 11 attacks—but Americans do not." Ivo Daalder, U.S. ambassador to NATO but at the time an analyst at the Brookings Institution, provided trenchant commentary on the polling results: "A very significant thing for Americans is the realization that our view of ourselves is not widely shared. Americans are in general totally convinced of our own essential goodness—that we are the most democratic, most liberal, most just people in the world and that we assume everybody else sees it that way. We are not very good at putting ourselves in the shoes of others, and therefore we don't necessarily understand that people don't share the view of us that we have of ourselves—and I think that's a major problem for our foreign policy." Marwan Bishara, an Israeli Arab who teaches international relations at the American University in Paris, told the Tribune that he sees an "asymmetric threat from terrorists" growing out of "the incredible quantitative difference of force and riches between North and South." He continued: "When people feel so inferior militarily and economically, they adopt asymmetric means—not the usual means—to achieve what they want." Addressing U.S. foreign policy, and referring to the Kyoto Protocol of 1997 on global warming; the 2001 antiracism conference in Durban, South Africa; the U.S. withdrawal in 2002 from the Anti-Ballistic Missile Treaty; and U.S. conduct at the United Nations Security Council, "where [the U.S.] tends to veto decisions that are adopted by all other countries," Bishara noted: "There's a general sense that America is pulling out and that the world is left with only American military hegemony and not American partnership." The alternative, Bishara wrote, is "to advance the importance of the human being, of human life, and of social and economic security."[28] All of this helps to provide a context for Chomsky's post–9/11 counsel to stop killing Muslims, which broadly refers to ending the illegal U.S. use and threat of force against Muslim countries and to complying with international law and human rights law in U.S. relations with Muslim countries. This would likely reduce the threat of terrorism targeted at the United States and, in turn, ease the threat to civil liberties.

A related distinction between Chomsky and Dershowitz is Chomsky's opposition to "aggressive war"—a phenomenon that the United States has initiated frequently, but which seldom is identified by name (when the United States does it) in the United States, as when Dershowitz misleadingly refers to aggressive war by the United States and Israel as "preventive," "preemptive," and "self-defense." Furthermore, whereas Dershowitz views the threat of terrorism against the United States and Israel as seemingly the greatest threat to those two countries and the world, Chomsky views aggressive war by states as a far greater threat. Even after 9/11, the facts show that the greatest threat to civilization, in addition to climate change and its effects, is not terrorism but aggressive war by states, which is a phenomenon to which the civilian population of the United States has been historically immune.

During World War I, for example, which began in 1914 with the Austria-Hungarian invasion of Serbia and the German invasions of Belgium, Luxembourg, and France, approximately 16 million people were killed, including 6.8 million civilians.[29] World War II—which featured the Nazi invasions of Poland, France, and Russia, the Nazi bombing of Britain, and the Japanese invasion of China—killed 62 to 78 million people, including 40 to 52 million civilians.[30] The totals included 757 American civilians killed during World War I and 1,700 American civilians killed during World War II. These figures can be compared, for example, to 1.5 million Russian civilians killed during World War I and 12 to 14 million Russian civilians killed during World War II. Meanwhile, the number of civilians killed due to acts of international terrorism committed on American soil in the twentieth century is 2,979: 2,973 killed on 9/11 and 6 killed on February 26, 1993, during the basement bombing of the North Tower of the World Trade Center. The fact is that the civilian population of the United States has not directly experienced the cataclysmic wars of the twentieth century that the civilian populations of other major nations have experienced on an immense scale. Those experiences for the most part have tempered the desire in other comparable countries to wage elective wars, while the United States, having never been invaded and occupied by a modern mechanized army or bombed for months on end by a powerful air force, has led the call to global war in response to the terrorist attacks on 9/11.

In a series of interviews that he was asked to conduct in the wake of 9/11, which were collected and published as a best-selling book titled *9-11*, Chomsky commented accordingly on the implications of the terrorist attacks that day (parentheses in original):

> The horrifying atrocities of September 11 are something quite new in world affairs, not in their scale and character, but in the target. For the United States, this is the first time since the War of 1812 that the national territory has been under attack, or even threatened. Many commentators have brought up a Pearl Harbor analogy, but that is misleading. On December 7, 1941, military bases in two U.S. colonies were attacked—not the national territory, which was never threatened. The U.S. preferred to call Hawaii a "territory," but it was in effect a colony. [Hawaii became a state in 1959.] During the past several hundred years the U.S. annihilated the indigenous population (millions of people), conquered half of Mexico (in fact, the territories of indigenous peoples, but that is another matter), intervened violently in the surrounding region, conquered Hawaii and the Philippines (killing hundreds of thousands of Filipinos), and, in the past half century particularly, extended its resort to force throughout much of the world. The number of victims is colossal. For the first time [due to 9/11], the guns have been directed the other way. That is a dramatic change.[31]

Rather than support the post–9/11 invasions of Afghanistan and Iraq, Chomsky has argued that the terrorist attacks on New York and Washington by about a dozen individuals should have been treated as a crime against the United States, not as an act of war ostensibly justifying the invasions and occupations of other countries:

> But to keep to the narrow question—the terrorism of others directed against us—we know quite well how the problem should be addressed, if we want to reduce the threat rather than escalate it. When IRA bombs were set off in London, there was no call to bomb West Belfast, or Boston, the source of much of the financial support for the IRA. Rather, steps were taken to apprehend the criminals, and efforts were made to deal with what lay behind the resort to terror. When a federal building was blown up in Oklahoma City [in 1995], there were calls for bombing the Middle East, and it probably would have happened if the source turned out to be there. When it was found to be domestic, with links to the ultra-right militias, there was no call to obliterate Montana and Idaho. Rather, there was a search for the perpetrator, who was found, brought to court, and sentenced, and there were efforts to understand the grievances that lie

behind such crimes and to address the problems. Just about every crime—whether a robbery in the streets or colossal atrocities—has reasons, and commonly we find that some of them are serious and should be addressed.[32]

There is little question that the U.S. resort to war against Muslim countries, in response to the events of 9/11, led to huge humanitarian catastrophes in Afghanistan and Iraq, increased the threat of terrorism targeted at the United States, with the total cost of both wars projected at $3 to $4 trillion.[33] Although Chomsky's comments seem eminently sensible, and have proven to be so a decade after they were first issued in a book published two months after 9/11, they sit far outside mainstream intellectual and political circles in the United States. In the meantime the law that was forged from the worst war in human history—for the most part enlightened in that it featured the prohibition of aggressive war by states—continues to be systematically violated most prominently in the Western world by the United States, even as the disregard of such law is arguably a major source of the terrorism targeted at it from abroad.

Due to the unprecedented tens of millions of casualties during World War II, the Allied powers, in order to outlaw and criminalize aggressive war—such as the German invasions of Poland (1939), France (1940), and Russia (1941)—prosecuted major Nazi war criminals in Nuremberg and played a leading role in the establishment of the United Nations and the UN Charter. In August 1945, the London Charter of the International Military Tribunal (the Nuremberg Charter), drafted by the United States, Britain, France, and the Soviet Union, established the Nuremberg Tribunal "for the just and prompt trial and punishment of the major war criminals of the European Axis." As the first of the three major crimes cited, the Nuremberg Charter defined a war of aggression as a "crime against peace" and the "planning, preparation, initiation or waging" of war "in violation of international treaties, agreements or assurances."[34] Two months later, in October, the tribunal indicted more than twenty German officials for committing crimes against peace (aggressive war), war crimes, and crimes against humanity.

A year after the indictment, the tribunal issued its judgment in September 1946. With respect to crimes against peace, it stated: "The charges in the Indictment that the [Nazi] defendants planned and waged aggressive wars are charges of the utmost gravity. War is essentially an evil thing. Its consequences are not confined to the belligerent states alone, but affect the whole world. To initiate a war of aggression, therefore, is not only an international crime; it is the supreme international crime differing only from other war crimes in that it contains within itself the accumulated evil of the whole."[35] Thus, under the Nuremberg precedent, and pursuant to the most calamitous war in human history, "the supreme international crime" under international law is aggressive war waged on a wholesale basis by states, not terrorism waged "asymmetrically" on a retail basis against such states.

The tribunal found twelve of the German defendants guilty of committing crimes against peace, including Hermann Goering, commander-in-chief of the German Luftwaffe; Joachim von Ribbentrop, Germany's minister of foreign affairs; and Wilhelm Keitel, supreme commander of the German armed forces. For their involvement in the planning and waging of aggressive war in Europe, Goering, Ribbentrop, and Keitel were sentenced to death by hanging.

One year after the Nuremberg Tribunal issued its judgment, the UN General Assembly directed the UN's International Law Commission (ILC) to "formulate the principles of international law recognized in the Charter of the Nuremberg Tribunal and in the judgment of the Tribunal."[36] A few years later, in 1950, the ILC issued the Principles of the Nuremberg Tribunal (the Nuremberg Principles) which, with respect to "crimes against peace," state:

> Principle VI
> The crimes hereinafter set out are punishable under international law:
>   (a) Crimes against Peace
>   (i) Planning, preparation, initiation or waging of a war of aggression or a war in violation of international treaties, agreements or assurances;
>   (ii) Participation in a common plan or conspiracy for the accomplishment of any of the acts mentioned under (i).[37]

Despite the intimate involvement of high American officials in the prosecution and punishment of major Nazi officials for planning and waging aggressive war—a "crime against peace" and "the supreme international crime"—there was very little discussion inside the United States about whether the U.S. invasion of Iraq in 2003 amounted to a war of aggression and crime against peace under the Nuremberg Principles.

Nearly simultaneous to the indictment of Nazi officials, the United Nations was established on October 24, 1945, with its principal purpose being, as stated in the first line of the preamble to the UN Charter, "to save succeeding generations from the scourge of war, which twice in our lifetime has brought untold sorrow to mankind."[38] Accordingly, the widely recognized cardinal rule of the charter requires UN member states to "refrain in their international relations from the threat or use of force against the territorial integrity or political independence of any state,"[39] thereby prohibiting the unilateral resort to force, and even the threat of force, as a legal policy option. There is little doubt that the prohibition against the resort to force and the waging of aggressive war were intended to be the major postwar legal constraints on the conduct of UN member states. Yet, when the

offered these observations about the firebomb attacks on Tokyo and Nagoya: "The American fliers hit the jackpot in the original Tokyo target, ten square miles expanded to seventeen square miles of ruin and homeless throngs. The Nagoya attack was disappointing only because, coming on the heels of the Tokyo smash, the fires it had stoked were checked by the city's entire population after only two square miles had been gutted by the aerial torch."[51]

On March 17, the United States firebombed Kobe, Japan's sixth largest city. The *Times* reported: "More than 300 Superfortresses flashed over Kobe in the dim early morning hours today and at low level sent some 2,500 tons of incendiary bombs crashing on Japan's principal port." According to General LeMay, "twelve square miles of Kobe were completely burned out."[52]

The Americans continued firebombing Japan over a five-month period, partially or mostly destroying over sixty Japanese cities. In the film *The Fog of War*, featuring former defense secretary McNamara, director Errol Morris graphically captured the extent of destruction by listing each Japanese city that was firebombed to a U.S. city of comparable size, while giving the percentage of destruction of each firebombed city in Japan:

51 percent of Tokyo (New York) destroyed
40 percent of Nagoya (Los Angeles)
35 percent of Osaka (Chicago)
55 percent of Kobe (Baltimore)
58 percent of Yokohama (Cleveland)
99 percent of Toyama (Chattanooga)
37 percent of Shimonoseki (San Diego)
69 percent of Nara (Boston)
42 percent of Kure (Toledo)
36 percent of Omuta (Miami)
50 percent of Wanayama (Salt Lake City)
35 percent of Kawasaki (Portland)
21 percent of Yawata (San Antonio)
63 percent of Kagoshima (Richmond)
69 percent of Okayama (Long Beach)
19 percent of Amagasaki (Jacksonville)
41 percent of Sasebo (Nashville)
23 percent of Moji (Spokane)
26 percent of Miya (Greensboro)
25 percent of Nobeoka (Augusta)
26 percent of Miyazaki (Davenport)
20 percent of Ube (Utica)
64 percent of Imabari (Stockton)

64 percent of Matsuyama (Duluth)
48 percent of Hiratsuka (Battle Creek)
48 percent of Tokuyama (Butte)
33 percent of Yokkaichi (Charlotte)
41 percent of Uyamaoa (Columbus)
39 percent of Okaki (Corpus Christi)
69 percent of Gifu (Des Moines)
86 percent of Fukui (Evansville)
85 percent of Tokushima (Ft. Wayne)
48 percent of Sakai (Fort Worth)
65 percent of Hachioji (Galveston)
31 percent of Kumamoto (Grand Rapids)
56 percent of Isezaki (Sioux Falls)
67 percent of Takamatsu (Knoxville)
50 percent of Akashi (Lexington)
81 percent of Fukuyama (Macon)
30 percent of Aomori (Montgomery)
32 percent of Okazaki (Lincoln)
66 percent of Shizuoka (Oklahoma City)
49 percent of Himeji (Peoria)
24 percent of Fukuoka (Rochester)
55 percent of Kochi (Sacramento)
42 percent of Shimizu (San Jose)
33 percent of Omura (Santa Fe)
41 percent of Chiba (Savannah)
56 percent of Ichinomiya (Springfield)
69 percent of Tsu (Topeka)
75 percent of Kuwana (Tucson)
68 percent of Toyohashi (Tulsa)
60 percent of Hamahatsu (Hartford)
42 percent of Numazu (Waco)
44 percent of Choshi (Wheeling)
78 percent of Kofu (South Bend)
43 percent of Utsunomiya (Sioux City)
69 percent of Mito (Pontiac)
22 percent of Senoai (Omaha)
65 percent of Tsuruga (Middletown)
12 percent of Nishinomiya (Cambridge)
65 percent of Nagaoka (Madison)
72 percent of Hitachi (Little Rock)
28 percent of Oita (St. Joseph)

44 percent of Saga (Waterloo)
55 percent of Kenosha (Not Decipherable)
55 percent of Kumagaya (Not Decipherable)

According to Grayling, "nearly half of the built-up areas of sixty-six Japanese cities was destroyed."[53] About the first-night firebombing of Tokyo, General LeMay said: "We scorched and boiled and baked to death more people in Tokyo on that night of March 9–10 than went up in vapor at Hiroshima and Nagasaki."[54]

The extent to which the United States bombed civilian populations in Japan, and the degree to which that bombing campaign functioned as an air-war model for future U.S. wars, was a significant point of analysis by Bruce Cumings, the preeminent American scholar of Korea. In a 2010 book *The Korean War*, Cumings wrote: "What hardly any Americans know or remember, however, is that we carpet-bombed . . . North [Korea] for three years with next to no concern for civilian casualties," and that the bombing was "an application and elaboration of the air campaigns against Japan and Germany" a few years earlier. He continued:

> After much experimentation and scientific study by Germany, Britain, and the United States, by 1943 it became clear that "a city was easier to burn down than to blow up." Combinations of incendiaries and conventional explosives, followed up by delayed-detonation bombs to keep firefighters at bay, could destroy large sections of a city, whereas conventional bombs had a much more limited impact. Magnesium-alloy thermite sticks, manufactured by the million and bundled together, did the trick; when supplemented by mixtures of benzol, rubber, resins, gels, and phosphorus, they formed unprecedentedly destructive blockbuster flaming bombs that could wipe out cities in a matter of minutes.

Cumings quoted General LeMay's claim that, during the Korean War, "we burned down every [sic] town in North Korea and South Korea." Cumings also reported that before napalm was used by American forces in Vietnam, "oceans of it were dropped on Korea silently or without notice in America, with much more devastating effect, since the DPRK [North Korea] had many more populous cities and urban industrial installations than did Vietnam."[55] With respect to the American bombing of Korea, North and South, Cumings wrote that "the scale of urban destruction quite exceeded that in Germany and Japan, according to U.S. Air Force estimates," and that most of North Korea's major cities "were obliterated." Those cities are listed here with the percentage of destruction: Pyongyang (75 percent), Chongjin (65 percent), Hamhung (80 percent), Hungnam (85 percent), Sariwon (95 percent), Sinanju (100 percent), and Wonsan (80 percent).[56]

Referring to another disturbing paradox concerning the relationship between the United States and yet another post–World War II instrument of international law, Cumings wrote: "The United Nations Genocide Convention defined the term as acts committed 'with intent to destroy, in whole or in part, a national, ethnical, racial or religious group.' This would include 'deliberately inflicting on the group conditions of life calculated to bring about its physical destruction in whole or in part.' It was approved in 1948 and entered into force in 1951—just as the USAF [United States Air Force] was inflicting genocide, under this definition and under the aegis of the United Nations Command, on the citizens of North Korea."[57] A decade later, the United States would bomb Indochina as intensively as it bombed Japan and Korea. About the line of succession of U.S. bombing campaigns, Grayling observed that without facing up to the commission of war crimes in Japan and Korea, the United States was bound to repeat the same practices in the future.[58]

In an apt summary of the enormous number of civilian casualties in World War II, Selden wrote that the war "remains unrivaled in the number of people killed and the scale of the mass destruction," although "it was not the bombing of cities [in Japan by the Americans and in Germany by the British] but Nazi genocide, the German invasion of the Soviet Union, and the Japanese slaughter of rural Asians that exacted the heaviest price in lives"; however, the U.S. strategy in Japan "of killing noncombatants through air power runs like a red line from the bombings of 1944–45 through the Korean and Indochinese wars to the Gulf, Afghanistan, and Iraq wars."[59]

Given this history of U.S. air wars, one could plausibly assert that there is an unacknowledged addiction—like smoking cigarettes in the 1950s—to bombing other countries. Unsurprisingly, in four published articles for *Huffington Post*, from November 2010 to March 2012,[60] Dershowitz does his part to push the addiction in both Israel and the United States, even beyond his support of Israel's bombings of Lebanon and Gaza. A good example is Dershowitz's March 2011 article titled "Israel Has the Right to Attack Iran's Nuclear Reactors Now." What is the alleged "right" under law for Israel and/or the United States to bomb Iran, as he has proposed? Aside from writing arbitrarily and without elaboration in any legal sense that "even the UN Charter authorizes a unilateral response to an armed attack," Dershowitz never identified any such legal right to bomb Iran.

What, then, was Dershowitz's factual basis for alleging an Israeli "right to attack Iran's nuclear reactors now"? Dershowitz supposedly identified it in the first sentence of his article: "Iran's *recent attempt to ship arms to Hamas* in Gaza is an act of war committed by the Iranian government against the Israeli government."[61] The words in italics were hyperlinked to a blog on the Fox News Web site, which reported that the Israeli military had seized fifty tons of weapons "allegedly en route from Iran to militants in the Gaza Strip."[62] Note that Fox News reported that the weapons were "allegedly" en route from Iran. I should also point out that the date of the Fox News report was March 16, 2011, and that the date of Dershowitz's article on *Huffington Post* was . . . March 16, 2011. Did Dershowitz somehow substantiate, that very day, a report by a blogger at Fox News that Iran had *actually*, and not merely *allegedly*, shipped weapons to Hamas? Dershowitz doesn't say.

Furthermore, Dershowitz's second sentence in the *Huffington Post* article stated: "The Israeli Navy seized the ship, loaded with weapons designed to kill Israeli civilians, and traced the weapons back to Iran."[63] According to Dershowitz, then, the weapons that were allegedly seized from Iran also were "designed to kill Israeli civilians." But there was no such allegation about "Israeli civilians" in Dershowitz's only referenced source (Fox News). And while most weapon systems can be used to target civilians, Dershowitz's claim that the end-use of the weapons was to "kill Israeli civilians" apparently was his own value-added accent to the Fox News account, which itself was grounded exclusively in Israeli government sources.[64] Thus, Dershowitz's claim that Iran had engaged in "an act of war" against Israel, and that Israel in turn had a "right" to attack Iran "now," was grounded solely on a report from Fox News, which itself referenced only the Israeli government, and which only "alleged" an Iranian connection to a supposed smuggled shipment of weapons.

And even assuming that Iran did ship weapons to Hamas, the weapons shipment was reportedly intercepted, and therefore never made it to Hamas to use against Israel. Thus, no Hamas military action against Israel, using the alleged shipment of smuggled weapons, ever occurred. Without an actual "armed attack" against Israel, it is not possible to assert, as Dershowitz did, an Israeli right to resort to force in response to an "armed attack."

Nor had Dershowitz exhibited any rigor while claiming that Iran had developed a nuclear weapons program. For example, in November 2010 on *Huffington Post*, Dershowitz wrote: "Under George Bush's watch, the United States issued its notorious National Intelligence Estimate of November 2007, which essentially denied that Iran was seeking to develop nuclear weapons. This report was known to be false at the time it was issued since American intelligence became aware of the nuclear weapons facility at Qum [Iran] before the report was issued."[65] Dershowitz neglected to reference a source for this assertion. And aside from the 2007 U.S. National Intelligence Estimate (NIE), which he simply disregarded, Dershowitz mentioned none of the several authoritative reports citing a lack of evidence of an Iranian nuclear weapons program.[66]

In addition, Dershowitz's reference to the 2007 NIE on Iran misstated its findings. In a declassified summary of the 2007 report, the NIE concluded as follows: "We judge with high confidence that in fall 2003, Tehran halted its nuclear weapons program; we also assess with moderate-to-high confidence that Tehran at a minimum is keeping open the option to develop nuclear weapons."[67] Thus, the 2007 NIE did not deny, as Dershowitz claimed, "that Iran was seeking to develop nuclear weapons"; rather, the NIE concluded that Iran was possibly "keeping open the option to develop nuclear weapons," while also reporting that, for now (2007), Iran has "halted its nuclear weapons program."[68]

Furthermore, there is no mention of any nuclear weapons facility at Qum in the summary of the 2010 NIE on Iran by James Risen and Mark Mazzetti in the *New York Times* in February 2012.[69] Nor is there any mention of any nuclear weapons facility at Qum in the equally authoritative June 2011 summary by Seymour Hersh in the *New Yorker* of the 2010 and 2011 NIE reports on Iran.[70] And, for the record, with respect to what Dershowitz referred to as the "notorious" 2007 NIE on Iran, Risen and Mazzetti reported in February 2012: "Recent assessments by American spy agencies are broadly consistent with a 2007 intelligence finding that concluded that Iran had abandoned its nuclear weapons program years earlier, according to current and former American officials. The officials said that assessment was largely reaffirmed in a 2010 National Intelligence Estimate, and that it remains the consensus view of America's 16 intelligence agencies."[71] Hersh likewise reported in June 2011: "The two most recent National Intelligence Estimates on Iranian nuclear progress, representing the best judgment of the senior officers from all the major American intelligence agencies, have stated that there is no conclusive evidence that Iran has made any effort to build the bomb since 2003."[72]

Similar problems arise when we consider Dershowitz's claims about Israel's so-called "preemptive" 1981 bombing of the Osirak nuclear reactor in Iraq. In his 2006 book *Preemption*, Dershowitz wrote:

> The Israeli military action most frequently cited in the current debate over preemption is the one-strike destruction of Iraq's nuclear reactor in 1981. As Professor Michael Reisman put it in the *American Journal of International Law*, "International law has been grappling with the claim of preemptive self-defense for decades. . . . The Israeli destruction of the Osirak reactor near Baghdad in 1981 was a quintessential preemptive action." Although the UN Security Council unanimously condemned Israel's attack as "in clear violation of the Charter of the United Nations and the norms of international conduct," as we shall see, Israel's preemptive action has—over time—become accepted as a proper and proportional example of anticipatory self-defense in the nuclear age. It is extremely relevant therefore to current options under consideration, especially with regard to Iran's efforts to become a nuclear power."[73]

Here Dershowitz appears to concede that Israel's attack on Iraq's Osirak nuclear reactor violated the UN Charter's prohibition against the use and threat of force and "the norms of international conduct"; yet, Dershowitz asserts, falsely, that Israel's "preemptive" bombing of the Osirak reactor has "become accepted" as "a proper and proportional example of anticipatory self-defense."

For one thing, it is odd that Dershowitz would endorse a statement characterizing the Israeli attack on the Osirak nuclear facility as a "quintessential preemptive action," which by definition is an armed response to an imminent military threat, given that Dershowitz in *Preemption* described the disposition of the Iraqi nuclear weapons threat in 1981 as neither imminent nor certain: "In spite of the lack of imminence and certainty to the threat posed by the Iraqi reactor, the Israeli government after much consideration concluded that the potential benefits [of bombing the Osirak reactor] outweighed the risks because the magnitude of the threat (even discounted by the lack of imminence and certainty) was so cataclysmic." "In other words," Dershowitz wrote, "even if there was only a 5 percent likelihood that Iraq would deploy a nuclear weapon against Israel in the succeeding ten years, the magnitude of the potential harm—hundreds of thousands, perhaps even millions of deaths and injuries to its civilian population—was more than enough to justify a preemptive strike."[74]

There was even less imminence, it seems, when we consider the assessments by independent experts of the nuclear weapons capability of the Osirak facility. Dan Reiter, for example, is a professor of political science at Emory University who has written extensively about the Israeli attack on the Osirak nuclear reactor.[75] In an article published in 2005 in *Nonproliferation Review*, Reiter wrote that Iraq "began to consider acquiring nuclear weapons as early as 1971 in reaction to fears of an Israeli nuclear arsenal." Reiter then described why the Osirak nuclear reactor was not suitable for nuclear weapons production:

> Starting around the end of 1974, Iraq began negotiating with France to purchase an additional nuclear reactor. The Iraqis wished to purchase a gas-graphite reactor, which would have generated enough plutonium to produce five to eight nuclear warheads per year. The French did not supply the gas-graphite reactor, and instead agreed in 1975 to supply a 70-megawatt (-MW) material-test research reactor called the Osiris model, supplemented with a smaller Isis reactor; this pair of reactors came to be known as Osirak. The French-supplied reactor, less efficient at plutonium production than a gas-graphite model, was a light water-moderated swimming-pool reactor, meaning that the reactor elements were submerged in a container of plain water. The reactor was part of Iraq's quest for a nuclear weapon.[76]

While Reiter reported that then vice president Saddam Hussein announced that the purchase of the French reactors was the first step in the production of an Arab atomic bomb, Reiter also reported that "the reactor itself was not well equipped to generate plutonium for a nuclear weapon," and that "illegal plutonium production would likely have caused a cutoff in the supply of nuclear fuel."[77]

Writing also in 2005 in a letter to *Atlantic Monthly*, Reiter explained further why "the French-supplied reactor at Osirak was not well-designed for plutonium production":

> More important, a rigorous inspection regime was in place to ensure that plutonium could not be produced and secretly diverted to a weapons program. The International Atomic Energy Agency was in the process of installing an extensive inspection regime that would probably have included twenty-four-hour camera surveillance and frequent on-site visits from IAEA inspectors (the reactor was not yet operative at the time of the attack). The French themselves had technicians on hand who filed frequent reports. France opposed Iraq's acquiring nuclear weapons, and would have suspended the supply of reactor fuel if evidence of plutonium production had been uncovered. The diversion of plutonium would have been difficult to conceal, given that it would have involved a number of non-routine activities, including possibly shutting down the reactor. Imad Khadduri, a former scientist in the Iraqi Atomic Energy Commission under Saddam Hussein, bluntly declares in his recent memoir that the idea that plutonium could be produced under this inspection regime without tipping off IAEA inspectors or French technicians is "delusional."[78]

And because Israel's 1981 strike on the Osirak reactor ultimately prompted Saddam Hussein to pursue a clandestine nuclear weapons program that was more geographically dispersed throughout Iraq to foil any future strikes on its nuclear facilities, a number of analysts have concluded that Israel's so-called preemptive strike hastened Iraq's nuclear weapons capability. For example, Reiter wrote that Israel's attack "may have actually increased Saddam's commitment to acquiring weapons."[79] Writing in the MIT journal *International Security*, Malfrid Braut-Hegghammer, a post-doctoral fellow at the Kennedy School of Government at Harvard, also wrote that the 1981 Israeli attack on Osirak "suggests that preventive attacks can increase the long-term proliferation risk posed by the targeted state."[80] Richard K. Betts, director of the Arnold A. Saltzman Institute of War and Peace Studies at Columbia University, concluded: "Contrary to prevalent mythology, there is no evidence that Israel's destruction of Osirak delayed Iraq's nuclear weapons program. The attack may actually have accelerated it."[81] And in *Foreign Policy*, Stephen M. Walt of Harvard University, who originally cited the sequence of sources just listed, wrote in March 2012 that "the destruction of Osirak led to an elite consensus that Iraq needed its own deterrent, and led Saddam Hussein to order a redoubling of Iraq's nuclear program in a more clandestine fashion." Walt argued that the Israeli preventive strike "reinforced Iraq's interest in acquiring a deterrent, and led Iraq to pursue it in ways that were more difficult to detect or prevent," and "that is what Iran is likely to do as well if Israel or the United States were foolish enough to strike them."[82]

Chomsky's perspective on Iran again stands in sharp contrast to Dershowitz's repeated appeals to the American public to support a U.S./Israeli bombing of Iran's nuclear sites. In an interview in 2007, for example, Chomsky said:

> Three years ago, the European Union and Iran made a bargain. Iran says they're enriching uranium for the development of nuclear energy. If that's what they're doing it's entirely within the framework of the Nuclear Non-Proliferation Treaty. . . . [I]n return—here's the other half of the bargain—the European Union would provide firm guarantees on security issues. The phrase "security issues" refers to U.S.-Israeli threats to bomb Iran, which are very serious. . . . However, Europe did not live up to its half of the bargain. Apparently under U.S. pressure, it backed off. It did not make any offer to provide any guarantees of security. Shortly after, Iran backed off from its side of the bargain. . . . They're back to enriching uranium, and we don't know for what purposes.
>
> No one wants Iran to get nuclear weapons. If there were a real interest in preventing that, what would happen is you would reduce the [U.S. and Israeli] threats, which are making it likely that that they'll develop them as a deterrent; implement the bargain that was made; and then move toward integrating Iran into the general international economic system; remove the sanctions, which are against the people, not the government; and just bring them into the world system. The U.S. refuses. Europe does what the U.S. orders them to do.[83]

More recently about Iran, in February 2012, Chomsky wrote:

> Why exactly is Iran regarded as such a colossal threat? The question is rarely discussed, but it is not hard to find a serious answer—though not, as usual, in the fevered pronouncements. The most authoritative answer is provided by the Pentagon and the intelligence services in their regular reports to Congress on global security. They report that Iran does not pose a military threat. Its military spending is very low even by the standards of the region, minuscule of course in comparison with the U.S.
>
> Iran has little capacity to deploy force. Its strategic doctrines are defensive, designed to deter invasion long enough for diplomacy to set in. If Iran is developing nuclear weapons capability, they report, that

would be part of its deterrence strategy. No serious analyst believes that the ruling clerics are eager to see their country and possessions vaporized, the immediate consequence of their coming even close to initiating a nuclear war. And it is hardly necessary to spell out the reasons why any Iranian leadership would be concerned with deterrence, under existing circumstances.

The regime is doubtless a serious threat to much of its own population—and regrettably, is hardly unique on that score. But the primary threat to the U.S. and Israel is that Iran might deter their free exercise of violence. A further threat is that the Iranians clearly seek to extend their influence to neighboring Iraq and Afghanistan, and beyond as well. Those "illegitimate" acts are called "destabilizing" (or worse). In contrast, forceful imposition of U.S. influence halfway around the world contributes to "stability" and order, in accord with traditional doctrine about who owns the world.[84]

In dark contrast to Chomsky once again, Dershowitz ultimately recommends the following course of action with respect to Iran's nuclear facilities: "Israel (with the help of the United States) should first try everything short of military action—diplomacy, threats, bribery, sabotage, targeted killings of individuals essential to the Iranian nuclear program, and other covert actions—but if all else fails, it (or the United States) must have the option of taking out the Iranian nuclear threat before it is capable of the genocide for which its leaders assert it is being built."[85]

For Dershowitz, what if Iran, at least for now, has no nuclear weapons program, as the U.S. National Intelligence Assessments have asserted? For him, the absence of an Iranian nuclear weapons program would not eliminate the necessity of a "preemptive" or "preventive" Israeli attack on Iran. In *Preemption*, Dershowitz drew an analogy as follows to the U.S. invasion of Iraq and the failure to find Iraqi WMD: "At every level, preventive decisions [to resort to force] must be based on uncertain predictions, which will rarely be anywhere close to 100 percent accurate. We must be prepared to accept some false positives (predictions of harm that would not have occurred) in order to prevent some predicted harms from causing irreparable damage."[86] Thus, by Dershowitz's logic, there should be no legally legitimate prohibition on the exercise of the use of force against Iran by the United States or Israel, given his jurisprudence of the rule of false positives, which, if universally applied, would permit even the Nazis to allude to their claim of the threat of Europe's Jews to the German nation as a mere mistake.

DERSHOWITZ'S AUTHORITARIANISM

It is feared by at least one constitutional law scholar that a second terrorist attack on the United States on the scale of 9/11 or worse would lead to the long-term destruction of civil liberties in the United States. In his 2006 book published by Yale University Press, *Before the Next Attack: Preserving Civil Liberties in An Age of Terrorism*, Bruce Ackerman, Sterling Professor of Law and Political Science at Yale University, wrote that "the next major attack may kill and maim one hundred thousand innocents, dwarfing the personal anguish suffered by those who lost family and friends on 9/11." The "political panic" that would ensue, Ackerman fears, would "threaten to leave behind a wave of repressive legislation far more drastic than anything imagined by the Patriot Act."[1] Ackerman is a political liberal and a civil libertarian who wrote his book to express a concern about the future of civil liberties in the United States. While he doesn't predict another major terrorist attack like 9/11, he would like to see the country better prepared from a civil liberties standpoint should another attack occur.

Despite a sensible premise, however, Ackerman's analysis goes badly wrong. His book, a study in his words of "lesser evils," credits the problematic work of Michael Ignatieff[2] and features the presentation of an "emergency constitution" of Ackerman's design, which he defines as "a limited state of emergency" to "allow for effective short-term measures that will do everything plausible to stop a second strike, but which firmly draws the line against permanent restrictions" on civil liberties.[3] "Above all else," Ackerman continues, "we must prevent politicians from exploiting momentary panic to impose long-lasting limitations on liberty."[4] Yet, Ackerman's protective remedy does unacceptable harm to civil liberties, given what it features, as he describes: "Defining the scope of emergency powers is a serious and sensitive business. But at its core, it involves the short-term detention of suspected terrorists to prevent a second strike. Nobody will be detained for more than forty-five days, and then only on reasonable suspicion. Once the forty-five days have elapsed, the government must satisfy the higher evidentiary standards that apply in ordinary criminal prosecutions. And even during the period of preventive detention, judges will be authorized to intervene to protect against torture and other abuses."[5] In addition to the surprise suggestion of preventive detention, Ackerman's procedural measures to protect civil liberties seem inadequate. In a follow-up volume published by Harvard University Press in 2010, Ackerman repeated his call for an emergency constitution featuring preventive detention and explained, as he did in his 2006 book, how a "super-majoritarian escalator" would function as a lever of constitutional protection permitting a short-term transfer of emergency powers to the president in the event of another attack. Thus, Ackerman wrote:

> Congress should authorize the president to act decisively in the imme-
> diate aftermath of a terrorist attack—and take emergency steps to
> preempt a second strike. But on the other hand, it should take special
> steps to prevent the president from exploiting momentary panic to
> impose long-lasting limitations on liberty.
>
> Here is a framework: My emergency statute begins by granting the
> president a broad range of extraordinary powers—but only for a week or
> two while Congress is considering the next step. His powers will then
> expire unless a majority of both Houses vote to continue them—but even
> this show of support only extends his emergency powers for two more
> months. The president must then return to Congress for reauthorization,
> and this time, a supermajority of 60 percent should be required; two
> months more, 70 percent; and 80 percent for every two-month extension
> thereafter. Except for the worst terrorist onslaughts, this "supermajoritar-
> ian escalator" will terminate extraordinary measures within a relatively
> short period.[6]

One problem with Ackerman's framework is that U.S. intelligence and federal law-enforcement agencies report to the president; in the context of Ackerman's state of emergency, and in the immediate aftermath of a terrorist attack, the Congress would be at the mercy of presidential discretion about information sharing, especially if the president was inclined to hold onto his or her emergency powers. The executive information monopoly would confer an advantage to the president in any institutional contest to extend or curtail the president's powers.

There is also a sordid history of "supermajoritarian" votes in the Congress that further problematizes Ackerman's proposal. For example, on August 7, 1964, the House voted 416 to 0 and the Senate 88 to 2 to back President Johnson's decision to bomb North Vietnam in response to the false reports from the president that two U.S. destroyers had been fired upon by North Vietnamese boats in the Gulf of Tonkin. This nearly unanimous congressional vote, which authorized the "Commander in Chief to take all necessary measures to repel any armed attack against the forces of the United States and to prevent further aggression," was a major gateway to open-ended U.S. war in Vietnam.[7] On September 14, 2001, the House voted 420 to 1 and the Senate 98 to 0 "to authorize the use of United States Armed Forces against those responsible for the recent attacks launched against the United States" on 9/11, which led to the U.S. invasion and drawn-out military occupation of Afghanistan. And in October 2002, the House voted 296 to 133 (69 percent majority) and the Senate 77 to 23 (77 percent majority) to authorize President George W. Bush to resort to military force against Iraq "as he determines to be necessary and appropriate" in order to "defend the national security of the United States against the continuing threat posed by Iraq."[8] This vote, with a 69 percent majority in the House and a 77 percent majority in the Senate, exceeded the 60 percent congressional supermajority required by Ackerman for a two-month extension of the president's emergency powers, nearly satisfies the 70 percent majority for a four-month extension, and is uncomfortably close to the 80 percent majority required for the indefinite extensions of the state of emergency. Given the history of supermajoritarian congressional deferrals to presidential authority, it seems that Ackerman's proposed state of emergency would likely facilitate a constitutional crisis rather than prevent one.[9]

In the approximate center among elite constitutional commentators is Philip B. Heymann, James Barr Ames Professor of Law at Harvard Law School and former deputy attorney general under President Bill Clinton. In his work on terrorism and civil liberties, Heymann, like Ackerman, zigzags between sensible and extreme positions. For example, Ackerman wrote: "I do not minimize the terrorist threat. But we shouldn't lose all historical perspective: terrorism is a very serious problem, but it doesn't remotely suggest a return to the darkest times of the Civil War or World War II."[10] He continued: "This fundamental point is erased by an unthinking repetition of war talk. If the struggle with terrorism counts as a 'war,' it is all too easy for lawyers and judges to cite the wartime precedents of Lincoln and Roosevelt as if they were germane to our present predicament. After all, war is war, isn't it?"[11]

Ackerman also is skeptical about whether federal judges would be willing to stand alone between any post-terror state of emergency and the Bill of Rights, even though he relies elsewhere in his book on judges to do so: "We will suffer grievous casualties in future attacks, but the only thing that threatens our polity is the war talk that we hear around us. It is precisely this rhetoric that will encourage courts to rubber-stamp presidential decisions to respond to terrorist attacks with escalating cycles of repression. If the courts don't challenge the language of war, they will ultimately acquiesce in the permanent destruction of our liberties."[12] Similarly, in his 2003 book published by MIT Press, *Terrorism, Freedom, and Security: Winning without War*, Heymann sensibly writes: "War on terrorism is the wrong theme. Reliance on the military is the wrong set of priority activities" against "opponents that do not have the powers of a state, or hope to defeat our armies, or destroy our powerful economy, or threaten to occupy our territory."[13]

Yet, in the same book, Heymann did not oppose or directly criticize the 2003 U.S. invasion of Iraq, and he supported the U.S. invasion of Afghanistan in response to 9/11: "Whatever one's views on the wisdom of trying to reduce the dangers of terrorism by attacking Iraq in 2003, the initial commitment to war in Afghanistan was plainly wise."[14] Heymann explains:

> Al Qaeda was able to recruit, train, plan, and marshal resources to attack far more easily because the government of Afghanistan tolerated and supported these activities. Much of the world was prepared to accept our expanded definition of national self-defense—the standard required by Article 51 of the UN Charter—when we declared that harboring those activities was a hostile threat to U.S. security. We have dealt with that state support by a military campaign that should also be a warning to other states. Such open help will not be available, risk free, in the future to groups threatening violence against U.S. citizens and interests at home or abroad.
>
> War in Afghanistan had other benefits. Much of the motivation for the attacks on September 11 may have been to turn the passive resentment of felt victimization into heroic hopes in much of Islam by showing the vulnerability of the United States to Islamic terrorists and proving its inability to retaliate effectively. This would increase enthusiasm for violent action in any pool of people deeply hostile to the United States. Our successful war in Afghanistan has helped deny these dangerous rewards to terrorists. . . .
>
> Other factors favored treating the conflict with the Taliban as a war. The conflict depended in far larger measure on the activities of the U.S. military than on intelligence agencies, the State Department, or the Justice Department. The number of armed and dangerous individuals we faced was beyond the operational capacity and beyond the physical reach of our judicial system. Useful or even necessary measures involving a significant amount of collateral damage depended for their legality on this being a war.[15]

Thus, on one hand, Heymann argued that war is the wrong way to respond to foreign groups like Al-Qaeda and the Taliban, which, as Heymann correctly observed, have no ability to defeat our armies, destroy our economy, or occupy our territory; yet, in the same book he supported the invasion and occupation of Afghanistan as the means to respond to the terrorist actions of Al-Qaeda. A decade later, the United States is still waging that "successful" war in Afghanistan, Al-Qaeda migrated out of Afghanistan, the Taliban remains, the Bush and Obama administrations expanded the war to Pakistan and Yemen, and the threat of terrorism against the United States apparently remains.

Despite these serious problems in their work, I don't doubt that Ackerman and Heymann are genuinely concerned about the long-term implications of the "war on terror" on civil liberties. However, both seem to reflect an elite conformist consensus about the presumptively benign disposition of U.S. policy toward the Muslim world, and neither one questions whether the genesis of the terrorist threat to the United States can be located in U.S. policy toward Muslim populations. For example, there is no mention in Ackerman's book (2006) or Heymann's (2003)—both of which focus on the threat of Muslim terrorism on the United States—of one of the worst humanitarian catastrophes in the Muslim world in modern times, which was brought about by the close sequence of the 1991 U.S. bombardment of Iraq during the "Gulf War" and the U.S.-led trade sanctions against Iraq from 1990 to 2003. A study published in the *New England Journal of Medicine* in September 1992 "provide[d] strong evidence that the [1991] Gulf war and trade sanctions caused a three-fold increase in mortality among Iraqi children under five years of age," which meant that "an excess of more than 46,900 [Iraqi] children died between January and August 1991."[16]

The continuing trade sanctions increased that death toll by a factor of ten within just a few years. A study published in the *American Journal of Public Health* in 2000 "examined the effect of sanctions on mortality among Iraqi children" and found that "the risk of dying increased dramatically" throughout the 1990s.[17] Also in 2000, authors of a study published in *Lancet* reported that during the 1990s "in the south/center of Iraq . . . under-5 mortality rose from 56 to 131 per 1000 live births."[18] And a UNICEF survey published in August 2000 estimated that, due to the U.S.-led sanctions against Iraq, "about half a million [Muslim] children under 5 years of age have died, who ordinarily would not have died."[19] Although this casualty toll of approximately 500,000 very young Muslim children was known worldwide in the years prior to 9/11,[20] there is no mention either by Ackerman or Heymann of the U.S.-led trade sanctions against Iraq and its consequences as being possibly relevant to the Muslim terrorism targeted at the United States. Nor did Heymann mention the embargo against Iraq and its impact on Iraqi children in his subsequent books on terrorism and civil liberties, *Protecting Liberty in an Age of Terror* (with Juliette N. Kayyem) (2005) and *Laws, Outlaws, and Terrorists* (with Gabriella Blum) (2010); nor did Ackerman in *The Decline and Fall of the American Republic* (2010).[21]

In fact, despite numerous reports linking U.S. policy toward the Muslim world to an increased threat of Muslim terrorism aimed at the United States, there is little discussion in these books by Ackerman or Heymann of U.S. policy toward the Muslim world. There is no discussion worth citing of the terrorism implications of U.S. economic, political, and military support of Israel's forty-five-year occupation and civilian settlement of the Palestinian territories. Nor is there any discussion of the Fourth Geneva Convention as applied to the Israeli settlements, or of Israel's illegal separation wall built on the Palestinian side of the Green Line.[22]

In *Before the Next Attack*, Ackerman explained, in a seemingly confused manner, that he intentionally avoided discussing U.S. and Israeli policy, since his focus was on "a very particular problem," that is, "how to respond to attacks, like September 11, which don't involve a serious threat of political takeover by the attackers." Thus, "from this vantage," recurrent references to Iraq and Israel "would muddle, not clarify, my argument." Yet, in the same paragraph, Ackerman wrote: "The entire aim of this book has been to move beyond a superficial view of terrorism as a technique, and insist that we can't assess any technique without a close attention to the political context in which it arises."[23] What is the "political context" in which terrorism targeted at the United States arises if not U.S. policy toward the people from whom the terrorism emanates? Indeed, in their 2010 book published by MIT Press, *Laws, Outlaws, and Terrorists: Lessons from the War on Terrorism*, Gabriella Blum, a professor of law at Harvard and former legal counsel for the Israel Defense Forces, and Heymann devote a substantial amount of space to the question of moral support for terrorism in the Muslim world and list "the ten possible sources of hostility" in Muslim countries toward the United States, including the following.

U.S. Military Imperialism. On this count, Blum and Heymann cite 2006 and 2010 Pew surveys in Muslim countries, a 2009 World Public Opinion poll, and a 2008 British MI5 internal research document, which reported that a majority of Muslims believe "that the American military presence in Iraq was 'an equal or greater danger to stability in the Middle East than the regime of Iranian president Mahmoud Ahmadinejad'" (Pew 2006), that a majority "are worried about a military threat from the United States" while fewer than 20 percent favor "the U.S.-led efforts to fight terrorism" (Pew 2010), that a majority "perceive U.S. military imperialism and aggression" as "a significant source of Muslim hostility" and "support Al-Qaeda's goal of pushing the United States 'to remove its bases and its military forces from all Islamic countries'" (World Public Opinion 2009), and that "the most pressing current threat is from Islamist extremist groups who justify the use of violence 'in defense of Islam'" (MI5 2008).

Our Contempt for and Disrespect of Islam. The authors report that polls "sustain the idea that there is a strong belief throughout the Muslim world that the United States is disrespectful toward Islam," that "the United States is attempting to undermine Islamic unity and spread Christianity," and that "the United States purposely tries to humiliate the Islamic world."

U.S. Cultural Imperialism. The authors note that "Western 'cultural saturation' is one of the top reasons for resentment against the United States, particularly among the politically radicalized Muslim population."

Our Position in the Arab-Israeli Conflict. Blum and Heymann also report that "the polls endorse the supposition that the United States' role in the Arab-Israeli conflict is a major source of Muslim hostility" against the United States. The hostility includes broad Muslim opposition to U.S. support for Israel in its conflict with the Palestinians and the Muslim "belief" that "the United States favors the expansion of Israel's national territory."

Our Abuse of Power. The authors note that in the Muslim world "substantial majorities see the United States as hypocritically failing to abide by international law while pressuring other countries to do so," and that "the United States is illegitimately wielding its power."

Economic Imperialism. "Huge majorities of those polled in predominately Muslim countries," Blum and Heymann write, "believe that the United States wants to 'maintain control over the oil resources of the Middle East'" and that "majorities in Muslim nations and some Western European nations view the entire war on terrorism as just 'an effort to control Mideast oil or dominate the world.'"[24]

Blum and Heymann also summarized the findings of the seven-year Gallup poll project, published in 2008 as *Who Speaks for Islam? What a Billion Muslims Really Think*,[25] which "found that the two beliefs most closely associated with the 7 percent of [Muslim] respondents who believed that 9/11 was completely justified" were "(1) that the West is denying respect to and is responsible for the humiliation of Islam, and (2) that Islam's territory and its culture are under aggressive attack from the West and must be defended." "Moreover," Blum and Heymann report, while citing the Gallup study, that "the politically radicalized individuals are significantly more likely to believe that Western societies do not 'show any concern for better coexistence with the Arab-Muslim world.'"[26]

While Blum and Heymann were astute and studious in identifying so thoroughly the sources of hostility in the Muslim world toward the United States, they advised a two-step U.S. response—about how to change what Muslims think: "Although we may not be able to, and should not, change all of the factors that incite Muslim hostility, designing a public diplomacy campaign with an accurate picture of the views of the Muslim world is a start. There is a second step. Besides weakening views of the United States that can lead to public support for terrorism, we must also seek to build up preexisting objections to [Muslim] terrorism and its target of innocent civilians."[27] In addition to recommending a U.S. "public diplomacy"[28] campaign aimed at the Muslim world in order to reduce moral support for terrorism aimed at the United States—as opposed to making any significant changes to U.S. economic, military, and foreign policies—the authors question whether the public diplomacy would work, since "the United States may lack the capacity to change the relevant root beliefs held by large numbers in Muslim countries by any material degree, as they may not be subject to argument and evidence."[29]

This is a very different set of policy recommendations compared to the proposals in the 2007 book *Less Safe, Less Free: Why America Is Losing the War on Terror* by David Cole, professor of law at the Georgetown University Law Center, and Jules Lobel, professor of law at the University of Pittsburgh School of Law. For example, in a chapter titled "A Preventive Foreign Policy," about the U.S. dependence on oil from the Middle East, Cole and Lobel write:

> A good part of our vulnerability to terrorists can be traced to our dependence on oil. Our dominant presence in the Middle East and our support of repressive governments there is largely attributable to the fact that we consume 25 percent of the world's oil but possess only 3 percent [of the population]. As a result, we are heavily dependent on the Middle East, and many of our priorities and policies are skewed by that fact of economic life. As a blue-ribbon committee sponsored by the Century Foundation noted, "the greater our dependence on foreign oil, the greater our exposure to the will of other nations and terrorists."[30]

About the Israel-Palestine conflict, Cole and Lobel write: "Resolution of the Israeli-Palestinian conflict is absolutely critical to reducing tensions in the Middle East and eliminating one of the most powerful rallying cries of Islamic terrorists. While it has long been noted that bin Laden focused on Palestine only belatedly, it can hardly be denied that that conflict plays a central role in fueling anti-American and pro-jihadist feeling around the world today."[31] Overall, Cole and Lobel conclude: "One cannot fight terrorism without understanding its roots." Blum and Heymann appeared to reach the halfway point of this essential aim, before proposing primarily a U.S. public diplomacy effort aimed at the Muslim world as opposed to any fundamental changes in U.S. policy.

While Ackerman, Heymann, and Blum seem ambivalent, at least in part, about what they think should be done about the problem of terrorism threatening the United States—Ackerman is concerned about the impact on civil liberties of terrorism targeting the United States but proposes a preventive detention program in response to the next terrorist attack; Heymann is opposed in principle to the war paradigm as the consensus U.S. response to the threat of terrorism but supports the U.S. invasion and occupation of Afghanistan and seems unsure about the invasion of Iraq; and Blum and Heymann skillfully detail the grievances in the Muslim world about U.S.

policies yet decline to recommend any significant changes to U.S. policy—the right-wing legal scholar, Richard Posner, presents a more assured, but more worrisome, approach to the threat of terrorism against the United States.

At the outset of his 2006 book published by Oxford University Press, *Not a Suicide Pact: The Constitution in a Time of National Emergency*, Posner, a judge for the United States Court of Appeals for the Seventh Circuit in Chicago and a senior lecturer at the University of Chicago Law School, describes the threat of terrorism against the United States as he sees it:

> Now, in the early years of the twenty-first century, the nation faces the intertwined menaces of global terrorism and proliferation of weapons of mass destruction. A city can be destroyed by an atomic bomb the size of a melon, which if coated with lead would be undetectable. Large stretches of a city can be rendered uninhabitable, perhaps for decades, merely by the explosion of a conventional bomb that has been coated with radioactive material. Smallpox virus bioengineered to make it even more toxic and vaccines ineffectual, then aerosolized and sprayed in a major airport, might kill millions of people. Our terrorist enemies have the will to do such things and abundant opportunities, because our borders are porous both to enemies and to containers. They will soon have the means as well.[32]

On one page, Posner writes, "I am not a Chicken Little,"[33] yet on the next page, and in contrast to the more measured assessment of the threat of terrorism to the United States as viewed by Ackerman and Heymann, he asserts: "The research that I have been conducting for the past several years on catastrophic risks, international terrorism, and national security intelligence has persuaded me that we live in a time of grave and increasing danger, comparable to what the nation faced at the outset of World War II."[34] Posner then identifies the enemy who is comparable today, in his view, to the threat of Nazi Germany: "[T]he external enemies whom Americans mainly fear are Islamist terrorists. And with good reason: they are numerous, fanatical, implacable, elusive, resourceful, resilient, utterly ruthless, seemingly fearless, apocalyptic in their aims, and eager to get their hands on weapons of mass destruction and use them against us."[35] Nor is the Islamist threat, for Posner, merely external; it is also internal and invisible. Thus, he writes: "Rooting out an invisible enemy in our midst might be fatally inhibited if we felt constrained to strict observance of civil liberties designed in and for eras in which the only serious internal threat (apart from spies) came from common criminals."[36]

Although he reports researching the Islamic threat for several years, it is surprising that there is no mention in his book, unlike the book by Cole and Lobel, of the Israel-Palestine conflict. The words "Palestine" or "Palestinian" make no appearance in Posner's book. Nor do the words "West Bank," "settlements," "Gaza," "Jerusalem," or "Fourth Geneva Convention." The word "Israel" appears once, in the book's conclusion, in the context of Posner's summary of a threat about which he provides little explanation of its origins: "What the current [U.S.] administration calls the 'war on terrorism' is not a conventional war. But it has essential features of a war, indeed of a total war. It is a violent conflict with a powerful resilient enemy that wants to injure the United States and Europe grievously, overthrow governments in the Middle East, Africa, and Central and Southeast Asia, destroy Israel, and force the United States to withdraw from the Eastern Hemisphere."[37] While this global threat against the Western world and Israel represents the core thesis of his book, Posner spends little time identifying, realistically, the tangible mechanisms by which the Islamist terrorists might plausibly achieve the conquest of Europe and Asia, as Nazi Germany and Imperial Japan failed to do, let alone what the origins of the Islamist threat might be. Even Satan enjoys the theory of the fallen angel as an explanation for his moral and ethical disposition, yet Posner gives no such courtesy to his Islamic demons. Thus, while Posner, like Ackerman and Heymann, ultimately accepts the premise of a benign U.S. foreign policy requiring little moral or legal scrutiny, Posner's analysis is far more belligerent and apocalyptic.

Posner then merges his orientalist notions about the presumably organic threat of Islamist terrorism with the status of civil liberties in the United States—to the detriment of civil liberties:

> The general argument of these chapters [in Not a Suicide Pact] is that the scope of constitutional liberties is rightly less extensive at a time of serious terrorist threats and rapid proliferation of means of widespread destruction than at a time of felt safety, but that the degree of curtailment required to protect us is not so great as to impair the feeling of freedom that is so important to Americans. It would leave the essential structure of constitutional liberties that the Supreme Court has been building since the 1950s and 1960s. That essential structure is one we can inhabit comfortably until the terrorist menace abates, however long that may be.[38]

On the following page, however, Posner writes: "Even torture may sometimes be justified in the struggle against terrorism, but it should not be considered *legally* justified. A recurrent theme of [Not a Suicide Pact] is that a nonlegal 'law of necessity' that would furnish a moral and political but not legal justification for acting in contravention of the Constitution may trump constitutional rights in extreme situations. The limits of legal codification as a method of social control are especially acute in the context of national security."[39] Thus, Posner's "law of necessity" embodies no actual law, would trump the Constitution, would be imbued with moral and political absolutes in the fight against the Islamist terrorists, and sounds a bit like martial law. Such views fail to leave me with that "feeling of freedom" that Posner promised.

In their books, Ackerman, Heymann, and Posner all mention Alan Dershowitz in the context of their work about terrorism and civil liberties, but they do so almost exclusively within the relatively narrow framework of Dershowitz's position on torture, which Dershowitz has stated, perhaps most emphatically, as follows:

> I am against torture as a normative matter, and I would like to see its use minimized. I believe that at least moderate forms of nonlethal torture are in fact being used by the United States and some of its allies today. I think that if we ever confronted an actual case of imminent mass terrorism that could be prevented by the infliction of torture, we would use torture (even lethal torture) and the public would favor its use. . . . I pose the issue as follows. If torture is, in fact, being used and/or would, in fact, be used in an actual ticking bomb terrorist case, would it be normatively better or worse to have such torture regulated by some kind of warrant, with accountability, recordkeeping, standards and limitations? This is an important debate, and a different one from the old, abstract Benthamite debate over whether torture can ever be justified. It is not so much about the substantive issue of torture as it is about accountability, visibility, and candor in a democracy that is confronting a choice of evils.[40]

Dershowitz's law school colleagues have responded to his views on torture. For example, Ackerman addressed the interrogation of detainees who might be preventively detained during his proposed forty-five-day post-attack state of emergency: "Do not torture the detainees. That should be an absolute, and judges should enforce it rigorously. The fact that many of the detainees are almost certainly innocent makes this ban exigent. Professor Alan Dershowitz has recently urged us to rethink this absolute prohibition. If we were confronted with a terrorist who could tell us where Al Qaeda would strike next, wouldn't it be right to torture him to save the lives of thousands?"[41] It seems that this summary reasonably reflects Dershowitz's position on torture,[42] to which Ackerman responded further:

> I am entirely unimpressed with the relevance of [Dershowitz's] musings to real-world emergency settings. Security services can panic in the face of horrific tragedy. With officials in disarray, with rumors of impending attacks flying about, and with an outraged public demanding instant results, there will be overwhelming temptations to use indecent forms of interrogation. This is the last place to expect carefully nuanced responses.
>
> Dershowitz recognizes the problem and proposes to solve it by inviting judges to serve as our collective superego, issuing "torture warrants" only in the most compelling cases. But judges are no more immune from panic than the rest of us. To offset the rush toward torture in an emergency, they would be obliged to make their hearings especially deliberate and

thoughtful. But if they slow the judicial proceedings down to deliberate speed for diligent review, the terrorists' second strike will occur before the torture warrant can issue. Serious deliberation is simply incompatible with the speedy response required in the aftermath of an attack.[43]

Heymann similarly responded to Dershowitz's position on torture: "Take the recommendation of my colleague Alan Dershowitz for judicially issued 'torture warrants' to substitute for torture at the discretion of intelligence agents pursuing a 'ticking bomb.' It will increase the use of torture."[44] Heymann then summarized Dershowitz's case for torture under extreme circumstances while emphasizing its impracticalities: "Dershowitz proposes to instead make torture acceptable and legal whenever a judge accepts the judgment of intelligence officials, before the torture, that: (1) there is a bomb in a public place; (2) the suspect knows where it is; (3) torture will get the truth, not a false story, out of him before the bomb explodes; and (4) the bomb won't be moved in the meantime."[45] Like Ackerman and Heymann, and writing in the *Progressive*, Alfred W. McCoy, the J.R.W. Smail Professor of History at the University of Wisconsin at Madison, also ably commented on Dershowitz's "ticking bomb" and "torture warrant" proposals:

> Number one: In the real world, the probability that a terrorist might be captured after concealing a ticking nuclear bomb in Times Square and that his captors would somehow recognize his significance is phenomenally slender. The scenario assumes a highly improbable array of variables that runs something like this: First, FBI or CIA agents apprehend a terrorist at the precise moment between timer's first tick and bomb's burst. Second, the interrogators somehow have sufficiently detailed foreknowledge of the plot to know they must interrogate this very person and do it right now. Third, these same officers, for some unexplained reason, are missing just a few critical details that only this captive can divulge. Fourth, the biggest leap of all, these officers with just one shot to get the information that only this captive can divulge are best advised to try torture, as if beating him is the way to assure his wholehearted cooperation.[46]

Posner, on the other hand, worst of all, asserts that the executive branch may have "a moral duty to torture" in extreme circumstances outside any legal framework whatsoever: "In evaluating the argument for authorizing government to resort to torture in extreme circumstances (somehow defined)—as advocated, for example, by Alan Dershowitz in his book *Why Terrorism Works* [2002]—we must consider the alternative of simply recognizing that in desperate circumstances, as when a terrorist has information that is absolutely vital to averting a catastrophic attack, the government will torture—will indeed be under a moral duty to torture—and that reliance on the executive's willingness to exercise raw power in extreme circumstances may be preferable to recognizing a legal right to do so."[47] Thus, Posner—a federal judge and professor of law—once again slips his way past what he seems to view repeatedly as the law's hindrance. And in his chapter on torture in *Not a Suicide Pact*, Posner wrote: "In the era of weapons of mass destruction, torture may sometimes be the only means of averting the death of thousands, even millions, of Americans. In such a situation it would be the moral and political duty of the president to authorize torture."[48]

Given that Ackerman, Heymann and Blum, and Posner are arguably the most prominent advocates of their points of view on terrorism (liberal, centrist, and right, respectively), that they reside at some of the most prestigious law schools in the United States (Harvard, Yale, and Chicago), and that they are published by the most prestigious academic publishers (Harvard, Yale, MIT, and Oxford), it is probably fair to say that they represent the state-of-the-art of academic scholarship about the threat of terrorism facing the United States and its implications for the survival of civil liberties. It also appears that Dershowitz shares an intellectual and political affiliation with the right-wing Posner, given that Dershowitz and Posner both promote an unnuanced view of the threat of "Islamic terrorism," support the idea of the political and moral necessity of torturing suspected terrorists in extreme circumstances, and would sacrifice civil liberties to the iron necessity of an endless war on terror.

Following the terrorist attacks on New York and Washington in September 2001, Dershowitz wrote a series of newspaper articles in which he began promoting a Brave New World on civil liberties in the United States. That approach was presented more comprehensively in his 2006 book *Preemption: A Knife That Cuts Both Ways*, which is Dershowitz's manifesto of a counterterrorist preventive state in the United States. We begin with the newspaper articles.

About a month after 9/11, Dershowitz wrote an opinion piece for the *San Francisco Chronicle* titled "Big Brother, Where Art Thou? Rethinking Civil Liberties in the Age of Terrorism," in which he began: "The Holocaust changed theology. The Civil War altered concepts of equality. And the terrorist attacks of Sept. 11 have changed the way many people think about good and evil—and about roving wiretaps, a national identity card, and other proposals formerly scorned. The transforming events that day and since have led many thoughtful people to reassess fundamental values. That is as it should be. Values, like rights, grow out of experience. History shows us that everything changes with experience, including religion, constitutional interpretation and moral values."[49]

How, exactly, should things change after 9/11? Dershowitz illustrates in the next sentence by invoking his hypothetical question about whether it should be U.S. practice "to shoot down a passenger jet about to crash into an occupied building."

Dershowitz concluded, without identifying anyone by name, that "almost every reasonable and thoughtful person now says shooting down the jet would be the only appropriate response." I present this hypothetical, and Dershowitz's response, as an example of the unique brand of grotesque simple-mindedness that he brings to the problem of terrorism targeting the United States and Israel, and for the assuredly violent and of his counterterrorism remedies.

In "Big Brother, Where Art Thou?"—which, given its title and substance, appeals literally to Big Brother, the dictator in Orwell's *1984*—Dershowitz also wrote: "Many thoughtful libertarians are rethinking their knee-jerk opposition to new technologies which may assist in fighting terrorism. I am one of them." He continued: "For example, I was immediately suspicious when I first heard of roving wiretaps, which would follow a specific person rather than a specific telephone. . . . I understand that the roving wiretap can play an important role in tracking potential terrorists who use cell phones briefly, then discard and replace them. I have begun to think hard about whether there are any real downsides to a roving warrant. There are not."[50] On reaching this conclusion, Dershowitz never mentioned the Fourth Amendment to the U.S. Constitution, which prohibits un-reasonable searches and seizures, and the issuance of warrants without probable cause. And on October 23, 2001, five days before Dershowitz's op-ed piece was published by the *San Francisco Chronicle*, the American Civil Liberties Union, in a report titled "How the Anti-Terrorism Bill Limits Judicial Oversight of Telephone and Internet Surveillance," and referring specifically to the roving wire-tap provisions of the final draft of the USA Patriot Act of October 2001, observed: "The Fourth Amendment to the Constitution requires that search warrants specify the place to be searched. This provides an important privacy protection" prevent-ing "random searches of the homes of innocent persons." The ACLU noted that the "specificity requirement of the Fourth Amendment means that law enforce-ment officers applying for a court order must specify the phone they want to tap"; yet, a roving wiretap "means that law enforcement agents can listen in on any phone the target might use because he is nearby."[51] The ACLU reported that the roving wiretap provisions in the Patriot Act would permit law enforcement to obtain the equivalent of a "blank warrant," which enables federal law enforcement agencies to use one search warrant to conduct multiple searches of a person's phone communications.[52]

The Electronic Frontier Foundation described the situation as follows:

> Imagine that the FBI could, with a single search warrant, raid every house or office that an individual suspect has visited over an entire year—every single place, whether or not the residents themselves are suspects. Suppose that the FBI could do this without ever having to identify the suspect in question. This is what Section 206 [of the Patriot Act] allows

in the communications context. Section 206 authorizes intelligence investigators to conduct "John Doe" roving surveillance—meaning that the FBI can wiretap every single phone line, mobile communications device or Internet connection that a suspect might be using, without ever having to identify the suspect by name. This gives the FBI a "blank check" to violate the communications privacy of countless innocent Americans. What's worse, these blank-check wiretap orders can remain in effect for up to a year.[53]

And the court charged with issuing the "blank checks" is the secret FISA Court,[54] which seldom denies or modifies a surveillance request from the Justice Department.[55]

And while Dershowitz wrote that there were no downsides to roving wiretaps, the Center for Constitutional Rights (CCR) issued its objections a year after the Patriot Act was signed into law in October 2001. In a report titled "The State of Civil Liberties One Year Later: Erosion of Civil Liberties in the Post 9/11 Era," CCR reported that "under the USA PATRIOT Act, the standards for wiretapping have been significantly weakened," given that the act "allow[s] the FBI to use concerns about foreign agents as a pretext for conducting criminal searches without probable cause, and to extend these searches, via roving wiretap, to individuals who are not the subject of a warrant."[56]

Around this time, in late 2002, Dershowitz was among five Harvard Law School faculty members who participated in a forum on the U.S. response to terrorism. Upon covering the event, the *Harvard Law Record* reported that, in addition to supporting "face recognition technology" as a counterterrorism measure, "Dershowitz also argued that roving wiretaps were better than traditional wiretaps, because they were less likely to record personal conversations of innocent people who were not the target of the wiretap."[57] This is, in fact, the opposite of what the American Civil Liberties Union, the Center for Constitutional Rights, and the Electronic Frontier Foundation all reported in detail about the roving wiretap provisions in the Patriot Act. Dershowitz's assertion that roving wiretaps protect innocent persons also was contradicted years later by a proposed amendment to the Patriot Act by Senator Dick Durbin (D-IL) and Congresswoman Barbara Lee (D-CA) in March 2011, who stated that the roving wiretap law "does not adequately protect innocent Americans from unwarranted government surveillance."[58]

In "Big Brother, Where Art Thou?"—the same October 2001 opinion piece that asked readers to "rethink" civil liberties after 9/11—Dershowitz wrote that "the events of Sept. 11 have also prompted me to rethink my opposition to national identity cards." Previously, Dershowitz's opposition to national ID cards, as he wrote, "grew primarily out of the misuse of such cards by the apartheid regime in South Africa and the totalitarian regimes in the Soviet Union and China," but "the ease with which several of the Sept. 11 hijackers managed to hide in open view" prompted him to conclude that "a foolproof national ID card has some real virtues," with few "compelling civil-libertarian arguments against" an ID card.

Just as Dershowitz asserted in the same op-ed piece that he had "thought hard" about any downsides to roving wiretaps, even as he ignored the legitimate objections of the ACLU that were issued days earlier, Dershowitz's claim that he could think of few civil libertarian arguments against a national ID card once again omitted any reference to the detailed opposition of the ACLU. In testimony to the U.S. House of Representatives in September 1998, three years to the month prior to 9/11, the ACLU's legislative counsel, Gregory T. Nojeim, stated: "The ACLU vigorously opposes the creation of a national ID card. . . . A national ID card or system of identification would substantially infringe upon the privacy rights of all U.S. citizens and is unnecessary to administer programs of the federal government." Nojeim continued: "A national ID system and the nationalized identification cards that would support it would inevitably violate the most basic of American liberties: the right to be left alone. Unlike children and workers in Nazi Germany, Soviet Russia, apartheid South Africa, Castro's Cuba or Saddam's Iraq, no American need fear the demand, 'Identity papers!' We are a free people who cherish our right to be individuals, to be left alone, and to start over, free from prying eyes (and grasping hands) of both Big Brother bureaucrats and snooping commercial interests."[59]

The problems with Dershowitz's claims about the benign nature of a national ID card were also evident in an October 2001 op-ed piece in the *New York Times* titled "Why Fear National ID Cards?," in which he asserted that a national ID card would enhance national security: "At many bridges and tunnels across the country, drivers avoid long delays at the toll booths with an unobtrusive device that fits on a car's dashboard. Instead of fumbling for change, they drive right through; the device sends a radio signal that records their passage. They are billed later. It's a tradeoff between privacy and convenience: the toll-takers know more about you—when you entered and left Manhattan, for instance—but you save time and money."

Rather than view with skepticism, from a privacy standpoint, electronic toll booth snooping, Dershowitz cites it as a model for the establishment of a national identity card: "An optional national identity card could be used in a similar way, offering a similar kind of tradeoff: a little less anonymity for a lot more security. Anyone who had the card could be allowed to pass through airports or building security more expeditiously, and anyone who opted out could be examined much more closely."[60] However, a national ID card would be genuinely "optional" only if a decision to opt-out did not lead to an increase in government suspicion and scrutiny. Dershowitz also claimed that a national ID card would result in "a lot more security." Yet, one month after Dershowitz's op-ed piece was published in the *Times*, ACLU legislative counsel Katie Corrigan seemed to respond directly to Dershowitz in her testimony to the House Committee on Government Reform:

> The rationale for creating a national ID system post–September 11 is to create a clear line between "us" (innocent people) and "them" (dangerous terrorists). Everyone would like an ID card that would put them squarely on the right side of the line and exempt them from suspicion and heightened security scrutiny when they board a plane or go to work. Unfortunately, none of the proposed identification systems would effectively sort out the "good" from the "bad." First, an identification card simply confirms that you are who you say you are. It does not establish motive or intent to attack a plane.[61]

Corrigan also observed: "A national ID card would set up the infrastructure for a surveillance society. Day to day, individuals could be asked for ID when they are walking down the street, applying for a job or health insurance, or entering a building. This type of daily intrusiveness would be joined with the full power of modern computer and database technology." Corrigan also quoted what California congressman Tom Campbell observed about a national ID card: "If you have an ID card, it is solely for the purpose of allowing the government to compel you to produce it. This would give the government the power to demand that we show our papers. It is a very dangerous thing."[62]

In addition to supporting roving wiretaps and a national ID card, Dershowitz is a post–9/11 proponent of the preventive detention of American citizens. In a chapter in *Preemption* titled "Preventive Measures against Terrorism," Dershowitz wrote that "deterrence is less effective" in the so-called war against terrorism, and thus "preventive mechanisms must assume a larger role."[63] In the section that follows, titled "Preventive Detention of Potential Terrorists," Dershowitz wrote: "One preventive mechanism that has been widely used during 'emergencies' has been the preventive detention of individuals or groups believed likely to engage in future acts of terrorism." Whereas Bruce Ackerman views the necessity of preventive detention as a limited, short-term response to the "next attack," Dershowitz would like us to consider preventive detention "as part of an overall preventive strategy."[64]

At one point, Dershowitz cited the words of U.S. Supreme Court Justice Robert Jackson, who wrote in 1950 in opposition to preventive detention: "The jailing of persons by the courts because of anticipated but as yet uncommitted crimes" cannot be reconciled with "traditional American law."[65] While Dershowitz represented Justice Jackson's words accurately, the fuller quote from Jackson is more compelling in its opposition to preventive detention: "It is . . . difficult to reconcile with traditional American law the jailing of persons by the courts because of anticipated but as yet uncommitted crimes. Imprisonment to protect society from predicted but unconsummated offenses is so unprecedented in this country and so fraught with danger of excess and injustice that I am loathe to resort to it."[66] Jackson is speaking here of the unprecedented nature of preventive detention under "traditional American law," which would not support the de facto state of emergency and preventive detentions in the United States that Dershowitz seems to favor.

In contrast to the views of Justice Jackson, and given, for him, the irreducible threat of terrorism, Dershowitz advised the United States, Israel, and Britain[67] to develop a legal "regulation" for preventive detention, which he described as "this increasingly important preventive mechanism": "The preventive detention of suspected future terrorists is likely to continue wherever terrorism is perceived as a serious threat. It is essential that democratic nations committed to the rule of law begin to develop a jurisprudence regulating this increasingly important preventive mechanism. It is fair to say that no nation has satisfied this important need."[68] Beyond the usual camouflage of his ritual incantations of "democratic nations" and "the rule of law," Dershowitz in fact proposes to subvert traditional American law, which has rejected preventive detention as abhorrent to the U.S. Constitution.

In addition to his support of roving wiretaps, a national ID card, and the legalization and regulation of preventive detention, Dershowitz also supports the legalization of torture, which he often qualifies by stating his opposition to torture on moral grounds. This means, as Dershowitz has explained, that while he is personally opposed to torture, he supports the legalization of torture with clear lines of legal authority and accountability. Thus, for example, in October 2006, Dershowitz wrote in the *Los Angeles Times*: "Although I personally oppose the use of torture, I recognize the reality that some forms of torture have been, are being and will continue to be used by democracies in extreme situations, regardless of what we say or what the law provides. In an effort to limit the use of torture to genuinely extreme 'ticking bomb' situations, rather than allowing it to become as routine as it obviously became at Abu Ghraib, I proposed that the president or a federal judge would have to take personal responsibility for ordering its use in extraordinary situations."[69]

Likewise, in November 2007, Dershowitz wrote in the *Wall Street Journal*: "Although I am personally opposed to the use of torture, I have no doubt that any president—indeed any leader of a democratic nation—would in fact authorize some forms of torture against a captured terrorist if he believed that this was the only way of securing information necessary to prevent an imminent mass casualty attack. The only dispute is whether he would do so openly with accountability or secretly with deniability. The former seems more consistent with democratic theory, the latter with typical political hypocrisy."[70]

What seems more consistent with "democratic theory" is the idea that elected officials will ultimately conform to what the electorate wants or does not want, not the other way around. If Dershowitz, the citizen, were genuinely opposed to torture, he would, it seems, oppose the practice of torture by his government rather than seek a "legal" accommodation to permit the practice to continue. In other words, actual opponents of torture—Amnesty International, Human Rights Watch, the ACLU, the Center for Constitutional Rights, Noam Chomsky, Richard Falk, and others—oppose torture by actually opposing torture. And given the political causes in the world worth supporting—including the abolition of nuclear weapons, aggressive war, poverty, hunger, disease, and so on—Dershowitz's crusade to legalize and regulate torture and preventive detention in the United States seems strange at best, while seeming to function as advocacy of authoritarianism in the guise of democratic accountability.

Furthermore, Dershowitz's hypothetical "ticking bomb" scenario, which he invokes to rationalize the legalization of torture, is a slippery slope, as he illustrates. In an op-ed piece in November 2007 in the Wall Street Journal titled "Democrats and Waterboarding," Dershowitz sought to demonstrate the efficacy of torture: "There are some who claim that torture is a nonissue because it never works—it only produces false information. This is simply not true, as evidenced by the many decent members of the French Resistance who, under Nazi torture, disclosed the locations of their closest friends and relatives."[71] Writing in response, and to this statement in particular, journalist Larisa Alexandrovna properly observed: "This statement defies logic. Even if in some instances Nazi tactics worked, why would anyone endorse them for any reason, especially a Jewish man?"[72] To which Dershowitz responded: "Alexandrovna distorts this factual evidence [that torture sometimes works] into an 'endorse[ment]' of torture as a moral matter, despite my clear statement of my personal opposition to the use of torture."[73] Thus, Dershowitz opposes torture "as a moral matter" by citing Nazi torture success to further his allegedly circumscribed case for torture. Note in this regard that Dershowitz cited the efficiencies of Nazi torture outside the realm of the ticking-bomb scenario—this to establish the efficacy of torture inside the realm of the ticking-bomb scenario, where the inherent practical constraints on "success" are far more severe.

Finally, assuming that Dershowitz is morally opposed to torture, he likely would have no qualms about citing the instruments of domestic and international law that prohibit torture; however, Dershowitz seldom if ever cites the laws banning torture, which include Common Article 3 of the Geneva Conventions,[74] the UN

Convention against Torture,[75] and the U.S. War Crimes Act of 1996.[76] And in the rare instances when Dershowitz attempts to identify such law, he misidentifies it. Clearly referring to and quoting from the UN Convention against Torture, Dershowitz misidentifies the convention as the "Geneva Convention against Torture." This occurs not once but twice in the only two textual references to the UN Convention against Torture in his 2002 book *Why Terrorism Works*,[77] which is a major source of Dershowitz's views on torture. This chronic mislabeling of basic sources of humanitarian law (referring to the Geneva Conventions as the "Geneva Accords") and human rights law (referring to the UN Convention against Torture as the "Geneva Convention against Torture"), coupled with his very infrequent references to such law, might cause Dershowitz's readers to doubt his familiarity with and support of the law that applies to issues about which he is considered an expert, including torture. For example, although Article 2 of the UN Convention against Torture harbors an unconditional prohibition against torture,[78] Dershowitz nevertheless reports his preferred method of torture—"a sterilized needle underneath the nail" to cause "excruciating pain."[79] Does Dershowitz here flout the absolute prohibition against torture, or is he merely ignorant of it? Either way, this is a strange brew from someone who proclaims a principled opposition to torture.

In addition to his support of the unamended roving wiretaps in the Patriot Act, a national ID card, preventive detention, and the legalization of torture, Dershowitz advocates the extrajudicial killing (or "targeted killing") of suspected terrorists by the United States and Israel. For example, in the *Jerusalem Post* in April 2004, Dershowitz wrote an article titled "Killing Terrorist Chieftains Is Legal."[80] In January 2008, Dershowitz published an article on *Huffington Post* titled "Targeted Killing Is Working, So Why Is the Press Not Reporting It."[81] A few hours after U.S. Special Forces killed Osama bin Laden in Pakistan in May 2011, Dershowitz wrote an instant analysis, published by *Huffington Post*, titled "Targeted Killing Vindicated."[82] And in his 2006 book *Preemption*, in a chapter titled "Preventive Measures against Terrorism," Dershowitz wrote twenty pages in support of the targeted killing practices of the government of Israel.[83] Before assessing Dershowitz's views further, we shall review, by way of contrast, how civil libertarians in the United States view the extrajudicial killing of suspected terrorists.

Writing for the *Guardian* in January 2012, Mary Ellen O'Connell—who is Robert and Marion Short Professor of Law at Notre Dame, chair of the International Law Association's Committee on the Use of Force, and vice president of the American Society of International Law—defined "targeted killing" as "the killing of certain individuals away from battle zones using military means, including missiles, bombs and commando raids." She observed: "The missiles and bombs are often delivered by drone aircraft. Given the munitions, it is the rare attack that spares the lives of bystanders—over 2,200 persons are estimated to have been killed in the three years of the Obama administration in Pakistan alone." O'Connell also observed: "Today, under the international legal definition of armed conflict, the United States is involved in such hostilities in one country only: Afghanistan. Beyond Afghanistan, any use of lethal force by designated authorities of the United States must follow the normal human rights limits on peacetime resort to lethal force." This means that while U.S. authorities "may engage in lethal force when necessary to save a human life immediately, if there is no alternative," in other cases "an attempt to arrest is required, followed by a fair trial within a reasonable period." O'Connell commented that "even if there was any data at all about assassination having a long-term positive impact on suppressing terrorism—which there is not—the data would not change the law and morality against it."[84]

Bill Quigley, professor of law at Loyola University in New Orleans and associate director of the Center for Constitutional Rights, pointed out that the Obama administration provides few details about the extrajudicial killing program of the United States: "U.S. civilian and military employees regularly target and fire lethal unmanned drone guided missiles at people across the world. Thousands of people have been assassinated. Hundreds of those killed were civilians. Some of those killed were rescuers and mourners. . . . But the government routinely refuses to provide any official information on local reports of civilian deaths or the identities of most of those killed." Quigley noted that "an investigation by the *Wall Street Journal* in November 2011 revealed that most of the time the U.S. did not even know the identities of the people being killed by drones in Pakistan."[85] Quigley also wrote: "There is incredible danger in allowing U.S. military and civilians to murder people anywhere in the world with no public or Congressional or judicial oversight. This authorizes the President and the executive branch, according to the ACLU and the Center for Constitutional Rights, to be prosecutor, judge, jury and executioner. . . . Continuation of flagrantly illegal drone attacks by the U.S. also risks justifying the exact same actions, taken by others, against us."[86] In fact, a few months earlier, Human Rights Watch reported that "about 40 other countries currently possess basic drone technology," that "the number is expected to expand significantly in coming years," and that "China, France, Germany, India, Iran, Israel, Italy, Russia, Turkey, and the United Kingdom either have or are currently seeking drones with attack capability."[87]

In August 2010, upon filing a lawsuit "challenging the government's asserted authority to carry out 'targeted killings' of U.S. citizens located far from any armed conflict zone," the American Civil Liberties Union and the Center for Constitutional Rights stated: "Outside of armed conflict, both the Constitution and international law prohibit targeted killing except as a last resort to protect against concrete, specific and imminent threats of death or serious physical injury.

An extrajudicial killing policy under which names are added to C.I.A. and military 'kill lists' through a secret executive process and stay there for months at a time is plainly not limited to imminent threats."[88]

In a report issued in May 2010, Philip Alston, the UN Special Rapporteur on Extrajudicial, Summary or Arbitrary Executions, identified the origins of the term "targeted killing": "It came into common usage in 2000, after Israel made public a policy of 'targeted killings' of alleged terrorists in the Occupied Palestinian Territories." Alston also observed that "in the 1990s, Israel categorically refused to admit to targeted killings, stating, when accused, that 'the [Israel Defense Forces] wholeheartedly rejects this accusation,' and 'there is no policy and there never will be a policy or a reality of willful killing of suspects.'"[89]

Today, and in recent years, both the United States and Israel readily employ a policy of extrajudicial killings. Dershowitz supports the extrajudicial killing policies of both countries. Writing in April 2004 in the *Jerusalem Post*, in an article titled "Killing Terrorist Chieftains Is Legal," Dershowitz supported the extra-judicial killing of Iraqi cleric Muqtada al-Sadr as follows: "The United States Army was recently given a highly specific military order. According to the top US commander in Iraq, Lt. General Ricardo Sanchez, the mission is to kill radical Shiite Cleric Muqtada al-Sadr. This order to target al-Sadr for extrajudicial killing is perfectly legitimate and lawful under the laws of war. Al-Sadr is a combatant, and it is proper to kill a combatant during an ongoing war unless he surrenders first. . . . Of course, his killing would be extrajudicial. Military attacks against combatants are not preceded by jury trials or judicial warrants."[90] Thus, Dershowitz argued on behalf of the nonexistent legal principle that it is perfectly legal for Country A to unilaterally invade and occupy Country B in violation of the most important rule of international law, for Country A to then label Country B a lawful field of battle in which the resistance leaders of Country B are "terrorists" and thus subject to "legal" assassination.

Dershowitz then sought to leverage the proposed U.S. targeted killing of Muqtada al-Sadr in Iraq to plead support for the Israeli targeted killing of Hamas leaders: "How then to explain the world's very different reaction to Israel's decision to target terrorist leaders, such as Sheikh Ahmed Yassin and Dr. Abdel Aziz Rantisi, the former leaders of Hamas. Surely, there is no legal or moral difference between Yassin and Rantisi [of Hamas] on the one hand, and Al-Sadr [of Iraq] on the other."[91] It is indeed the case that there is no moral and legal difference between Yassin, Rantisi, and Al-Sadr, on one hand, and the American and Israeli military on the other, in the sense that all sides are obliged to follow the law. Yet, in a March 2004 press release titled "Amnesty International Strongly Condemns the Assassination of Sheikh Yassin," which included information that Dershowitz omitted about the Israeli killing of Yassin, AI reported:

Amnesty International condemns the extrajudicial execution, by the Israeli army, of Hamas' leader Sheikh Ahmad Yassin this morning in the Gaza Strip. The attack also resulted in the unlawful killing of seven other Palestinians and the injury of many more. . . . The assassination of Sheikh Yassin is likely to further escalate the spiral of violence which has claimed the lives of some 2,500 Palestinians and 900 Israelis, most of them civilians, in the past three and a half years. . . . Israel has resorted to extrajudicial executions for several years without offering proof of guilt or right of defence. Some 200 Palestinians have been assassinated by the Israeli army in the past three and a half years. Such attacks have also resulted in the unlawful killing of more than 100 bystanders, including dozens of children. Amnesty International has repeatedly condemned these acts as unlawful.[92]

While supporting, in the *Jerusalem Post* in April 2004, Israel's policy of extrajudicial assassinations in Israel-occupied Palestinian territory, Dershowitz mentioned none of these details reported by Amnesty International a month earlier.

Overall, citing statistics from September 29, 2000 to December 13, 2006, B'Tselem reported that "Israel's targeted killing attacks have killed 339 Palestinians, 210 of them the target of the attack and 129 of them civilian bystanders."[93] B'Tselem also reported that from September 2000 to August 2011, Israel's targeted killings had killed 425 Palestinians, 251 of them the target of the attack and 174 of them civilian bystanders.[94] To my knowledge, Dershowitz has never cited these and other fatality figures from the human rights organizations when he writes in support of Israel's policy of extrajudicial killings. Furthermore, the figures just cited mean, in part, that from 2006 to 2011, Israel's targeted attacks had killed a total of eighty-six Palestinians—forty-one targeted persons and forty-five civilian bystanders. Thus, from 2006 to 2011, the targeted killing practice of Israel killed fewer targeted persons (41) than civilian bystanders (45). Yet, in January 2008 in an article published by *Huffington Post*, Dershowitz claimed that Israel's targeted killings were "pinpointed," even though the percentage of civilian bystanders killed from 2006 to 2011 was rising.

Throughout his discourse on "rethinking civil liberties" in the post–9/11 era, where he advocates on behalf of a U.S. counterterrorist "preventive state" featuring electronic surveillance, a national ID card, preventive detention, torture, and extrajudicial killings, Dershowitz hardly mentions the Bill of Rights. For example, although much of his "jurisprudence of the preventive state" appears in *Huffington Post*, I don't recall reading any references to the Bill of Rights in Dershowitz's articles on that Web site. A Google search shows no such references.[95] In his 2006 book *Preemption: A Knife That Cuts Both Ways*, which is Dershowitz's manifesto of the preventive state, Dershowitz mentions the Bill of Rights once (in the context of an historical artifact pertaining to justices of the peace and preventive confinement in the United States).[96] The fact that the contemporary Dershowitz takes little notice of the Bill of Rights—in the context of his post–9/11 plea to "rethink civil liberties"—represents a dramatic turnaround, given Dershowitz's published views about the Bill of Rights from the 1960s and 1970s, as detailed in chapter 3.

At that time, Dershowitz wrote: "The civil liberties of all Americans—the right to be free from unwarranted government intrusion, to speak critically of those in power, to be treated fairly and with due process—have been seriously curtailed over the past few years." Dershowitz accused President Nixon of "tak[ing] aim at the Fourth Amendment's protection against unreasonable searches and seizures," and for "audaciously claim[ing] to be exempt from the requirement that a court approved warrant be obtained before it may tap or bug conversations involving the national security." Dershowitz observed that "in 1969 and 1970 alone, more than 40,000 days of tapping and bugging were conducted without court approval" and that "the number of innocent conversations illegally monitored in recent years is truly staggering." Dershowitz also wrote that "the Eighth Amendment's right to reasonable bail has also been undercut by the Administration's preventive detention law, which authorizes the imprisonment of suspects not because of what they have done, but because of what it is predicted they might do at some future time." Dershowitz added that "the implications of preventive imprisonment based on future predictions are frightening to contemplate."[97] Thus, if Dershowitz once supported those aspects of the Bill of Rights, evidence in his own writings indicates that he does not support them today. This conclusion is consistent with Dershowitz's post–9/11 thinking, which, as he wrote in "Big Brother, Where Art Thou? Rethinking Civil Liberties in the Age of Terrorism," was to "reassess our fundamental values," including with regard to "constitutional interpretation."

From where, then, if not the U.S. Constitution and the Bill of Rights, does Dershowitz derive the legal and philosophical authority to urge Americans to reconsider our rights and liberties? The source that he most frequently references with specificity, including with regard to precedent, is the Bible. Dershowitz's *Preemption*, in fact, begins with an inscription to his friend, Irwin Cotler, and a salutation to the pursuit of justice on behalf of the Bible: "This book is dedicated to my dear friend and colleague of forty years, the Honorable Irwin Cotler, Attorney General and Minister of Justice of Canada, who always carries out the biblical command to pursue justice, and who inspires me and so many others by his constant example and his unwavering commitment to principle."[98] Why would a U.S. civil libertarian pay such homage to "the biblical command to pursue justice"—while failing to cite the Bill of Rights—in the context of a post–9/11 call to "rethink" civil liberties in the United States? For one thing, to note only a few examples of biblical justice, the Bible favors the death penalty for a variety of acts, including adultery, sodomy, a woman found not to have been a virgin on the night of her wedding, and witchcraft. In fact, Dershowitz's jurisprudence of the preventive state in *Preemption* at times seems informed more by a parade of references to the ancient cultural customs of the Bible and rabbinical teachings than by enlightened Western law.

In the introduction to *Preemption*, for example Dershowitz wrote: "One early, if incomplete, effort at constructing a jurisprudence of preemption was undertaken by the twelfth century Jewish scholar Maimonides. He began with the biblical rule, 'If a thief is caught breaking in and is struck so that he dies, the defendant is not guilty of bloodshed.' This rule was explained as presuming that a nighttime thief anticipated confronting and killing the homeowner, whereas a daytime thief intended merely to steal property from a vacant house. The Talmud generalized this interpretation into a rule of anticipatory self-defense: 'If a man comes to kill you, you kill him first.'"[99] In chapter 1, "A Brief History of Preemption, Prevention, and Prediction," Dershowitz wrote:

> From the beginning of recorded history, societies have worried about dangerous people who had not "yet" done the harm it was believed—or predicted—they would do. Preventive imprisonment, even in times when places of confinement were primitive, was employed in some systems. For example, the Bible requires two witnesses to convict a murderer. If only one credible witness testified, the defendant had to be acquitted, but that did not necessarily mean that the dangerous killer would be allowed to go free and perhaps murder again. Instead, he was placed in a locked room, where he was sometimes fed a lethal concoction of water and grain calculated to cause his stomach to burst. The rabbis justified this extra-biblical punishment as necessary to prevent lawlessness. I suspect that most societies developed similar informal or extrajudicial mechanisms for dealing with obviously dangerous people who could not be convicted of past crimes.[100]

Dershowitz concluded the chapter as follows: "This brief historical account of one paradigmatic genre of preemption—preventive confinement of individuals believed to be dangerous—is intended to illustrate a more general phenomenon, namely, that preemptive actions of many kinds have been far more common in practice than they appear in theory. Similar historical accounts, though with varying content and rationalizations, could be provided for other preemptive mechanisms as well. For example, as we shall now see, preemptive military attacks on enemies who may themselves be contemplating attack are at least as old as the

Bible."[101] In his next chapter, "Preemptive Military Action: From Surgical Strike to All-Out War," and after leading with the book of Genesis in his list of historical examples[102]—all depicting preemptive and preventive wars favorably—Dershowitz cited other precedents of preemptive military action from the Bible:

> The Bible contains several instances of preemptive military action, most famously in the Book of Esther, which recounts how King Ahasuerus of Persia (sometimes referred to as Xerxes) was instigated by his adviser Haman to mandate the destruction of the Jewish people within his kingdom, because their customs were "different" and did "not obey the King's laws." Dispatches were then sent by couriers to all the king's provinces with the order to "kill and annihilate all the Jews—young and old, women and little children—on a certain day, the thirteenth day of the twelfth month . . . and to plunder their goods." After a convoluted plot by the Jew Mordechai and his niece Queen Esther to turn the king against Haman, Ahasuerus commanded the execution of Haman, but the law forbade him to rescind his order to kill the Jews, "for no document written in the king's name and sealed with his ring can be revoked." So the King issued another order granting the Jewish people "the right to assemble and protect themselves" from anyone preparing to carry out the first order. This order bestowed on the Jews the right "to destroy, kill and annihilate any armed force . . . that might attack them and their women and children. . . ." That right of preemptive self-defense came into operation on the thirteenth day of the twelfth month, the same day specified in the initial order for their destruction. On that day "the enemies of the Jews had hoped to overpower them, but now the tables were turned and the Jews got the upper hand over those who hated them," because "the people of all the other nationalities were afraid of them," knowing that Mordechai "was prominent in the palace." And so "the Jews struck down all their enemies with the sword, killing and destroying them. . . ." In this biblical account, the Jewish people acted in anticipatory self-defense against an imminent and certain threat of genocide and were praised for it.[103]

Dershowitz in fact made over twenty references to the Bible in *Preemption*.[104] In contrast, Dershowitz made one reference, at best, to the Bill of Rights,[105] no references to the Fourth Amendment (which prohibits unreasonable searches and seizures and the issuance of warrants without probable cause), no references to the Fifth Amendment (which provides that a person cannot be deprived of life, liberty, or property without due process of law), and no references to the Eighth Amendment (which prohibits excessive bail, and cruel and unusual punishment).

While citing anecdotal evidence in *Preemption* to claim that important historical figures from Maimonides to Machiavelli to Thomas More supported preventive detention, Dershowitz never mentioned the American revolutionaries, including James Madison—the author of the Bill of Rights, or Patrick Henry, Robert Yates, Samuel Bryon, and George Mason—the principal supporters of a Bill of Rights. The lone exception in this regard was Dershowitz's reference, once again, to John Adams, about whom Dershowitz wrote in *Preemption*: "A related phenomenon [to preventive detention[106]] is the age-old right of self-defense. John Adams, in his closing argument on behalf of the British soldiers accused of perpetrating the Boston Massacre, invoked what he called 'the first and strongest principle in our nature,' preventing our own deaths by killing those about to attack us."[107] It seems that Dershowitz saw a great deal of utility in his retelling of the Boston Massacre, given its preeminence, along with the Bible, in his post–9/11 "jurisprudence" of the preemptive/preventive state.

12

CHOMSKY'S ANTI-AUTHORITARIANISM

In an appearance on the PBS show *Firing Line*, in April 1969, William F. Buckley introduced his guest for the evening, Noam Chomsky, as follows, with Chomsky's reply in full:

Buckley (introducing Noam Chomsky):

Professor Noam Chomsky is listed in anybody's catalog as among the half-dozen top heroes of the New Left. This standing he achieved by adopting over the past two or three years a series of adamant positions rejecting, at least, American foreign policy, at most, America itself. His essays and speeches are collected in his new book, *American Power and the New Mandarins*. Usually Mr. Chomsky writes nonpolitical books, for instance, *Syntactic Structures* in 1957, *Cartesian Linguistics* in 1966, and *Topics in the Theory of Generative Grammar*, 1965. He is a highly esteemed student of modern language and linguistics who teaches nowadays at the Massachusetts Institute of Technology and has taught before at Berkeley, Columbia, and other strife-torn universities [Buckley and Chomsky smile]. He is a member of many organizations and learned societies, including, I am sure he would want me to mention, the Aristotelian Society of Great Britain. In one of his essays, Mr. Chomsky writes: "By accepting the presumption of legitimacy of debate on certain issues, such as this one [the U.S. war in Vietnam], one has already lost one's humanity." I should like to begin by asking him why, under the circumstances, if by being here he stands to lose his humanity, he consented to appear in the first place?

Chomsky (responding to Buckley):

> Because . . . first of all, I didn't quite put it in those terms, I don't think. I think there are certain issues, for example, like Auschwitz, such that by consenting to discuss them one degrades oneself and to some degree loses one's humanity. And I think that that's true. Nevertheless, I can easily imagine circumstances in which I would have been glad to debate Auschwitz, for example, if there were some chance that by debating Auschwitz it might have been possible to eliminate it, or to at least mitigate the horror of what was going on. And I feel the same way about Vietnam.[1]

As an early, unsolicited statement of his abhorrence of the Nazis and the atrocities they committed, which he views as almost literally unspeakable, Chomsky's reference to Auschwitz as an archetype of Nazi atrocities is worth noting in the context of Dershowitz's charges years later that "Professor Noam Chomsky took up the cause of a notorious neo-Nazi Holocaust denier named Robert Faurisson," who claimed that the Nazi gas chambers never existed.[2] Dershowitz issued this charge, although—as Milan Rai reported in his 1994 book *Chomsky's Politics*—"anyone with the slightest knowledge of Chomsky's work will know, as Brian Morton points out, that from his earliest writings to his latest, 'Nazism has served him as a benchmark of pure and unquestionable evil.'"[3]

To illustrate further, in the very first pages of *American Power and the New Mandarins*, published in 1969, Chomsky wrote essentially the same thing that he would say to Buckley later that year:

> For the most part, these essays are elaborated versions of lectures given over the past few years. During these years, I have taken part in more conferences, debates, forums, teach-ins, meetings on Vietnam and American imperialism than I care to remember. Perhaps I should mention that, increasingly, I have had a certain feeling of falseness in these lectures and discussions. This feeling does not have to do with the intellectual issues. The basic facts are clear enough: the assessment of the situation is as accurate as I can make it. But the entire performance is emotionally and morally false in a disturbing way. It is a feeling that I have occasionally been struck by before. For example, I remember reading an excellent study of Hitler's East European policies a number of years ago in a mood of grim fascination. The author was trying hard to be cool and scholarly and objective, to stifle the only human response to a plan to enslave and destroy millions of subhuman organisms so that the inheritors of the spiritual values of Western civilization would be free to develop a higher form of society in peace. Controlling this elementary human

reaction, we enter into a technical debate with the
it technically feasible to dispose of millions of boa.
evidence that the Slavs are inferior beings? Must they be gi
foot or returned to their "natural" home in the East so that this gre.
ture can flourish, to the benefit of all mankind? Is it true that the Jews a.
a cancer eating away at the vitality of the German people? And so on.
Without awareness, I found myself drawn into this morass of insane
rationality—inventing arguments to counter and demolish the construc-
tions of the [Martin] Bormanns and the [Alfred] Rosenbergs.[4]

By entering into the arena of argument and counterargument, of
technical feasibility and tactics, of footnotes and citations, by accepting
the presumption of legitimacy of debate on certain issues, one has already
lost one's humanity. This is the feeling that I find almost impossible to
repress when going through the motions of building a case against the
American war in Vietnam. Anyone who puts a fraction of his mind to
the task can construct a case that is overwhelming; surely this is now
obvious. In an important way, by doing so he degrades himself, and insults
beyond measure the victims of our violence and moral blindness.[5]

An obviously misleading interpretation of this eloquent statement would be that
Chomsky was "fascinated" with Nazi policy in Eastern Europe, or that Chomsky
once pondered whether the Jews were a "cancer" in Germany in the 1930s. Yet,
this roughly resembles the level of analysis that Dershowitz would apply years
later to his claim—which he stated in *Chutzpah* (1991), *The Case for Israel* (2003),
The Case for Peace (2005), and *The Case against Israel's Enemies* (2008)—that
Chomsky supported Faurisson's substantive claims about the Nazis and the
Holocaust.

Dershowitz's suggestion that Chomksy, like Faurisson, is a Holocaust denier not
only adds to his portfolio of ugly insults of prominent American intellectuals, but
also should be seen in the completely clear context of Chomsky's lifelong record
of contempt for the Nazis. Thus, in his 1974 book *Peace in the Middle East?
Reflections on Justice and Nationhood*, Chomsky referred to the Holocaust as "the
most fantastic outburst of collective insanity in human history."[6] And here is
Chomsky speaking to James Peck in an interview published in 1987:

I suppose I am also a child of the Depression. Some of my earliest
memories, which are very vivid, are of people selling rags at our door, of
violent strikebreaking, and other Depression scenes. Whatever the reason
may be, I was very much affected by events of the 1930s, the Spanish Civil
War, for example, though I was barely literate. The first article I wrote was
an editorial in the school newspaper on the fall of Barcelona, a few weeks
after my tenth birthday. The rise of Nazism also made a deep impression,

ve were practically the only Jewish family in
ınd German Catholic neighborhood in which
r the Nazis until December 1941.[7]

ersity in 1985 about the U.S. overthrow of the
emalan government of Jacobo Arbenz and its replace-
atorship, Chomsky stated: "In Guatemala, in 1954, we
ıd destroy Guatemala's one attempt at democracy. There
eformist-capitalist democratic regime which we managed
to ove⌐ a literal hell-on-earth, probably the country which comes
closest in the mporary world to Nazi Germany. And we repeatedly
intervened to keep it that way."[8] (Years later, in 1999, the Guatemalan Commission
for Historical Clarification, referred to informally as the Guatemalan Truth
Commission, reported that "acts of genocide" had been committed against the
Mayans of Guatemala and that U.S.- and Israel-supported Guatemalan "state
forces and related paramilitary groups were responsible for 93 percent of the
violations documented."[9])

Chomsky not only has repeatedly denounced the atrocities of the Nazi regime
in Germany, he has helped to expose the Nazi and neo-Nazi network within the
U.S.-supported military dictatorships in Latin America, including in *The
Washington Connection and Third World Fascism* (1979), coauthored with Edward
S. Herman, which includes an eleven-page section titled "The Nazi Parallel," and
which reported:

- "Fascist ideology has flowed into Latin America directly and indirectly.
Large numbers of Nazi refugees came to Latin America during and after
World War II, and important ingredients of fascist ideology have been
indirectly routed into that area through the U.S. military and intelligence
establishment."[10]
- "The ideology designated the 'National Security Doctrine' (NSD) now
prevails among the military elites that rule at least eight Latin American
states—Argentina, Bolivia, Brazil, Chile, Ecuador, Paraguay, Peru, and
Uruguay. The doctrine has three main elements: (1) that the state is
absolute and the individual is nothing; (2) that every state is involved in
permanent warfare, its present form being Communism versus the Free
World; and (3) that control over 'subversion' is possible only through
domination by the natural leadership in the struggle against subversion,
namely the armed forces. The first two elements of the NSD closely
parallel Nazi ideology."[11]
- "In Nazi Germany too, as in other totalitarian societies, a primary aim
of the controlling leadership was the destruction of any organizational

threat that might challenge the attainment of 'state' ends; and unions, students and professional organizations, and community groups and political parties were infiltrated, harassed, destroyed, or brought under state control."[12]

• "The analogy here with the Latin America experience is striking, although it has been diligently avoided in the mass media of the United States. The National Security States, like Hitler, have used informers and force to destroy or bring under state control all protective organizations of the working class, peasants, rural workers and sub-proletariat."[13]

• "From the inception of this process and especially since the Brazilian coup of 1964, the churches have been pressed into opposition to subfascism, just as under Nazism, as the last institutional refuge of the population against state terror and state-protected and state-sponsored exploitation."[14]

Another setting for Chomsky's anti-Nazi views, his 1991 book *Deterring Democracy*, was published the same year as Dershowitz's *Chutzpah*, and included multiple denunciations of the Nazis and the neo-Nazi military governments in Central and South America.[15] Thus, while Dershowitz was asserting in *Chutzpah* in 1991 that Chomsky had supported "the merits"[16] and "the substance"[17] of Faurisson's denial of the existence of Nazi gas chambers and the Holocaust, Chomsky's readers were seeing something quite different in print in Chomsky's own words.

The matter of taking the time and space here to document a small portion of the record of Chomsky's abhorrence of the Nazis might seem unnecessary and perplexing. Yet, a book published in 2004 *The Anti-Chomsky Reader*, claimed that Chomsky "plays an important role in the neo-Nazi movement of our time," and that "much like a bigamist who must constantly strain to keep one of his wives secret from the other, Chomsky and his most determined supporters try to prevent his liberal and left-wing followers from knowing too much about his other life, the neo-Nazi one," in which Chomsky is the "grand patron of the neo-Nazi movement."[18] The same book claims that aspects of Chomsky's political work "amounts to a justification of Nazi Germany."[19] In the only back-cover endorsement to the book, edited by Peter Collier and David Horowitz, Dershowitz wrote: "Finally the smoking gun that conclusively proves what many have long known: that Chomsky simply cannot be trusted."[20]

In the context of Dershowitz's charges against Chomsky about Robert Faurisson, and for the purposes of this chapter, a second review exercise is necessary—on Chomsky's long history of defending academic freedom, free speech, and human rights. On October 14, 1973, the *New York Times* reported that "Noam Chomsky, the authority on linguistics; Representative Bella Abzug, Democrat of Manhattan; Allen Ginsburg, the poet; E. Y. Harburg, the lyricist; and Paddy Chayefsky, the playwright" had given their support to the "campaign to enable Leopold Trepper, who ran an anti-Nazi underground organization for the Soviet Union in Eastern Europe before and during World War II, to emigrate from Poland." The *Times* reported that "for several years sympathizers in Western Europe and the United States have been pressing the Polish Government to allow Mr. Trepper, a leader of the Jewish community, to leave." From the mid-1930s to the fall of Hitler, Trepper was head of "Red Orchestra," an anti-Nazi spy ring that reportedly "cost the lives of 200,000 German soldiers." A colleague of Trepper's told the *Times* that Poland had refused to permit Trepper to emigrate due to "the anti-Jewish campaign that began in Poland in 1969 and is still going on."[21] Chomsky and the others had acted in support of Trepper's right to leave Poland.

A year later, on January 31, 1974, the *New York Times* reported: "Yugoslavia's Communist party is finding itself subjected to growing international criticism for a bitter campaign to oust eight nonconformist Marxist professors at Belgrade University. The campaign has stirred wide protest in the West, especially among scholars concerned about academic freedom." In the United States, these included, as the *Times* reported, "the sociologist Daniel Bell of Harvard, the linguist Noam Chomksy of the Massachusetts Institute of Technology, Robert S. Cohen, the Boston University physicist and philosopher, the philosopher Charles Frankel of Columbia, Stanley Hoffmann, Harvard professor of government, and the philosopher Herbert Marcuse of the University of California at San Diego." President Tito of Yugoslavia had accused the eight professors at Belgrade University of being "anarcho-liberals" defiant of Communist party "discipline and doctrine."[22] Chomsky and the others had acted on behalf of the professors to prevent their ouster by Tito.

A few days later, on February 3, 1974, following Irving Howe's review in the *New York Times* of *The Case Worker* by the Jewish Hungarian writer George Konrád,[23] Chomsky wrote in the *Times*: "George Konrád, the author of the novel 'The Case Worker' which Irving Howe praised so highly in last week's Book Review, is currently in disfavor in Hungary." As a result, and as Chomksy reported, Konrád lost his research position at the Sociological Institute of the Hungarian Academy of Sciences, his freedom to travel, and the right to publish in Hungary. Chomsky added that "several other writers, including some associates of George Lukács," the Marxist Hungarian writer and philosopher, "have been similarly treated." Chomsky stated: "Hungary is still more liberal than other Eastern bloc countries, and I hope that the American publication of 'The Case Worker' will persuade the Hungarian authorities to restore Mr. Konrád's—and his colleagues'— right to work, publish and travel."[24]

The next day, on February 4, 1974, the *Times* reported that "a group of American scholars and writers has called on the Iranian Government to free from prison 12 Iranian journalists, writers and filmmakers, seven of whom they said had been sentenced to death for plotting against the royal family" of Shah Mohammad Reza Pahlavi, the U.S.-backed authoritarian ruler of Iran. The Americans, which included, as the *Times* reported, "Kurt Vonnegut Jr., Eric Bentley, Noam Chomsky and Dorothy Day, editor of The Catholic Worker," alleged that the twelve Iranians had been "arbitrarily arrested and brought before a military tribunal solely on the basis of 'confessions' obtained after torture."[25]

Thus, from January 31 to February 4, 1974—a period of five days—and in addition to Chomsky's support the year before of the right of Leopold Trepper to leave Poland, the *New York Times* published two brief news items and a letter noting Chomsky's support for eight professors in Yugoslavia, one writer in Hungary, and twelve journalists, writers, and filmmakers in Iran. Given the number of people involved, and the diversity of their nationalities and academic and artistic interests, it is unlikely that Chomsky would have been familiar with the work of each one. It is thus rather obvious that Chomsky was defending, if not the content of such work, then the right of academic and artistic expression.

I could continue for quite some time itemizing, as before, the occasions in which Chomsky loaned his name to a defense of the rights of academics, writers, artists, and others. To quickly list a few more: Chomsky, Howard Zinn, Simone de Beauvoir, and hundreds of academics and intellectuals signed a petition to protest the Indian government's detention of "tens of thousands of political prisoners . . . who have been rotting in Indian jails for several years without proper trials" while being subjected "to the most inhuman conditions as well as to physical torture."[26] Thus, was it the aim of Chomksy, Zinn, and the others to defend the detailed political views and conduct of each of the "tens of thousands" of prisoners? Or was the motivation to defend in principle the human rights of those imprisoned without trial? Similarly, in the 1970s Chomsky was a member of the Committee to Free Martin Sostre, "a black Puerto Rican" who, since 1968, had been "serving a 21-to-30 year sentence" in the state of New York for "selling $15 worth of heroin" in a bookstore in Buffalo.[27] Was Chomsky's interest here to defend the sale of heroin or, say, the constitutional ban against cruel and unusual punishment or racial discrimination in sentencing?

These are not difficult distinctions to grasp. Yet, when Chomsky signed a petition in 1979—"in the company of hundreds of others";[28] with "roughly five hundred others"[29]—defending the academic freedom of a French professor of literature, Robert Faurisson, who had been suspended from his job as a lecturer at the University of Lyon after claiming that the Nazi gas chambers did not exist—the distinction between a principled defense of academic freedom and the substance of Faurisson's claims should have been clear. That key distinction, however, in many cases, somehow vanished. For example, while referring to the Faurisson petition as "scandalous" in an influential 1980 article in the French literary magazine *Esprit*, French historian Pierre Vidal-Naquet never quoted from the operative part of the petition, which read as follows:[30] "We strongly protest these efforts to deprive Professor Faurisson of his *freedom of speech* and expression, and we condemn the shameful campaign to silence him. We strongly support Professor Faurisson's just *right of academic freedom* and we demand that university and government officials do everything possible to ensure his safety and the free exercise of his legal rights" (emphasis added).[31] A year later, in 1981, Vidal-Naquet published an article titled "On Faurisson and Chomsky," in which he again declined to cite this key paragraph from the petition, even while purporting to have reproduced the text of the petition in full; the same deletion was repeated in Vidal-Naquet's 1992 book *Assassins of Memory: Essays on the Denial of the Holocaust*.[32]

Furthermore, immediately after quoting from the petition, and while declining to reproduce the key words "freedom of speech" and "academic freedom" and thus negating the reasons for Chomsky's signature on it, Vidal-Naquet implied that Chomksy signed the petition because he had found some "truth" in Faurisson's claims:

> What is scandalous about the petition is that it never raises the question of whether what Faurisson is saying is true or false, that it even presents his conclusions or "findings" as the result of a historical investigation, one, that is, in quest of the truth. To be sure, it may be argued that every man has a right to lies and falsehood, and that individual freedom entails that right, which is accorded, in the French liberal tradition, to the accused for his defence. But the right that the forger demands should not be conceded to him in the name of truth.[33]

Without advocating on behalf of the truth of Faurisson's claims, Chomsky situated the issue at stake with respect to the Faurisson affair years later: "A professor of French literature was suspended from teaching on grounds that he could not be protected from violence, after privately printing pamphlets questioning the existence of gas chambers. He was then brought to trial for 'falsification of History,' and later condemned for this crime, the first time that a modern Western state openly affirmed the Stalinist-Nazi doctrine that the state will determine historical truth and punish deviation from it."[34]

The Faurisson affair, with respect to Chomsky's involvement, had its origins in December 1978 and January 1979, when Faurisson "published two letters in the French newspaper *Le Monde* claiming that the gas chambers used by the Nazis to exterminate the Jews did not exist." Faurisson was suspended from teaching and, following a television interview in France in which Faurisson repeated these claims, "was found guilty of defamation and incitement to racial hatred" and "given a suspended three-month prison term."[35] Subsequent to these events, and with hundreds of others, Chomksy signed a petition of protest, which he neither wrote nor initiated.[36]

Pursuant to criticism in France of Chomsky's signature on the petition, and in response to a request from a friend of Chomsky's to explain his reasons for signing the petition, Chomksy wrote a statement, which he titled "Some Elementary Comments on the Rights of Free Expression." By way of introduction, Chomsky wrote: "The remarks that follow are sufficiently banal so that I feel that an apology is in order to reasonable people who may happen to read them. If there is, nevertheless, good reason to put them on paper—and I fear that there is—this testifies to some remarkable features of contemporary French intellectual culture." Chomsky then wrote:

> Before I turn to the subject on which I have been asked to comment, two clarifications are necessary. The remarks that follow are limited in two crucial respects. First: I am concerned here solely with a narrow and specific topic, namely, the right of free expression of ideas, conclusions and beliefs. I have nothing to say here about the work of Robert Faurisson or his critics, of which I know very little, or about the topics they address, concerning which I have no special knowledge. Second: I will have some harsh (but merited) things to say about certain segments of the French intelligentsia, who have demonstrated that they have not the slightest concern for fact or reason, as I have learned from unpleasant personal experience that I will not review here.[37]

Chomsky continued:

> Some time ago I was asked to sign a petition in defense of Robert Faurisson's "freedom of speech and expression." The petition said absolutely nothing about the character, quality or validity of his research, but restricted itself quite explicitly to a defense of elementary rights that are taken for granted in democratic societies, calling upon university and government officials to "do everything possible to ensure the safety and the free exercise of his legal rights." I signed it without hesitation.
>
> The fact that I had signed the petition aroused a storm of protest in France. In the *Nouvel Observateur*, an ex-Stalinist who has changed allegiance but not intellectual style published a grossly falsified version of the contents of the petition, amidst a stream of falsehoods that merit no comment. This, however, I have come to regard as normal. I was considerably more surprised to read in *Esprit* (September 1980) that

Pierre Vidal-Naquet found the petition "scandaleuse," citing specifically that fact that I had signed it (I omit the discussion of an accompanying article by the editor that again merits no comment, at least among people who retain a commitment to elementary values of truth and honesty).

Vidal-Naquet offers exactly one reason for finding the petition, and my act of signing it, "scandaleuse": the petition, he claims, presented Faurisson's "'conclusions' comme si elles etaient effectivement des decouvertes [as if they had just been discovered]." Vidal-Naquet's statement is false. The petition simply stated that Faurisson had presented his "findings," which is uncontroversial, stating or implying precisely nothing about their value and implying nothing about their validity. Perhaps Vidal-Naquet was misled by faulty understanding of the English wording of the petition; that is, perhaps he misunderstood the English word "findings." It is, of course, obvious that if I say that someone presented his "findings" I imply nothing whatsoever about their character or validity; the statement is perfectly neutral in this respect. I assume that it was indeed a simple misunderstanding of the text that led Vidal-Naquet to write what he did, in which case he will, of course, publicly withdraw that accusation that I (among others) have done something "scandaleuse" in signing an innocuous civil rights petition of the sort that all of us sign frequently.[38]

After responding further to the criticism from French intellectuals, Chomsky began the final paragraph of his statement as follows:

Let me add a final remark about Faurisson's alleged "anti-Semitism." Note first that even if Faurisson were to be a rabid anti-Semite and fanatic pro-Nazi—such charges have been presented to me in private correspondence that it would be improper to cite in detail here—this would have no bearing whatsoever on the legitimacy of the defense of his civil rights. On the contrary, it would make it all the more imperative to defend them since, once again, it has been a truism for years, indeed centuries, that it is precisely in the case of horrendous ideas that the right of free expression must be most vigorously defended; it is easy enough to defend free expression for those who require no such defense.[39]

Indeed, the circumstances of the episode involving Faurisson, who was a mere pamphleteer, seemed less noxious than the horrific set of circumstances presented to the Jewish residents of Skokie, Illinois, in the 1970s, and eventually confronted by the U.S. Supreme Court in 1978 in *National Socialist Party v. Village of Skokie* (also cited as *Smith v. Collin*). In essence, an American neo-Nazi group, while intending to wear Nazi uniforms with swastikas, sought to hold an assembly at the city hall in Skokie, Illinois, a suburb of Chicago with a majority Jewish population, including Holocaust survivors. At the outset of her book *When the Nazis Came to Skokie: Freedom for Speech We Hate* (University Press of Kansas, 1999), Philippa Strum graphically described the circumstances of the case that eventually went to the U.S. Supreme Court:

> Francis Joseph Collin, known as Frank, called himself a Nazi. He believed that Jews and African Americans were biologically inferior and that the only way the United States could remain strong was to deprive Jews of citizenship and send all black Americans back to Africa. While he claimed not to advocate the immediate death of Jews, his idol was Adolf Hitler, the German Nazi leader who attempted to eradicate European Jews by having six million of them murdered in concentration camps during World War II.
>
> Frank Collin wasn't German. He was an American, born in Illinois. He never traveled outside the United States. As do all Americans, he possessed inalienable rights, among them the right to believe and to speak in public about whatever obnoxious ideas he chose.
>
> The place Collin and his two dozen uniformed followers chose to proclaim their Nazism in 1977, however, was the Chicago suburb of Skokie, the home of thousands of Holocaust survivors. These residents were among the minority of European Jews who had managed to escape death in Hitler's concentration camps and immigrate to the United States at the end of World War II. By 1977 they too were American citizens with inalienable rights. One of their rights, they believed, was to live peacefully and safely, dealing as best they could with their unspeakable memories of families brutally separated, of forced labor and starvation, and of those who were forced into gas chambers to die. They shuddered at the idea of American Nazis appearing in their town, wearing the same uniforms as the German Nazis who had enslaved them and killed their families.
>
> The psychological damage Collin's presence would inflict upon them gave *them* a right, they thought, that outweighed Collin's claim to parade his ideas in their village, and they were equally sure the American government would recognize that. So they went to court to keep Collin and his obnoxious ideas out of Skokie.[40]

Ultimately, however, the Illinois Supreme Court ruled that Collin and his band of Nazis had a First Amendment right to assemble, and the U.S. Supreme Court denied the petition by the Village of Skokie to review that decision.

Due to its legal representation of Collin and his Nazi cohort, and evocative of the reaction against Chomsky, the American Civil Liberties Union was subjected to a severe backlash within the country at large and from its membership. In a news item in August 1977 titled "A.C.L.U. Members Resign over Defense of Nazis," the *New York Times* reported:

> The legal defense of Nazis by the American Civil Liberties Union has set off a wave of resignations among members of the A.C.L.U., an official of the organization says. David Hamlin, executive director of the A.C.L.U.'s Illinois chapter, said yesterday that 1,000 out of 8,000 members have quit the state branch of the A.C.L.U., which is devoted to upholding free speech and other constitutional rights. Mr. Hamlin said 2,100 persons have resigned from the national organization since the Illinois branch began its legal battle to allow the Chicago-based Nazi organization to hold a parade in Skokie, a heavily Jewish suburb of Chicago.[41]

And in her book, Strum reported: "By September 1977, David Goldberger and the rest of the ACLU staff were reeling from the public response to the case. . . . So much of the national press was writing about Skokie and interviewing [Holocaust] survivors there that it was hard to find new faces for their stories. Many of [the journalists] turned their attention instead to what Goldberger called 'the growing flood of criticism and outright verbal abuse' and to the increasing number of resignations by ACLU members."[42]

Strum also reported how Ira Glasser, who would replace Aryeh Neier as the A.C.L.U.'s executive director in 1978, described the backlash as "threaten[ing] to cripple the ACLU" and told New York members that "all our programs were in jeopardy." Yet, Glasser defended the organization's decision to represent the Nazis in its suit against the Skokie ordinances that prohibited the Nazis to assemble:

> It is the same kind of law that was used in Birmingham, Alabama, and throughout the South to stop civil rights demonstrators. . . . Of course, there is a vast moral difference between the Nazis' speech in Skokie and Martin Luther King's demonstrations in the South. What we must all decide, however, is . . . whether it is in our best interests—yours and mine—for the ACLU to have entered the Skokie case in order to strike down the anti-demonstration law. We defend the First Amendment for everybody because there is no other way to defend it for ourselves.[43]

This was precisely the principled basis of Chomsky's defense of Faurisson's speech and academic rights, as stipulated not only in the original petition, cited earlier, but in the statement that Chomksy wrote to respond to the criticism of his signature on the petition.

Note that Chomsky had signed the petition in 1979, a mere one year after the ACLU's defense of the speech and assembly rights of the American Nazis, and the decisions by the Illinois Supreme Court and the U.S. Supreme Court. Furthermore, Dershowitz wrote in 1991 in *Chutzpah* that he had "defend[ed]" the "rights of Nazis to march through the Jewish community of Skokie."[44] Yet, in that very same book, and subsequent ones, Dershowitz accused Chomsky of Holocaust denialism for supporting the same principled right of free speech with respect to Faurisson.

Dershowitz also wrote, falsely: "Chomsky went even further. After signing the petition, he wrote an essay that he allowed to be used as a foreword to Faurisson's next book about his career as a Holocaust denier."[45] Dershowitz published these words in 2003. Yet, more than twenty years earlier, Chomsky had detailed how the statement that he wrote, in response to the criticism of his name on the petition, was issued as the foreword to a book by Faurisson. In an article in the *Nation* in February 1981 titled "His Right to Say It," Chomsky described how he had responded to a request from a friend, Serge Thion:

> Thion then asked me to write a brief statement on the purely civil libertarian aspects of this [Faurisson] affair. I did so, telling him to use it as he wished. . . . I later learned that my statement was to appear in a book in which Faurisson defends himself against the charges soon to be brought against him in court. While this was not my intention, it was not contrary to my instructions. I received a letter from Jean-Pierre Faye, a well-known anti-Fascist writer and militant, who agreed with my position but urged me to withhold my statement because the climate of opinion in France was such that my defense of Faurisson's right to express his views would be interpreted as support for them. I wrote to him that I accepted his judgment, and requested that my statement not appear [in Faurisson's book], but by then it was too late to stop publication.[46]

While claiming more than twenty years later that Chomsky "wrote an essay that he allowed to be used as a foreword to Faurisson's book," Dershowitz did not bother to acknowledge Chomsky's explanation to the contrary.

Rather than retract his claim, issued in 2003 in *The Case for Israel*, that Chomsky had "flirted with Holocaust denial," Dershowitz embellished it further in his 2005 book *The Case for Peace*, where he ominously asks in a bold-type section heading: "Who Is Noam Chomsky?" Dershowitz then wrote: "But not many are aware of the even darker side of [Chomsky's] record—including supporting, praising, and working with Holocaust deniers. Chomsky's most notorious bedfellow is Robert Faurisson, who called the Holocaust a 'hoax,' denied the existence of gas chambers, claimed that the diary of Anne Frank was a 'forgery,' and described the Jewish claims for Holocaust reparations as a 'fraud.'"[47] Assuming, for a moment (falsely), that Faurisson is one of Chomsky's "bedfellows" in Holocaust denialism, who are the others? Dershowitz doesn't say. But to support his claim that Chomsky and Faurisson are co-conspirators in Holocaust denialism, Dershowitz references "Chomsky and Holocaust Denial" by Werner Cohn,[48] author of the claims, cited earlier, that Chomsky "plays an important role in the neo-Nazi movement of our time," that "Chomsky and his most determined supporters try to prevent his liberal and left-wing followers from knowing too much about his other life, the neo-Nazi one," and that Chomsky is the "grand patron of the neo-Nazi movement."[49] Thus, Dershowitz not only wrote the only book-cover blurb for the book in which these statements were made, he went on to cite this very same essay in footnoting his claim that Chomsky "supports, praises, and works with Holocaust deniers." Dershowitz also implied that Chomsky shares Faurisson's views that the Holocaust was a hoax, that the Nazi gas chambers did not exist, and that the diary of Anne Frank was a forgery. Yet, in his February 1981 article in the *Nation*, Chomsky wrote: "Faurisson's conclusions are diametrically opposed to views I hold and have frequently expressed in print."[50] Dershowitz never cited those words either, published in 1981, while accusing Chomsky in 2005 of being Faurisson's bedfellow in Holocaust denialism.

In addition to the problems noted previously, there are other issues worth reviewing in the context of Dershowitz's long-standing effort to mark Chomsky as a Holocaust denier. In his 1991 autobiography *Chutzpah*, Dershowitz described Meir Kahane, the Jewish American founder of the Jewish Defense League, as a "Jewish racist," and explained why he defended Kahane's right to free speech: "I decided that I would not impose a double standard on the rights of a Jewish racist . . . as distinguished from other bigots. Whatever rights any racist, sexist, or other –ist would be entitled to, Kahane and his audiences should have as well."[51] Also in *Chutzpah*, Dershowitz wrote: "While condemning Kahane's ideas on their merits, I defended his right to state them."[52] Thus, Dershowitz defends the identical right of Kahane, a Jewish terrorist, to express his ideas—without, he asserted, endorsing those ideas—that Chomsky defended with respect to Faurisson. Yet, while Dershowitz is prolifically and viciously critical of Chomsky's defense of Faurisson's rights, Chomsky has not criticized Dershowitz's defense of Kahane's rights, although he would have had grounds to do so, given that Kahane was not subjected to state censorship, while Faurisson was.

Furthermore, Kahane was a notorious proponent of politically motivated violence in the United States in the "self-defense" of American Jews who, in Kahane's view, faced a Nazi-like threat of annihilation in the United States. On its Web site, the Anti-Defamation League describes Kahane's views as follows: "In Rabbi Kahane's gross distortion of the position of Jews in America, American Jews were living in a fiercely hostile society, facing much the same dangers as the Jews in Nazi Germany or those in Israel surrounded by 100-million Arab enemies. Rabbi Kahane believed that the major Jewish organizations in the United States had failed to protect America's Jews from anti-Semitism, which he saw as 'exploding' all over the country.... In fact, Kahane consistently preached a radical form of Jewish nationalism which reflected racism, violence and political extremism." The same ADL Web page lists many dozens of acts of violence committed by the Jewish Defense League, or supported by it, well before 1991, the publication date of *Chutzpah*.[53]

Also, according to the *Jerusalem Post*'s English-language Internet edition:

> Kahane was known in the United States and Israel for political and religious views that included proposing emergency Jewish mass-immigration to Israel due to the imminent threat of a "second Holocaust" in the United States, advocating that Israel's secular democracy be replaced by a state modeled on Jewish religious law, and promoting the idea of a Greater Israel in which Israel would annex the West Bank and Gaza Strip. In order to keep Arabs, whom he stated would never accept Israel as a Jewish state, from demographically destroying Israel, he proposed paying Arabs to leave Israel and those territories voluntarily, and forcibly removing those who would not.[54]

In *Chutzpah*, Dershowitz recalled an exchange with Kahane during one of their debates, from which Dershowitz provided a verbatim excerpt. In it, at a minimum, Dershowitz failed to oppose Kahane's suggestion to remove Arabs from Israel and the Israel-occupied territories:

> [Kahane:] "Assuming that the Arabs become saints—and they sit down democratically, and they reproduce saints—I don't want to live under a majority of Arab saints. So the question that I ask of people who are upset at the things I say, is: What is your answer to the voting question? Do the Arabs have a right to become a majority, democratically, peacefully, in the state of Israel?"
>
> [Dershowitz:] "I tried to answer in a manner consistent with both my Jewish and democratic values. Rabbi Kahane would throw up his hands and say there is no room for democracy, there is nothing Jewish about democracy. I beg to differ. The vast majority of Jews in this world support both Zionism and democracy. The false dichotomy that Rabbi Kahane is seeking to impose on us is not correct, and the ultimate implications of his dangerous view are that once the Arabs are expelled from Israel, then Jews who do not fit Rabbi Kahane's particularistic definition of his kind of Jew will also be expelled."[55]

For Dershowitz, in this passage, the "dangerous view" does not appear to be the expulsion of Arabs from Israel, and possibly from the West Bank, but the fate of certain Jews "once the Arabs are expelled from Israel."

In addition, as he notes in *Chutzpah*, Dershowitz had a long-standing relationship of a sort with Kahane.[56] This included debating Kahane, as Dershowitz tells it: "My debates with Meir Kahane are a story in themselves. For years no prominent Jew—certainly no members of the Jewish establishment—would debate Kahane or share a platform with him. Because of his ultraright views and advocacy of violence to rid Israel of Arabs, the major Jewish organizations had imposed a virtual shroud of censorship around him."[57] Thus, despite Kahane's open advocacy of the expulsion of Israeli Arabs from "Greater Israel," and nearly alone among establishment Jews, Dershowitz was willing to "share a platform with him." One might ask, however: Where was the compelling interest for Dershowitz to do so? Dershowitz answered: "I had long opposed these attempts at censorship" of Kahane.[58] But it's only "censorship" when governments do it as, for example, in the case of Faurisson; when private organizations or individuals do it, it's merely an expression of personal preference and, in this instance, as the ADL observed, civilized values.

There are other disturbing aspects of Dershowitz's involvement in the Faurisson affair. In at least ten endnotes in his 2003 book *The Case for Israel*, Dershowitz referenced a lecture that Chomsky had given at Harvard University on November 25, 2002, at the invitation of the Harvard Anthropology Department. Chomsky's lecture at Harvard was Dershowitz's single-most referenced source of Chomsky's work in *The Case for Israel*—the same book in which Dershowitz referred to "Chomsky's flirtation with Holocaust denial."[59] Yet, in that very same lecture, Chomsky referred to the Nazis as "the worst mass murderers, maybe in history."[60] Dershowitz never quoted or otherwise referred to that statement by Chomsky, despite prolifically citing the very same source in which Chomsky spoke those words.

Two years later, in *The Case for Peace*, Dershowitz introduced a section on Chomsky by accusing him of "extreme hatred of the United States and Israel."[61] Yet, Dershowitz no doubt was familiar with the words of Stephen Caton, chair of Harvard University's Anthropology Department, who introduced Chomsky to the Harvard audience in that same lecture by Chomsky on November 25, 2002, and who eloquently identified Chomsky's allegiance to a better tradition of the United States than loyalty to its aggressive wars:

> It is an honor and a great pleasure to introduce Professor Chomsky. . . .
> We are located just a few miles from Concord, Massachusetts, and Walden Pond, the site of Henry David Thoreau's experiment of living in the woods and living independently. And, of Thoreau, Emerson once said: "No truer American existed than Thoreau." This was not the least because of his classic essay, on the duty of "Civil Disobedience," which has ever since formed a statement about protest and dissidence, not only in American politics, but elsewhere.

In an important sense, our speaker today is heir of that tradition, a tradition that today is very much in danger of being forgotten and disappearing. His is the voice of a highly informed and reasoned dissent from prevailing points of view in the media and in the U.S. government. Indeed, it is rare to find a public intellectual who so painstakingly unearths facts, then analyzes them in such a systematic manner so as to explain what we are up to. . . .

He was willing to go to jail when he refused to pay his taxes during the Vietnam War as a protest against what he deemed to be illegal and unjust policies of our government. And he has had to endure intimidation of various kinds in his courageously outspoken views on the Middle East and other areas of the world. . . . Let me just say in conclusion that what Emerson said of Thoreau, one could repeat of Chomsky, that "Perhaps no truer American exists today."[62]

It is difficult to fathom why an American civil libertarian, which Dershowitz perhaps once was, would transpose an essential element of civil libertarianism—dissent from the lawless conduct of one's own government—into a claim that Chomsky "hates" his country. Indeed, to characterize Chomsky's exemplary dissent from perpetual war—waged illegally by government officials in the name of the American people with public funds that would serve this country far better if they were not spent on illegal, aggressive war—as "extreme hatred of the United States," is an attack on dissent itself. So are Dershowitz's tireless insults of the other "haters," "bigots," and "enemies" already noted in this volume, who also have dissented from U.S. government policies for similar reasons.

Another peculiar feature of Dershowitz's accusations about Chomsky's "flirtation" with Nazism is the fact that it was Chomsky, and not Dershowitz, who worked assiduously to expose the Nazi legacy in Latin America, including the U.S.- and Israel-supported fascist military dictatorships in Central America. Recall Chomsky's statement in 1985 at Harvard that "probably the country which comes closest in the contemporary world to Nazi Germany" was post-1954 Guatemala.[63] The date, 1985, is significant, since by then, the major human rights organizations at the time—Amnesty International and Americas Watch[64]—had issued reports on Guatemala that supported Chomsky's assertion. In reading excerpts from the reports quoted further on by Amnesty International and Americas Watch, and the practices and policies of the neo-Nazi fascism that the reports invoke, note that it was Chomsky, not Dershowitz, who spent years bitterly opposing the fascist dictatorships of Central America, and that it was Dershowitz, not Chomsky, who would do more than "flirt" years later with such pillars of totalitarianism as unending war, preventive detention, torture, extrajudicial killings (state-sponsored murder), and the rejection of enlightened law.

In its 1981 report "Guatemala: A Government Program of Political Murder," Amnesty International introduced its findings as follows: "The human rights issue that dominates all others in the Republic of Guatemala is that people who oppose or are imagined to oppose the government are systematically seized without warrant, tortured and murdered, and that these tortures and murders are part of a deliberate and long-standing program of the Guatemala Government."[65] In its 1982 report "Human Rights in Guatemala: No Neutrals Allowed," Americas Watch reported:

> Against this background [of extreme wealth disparities, an economic crisis, and an armed conflict between the government and anti-government insurgents], we examined the status of civil and political rights in Guatemala. We came away profoundly disturbed by the policies and attitudes of the Rios Montt government. That government, whose legitimacy and authority derive only from the military, is committed, and has been committed from the outset, to a military solution. Indeed, we believe that the government of Rios Montt is committed to total war. . . .
>
> Obviously, such a policy of total war ensures that fundamental rights, such as the right to life, the right to physical integrity, the right to personal security and the right to liberty, will be little respected. Massacres of Indians that may be committed by the Guatemalan armed forces cannot be blamed solely on undisciplined, rogue troops. They flow directly from the announced policies of the Rios Montt government that recognize no neutrals.
>
> The total war policies of the government of President Rios Montt are reflected in its decrees. Those decrees . . . abolish virtually all the rights of Guatemalans. Indeed, our close examination of the decrees promulgated by President Rios Montt since the March 23 coup persuades us that the Guatemalan Government has overtly abandoned the rule of law and that it has overtly substituted a system of government that is both despotic and totalitarian.[66]

In 1984, Americas Watch reported that "the killing continues" in Guatemala, that "the government of Guatemala continues to engage in the systematic use of torture as a means of gathering intelligence and coercing confessions," and that "there has been a sharp increase in the incidence of disappearances, both urban and rural."[67]

Coincidental to these reports is the fact that by the mid-1970s and into the 1980s, Guatemala's main military supplier was Israel—a fact about which Dershowitz has written nothing. In a lengthy analysis in 1986 titled "Israel and Guatemala: Arms, Advice and Counterinsurgency," Cheryl Rubenberg reviewed the Israel-Guatemala military relationship:

In 1975 [following an Israel-Guatemala arms agreement], Israeli-made Arava aircraft (adaptable for counterinsurgency tasks) arrived in Guatemala, followed by deliveries of armored cars, artillery and small arms, including [Israel-made] Uzi submachine guns and the [Israel-made] Galil assault rifle, which became standard issue for the Guatemalan army. Israeli technicians and military advisers accompanied the Aravas.... In 1977, a series of events resulted in Israel becoming Guatemala's principal arms supplier and primary source of counterinsurgency advice.

Three months after Jimmy Carter became president in January 1977, the [U.S.] State Department issued a report condemning human rights violations in Guatemala. The Guatemalan regime retorted that it would reject in advance any military aid from a government which dared to impose conditions or interfere in its internal affairs. At Carter's request, Congress suspended military aid to Guatemala, and the administration included Guatemala on a list of "gross and consistent violators of human rights."

The Israeli government immediately stepped in to fill the vacuum and a flourish of activity ensued. Israel did not put "strings" on its arms or advice and was indifferent to the repressive practices of the Guatemalan regime. The flow of arms and "agricultural development" advisors picked up considerably.[68]

Ultimately, according to Rubenberg, Guatemala bought armed patrol boats, tanks and armored cars, other weapons and munitions, military communications equipment, radar systems, and field kitchens from Israel. "By 1980," Rubenberg wrote, "the Guatemalan army was fully equipped with Galil rifles at a cost of $6 million."[69] In her 1987 book *Israeli Foreign Policy: South Africa and Central America*, Jane Hunter reported that "Uzis and the larger Galil assault rifles used by Guatemala's special counterinsurgency forces accounted for at least half of the estimated 45,000 Guatemalan Indians killed by the [Guatemalan] military since 1978."[70]

Hunter also reported that "Israeli advisers have worked with the feared G-2 police intelligence unit," which "has been largely responsible for the death squad killings over the last decade."[71] Israel also "bestowed upon Guatemala the technology needed by a modern police state," according to Hunter, including computer systems used by "the nerve center of the armed forces" and "to sort through dossiers and to distribute lists of those marked for death."[72] Rubenberg reported that "by early 1982, there were at least 300 Israeli advisors in Guatemala."[73]

And it wasn't merely Guatemala that enjoyed Israel's business as an arms supplier and counterinsurgency adviser. Leslie Gelb of the *New York Times* reported in 1982 that "Israel entered the Central American arms market in the mid-1970s, largely to supply small arms to the Nicaraguan regime headed by Anastasio

Somoza Debayle," and that "those supplies continued nearly until the collapse of the Somoza regime despite entreaties by the Carter Administration to stop much earlier."[74] And Hunter reported that "between the 1977 U.S. cutoff [under President Carter] and the resumption [under President Reagan] of U.S. aid in 1981, El Salvador obtained over 80 percent of its weapons from Israel."[75] While Rubenberg wrote that "Israel's increasingly visible presence throughout the Third World, including such disparate places as the Philippines, South Africa, Sri Lanka, Botswana, El Salvador and Argentina, raises a number of questions about the objectives and character of Israel's foreign policy,"[76] Hunter observed that "the export markets open to Israel are frequently among the world's most unsavory; indeed, to be off limits to the superpowers, they often are located inside the very gates of hell," including "the white clique in South Africa, Somoza of Nicaragua, Duvalier of Haiti [and] Mobutu of Zaire."[77]

Surely, as a leading American expert on Israel for the past several decades, Dershowitz would have been knowledgeable about Israel's support for the post–World War II fascist military dictatorships in Central America. Yet, in the four books in which he accused Chomksy of having Nazi and neo-Nazi sympathies—from *Chutzpah* in 1991 to *The Case against Israel's Enemies* in 2006—Dershowitz never mentioned the word "Guatemala," or otherwise reviewed in any way Israel's close military support of post-1954 Guatemala.[78] The same search results apply to the words "Nicaragua," "Somoza," and "El Salvador." In other words, Dershowitz launched his Nazi "flirtation" campaign against Chomsky in *Chutzpah* in 1991 after more than a decade of Israeli military sales to the neo-Nazi governments in Latin America—a fact that Dershowitz ignored while Chomsky did not. A brief survey follows.

On the first page of *The Washington Connection and Third World Fascism*, published in 1979, Chomsky and Herman wrote: "Since 1960 over 18 Latin American regimes have been subjected to military takeovers." This fact and its consequences would occupy much of what Chomsky and Herman would write about in subsequent books and articles, including *The Real Terror Network: Terrorism in Fact and Propaganda* (1982) by Herman and *Turning the Tide: U.S. Intervention in Central America and the Struggle for Peace* (1985) by Chomsky. Chomsky and Herman continued: "U.S. influence has been crucial in this process [of military takeovers in Latin America], in some cases by means of deliberate subversion or even direct aggression, but invariably important given the substantial economic and military penetration and presence of the superpower." The authors then noted: "The fate of Guatemalan democracy, subverted by the CIA in 1954 in favor of a regime of torture and oppression, can be matched with that of Iran a year earlier; and the Philippines, brutally subjugated at the turn of the century, has now been stripped of its short-lived democratic façade without a word of protest by the United States. This, and the subsequent sharp increases in economic and military aid to the martial law government of Marcos, not only reflect a familiar and traditional pattern, they are also compelling evidence of approval and support."[79]

About Guatemala, Herman wrote in *The Real Terror Network*:

> Another extremely important reflection of a resurgence of [Guatemalan state] terrorism has been the growth of "disappearances," a phenomenon mentioned by Hannah Arendt as one of the last and most terrible phases in the evolution and degeneration of totalitarian states. The term refers to cases where individuals are seized by military, paramilitary or police agents of the state, who secretly murder and dispose of the bodies of their victims, often after torture, always without acknowledgment and admitted responsibility of the state. Disappearance, as described by a report on this subject by [Amnesty International], is "a particular government practice applied on a massive scale in Guatemala after 1966, in Chile since late 1973, and in Argentina after March 1976." It was a tactic used by the Nazis in the occupied territories in the 1940s under the Nacht und Nebel (Night and Fog) Decree to dispose of those resisters "endangering German security" by means of what Field Marshall Wilhelm Keitel described as "effective intimidation." The victims, in Germany as in Chile, were subject to an often violent arrest, torture, secret imprisonment and usually death.[80]

Also about Guatemala, Chomsky wrote in *Turning the Tide*:

> In a brief report of the murder of yet another professor at the national university [of Guatemala], the [*New York*] *Times* noted in passing that more than 40,000 people have disappeared and more than 95,000 "have died in political violence here since 1954" according to "the Mexican-based Guatemalan Human Rights Commission": to translate from Newspeak, some 140,000 have been eliminated by the governments installed and kept in power by the US since the US overthrew Guatemalan democracy in 1954 (the crucial fact, regularly omitted in news reports and editorial comment), according to a Human Rights Commission which is Mexican-based because its members could not long survive in Guatemala. In May 1982, the conservative Guatemalan Conference of Catholic Bishops stated that "never in our history have such extremes been reached, with the assassinations now falling into the category of genocide."[81]

In short, while the Israeli government played a key role for a time in arming and supporting the military dictatorships of Central America, it was the United States that mainly conducted the post–World War II orchestra of fascist regimes

---

throughout Latin America. While falsely accusing Chomsky of having Nazi and neo-Nazi sympathies, Dershowitz did nothing to oppose the far-right governments in Latin America; this while Chomsky and Herman generated valuable first-rate scholarship and thereby contributed to the downfall of the neo-Nazi governments in Latin America, where both are highly esteemed as anti-fascist intellectuals.

The result is similar when we apply the relative "truth" standards of Chomsky on the one hand, and Dershowitz on the other, to Israel's occupation of the Palestinian territories, where Chomsky also is highly regarded. Whereas Chomsky wrote, over forty years ago, that it is the responsibility of intellectuals to tell the truth and expose the lies of governments—on behalf of human rights and in opposition to the coercive powers of the state—it seems that Dershowitz's view of his role as an influential intellectual is the opposite in each of those respects. From the start Chomsky has denounced state terrorism quite literally on a global scale—from East Timor to Nicaragua to the West Bank. In contrast, with a one-client practice in the court of public opinion, Dershowitz is a leading advocate of the coercive powers of the state in virtually every conceivable realm: what Dershowitz depicts as "preemptive" and "preventive" wars are in fact wars of aggression—the "supreme international crime" in international law; Dershowitz's support for extrajudicial killings is support for state-sanctioned murder; his well-known support of torture in ticking-bomb scenarios, with a presidential or court signature, would formally establish state-sanctioned torture in the United States; his apparent support of the surveillance state and preventive detention as counterterrorism measures is squarely within the tradition of the extinct neo-Nazi governments of Latin America. To paraphrase Henry Stimson, there is something wrong with a country where few people question this. Finally, Dershowitz openly markets his dystopian "preventive state" by campaigning for a "reinterpretation of constitutional principles," which is Dershowitz's would-be coup against the Bill of Rights.

"Big Brother, Where Art Thou?" Thou art, of all places, at Harvard Law School.

13

ON KILL COURTS AND TORTURE WARRANTS

On September 30, 2011, Anwar al-Awlaki, a U.S. citizen, was killed in Yemen by "a barrage of Hellfire missiles" fired from an aerial drone pursuant to the personal approval of President Obama.[1] At the White House that day, Obama announced the killing: "Earlier this morning, Anwar Awlaki ... was killed in Yemen. The death of Awlaki is a major blow to Al Qaeda's most active operational affiliate. Awlaki was the leader of external operations for Al Qaeda in the Arabian Peninsula. In that role he took the lead in planning and directing the efforts to murder innocent Americans. He directed the failed attempt to blow up an airplane on Christmas Day in 2009."[2] Whether those charges were accurate or not is hard to say; I will revisit them momentarily. More importantly, perhaps, they were issued solely by the president, with no opportunity for Awlaki to defend himself in a court of law before he was executed by the government in a covert operation with remote-controlled missiles, as David Cole has observed.[3]

Obama's announcement was an unprecedented demonstration of presidential disregard of the Fifth Amendment's guarantee of due process, not to mention other U.S. law that prohibits "murder" and "assassinations." The targeted killing of Awlaki—who, as reported by the *New York Times*, was included on President Obama's "kill list" and whose killing was, in the president's words, "an easy one" to authorize[4]—is presented here as a case study of how the U.S. war on terrorism is infecting the Bill of Rights with ongoing lawless executive conduct at home and abroad. And like the Faurisson affair and the Nazis in Skokie discussed in the previous chapter, the constitutionally relevant issue here is not whether we liked Anwar al-Awlaki or approved of the contents of his political speech, but whether the Bill of Rights applies to all U.S. citizens, and whether the president can pick and choose who deserves to have those rights and who doesn't.

The constitutional and statutory law context of the killing of Anwar al-Awlaki is summarized briefly as follows: The Fifth Amendment to the U.S. Constitution specifies: "No person shall be … deprived of life, liberty, or property, without due process of law." *Black's Law Dictionary* defines "due process" as "the conduct of legal proceedings according to established rules and principles for the protection and enforcement of private rights, including notice and the right to a fair hearing before a tribunal with the power to decide the case." That same reference quoted the words of Alexander Hamilton: "The words 'due process' have a precise technical import, and are only applicable to the process and proceedings of the courts of justice." It also cited two U.S. Supreme Court decisions: "The words 'due process of law' were undoubtedly intended to convey the same meaning as the words 'by the law of the land,' in Magna Carta"; and: "An elementary and fundamental requirement of due process in any proceeding which is to be accorded finality is notice reasonably calculated, under all the circumstances, to apprise interested parties of the pendency of the action and afford them an opportunity to present their objections."[5] In addition, Title 18, section 1119, of the United States Code, "Foreign Murder of United States Nationals," bans the "murder" of U.S. citizens abroad,[6] while a series of executive orders issued by several of our most recent presidents prohibit "assassinations."[7] Despite the extremely serious constitutional and legal issues implicated in his order to kill the U.S. citizen Anwar al-Awlaki, President Obama referenced no part of the Constitution or any law in his announcement of the targeted killing of Awlaki.

Four months later, on February 4, 2012, veteran national security reporter Michael Isikoff issued a report for NBC News about "a confidential Justice Department memo" pertaining to the Awlaki episode. Isikoff's piece was called "Justice Department Memo Reveals Legal Case for Drone Strikes on Americans." The memo itself was titled "Lawfulness of a Lethal Operation Directed against a U.S. Citizen Who Is a Senior Operational Leader of Al-Qa'ida or an Associated Force."

While presenting its case, the Justice Department document placed repeated emphasis on an "imminent threat" justification for killing Awlaki, including as follows (emphasis added):

> • "Targeting a member of an enemy force who poses an *imminent threat* of violent attack to the United States is not unlawful. It is a lawful act of national self defense";[8]
> • "A lethal operation against a U.S. citizen who is a senior operational leader of al-Qa'ida or its associated forces" and "who himself poses an imminent threat of violent attack against the United States, would not

violate the Constitution";[9]

• "In these circumstances, the 'realities' of the conflict and the weight of the government's interest in protecting its citizens from an *imminent attack* are such that the Constitution would not require the government to provide further process to such a U.S. citizen before using lethal force."[10]

At the same time, the Justice Department deployed a modified meaning of "imminent threat" that was not consistent with the customary legal meaning of the term: "Certain aspects of this legal framework require additional explication. First, the condition that an operational leader present an 'imminent' threat of violent attack against the United States does not require the United States to have clear evidence that a specific attack on U.S. persons and interests will take place in the immediate future."[11]

In his report for NBC News and quoting the Justice Department memo, Isikoff wrote that the Justice Department deployed a "broader concept of imminence," and cited Jameel Jaffer, deputy legal director of the ACLU, who told Isikoff that the memo "redefines the word imminence in a way that deprives the word of its ordinary meaning."[12] *Black's Law Dictionary* gives the ordinary meaning of the term: An "imminent danger" is "an immediate, real threat to one's safety that justifies the use of force in self-defense." In short, the government cannot credibly justify a targeted killing of a U.S. citizen without due process by, at one moment, featuring an "imminent threat" justification and at the next moment allowing that the alleged threat posed by the person who had already been killed may not have been "imminent" within the obvious meaning of the word.

Isikoff also wrote that the Justice Department memorandum deployed an "expansive definition of self-defense" when it claimed legal authority for the targeted killing of Awlaki. The memo invoked "national self-defense" or "self-defense" on ten separate occasions while citing U.N. Charter Article 51 as the lone legal source of its self-defense claim.[13] But as Mary Ellen O'Connell noted in a legal analysis for CNN titled "Killing Awlaki Was Illegal, Immoral, and Dangerous": "[Obama administration] officials also assert we have a right to kill persons who pose an 'imminent' threat under the law of self-defense. In fact, the law of self-defense, found in the U.N. Charter, permits force in self-defense on the territory of a state if the state is responsible for a significant armed attack. Yemen is not responsible for any significant armed attacks."[14] As O'Connell suggests, the resort to the use of force by one state against another in self-defense relies on a rigorous standard of "armed attack" involving real military forces engaged in a genuinely imminent or actual assault on the territorial borders of another state, as I have already discussed (see chapter 8). This standard of self-defense by resort to military force—which is the only exception to the UN Charter's predominate prohibition against the resort to military force—is not met by the Justice Department's focus on a targeted individual who had no ability to engage in an "armed attack" against the United States as the term is defined under international law.

The Justice Department's memo also asserted that "the United States is in an armed conflict with al-Qa'ida and its associated forces, and Congress has authorized the President to use all necessary and appropriate force against those entities." The memo cited the 2001 congressional Authorization to Use Military Force (AUMF) to support this statement.[15] However, Awlaki was not a proven member of Al-Qaeda and "associated forces" is not mentioned in the 2001 AUMF, which authorized President George W. Bush "to use all necessary and appropriate force against those nations, organizations, or persons he determines planned, authorized, committed, or aided the terrorist attacks that occurred on September 11, 2001, or harbored such organizations or persons, in order to prevent any future acts of international terrorism against the United States by such nations, organizations or persons."[16] More than a decade later, the Obama administration's Justice Department claims in essence that this authorization permits war on an indefinite basis, including against persons who had nothing to do with 9/11. From there, the Justice Department also asserted that "the AUMF itself does not set forth an express geographic limitation on the use of force it authorizes,"[17] thereby claiming that the 2001 congressional authorization of force recognizes neither a geographic limit nor a time limit on the U.S. use of force in response to 9/11. This interpretation of the 2001 AUMF amounts to a legal claim to wage perpetual war on a global scale.

In addition to modifying the customary legal meaning of "imminent threat," "self-defense," and "armed attack," and infusing the 2001 AUMF with a multi-decadal time span, a global geographic range, and a new reach to "associated forces," the Justice Department similarly interpreted the Title 18 U.S. domestic law prohibition against government murder of a U.S. citizen abroad and President Reagan's Executive Order 12333 banning assassinations.

Title 18 (section 1119(b)) states: "A person who, being a national of the United States, kills or attempts to kill a national of the United States while such national is outside the United States but within the jurisdiction of another country shall be punished as provided under sections 1111, 1112, and 1113."[18] With regard to Title 18 (section 1119(b)), the Justice Department memo argued:

> Because the person who would be the target of the kind of operation discussed here would be a U.S. citizen, it might be suggested that section 1119(b) would prohibit such an operation [the targeted killing of Awlaki].

Section 1119, however, incorporates the federal murder and manslaughter statutes, and thus its prohibition extends only to "unlawful killing[s]."[19]

The Justice Department thus claimed in essence that because it has asserted that the U.S. targeted killing of Awlaki in Yemen was a "lawful" killing (under the "self-defense" against an "imminent threat" claim), the federal prohibition against murder in Title 18 does not apply to the U.S. government's killing of Awlaki.[20]

While referring to the executive order banning assassination, the Justice Department fell back on its questionable assertions with regard to "imminent threat" and "self-defense" and simply claimed: "A lawful killing in self-defense is not an assassination. In the Department's view, a lethal operation conducted against a U.S. citizen whose conduct poses an imminent threat of violent attack against the United States would be a legitimate act of national self-defense that would not violate the assassination ban."[21]

Finally, there is in fact no executive authority in the U.S. Constitution that permits the president to authorize a targeted killing of a U.S. citizen abroad who is outside a war zone and who poses no imminent violent threat to the United States or its citizens. Perhaps for that reason, no president before Obama, as far as we know, had ever ordered a targeted killing abroad of a U.S. citizen under a similar set of circumstances in the history of the United States.

The Justice Department's claims seeking to legally certify the targeted killing of Anwar al-Awlaki—first reported by Michael Isikoff in February 2012—were re-stated by Attorney General Eric Holder in a speech at the Northwestern University School of Law in March 2012,[22] and in a letter to Senator Patrick Leahy of Vermont, who chairs the Senate Judiciary Committee, on May 22, 2013.[23] In addition to that body of legal claims purporting to justify the killing of Awlaki, President Obama articulated the same set of factual justifications for killing Awlaki that he first mentioned in September 2011. Thus, in a May 23 speech, Obama asserted that Awlaki:

- was "the chief of external operations for AQAP [Al-Qaeda in the Arabian Peninsula]";
- "was actively plotting to kill U.S. citizens";
- "was involved in planning to blow up an airliner in 2009";
- had "hosted [Farouk Abdulmutallab in Yemen], approved his suicide operation [to blow up a Detroit-bound airliner above the United States on Christmas Day, 2009], helped him to tape a martyrdom video to be shown after the attack, and [instructed Abdulmutallab] to blow up the airplane when it was over American soil."[24]

Responding to the charge that Awlaki was an "operational leader" of Al-Qaeda in Yemen, American journalist Jeremy Scahill, a leading expert on U.S. drone policy who has spent extensive amounts of time in Yemen, including while investigating the killing of Awlaki, wrote that the president had "bestowed upon Awlaki a label that had never been attached to him before, despite all his reported associations with al Qaeda."[25] Obama also claimed in 2011 that Awlaki "directed the failed [underwear bomber] attempt to blow up an airplane on Christmas Day in 2009."[26] About that charge, Scahill wrote: "Awlaki's role in the 'underwear plot' was unclear."[27] Scahill also wrote:

> While U.S. media outlets, terror 'experts' and prominent government officials were identifying Awlaki as a leader of AQAP [Al-Qaeda in the Arabian Peninsula], those allegations were dubious. Awlaki had entered dangerous territory in openly praising terrorist attacks on the United States and calling for Muslims in America to follow the example of Nidal Hassan [who shot and killed 13 people and injured 30 at Fort Hood, Texas, in November 2009]. But the available evidence regarding al Qaeda's relationship with Awlaki in 2010 suggests that Awlaki was not an operational member of the group but was seeking out an alliance with like-minded individuals.[28]

Both Scahill, in his book *Dirty Wars: The World Is a Battlefield*, and Gregory Johnsen, a Near East studies scholar at Princeton University, in his book *The Last Refuge: Yemen, al-Qaeda, and America's War in Arabia*, reported that prior to the attempted bombing of the airplane on Christmas Day, 2009, Awlaki met in Yemen with Farouk Abdulmutallab (the underwear bomber), and subsequently issued public statements that supported the attempted bombing. Neither Scahill nor Johnsen, however, reported evidence of an operational role played by Awlaki in the attempted bombing, and before he was killed Awlaki denied any such role.[29] This is not to say that Awlaki did not do what the president had charged; however, there is informed opinion in the journalistic and scholarly literature that raises doubts about the precision of Obama's factual allegations that served as the public justification for Awlaki's targeted killing by the government.

There is no doubt that Awlaki's public statements eventually supported the idea of terrorist attacks on U.S. civilians, including with regard to the attempted suicide bombing of the U.S. airplane on Christmas 2009. In that sense Awlaki crossed a line—perhaps not in terms of the constitutionality of such speech, but with the fact of his public support of the killing of U.S. civilians, which he justified as follows:

> The American people live [in] a democratic system and that is why they are held responsible for their policies. The American people are the ones

who have voted twice for Bush the criminal and elected Obama, who is not different from Bush as his first remark stated that he would not abandon Israel, despite the fact that there were other antiwar candidates in US elections, but they won very few votes. The American people take part in all its government's crimes. If they oppose that, let them change their government. They pay the taxes which are spent on the army and they send their sons to the military, and that is why they bear responsibility.[30]

There is no enlightened law or moral principle that permits the killing of civilians as collaborators in retaliation for harm to another population by the government of those civilians, as Awlaki suggested with respect to American civilians, and as Dershowitz suggested with respect to Lebanon's civilians during the Israel-Lebanon conflict in summer 2006, when he wrote a piece for *Huffington Post* titled "Lebanon is Not a Victim": "When a nation chooses sides in a war, especially when it chooses the side of terrorism, its civilians pay a price for that choice. This has been true of every war. We must stop viewing Lebanon as a victim and begin to see it as a collaborator with terrorism."[31] If it is not morally or legally sound, which it is not, for Awlaki to assert that American civilians are fair game as targets for terrorism given the policies of their government, then the same moral and legal condemnation must apply to Dershowitz's argument with respect to Lebanon's civilians (see chapter 8).

Given the tenuous nature of the government's factual case against Awlaki, it seems likely that Awlaki was targeted because of his inflammatory speech rather than for any operational role in Al-Qaeda in the Arabian Peninsula. Awlaki gave numerous abhorrent speeches, as Scahill notes: "Awlaki's own words crossed a line during this time [late 2009], as he lent his powerful endorsement to specific acts of terrorism on U.S. targets."[32] But if Awlaki was killed for his ideas rather than his actions, then his killing likely amounted to a prohibited assassination of a U.S. citizen. In addition, if the government had probable cause to suspect that Awlaki had transitioned from mere advocacy of reprehensible ideas to a criminal conspiracy to kill Americans, then the president could have charged Awlaki with one or more crimes and requested his extradition from Yemen to stand trial in the United States.

In this light, President Obama's claim, in his May 23 speech, that he was logistically unable to arrest Awlaki in Yemen,[33] including while Awlaki was living in a small village in a remote area,[34] is not credible. According to the *New York Times*, prior to his death Awlaki had been the subject of a "two-year manhunt" by the United States in Yemen.[35] It is hardly believable that the United States lacked the law enforcement and intelligence assets, in addition to the political resources, to apprehend a U.S. citizen in Yemen over a two-year period who allegedly was an imminent violent threat to the United States and its citizens. Furthermore, there is no published evidence to my knowledge of any U.S. request to have Awlaki extradited from Yemen.

Moreover, two weeks after Anwar al-Awlaki was killed, his 16-year-old son, Abdulrahman al-Awlaki, also a U.S. citizen, was killed in Yemen by a missile fired from a drone while he and his cousins were eating food outdoors.[36] Samir Khan and Jude Kenan Mohammad, both U.S. citizens, also were killed by U.S. drone strikes—Khan was killed with Anwar al-Awlaki in Yemen and Mohammad was killed in a signature drone strike in Pakistan.[37] No one among these three was ever charged with a crime and the teenage son of Anwar al-Awlaki had no involvement whatsoever with Al-Qaeda. When Obama admitted on May 23 that his administration had killed these three U.S. citizens with drone strikes (in addition to Awlaki), he mentioned none of them by name and provided no additional details.[38]

After it had been reported that the Obama administration had targeted Anwar al-Awlaki for killing, but before he was killed, the American Civil Liberties Union and the Center for Constitutional Rights filed a lawsuit on behalf of Awlaki's father, Nasser al-Awlaki, challenging the government's asserted authority to carry out targeted killings of U.S. citizens located outside a war zone. The civil liberties groups charged that "the authority contemplated by the Obama administration is far broader than what the Constitution and international law allow," that "both the Constitution and international law prohibit targeted killing except as a last resort to protect against concrete, specific, and imminent threats of death or serious physical injury," and "an extrajudicial killing policy under which names are added to CIA and military 'kill lists' through a secret executive process and stay there for months at a time"—as in Awlaki's case—"is plainly not limited to imminent threats." The civil liberties groups also charged that "targeting individuals for execution who are suspected of terrorism but have not been convicted or even charged—without oversight, judicial process, or disclosed standards for placement on kill lists" is a violation of the due process rights of the targeted citizens. A U.S. federal court dismissed the suit in October 2011 on procedural grounds, claiming that Awlaki's father had no judicial standing to sue the government.[39]

Robert Wright, a columnist for the online edition of the *New York Times*, also composed a relevant list of comments and questions about the targeted killing of Awlaki:

> I wouldn't have believed you if you'd told me 20 years ago that America
> ...eday be routinely firing missiles into countries it's not at war
> ...at matter, I wouldn't have believed you if you'd told me a few

months ago that America would soon be plotting the assassination of an American citizen who lives abroad. Shows you how much I know.

President Obama, who during his first year in office oversaw more drone strikes in Pakistan than occurred during the entire Bush presidency, last week surpassed his predecessor in a second respect: he authorized the assassination of an American—Anwar al-Awlaki, the radical Imam who after 9/11 moved from Virginia to Yemen, a base from which he inspires such people as the Fort Hood shooter and the would-be underwear bomber.

Students of the law might raise a couple of questions:

1) Doesn't it violate international law to fire missiles into Pakistan (especially on a roughly weekly basis) when the Pakistani government has given no formal authorization?

2) Wouldn't firing a missile at al-Awlaki in Yemen compound the international-law question with a constitutional question—namely whether giving the death penalty to an American without judicially establishing his guilt deprives him of due process?[40]

Despite significant concerns about the legality of these targeted killings, on May 23 Obama announced that he would seek an additional step to establish the practice indefinitely. As a supplement to his indifference to the Fifth Amendment's guarantee of due process, President Obama added insult to injury by proposing what the *Guardian* called a "kill court" that would institutionalize, with a veneer of legality, the president's "kill list"[41] and the targeted killing of suspected terrorists that flows from it. This presumably would include U.S. citizens, given the immediate context of the targeted killings of Awlaki, Awlaki's 16-year-old son, and the two other U.S. citizens.

In a report titled "Obama Drone Oversight Proposal Prompts Concern over 'Kill Courts,'" the *Guardian* reported that "proposals to vet future US drone strikes risk creating 'kill courts,' according to human rights campaigners who say Barack Obama's promise of new legal oversight does not go far enough to end what they regard as extrajudicial executions," and the proposals "highlight how little change Obama is proposing to the underlying principle that the U.S. has a legal right to kill suspected terrorists abroad without trial." Zeke Johnson, director of Amnesty International's Security with Human Rights Campaign in the United States, said: "What's needed on drones is not a 'kill court' but rejection of the radical redefinition of 'imminence' used to expand who can be killed, as well as independent investigations of alleged extrajudicial executions and remedy for victims."[42]

A U.S. "kill court" to oversee U.S. targeted killings would likely operate in a fashion similar to the FISA court, which was established to oversee U.S. surveillance of phone calls "without a probable-cause warrant so long as one of the parties to the communication is believed outside the United States."[43] In a 2013 letter to Senator Harry Reid, the Justice Department's Office of Legislative Affairs informed the senator that in 2012 the department had submitted 1,789 requests to the FISA court to conduct electronic surveillance, and that "the FISC [FISA court] did not deny any applications in whole or in part."[44] An April 2012 DOJ letter to Congress, according to Bill Quigley, reported: "In 2011, the government asked FISA judges 1,676 times to conduct electronic surveillance for foreign intelligence services. There were zero denials." And: "In 2010, the government asked FISA judges 1,511 times to conduct electronic surveillance for foreign intelligence purposes. There were zero denials."[45] According to David Kris, who "headed the Justice Department's National Security Division between 2009 and 2011," the FISA Amendments Act of 2008, which George W. Bush signed and which in December 2012 President Obama extended for another five years,[46] "gives the government nearly carte blanche spying powers." Kris observed that the Bush and Obama administrations have "interpreted the law to mean that as long as the real target is al-Qaeda, the government can wiretap purely domestic e-mails and phone calls."[47]

That the secret FISA court provides a façade of oversight of the executive branch while backing the government's violation of the Fourth Amendment ban against unreasonable searches and seizures was validated further in June 2013, when the *Guardian* reported:

> The [U.S.] National Security Agency is currently collecting the telephone records of millions of U.S. customers of Verizon, one of America's largest telecom providers, under a top secret court order issued in April.
>
> The order, a copy of which has been obtained by the Guardian, requires Verizon on an "ongoing, daily basis" to give the NSA information on all telephone calls in its systems, both within the U.S. and between the U.S. and other countries.
>
> The document shows for the first time that under the Obama administration the communication records of millions of U.S. citizens are being collected indiscriminately and in bulk—regardless of whether they are suspected of any wrongdoing.
>
> The secret Foreign Intelligence Surveillance Court [FISA Court] granted the order to the FBI on April 25, giving the government unlimited authority to obtain the data for a specified three-month period ending on July 19.[48]

Responding to the *Guardian* report, the Center for Constitutional Rights issued a statement that began: "As far as we know this order from the FISA court is the broadest surveillance order to ever have been issued: it requires no level of suspicion and applies to all Verizon subscribers anywhere in the U.S."[49] On June 19, following an interview with Noam Chomsky, the *Guardian* reported: "The actions of the US government in spying on its and other countries' citizens have been sharply criticised by Noam Chomsky, the prominent political thinker, as attacks on democracy and the people." Chomsky told the *Guardian*: "Governments should not have this capacity."[50] It thus could be argued that the de facto function of the FISA court overall is not to oversee the constitutionality of the government's surveillance policies but to provide a quasi-judicial mechanism that allows the government to electronically search and seize what it wants without regard to the Fourth Amendment.

Meanwhile, in news media interviews in June 2013, Dershowitz supported the Obama administration's NSA phone surveillance of millions of American citizens without probable cause: "Even Benjamin Franklin was wrong when he said those who would give up any privacy or rights in the name of security deserve neither. That's nonsense. That's hyperbole. That's extremism. That's the kind of thing we expect from the guy who broke the story for the Guardian, Glenn Greenwald, who never met a terrorist he didn't like and never met an American government official he liked."[51] For the record, what Ben Franklin actually said was (emphasis added): "Those who would give up *essential Liberty*, to purchase a little temporary Safety, deserve neither Liberty nor Safety."[52] Given the context in which he cited Franklin and applied his words,[53] Dershowitz was presumably arguing either that the Fourth Amendment ban on unreasonable searches and seizures is not an "essential liberty" or is not jeopardized by the government's confirmed ongoing collection of the phone records of millions of Americans not suspected of a crime. Either way, once again, it is Dershowitz's claims that are extreme.

The FISA court and the proposed "kill court"—in Obama's words "the establishment of a special court to evaluate and authorize lethal action"[54]—also resemble the recommendation from Alan Dershowitz to establish a torture court in the United States to issue "torture warrants" that would authorize the president to approve requests to torture suspected terrorists in ticking-bomb scenarios, and thus regulate the practice.[55] This recommendation included Dershowitz's suggestion in his 2002 essay "The Case for Torture Warrants," that "a sterilized needle underneath the nail might be one such approved method" of torture.[56] That proposal is evocative of the Nazi legalization of torture as described by German lawyer Ingo Müller in his 1991 book *Hitler's Justice: The Courts of the Third Reich*, published by Harvard University Press:

> The [German] judicial system also quickly learned to live with the fact that defendants appeared in court bearing signs of torture or testified that confessions had been extracted from them by force. In the beginning, these cases caused judges acute embarrassment, and the minister of justice was unable to accept such police interference in the operations of

the court. A committee of top legal advisers from the Ministry of Justice and the Gestapo found a practical solution, however: they legalized the terror, to such an extent that they even established a "standard club" to be used in beatings, so that torture would at least be regularized.[57]

The proposed U.S. "kill court" and "torture court," if established, would likely enable rather than restrain unconstitutional killings and illegal torture, just as the FISA court appears to have enabled rather than restrain the electronic surveillance of millions of Americans. And once the government has "legalized" in a procedural sense otherwise illegal surveillance, targeted killings, and torture, who could say that the post–9/11 political leadership in the United States had not succeeded in overthrowing the Bill of Rights and crossing the line to authoritarianism?

Meanwhile, the "red line" that Cornell scholar Mark Selden observed, "of killing noncombatants through air power," beginning with the U.S. firebombing and nuclear bombing of Japan and continuing "through the Korean and Indochinese wars to the Gulf, Afghanistan, and Iraq wars," has been extended by President Obama to the killing of noncombatants in Pakistan and Yemen through his signature drone war. These drone strikes virtually guarantee an ongoing supply in those lands of advocates of retaliatory terrorism against the United States. In turn, one shouldn't expect any let up in the opportunistic subversion of the Bill of Rights without an end to the countless U.S. wars and military actions abroad, which have yet to be rigorously subjected to moral and legal scrutiny inside the United States; that is, except, in the beginning, by Noam Chomsky in *American Power and the New Mandarins* (1967),[58] Howard Zinn in *Vietnam: The Logic of Withdrawal* (1967),[59] Richard Falk in *Vietnam and International Law* (1967),[60] and that superb generation of antiwar academics, intellectuals, and activists.

In their 2005 debate at Harvard University, Alan Dershowitz derisively characterized a number of Noam Chomsky's political claims as emanating from "Planet Chomsky," thus dismissing Chomsky's legitimate concerns, in this instance, with the political independence of the major U.S. news outlets and whether or not a succession of U.S. administrations genuinely supported a two-state solution in the Israel-Palestine conflict consistent with international law.[61] However, if you support the Bill of Rights in the United States and human rights abroad, in addition to an enlightened American society and a peaceful world order, "Planet Chomsky" isn't your worry, but a "Planet Dershowitz" might be.

In recent years, it's been Chomsky who has spoken on behalf of the enlightened traditions of Anglo-American law dating back to the Magna Carta,[62] not Dershowitz, and it's been the MIT linguistics professor who has spoken most recently in support of the presumption of innocence,[63] not the Harvard law professor. Meanwhile, Dershowitz has been advancing a jurisprudence of the counterterrorist "preventive state" that would date and discredit longstanding Western legal traditions as anachronistic and obsolete because they tie the hands of the United States and Israel in the conduct of their serial wars and military incursions.[64] Conversely, it is Chomsky who supports the rule of law in international affairs, including as applied to the pivotal Israel-Palestine conflict, and Enlightenment traditions of law and liberty in the United States. Unfortunately for us all, it looks as if the Dershowitzian vision of the authoritarian counterterrorist "preventive state" may indeed become an American nightmare, while the Chomskyan vision of an enlightened and peaceful society remains a dream.

NOTES

CHAPTER 1: METAPHORS

1. "Noam Chomsky v. Alan Dershowitz: A Debate on the Israeli-Palestinian Conflict," video and transcript, *Democracy Now!* at http://www.democracynow.org/2005/12/23/noam_chomsky_v_alan_dershowitz_a, December 23, 2005.

2. Noam Chomsky, *Fateful Triangle: The United States, Israel & The Palestinians* (Boston: South End Press, 1983), 39.

3. Norman Finkelstein, *Knowing Too Much: Why the Jewish American Romance with Israel Is Coming To an End* (New York: OR Books, 2012), xix.

4. "Noam Chomsky v. Alan Dershowitz: A Debate on the Israeli-Palestinian Conflict."

5. Alan Dershowitz, *The Case for Peace: How the Arab-Israeli Conflict Can Be Resolved* (Hoboken: Wiley, 2005), 12. Dershowitz wrote: "All reasonable people acknowledge that the final borders will incorporate Israel's large permanent settlements (reall towns   such as Maale Adumim) into Israel, and that these suburbs of Jerusalem will become contiguous with Jewish Jerusalem. That is the reality on the ground, as former president Bill Clinton, President George W. Bush, and Palestinian president Mahmoud Abbas recognize." See also, Alan Dershowitz, "A Settlement Freeze Can Advance Israeli-Palestinian Peace," *Huffington Post*, July 12, 2012. Here, Dershowitz wrote: "The first issue on the table should be the rough borders of a Palestinian state. Setting those would require that the West Bank be realistically divided into three effective areas:

Those that are relatively certain to remain part of Israel, such as Maale Adumim, Gilo and other areas close to the center of Jerusalem;

Those that are relatively certain to become part of a Palestinian state, such as Ramallah, Jericho, Jenin and the vast majority of the heavily populated Arab areas of the West Bank beyond Israel's security barrier;

Those reasonably in dispute, including some of the large settlement blocs several miles from Jerusalem such as Ariel (which may well remain part of Israel, but subject to negotiated land swaps)."

6. Alan Dershowitz, *The Case for Peace: How the Arab-Israeli Conflict Can Be Resolved* (Hoboken: Wiley, 2005), 12, 13, 15.

7. The Geneva Accord, Article 4, at http://www.nationsonline.org/oneworld/geneva_accord_article1-4.htm.

8. Alan Dershowitz, "The Case against the Left and Right One-State Solution," *Huffington Post*, March 21, 2012.

9. Alan Dershowitz, "Ed Koch: The Death of a Liberal Israel Lover," *Huffington Post*, February 4, 2013. Dershowitz wrote that "much of the left is opposed to the very existence of a Jewish Zionist state even on the 1948 lines."

10. Noam Chomsky, *American Power and the New Mandarins* (New York: Pantheon Books, 1969), 11.

11. Ibid., 46.

12. Ibid., 59.

13. Ibid., 333.

14. Noam Chomsky, *Failed States: The Abuse of Power and the Assault on Democracy* (New York: Metropolitan, 2006), 3.

15. Chomsky, *Fateful Triangle*, 3.

16. Noam Chomsky, *Hopes and Prospects* (Chicago: Haymarket, 2010), 5.

17. Chalmers Johnson, *Blowback: The Costs and Consequences of American Empire* (New York: Metropolitan, 2000).

18. Jonathan Turley, "10 Reasons the US is No Longer the Land of the Free," *Washington Post,* January 14, 2012.

Chapter 2. Chomsky at MIT, 1965–1973

1. "An Open Letter to President Johnson" (display advertisement), *Washington Post*, March 22, 1965.

2. Stanley Karnow, *Vietnam: A History*, 2nd edition (New York: Penguin, 1997), 267.

3. Ibid., 27.

4. Robert S. McNamara, James G. Blight, and Robert K. Brigham, *Argument without End: In Search of Answers to the Vietnam Tragedy* (New York: Public Affairs, 1999), 172; "Seven G.I.s Slain in Vietcong Raid: 80 Are Wounded: 2 U.S. Compounds Attacked 240 Miles from Capital," *New York Times*, February 7, 1965.

5. "Capital Is Tense: But President Asserts Nation Still Opposes Widening of War: U.S. Jets Bomb North Vietnam," *New York Times*, February 8, 1965.

6. McNamara, Blight, and Brigham, *Argument without End*, 173–174, 207–209.

7. "McNamara Gives Details of Raids: Says Damage 'Considerable' in Retaliatory Strike," *New York Times*, February 8, 1965.

8. Robert S. McNamara, *In Retrospect* (New York: Times Books, 1995), 171.

9. McNamara, Blight, and Brigham, *Argument without End*, 172.

10. Ibid.

11. Ibid., 172–173.

12. "3,500 U.S. Marines Going to Vietnam to Bolster Base; 2 Battalions for Danang Are First Land Combat Troops Committed by Washington," *New York Times*, March 7, 1965.

13. "An Open Letter to President Johnson."

14. Karnow, *Vietnam*, 696.

15. "Robert McNamara and the Ghosts of Vietnam," *New York Times*, August 10, 1997.

16. McNamara, Blight, and Brigham, *Argument without End*, xxi.

17. Ziad Obermeyer, Christopher J. L. Murray, and Emmanuela Gakidou, "Fifty Years of Violent War Deaths from Vietnam to Bosnia: Analysis of Data from the World Health Survey Programme," *British Medical Journal* (June 28, 2008): 1482–1486.

18. Benedict F. Kiernan, *The Pol Pot Regime: Race, Power, and Genocide in Cambodia under the Khmer Rouge, 1975–1979* (New Haven: Yale University Press, 2002), 24.

19. "Take-Over Ends Strife in Laos That Outsiders Had Intensified," *New York Times*, August 24, 1975.

20. Edward S. Herman and Noam Chomsky, *Manufacturing Consent: The Political Economy of the Mass Media* (New York: Pantheon, 2002), 260, 253–260.

21. About the invasion of the Dominican Republic, Noam Chomsky and Edward S. Herman wrote in 1979: "It will be recalled that the U.S. invaded the Dominican Republic in 1965 to prevent the displacement of the relatively benign fascist regime of Donald Reid Cabral by the Constitutionalist regime of Juan Bosch, who had been overthrown by a military coup in 1963—without eliciting any U.S. intervention to save *him* and his brief experiment in democratic government. The rationalization of Lyndon Johnson and his spokesmen, alleging an imminent threat of Communism, were convincingly shown by Theodore Draper and others to have been a hypocritical cover for a positive preference for fascism over a less reliable and less controllable democratic reformist government. The invasion of 1965 reestablished a firm grip on the island. As Bosch put it in June 1975: 'This country is not pro-American, it is United States property.'" See Chomsky and Herman, *The Washington Connection and Third World Fascism: The Political Economy of Human Rights—Volume I* (Boston: South End Press, 1979), 243.

22. "Only 100 Turn Out for M.I.T. Teach-In," *Boston Globe*, May 16, 1965.

23. "Author Mailer to Speak at Teach-In Here," *Boston Globe*, July 11, 1965.

24. "Cheers, Jeers, Eggs, Paint Greet Marching Thousands," *Boston Globe*, October 17, 1965.

25. Michael S. Foley, *Confronting the War Machine: Draft Resistance During the Vietnam War* (Chapel Hill: University of North Carolina Press, 2003), 28–29.

26. Karnow, *Vietnam*, 696.

27. McNamara, *In Retrospect*, 243.

28. Bernd Greiner, *War without Fronts: The USA in Vietnam* (New Haven: Yale University Press, 2009), 28, 29.

29. Display advertisement, "On Vietnam," *New York Times*, June 5, 1966.

30. Ibid.

31. Ibid.

32. Display advertisement, "Mr. President: Stop the Bombing," *New York Times*, January 15, 1967; January 22, 1967.

33. "Professors from 80 Schools Ask: 'Mr. President, Stop the Bombing,'" *Harvard Crimson*, January 16, 1967.

34. "Profiles in Science: National Library of Medicine: The Salvador E. Luria Papers: Politics, Science and Social Responsibility," at http://profiles.nlm.nih.gov/QL/Views/Exhibit/narrative/politics.html.

35. Noam Chomsky, "A Special Supplement: The Responsibility of Intellectuals," *New York Review of Books*, February 23, 1967.

36. See I. F. Stone, "Vietnam: An Exercise in Self-Delusion," *New York Review of Books*, April 22, 1965; "Fulbright: From Hawk to Dove (Part 2)," *New York Review of Books*, January 12, 1967.

37. See Bernard Fall, "Vietnam: The Undiscovered Country," *New York Review of Books*, March 17, 1966; "The View from Vietnam," *New York Review of Books*, February 9, 1967.

38. See Jean Lacouture, "Vietnam: The Lessons of War," *New York Review of Books*, March 3, 1966; "Vietnam: The Turning Point," *New York Review of Books*, May 12, 1966.

39. Stone, "Vietnam: An Exercise in Self-Delusion."

40. Stone, "Fulbright: From Hawk to Dove."

41. Fall, "Vietnam: The Undiscovered Country."

42. Lacouture, "Vietnam: The Turning Point."

43. Display ad, "On Vietnam," *New York Times*, June 5, 1966.

44. Stone, "Vietnam: An Exercise in Self-Delusion."

45. Stone, "Fulbright: From Hawk to Dove."

46. Chomsky, "A Special Supplement: The Responsibility of Intellectuals."

47. "Biggest Anti-War Rally in Hub Set for Monday," *Boston Globe*, October 12, 1967.

48. Foley, *Confronting the War Machine*, 96–97, 99.

49. Ibid., 105.

50. Norman Mailer, *The Armies of the Night: History as a Novel, the Novel as History* (New York: Plume, 1994, first edition published by Signet, 1968), 113, 114.

51. Ibid., 180.

52. "M.I.T. Prof. Arrested on March," *Boston Globe*, October 22, 1967.

53. "Blood Poured on Baltimore Draft Files: Priest, Minister, and 2 Others Seized," *New York Times*, October 28, 1967.

54. "Cardinal Scores Berrigan for 'Damaging' Act," *New York Times*, May 27, 1968.

55. To the Editor, Noam Chomsky, Robert S. Cohen, and Howard Zinn, "Father Berrigan's Action," *New York Times*, August 23, 1970.

56. Robert F. Barsky, *Noam Chomsky: A Life of Dissent* (Cambridge: MIT Press, 1997), 124.

57. Ibid.

58. "Chomsky among 60 Seized at Protest," *New York Times*, April 18, 1972.

59. "Police Arrest 94 in Capitol Protest," *Washington Post*, May 25, 1972.

60. "Ellsberg Admits Leak, Is Freed on Bond," *Boston Globe*, June 29, 1971.

61. "Ellsberg Lawyers Weigh New Motion for Dismissal," *New York Times*, April 30, 1973.

62. "F.B.I. Tap Picked Up Calls Ellsberg Made in 1969–'70," *New York Times*, May 11, 1973; "Week-Long Hunt: Pentagon Papers Trial Was Ended in Part Over Lost Material," *New York Times*, May 15, 1973.

63. "Ellsberg Judge's Act Cited in Plan to Ask End of Trial," *New York Times*, May 7, 1973.

64. "New Trial Barred: But Decision Does Not Solve Constitutional Issues in Case," *New York Times*, May 12, 1973.

65. "Chomsky, 3 Others Face U.S. Jury," *Boston Globe*, October 12, 1971.

66. "Ellsberg Says War Papers Taught Him: Distrust Authority," *Boston Globe*, October 14, 1971.

67. "Professors Cite 1st Amendment in Opposing Papers Testimony," *Boston Globe*, October 23, 1971.

68. "Scholars Seeking Right Not to Disclose Sources," *New York Times*, October 25, 1971.

69. "Popkin Faces Jail Sentence in Contempt of Court Case," *Harvard Crimson*, March 22, 1972; "Grand Jury Discharged, Popkin Freed," *Boston Globe*, November 28, 1972.

70. "Popkin Faces Jail Sentence in Contempt of Court Case."

71. "Grand Jury Discharged, Popkin Freed."

72. Ibid.

73. "Justice Dept. May Try to Link Ellsberg to Hanoi," *Boston Globe*, January 10, 1972.

74. "Professors Cite 1st Amendment in Opposing Papers Testimony."

75. See "Papers Probe Halted in Boston," *Boston Globe*, October 30, 1971; "Grand Jury Told to Halt Pentagon Papers Quiz," *Los Angeles Times*, October

30, 1971; "Legal Obstacles Blocking Boston Grand Jury in Its Investigation of the Release of Pentagon Papers," *New York Times*, November 1, 1971; "Grand Juries: Strange Doings by the Honest Countrymen," *New York Times*, November 7, 1971; "U.S. Courts Back War Papers Case," *New York Times*, November 30, 1971; "War-Papers Probe Can Resume, but Sen. Gravel Keeps Immunity," *Boston Globe*, November 30, 1971; "Ellsberg Indicted Again in Pentagon Case," *New York Times*, December 31, 1971; "Ellsberg Case Takes a Twist," *New York Times*, January 9, 1972.

76. Noam Chomsky and Howard Zinn (eds.), *The Pentagon Papers: The Senator Gravel Edition: Critical Essays: Volume Five and Index to Volumes 1–4* (Boston: Beacon Press, 1971), 281.

77. *The Pentagon Papers: The Senator Gravel Edition: The Defense Department History of United States Decisionmaking on Vietnam, Volume 4* (Boston: Beacon Press, 1971), 22.

78. "Israel Shenker, 82, a Reporter with the Instincts of a Scholar, Dies," *New York Times*, June 17, 2007.

79. "A Linguistics Expert Believes That Academicians Should Also Be Activists," *New York Times*, October 27, 1968.

80. Ibid.

81. "Chomsky Tells of Trip to Hanoi," *New York Times*, May 20, 1970.

82. "American Power and the New Mandarins," *New York Times*, March 16, 1969; "Books of the Times: Why Are We in Vietnam?" *New York Times*, March 18, 1969; "At War With Asia," *New York Times*, January 17, 1971; "Should We Have War Crime Trials?" *New York Times*, March 28, 1971; "Books of the Times: The Burden of Noam Chomsky," *New York Times*, August 2, 1973; "For Reasons of State; The World of Nations; The Intellectuals and the Powers," *New York Times*, September 30, 1973.

83. "American Power and the New Mandarins," *New York Times*, March 16, 1969.

84. "Books of the Times: Why Are We in Vietnam," March 18, 1969.

85. Hans J. Morgenthau, "We Are Deluding Ourselves in Vietnam," *New York Times Magazine*, April 18, 1965.

86. "At War With Asia," *New York Times*, January 17, 1971.

87. Ibid.

88. Ibid.

89. Noam Chomsky, *At War With Asia* (New York: Pantheon, 1970), 268–269.

90. See "'We Are Deluding Ourselves in Vietnam,'" Hans J. Morgenthau, *New York Times Magazine*, April 18, 1965.

91. "The Burden of Noam Chomsky," *New York Times*, August 2, 1973.

92. Noam Chomsky, *For Reasons of State* (New York: Pantheon, 1973), 11–12.

93. "The Burden of Noam Chomsky," *New York Times*, August 2, 1973.

94. Richard Falk, Gabriel Kolko, and Robert J. Lifton (eds.), *Crimes of War: A*

Legal, Political-Documentary, and Psychological Inquiry into the Responsibility of Leaders, Citizens, and Soldiers for Criminal Acts in Wars (New York: Random House, 1971).

95. See John Duffett (ed.), *Against the Crime of Silence: Proceedings of the Russell International War Crimes Tribunal* (New York: O'Hare Books, 1968).

96. Noam Chomsky, *American Power and the New Mandarins* (New York: Pantheon, 1969), 221–222.

97. Ibid., 231–232.

98. Ibid., 239.

99. "Lieutenant Accused of Killing 109 Civilians," *St. Louis Post-Dispatch*, November 13, 1969.

100. Chomsky, *At War With Asia*, 102.

101. Ibid., 102–103.

102. Ibid., 103.

Chapter 3. Dershowitz at Harvard, 1967–1973

1. Richard Archer, *As If an Enemy's Country: The British Occupation of Boston and the Origins of Revolution* (New York: Oxford University Press, 2010), 198.

2. Ibid., 193, 195, 196, 200,

3. Ibid., 196, 197, 200.

4. Ibid., 201.

5. Alan M. Dershowitz, *America on Trial: Inside the Legal Battles That Transformed Our Nation* (New York: Warner Books, 2004), 54–55.

6. Ibid., 33–34. Dershowitz wrote: "In his memoirs, [John] Adams justified his participation in the trial as an attempt to uphold the rule of law in the colonies: 'To depend upon the perversion of the law, and the corruption or partiality of juries, would insensibly disgrace the jurisprudence of the country and corrupt the morals of the people,' he wrote. Yet it now seems that Adams's participation in the trial may also have reflected his disdain for the lower-class zealots who had provoked the British officers."

7. Ibid., 55.

8. Frederic Kidder, *The History of the Boston Massacre, March 5, 1770* (Albany: J. Munsell, 1870).

9. Hiller Zobel, *The Boston Massacre* (New York: W.W. Norton, 1970).

10. Ibid., 198–199.

11. See Peter Pringle and Philip Jacobson, *Those Are Real Bullets: Bloody Sunday, Derry, 1972* (New York: Grove Press, 2000); Don Mullan, *Bloody Sunday: Massacre in Northern Ireland* (Niwot, CO: Roberts Rinehart Publishers, 1997).

12. James A. Michener, *Kent State: What Happened and Why* (New York: Fawcett, 1982).

13. Elena Poniatowska, *Massacre in Mexico*, translated by Helen R. Lane

(Columbia: University of Missouri Press, 1991).

14. See Archer, *As If an Enemy's Country*, xi.

15. Ibid., xvi.

16. Francis Jennings, *The Invasion of America: Indians, Colonialism, and the Cant of Conquest* (Chapel Hill: University of North Carolina Press, 1975), 187–188.

17. Neal Salisbury, *Manitou and Providence: Indians, Europeans, and the Making of New England* (New York: Oxford University Press, 1982), 221–222.

18. Alfred A. Cave, *The Pequot War* (Amherst: University of Massachusetts Press, 1996), 151.

19. Jennings, *The Invasion of America*, 220.

20. Salisbury, *Manitou and Providence*, 222.

21. Noam Chomsky, *Year 501: The Conquest Continues* (Boston: South End Press, 1993), 263.

22. Ibid., 21, 23.

23. Alan Dershowitz, "Terrorism & Preventive Detention: The Case of Israel," *Commentary* (December 1970): 67–78.

24. Alan Dershowitz, *Why Terrorism Works: Understanding the Threat, Responding to the Challenge* (New Haven: Yale University Press, 2002), 187.

25. Ibid., 187–188.

26. Ibid., 188–189.

27. Dershowitz, "Terrorism & Preventive Detention."

28. Norman Finkelstein, *Beyond Chutzpah: On the Misuse of Anti-Semitism and the Abuse of History* (Berkeley: University of California Press, 2005), 147–149.

29. Fawzi El-Asmar, Letter to the Editor, *Commentary* (June 1971).

30. Alan Dershowitz, Letter to the Editor, *Commentary* (June 1971).

31. Felicia Langer, Letter to the Editor, *Commentary* (June 1971).

32. Israel Shahak, Letter to the Editor, *Commentary* (June 1971).

33. Alan Dershowitz, Letter to the Editor, *Commentary* (June 1971).

34. "Professor Says Israel Is 'Racist,'" *Boston Globe*, April 18, 1973.

35. Alan Dershowitz, "Shahak, Best Proof of Freedom of Speech," *Boston Globe*, April 29, 1973.

36. Noam Chomsky, Letter to the Editor, "Shahak, A Man of Honor and Principle," *Boston Globe*, May 17, 1973.

37. Alan Dershowitz, Letter to the Editor, "Dershowitz Replies," *Boston Globe*, May 25, 1973.

38. Noam Chomsky, Letter to the Editor, "In Defense of Shahak," *Boston Globe*, June 5, 1973.

39. Alan Dershowitz, *Chutzpah* (Boston: Little, Brown, 1991).

40. Robert F. Barsky, *Noam Chomsky: A Life of Dissent* (Cambridge: MIT Press, 1997), 170–171.

41. Robert F. Barsky, *The Chomsky Effect: A Radical Works Beyond the Ivory*

Tower (Cambridge: MIT Press, 2007), 181.

42. Michael S. Foley, *Confronting the War Machine: Draft Resistance during the Vietnam War* (Chapel Hill: University of North Carolina Press, 2003).

43. Display ad, "The Time Has Come to End American Combat Operations and to Withdraw the American Military Presence in Vietnam," *Boston Globe*, October 14, 1969.

44. "1969: Millions March in U.S. Vietnam Moratorium," BBC News, October 15, 1969.

45. Display ad, "Our Government Should Put into Effect at Once a Plan for the Orderly Cessation THIS YEAR of all American Military Operations in Vietnam and Neighboring Countries," *Boston Globe*, April 22, 1970.

46. Display ad, "Quit Vietnam—Harvard Law Faculty," *Boston Globe*, May 14, 1970.

47. Display ad, "WE, the Above Signed Members of the LEGAL PROFESSION in Greater Boston, Urge That the Administration . . . ," *Boston Globe*, March 11, 1971.

48. Richard Falk, Chair, John H. E. Fried, Rapporteur, *The Consultative Council of the Lawyers Committee on American Policy Towards Vietnam: Vietnam and International Law* (Flanders, NJ: O'Hare, 1967), reissued as *Vietnam and International Law: An Analysis of International Law and the Use of Force, and the Precedent of Vietnam for Subsequent Interventions* (Northampton, MA: Aletheia Press, 1990), 93–94.

49. "20 Legal Scholars Endorse Shea's Vietnam Bill," *Boston Globe*, March 15, 1970.

50. "The Shea Bill Testing the War," *Harvard Crimson*, April 11, 1970.

51. See display ad, *Boston Globe*, October 14, 1969, and the list of legal scholars who supported the Shea Bill in "20 Legal Scholars Endorse Shea's Vietnam Bill."

52. "Law Schools: Student Lawyers & Viet Nam," *Time*, March 1, 1968.

53. See *U.S. v. Spock* 416 F.2d 165, 1969, at http://bulk.resource.org/courts.gov/c/F2/416/416.F2d.165.7205-7208_1.html. The U.S. First Circuit Court of Appeals, upon deciding an appeal in the conviction of Benjamin Spock, William Sloane Coffin, Michael Ferber, and Mitchell Goodman, ruled: "These are appeals by four defendants convicted under a single count indictment for conspiracy. We reverse."

54. See 50 U.S.C. § 462(b)(3), at http://www.law.cornell.edu/uscode/html/uscode50a/usc_sec_50a_00000462——000-.html.

55. Alan Dershowitz, "The Trial of Dr. Spock," *New York Times*, September 14, 1969.

56. Ibid.

57. Ibid.

58. Alan Dershowitz, "The Erosion of Our Rights," *Boston Globe*, September 25, 1972.

59. "The Supreme Court on Trial," *Boston Globe*, October 3, 1972.

60. "A Bill of Complaint: The People's Need to Know," *Boston Globe*, January 21, 1973.

61. Ibid.

62. Ibid.

63. "A Threat to Liberty," *Boston Globe*, January 31, 1969.

64. "Make Legal Haste Wisely," *New York Times*, March 22, 1969.

65. "Jail without Guilt," *Boston Globe*, August 17, 1969.

66. Alan Dershowitz, *Preemption: A Knife That Cuts Both Ways* (New York: W.W. Norton, 2006), xiii, 190–250.

67. Ibid., 1.

68. Ibid., 2–3.

69. Ibid., 3.

70. Ibid., 7–8.

71. Ibid., 59.

72. Ibid., 61–63.

73. Ibid., 63–64.

74. Ibid., 63–67.

75. Ibid., 1–3.

76. Ibid., 76–77.

CHAPTER 4. AGGRESSIVE WARFARE → TERRORISM → COUNTERTERRORISM → AUTHORITARIANISM

1. International law violations here feature U.S. or U.S.-supported violations of the UN Charter's prohibition of the threat and use of force by states, violations of international humanitarian law, including the Fourth Geneva Convention (1949) and Protocol I Additional to the Fourth Geneva Convention (1977), and international human rights law, including the Convention on the Prevention and Punishment of the Crime of Genocide (1948), Convention Relating to the Status of Refugees (1951), Convention on the Elimination of All Forms of Racial Discrimination (1965), International Covenant on Civil and Political Rights (1966), International Covenant on Economic, Social, and Cultural Rights (1966), International Convention on the Suppression and Punishment of the Crime of Apartheid (1973), Convention Against Torture (1984), Convention on the Rights of the Child (1989), and the International Convention for the Protection of All Persons from Enforced Disappearance (2006).

2. "Aggressive Warfare" here incorporates violations of the sources of international law listed in note 1 when they are directed against another state or an ethnic, racial, or religious group.

3. Alan Dershowitz, "The Preventative State," *Big Think*, January 16, 2008, at http://bigthink.com/ideas/3423.

4. Alan Dershowitz, *Preemption: A Knife That Cuts Both Ways* (New York: W.W. Norton, 2006).

5. "History Did Not Begin with the Qassams," *Haàretz*, January 14, 2009.

6. Noam Chomsky, *9-11* (New York: Seven Stories Press, 2001). See also: Chomsky, *Power and Terror: Post–9/11 Talks and Interviews* (New York: Seven Stories Press, 2003); Chomsky, *9-11: Was There an Alternative?* (New York: Seven Stories Press, 2011).

7. Noam Chomsky, *Fateful Triangle: The United States, Israel, and the Palestinians* (Boston: South End Press, 1983); *Middle East Illusions: Reflections on Justice and Nationhood* (Lanham, MD: Rowman & Littlefield, 2003); *Hegemony or Survival: America's Quest for Global Dominance* (New York: Metropolitan, 2003), 157–167; *Failed States: The Abuse of Power and the Assault on Democracy* (New York: Metropolitan, 2006), 171–204.

8. Noam Chomsky, *Deterring Democracy* (New York: Hill and Wang, 1992).

9. Noam Chomsky, "U.S. Iraq Policy: Motives and Consequences," Alternative Radio, January 30, 1999, www.alternativeradio.org/products/chon148; Noam Chomsky, Edward Herman, Edward Said, and Howard Zinn, "Sanctions Are Weapons of Mass Destruction," in Anthony Arnove (ed.), *Iraq under Siege: The Deadly Impact of Sanctions and War* (Boston: South End Press, 2000); Noam Chomsky, *Hegemony or Survival: America's Quest for Global Dominance* (New York: Metropolitan, 2003).

10. Noam Chomsky, *Hegemony or Survival: America's Quest for Global Dominance* (New York: Metropolitan, 2003); Noam Chomsky and David Barsamian, *Imperial Ambition: Conversations on the Post–9/11 World* (New York: Metropolitan, 2005); Noam Chomsky, *Failed States: The Abuse of Power and the Assault on Democracy* (New York: Metropolitan, 2006).

11. Chomsky and Barsamian, *Imperial Ambition*; Chomsky, *Failed States*.

12. Noam Chomsky and Ilan Pappé, Frank Barat (ed.), *Gaza in Crisis: Reflections on Israel's War against the Palestinians* (Chicago: Haymarket Books, 2010).

13. Noam Chomsky, *Hopes and Prospects* (Chicago: Haymarket Books, 2010); Chomsky, *Failed States*.

14. "Professor Noam Chomsky—In Interview," PublicServiceEurope, October 28, 2011, at http://www.publicserviceeurope.com/article/1047/professor-noam-chomsky-in-interview; Chomsky, *Hopes and Prospects*.

15. Joy Gordon, *Invisible War: The United States and the Iraq Sanctions* (Cambridge: Harvard University Press, 2010), 87.

16. Chomsky.Info: The Noam Chomsky Website; Bios: MIT Linguistic Program; www.chomsky.info/bios/2002——htm.

17. Noam Chomsky, "A Review of B. F. Skinner's *Verbal Behavior*," *Language* 35, no. 1 (1959): 26–58.

18. Ted Honderich (ed.), *The Oxford Companion to Philosophy* (New York:

Oxford University Press, 1995), 132.

19. Chomsky.Info: The Noam Chomsky Website; Bios: MIT Linguistic Program.

20. See MIT Linguistics; Department of Linguistics and Philosophy; Faculty; Noam Chomsky, at http://web.mit.edu/linguistics/people/faculty/chomsky/ index.html.

21. Ibid.

22. "Noam Chomsky," Wikipedia, at http://en.wikipedia.org/wiki/ Noam_Chomsky. Chomsky's list of published books include: *Aspects of the Theory of Syntax* (1965); *Cartesian Linguistics* (1966); *Sound Pattern of English* (with Morris Halle) (1968); *Language and Mind* (1968); *American Power and the New Mandarins* (1969); *At War With Asia* (1970); *For Reasons of State* (1973); *Peace in the Middle East?* (1974); *Reflections on Language* (1975); *The Political Economy of Human Rights, vols. I and II* (with Edward S. Herman) (1979); *Rules and Representations* (1980); *Lectures on Government and Binding* (1981); *Radical Priorities* (1981); *Towards a New Cold War* (1982); *Fateful Triangle* (1983); *Turning the Tide* (1985); *Knowledge of Language* (1986); *Pirates and Emperors* (1986); *On Power and Ideology* (1987); *Language and Problems of Knowledge* (1988); *The Culture of Terrorism* (1988); *Manufacturing Consent* (with Edward S. Herman) (1988); *Necessary Illusions* (1989); *Deterring Democracy* (1991); *Year 501* (1993); *Rethinking Camelot* (1993); *Letters from Lexington* (1993); *World Orders, Old and New* (1994); *The Minimalist Program* (1995); *Powers and Prospects* (1996); *The Common Good* (1998); *Profit Over People* (1999); *The New Military Humanism* (1999); *New Horizons in the Study of Language and Mind* (2000); *Rogue States* (2000); *A New Generation Draws the Line* (2000); *9-11* (2001); *Understanding Power* (2002); *Hegemony or Survival* (2003); *Failed States* (2006); *The Chomsky-Foucault Debate* (2006); *What We Say Goes* (2007); and *Hopes and Prospects* (2010).

23. "Chomsky Is Citation Champ," *MIT News*, April 15, 1992, at http://web.mit.edu/newsoffice/1992/citation-0415.html.

24. Alan M. Dershowitz, Biographical Statement, at http://www.alandershowitz. com/detailed.php; Harvard Law School, Alan M. Dershowitz, at http://www.law.harvard.edu/faculty/directory/index.html?id=12.

25. Alan M. Dershowitz, Biographical Statement.

26. Dershowitz's books include: *The Best Defense* (1983), *Reversal of Fortune* (1986), *Chutzpah* (1991), *Supreme Injustice* (2001), *Letters to a Young Lawyer* (2001), *Shouting Fire* (2002), *Why Terrorism Works* (2002), *The Case for Israel* (2003), *The Case for Peace* (2005), *Preemption* (2006), and *The Case against Israel's Enemies* (2008).

27. Alan M. Dershowitz, Biographical Statement.

28. Alan M. Dershowitz, Faculty Bibliography, Harvard Law School, at http://www.law.harvard.edu/faculty/bibliography.html.

29. Alan M. Dershowitz, Biographical Statement.

30. Dershowitz, *Preemption*; Alan Dershowitz, *Is There a Right to Remain Silent? Coercive Interrogations and the Fifth Amendment* (New York: Oxford University Press, 2008); Alan Dershowitz, "The Preventative State," *Big Think*, January 16, 2008; "To Torture or Not to Torture," *New York Times*, September 17, 2008.

31. Dershowitz, "The Preventative State."

32. Ibid.

33. Ibid.

34. Ibid.

35. See, for example: Amnesty International, "Suffocating Gaza: The Israeli Blockade's Effects on Palestinians," June 1, 2010, http://www.amnesty.org/en/news-and-updates/suffocating-gaza-israeli-blockades-effects-palestinians-2010-06-01; "UN Human Rights Envoy Says Gaza a Prison for Palestinians," *Haaretz*, September 29, 2006; B'Tselem, "Gaza Prison: Freedom of Movement to and from the Gaza Strip on the Eve of the Disengagement Plan," March 2005, http://www.btselem.org/publications/summaries/200503_gaza_prison.

36. See, for example: B'Tselem, "Gaza Strip: Background on the Gaza Strip," at http://www.btselem.org/gaza_strip; B'Tselem, "The Siege on Gaza," at http://www.btselem.org/gaza_strip/siege; "Gaza under Blockade," BBC News, July 6, 2010; Amnesty International, "Israel/Occupied Palestinian Territories: Gaza Blockade: Collective Punishment," July 4, 2008, http://www.amnesty.org/en/library/info/MDE15/021/2008/en.

37. See, for example: B'Tselem, "Gaza Updates," February 10, 2005 to February 1, 2012, at http://www.btselem.org/ota?year[value][year]=&tid=12; Human Rights Watch, "Israel/Occupied Palestinian Territories: Events of 2009: World Report 2010," at http://www.hrw.org/world-report-2010/israel-occupied-palestinian-territories-opt; Amnesty International, "Israel/Gaza: Operation 'Cast Lead': 22 Days of Death and Destruction," July 2009, http://www.amnesty.org/en/library/info/MDE15/015/2009.

38. "Terrorism Causes Occupation, Not Vice Versa," *Huffington Post*, August 11, 2006.

39. "The Palestinian Leadership Is Responsible for the Continuing Israeli Occupation of the West Bank," *Huffington Post*, December 9, 2010.

40. United Nations General Assembly: A/Res/42/159, December 7, 1987.

41. Noam Chomsky, *Necessary Illusions: Thought Control in Democratic Societies* (Boston: South End Press, 1999), 85.

CHAPTER 5. ON SEPTEMBER 29, 2000

1. "Intifada" refers to the Palestinian uprising against the Israeli occupation of the Palestinian West Bank and the Gaza Strip.

2. Dennis Ross, *The Missing Peace: The Inside Story of the Fight for Middle East*

Peace (New York: Farrar, Straus and Giroux, 2004), 727.

3. Aaron David Miller, *The Much Too Promised Land: America's Elusive Search for Arab-Israeli Peace* (New York: Bantam Books, 2008), 307.

4. Ross, *The Missing Peace*, 727, 728.

5. Ibid., 728.

6. Avi Shlaim, *The Iron Wall: Israel and the Arab World* (New York: W.W. Norton, 2001), 250–253.

7. "Sharon Touches a Nerve, and Jerusalem Explodes," *New York Times*, September 29, 2000.

8. "Battle at Jerusalem Holy Site Leaves 4 Dead and 200 Hurt," *New York Times*, September 30, 2000.

9. "Mideast Violence Continues to Rage: Death Toll Rises," *New York Times*, October 1, 2000.

10. "Violence Spreads to Israeli Towns; Arab Toll at 28," *New York Times*, October 2, 2000.

11. "Clinton's Chance to Broker Pact May Be Gone," *New York Times*, October 2, 2000.

12. "As Arabs and Israelis Fight On, Albright Seeks Talks," *New York Times*, October 3, 2000.

13. "At Arms Again, Suddenly," *New York Times*, October 3, 2000.

14. "Israelis Criticized for Using Deadly Force Too Readily," *New York Times*, October 4, 2000.

15. United Nations Security Council, S/Res/1322, October 7, 2000.

16. Alan Dershowitz, *The Case for Israel* (Hoboken: Wiley, 2003), 8, 9, 10.

17. Ibid., 10.

18. Alan Dershowitz, *The Case for Peace: How the Arab-Israeli Conflict Can Be Solved* (Hoboken: Wiley, 2005), 44.

19. Ibid., 119.

20. Alan Dershowitz, *Why Terrorism Works: Understanding the Threat, Responding to the Challenge* (New Haven: Yale University Press, 2002), 78.

21. "The Sharon Victory: The Overview; Sharon Easily Ousts Barak to Become Israel's Premier," *New York Times*, February 7, 2001.

22. Anti-Defamation League, "Major Terrorist Attacks in Israel," as of May 11, 2011, at http://www.adl.org/israel/israel_attacks.asp.

23. Amnesty International, "Israel and the Occupied Territories: Civilian Lives Must Be Respected," October 2, 2000, http://www.amnesty.org/fr/library/asset/MDE15/032/2000/fr/62d4114e-dd45-11dd-969e-85a7b54dc46a/mde150322000en.pdf.

24. Amnesty International, "Israel/Occupied Territories/Lebanon: Amnesty International Calls for UN investigation," October 9, 2000, at http://www.commondreams.org/news2000/1009-07.htm.

25. Ibid.

26. Human Rights Watch, "Israel, the Occupied West Bank and Gaza Strip, and the Palestinian Authority Territories: Investigation into Unlawful Use of Force in the West Bank, Gaza Strip, and Northern Israel," October 2000, at www.hrw.org/reports/2000/israel.

27. See, Defence for Children International, at http://www.defenceforchildren.org/.

28. "Breakdown of Palestinian Child Deaths (29 September 2000–31 December 2000)," Defence for Children International, Palestine Section, December 31, 2000, as of May 12, 2011 at http://www.dci-pal.org/english/display.cfm?DocId=160&CategoryId=2.

29. "Question of the Violation of Human Rights in the Occupied Arab Territories, Including Palestine: Update to the Mission Report on Israel's Violations of Human Rights in the Palestinian Territories Occupied Since 1967, Submitted by Giorgio Giacomelli, Special Rapporteur to the Commission on Human Rights at Its Fifth Special Session," United Nations Economic and Social Council: Commission on Human Rights, March 16, 2001, E/CN.4/2001/30.

30. "Question of the Violation of Human Rights in the Occupied Arab Territories, Including Palestine: Report of the Human Rights Inquiry Commission Established Pursuant to Commission Resolution S-5/1 of 19 October 2000," United Nations Economic and Social Council: Commission on Human Rights, March 16, 2001, E/CN.4/2001/121.

31. "Question of the Violation of Human Rights in the Occupied Arab Territories, including Palestine: Report of the Special Rapporteur of the Commission on Human Rights on the Situation of Human Rights in the Palestinian Territories Occupied by Israel Since 1967," October 4, 2001, A/56/440.

32. Dershowitz, *The Case for Israel*, 10.

33. Ibid., 119.

34. See, for example: Clayton E. Swisher, *The Truth about Camp David: The Untold Story about the Collapse of the Middle East Peace Process* (New York: Nation Books, 2004); Charles Enderlin, *Shattered Dreams: The Failure of the Peace Process in the Middle East: 1995–2002*, translated by Susan Fairfield (New York: Other Press, 2003); Norman Finkelstein, "The Camp David II Negotiations: How Dennis Ross Proved the Palestinians Aborted the Peace Process," *Journal of Palestine Studies*, vol. 36, no. 1 (Winter 2007), at http://www.palestine-studies.org/journals.aspx?id=7317&jid=1&href=fulltext; Ron Pundak, "From Oslo to Taba: What Went Wrong?" *Survival*, vol. 43, no. 3 (Autumn 2001): 31–46; Benny Morris, "Camp David and After: An Exchange (1. An Interview with Ehud Barak)," *New York Review of Books*, vol. 49, no. 10 (June 13, 2002); Hussein Agha and Robert Malley, "Camp David and After: An Exchange (2. A Reply to Ehud Barak)," *New York Review of Books*, vol. 49, no. 10

(June 13, 2002); Ethan Bronner, "Exhausted Are the Peacemakers" (review of *The Missing Peace* by Dennis Ross), *New York Times*, August 8, 2004.

35. Dershowitz, *The Case for Israel*, 118.

36. See Dershowitz's references to Ross's views about the July 2000 Camp David summit and related matters: Alan Dershowitz, *The Case against Israel's Enemies: Exposing Jimmy Carter and Others Who Stand in the Way of Peace* (Hoboken: Wiley, 2008), 26–27, 41, 69; Dershowitz, *The Case for Peace*, 8, 36, 37–38, 39, 55, 108; Dershowitz, *The Case for Israel*, 118.

37. Ross, *The Missing Peace*, 667–668.

38. Ibid., 674.

39. Ibid., 684.

40. Ibid., 688.

41. Ibid., 729.

42. Ibid., 752.

43. Jimmy Carter, *Palestine Peace Not Apartheid* (New York: Simon & Schuster, 2006), 150.

44. Ross, *The Missing Peace*, 755.

45. Jeremy Pressman, "Lost Opportunities: The Missing Peace: The Inside Story of the Fight for Middle East Peace," *Boston Review* (December 2004 / January 2005).

46. Ross, *The Missing Peace*, 753–754, 754–755, 756.

47. Ibid., 757.

48. Elsa Walsh, "The Prince: How the Saudi Ambassador Became Washington's Indispensable Operator," *New Yorker*, March 24, 2003.

49. Ross, *The Missing Peace*, 752–753.

50. "Geography of Israel," Wikipedia, at http://en.wikipedia.org/wiki/Geography_of_Israel#cite_note-IsraelCountryStudy-0.

51. Dershowitz, *The Case for Israel*, 118.

52. Nor does Ross's book confirm Bandar's "insider's" access to the final status negotiations in 2000, beyond a single meeting between Ross and Bandar in London in December 2000 and Bandar picking up Arafat at the airport on January 2, 2001. See Ross, *The Missing Peace*, 747–748, 756.

53. Dershowitz, *The Case for Israel*, 117–122, 251–252.

54. Ibid., 118–119.

55. "'Moratinos Document': The Peace That Nearly Was at Taba," *Ha'aretz*, February 14, 2002.

56. Yossi Beilin, The Path to Geneva: The Quest for a Permanent Agreement, 1996–2004 (New York: RDV Books, 2004), 249.

57. Ibid., 249–250.

58. Benny Morris, *One State, Two States: Resolving the Israel/Palestine Conflict* (New Haven: Yale University Press, 2009), 133–134.

59. "The New New Historians," *New York Times*, November 9, 2003.

60. "And Yet So Far: A Special Report: Quest for Mideast Peace: How and Why It Failed," *New York Times*, July 26, 2001.

61. Morris, "Camp David and After: An Exchange (1. An Interview with Ehud Barak)."

62. Ibid.

63. Ibid.

64. Ross, *The Missing Peace*, xv.

65. Ibid., xii.

66. Agha and Malley, "Camp David and After: An Exchange (2. A Reply to Ehud Barak)."

67. Ross, *The Missing Peace*, 725–726.

68. Ibid.

69. Noam Chomsky, *Failed States: The Abuse of Power and the Assault on Democracy* (New York: Metropolitan Books, 2006), 179, 181.

70. Richard Falk, *Unlocking the Middle East: The Writings of Richard Falk* (Northampton: Olive Branch Press, 2003), 226.

71. Edward W. Said, *The End of the Peace Process: Oslo and After* (New York: Vintage, 2001), 360–361.

72. Norman Finkelstein, *Beyond Chutzpah: On the Misuse of Anti-Semitism and the Abuse of History* (Berkeley: University of California Press, 2005), 96–106; 308–311.

73. Ibid., 96.

74. Finkelstein, "The Camp David II Negotiations: How Dennis Ross Proved the Palestinians Aborted the Peace Process."

75. Anti-Defamation League, "Major Terrorist Attacks in Israel."

CHAPTER 6. THE FOURTH GENEVA CONVENTION

1. "International Humanitarian Law: Answers to Your Questions," International Committee of the Red Cross, October 2002, 4, at http://www.icrc.org/eng/assets/files/other/icrc_002_0703.pdf.

2. "International Humanitarian Law: Treaties and Documents: 1949 Conventions and Additional Protocols," International Committee of the Red Cross, at http://www.icrc.org/ihl.nsf/CONVPRES?OpenView.

3. "International Humanitarian Law: Treaties and Documents: Convention (IV) Relative to the Protection of Civilian Persons in Time of War, Geneva, 12 August 1949," International Committee of the Red Cross, at http://www.icrc.org/ihl.nsf/FULL/380?OpenDocument.

4. Ibid.

5. United Nations Security Council (UNSC), S/Res/271, September 15, 1969.

6. UNSC, S/Res/446, March 22, 1979.

7. UNSC, S/Res/799, December 18, 1992.

8. UNSC, S/Res/904, March 18, 1994.

9. United Nations General Assembly (UNGA), A/Res/2727, December 15, 1970.

10. UNGA, A/Res/2851, December 20, 1971.

11. The vote on UNGA A/Res/2727, December 15, 1970, was 52 to 20 with 43 abstentions. The vote on UNGA A/Res/2851, December 20, 1971, was 53 to 20 with 46 abstentions. For vote tallies on these and other UNGA and UNSC resolutions, see the United Nations Bibliographic Information System (UNBISnet) at http://www.un.org/Depts/dhl/unbisnet/index.html#voterecords.

12. The vote on UNGA A/Res/3005, December 15, 1972, was 63 to 10 with 49 abstentions.

13. UNGAA/Res/3092(A), December 7, 1973.

14. UNGAA/Res/3240(B), November 29, 1974.

15. UNGAA/Res/3525(B), December 15, 1975.

16. UNGAA/Res/31/106(B), December 16, 1976.

17. UNGA A/Res/32/5, October 28, 1977; UNGA A/Res/33/113(A), December 18, 1978; UNGAA/Res/34/90(B), December 12, 1979; UNGA A/Res/35/122(A), December 11, 1980; UNGAA/Res/36/147(A), December 16, 1981; UNGA A/Res/37/88(A), December 9, 1982; UNGAA/Res/39/95(B), December 14, 1984; UNGA A/Res/40/161(B), December 16, 1985; UNGAA/Res/41/63(B), December 3, 1986; UNGA A/Res/42/160(B), December 8, 1987; UNGAA/Res/43/58(B), December 6, 1988; UNGA A/Res/44/48(B), December 8, 1989; UNGAA/Res/45/74(B), December 11, 1990; UNGA A/Res/46/47(B), December 9, 1991; UNGAA/Res/47/70(B), December 14, 1992; UNGA A/Res/48/41(B), December 10, 1993; UNGAA/Res/49/36(B), December 9, 1994; UNGA A/Res/50/29(B), December 6, 1995.

18. UNGA A/Res/51/132, December 13, 1996; UNGA A/Res/52/65, December 10, 1997; UNGAA/Res/53/54, December 3, 1998; UNGA A/Res/54/77, December 6, 1999; UNGA A/Res/55/131, December 8, 2000; UNGA A/Res/56/60, December 10, 2001; UNGA A/Res/57/125, December 11, 2002; UNGA A/Res/58/97, December 9, 2003; UNGA A/Res/59/122, December 10, 2004; UNGAA/Res/60/105, December 8, 2005; UNGA A/Res/61/117, December 14, 2006; UNGAA/Res/62/107, December 17, 2007; UNGA A/Res/63/96, December 5, 2008; UNGA A/Res/64/92, December 10, 2009; UNGA A/Res/65/103, December 10, 2010.

19. UNGA A/Res/65/104, January 20, 2011.

20. UNGA A/Res/51/133, December 13, 1996; UNGA A/Res/52/66, December 10, 1997; UNGAA/Res/53/55, December 3, 1998; UNGA A/Res/54/78, December 6, 1999; UNGA A/Res/55/132, December 8, 2000; UNGA A/Res/56/61, December 10, 2001; UNGA A/Res/57/126, February 24, 2003; UNGA A/Res/58/98, December 17, 2003; UNGA A/Res/59/123, January 25, 2005; UNGA

A/Res/60/106, January 18, 2006; UNGAA/Res/61/118, January 15, 2007; UNGA A/Res/62/108, January 10, 2008; UNGA A/Res/63/97, December 18, 2008; UNGA A/Res/64/93, January 19, 2010.

21. "Legal Consequences of the Construction of a Wall in the Occupied Palestinian Territory: Advisory Opinion of 9 July 2004," International Court of Justice, para. 163, at http://www.icj-cij.org/docket/files/131/1671.pdf.

22. "Legal Consequences of the Construction of a Wall in the Occupied Palestinian Territory: Summary of the Advisory Opinion of 9 July 2004," International Court of Justice, July 9, 2004, 9, at http://www.icj-cij.org/docket/files/131/1677.pdf.

23. Ibid., 10.

24. "Legal Consequences of the Construction of a Wall in the Occupied Palestinian Territory," para. 163.

25. See "International Court of Justice: Legal Consequences of the Construction of a Wall in the Occupied Palestinian Territory (Request for Advisory Opinion): Summary of the Advisory Opinion of 9 July 2004," Declaration of Judge Buergenthal, July 9, 2004.

26. "International Committee of the Red Cross: Implementation of the Fourth Geneva Convention in the Occupied Palestinian Territories: History of a Multilateral Process (1997–2001): Annex 2: Conference of High Contracting Parties to the Fourth Geneva Convention: Statement by the International Committee of the Red Cross," December 5, 2001.

27. Amnesty International, "Israel: Respect of Fourth Geneva Convention Must Be Ensured by High Contracting Parties Meeting in Geneva" (press release), December 4, 2001.

28. Amnesty International, "US Veto Effectively Gives Israel 'Green Light' to Expand Illegal Settlements" (press release), February 22, 2011.

29. Human Rights Watch, "Center of the Storm: A Case Study of Human Rights in Hebron District," April 2001.

30. Human Rights Watch, "Israel, the Occupied West Bank and Gaza Strip, and the Palestinian Authority Territories: In a Dark Hour: The Use of Civilians during IDF Arrest Operations," April 2002.

31. Human Rights Watch, "Israel: US Veto on Settlements Undermines International Law," February 18, 2011.

32. B'Tselem, "International Humanitarian Law," at http://www.btselem.org/English/International_Law/Humanitarian_Law.asp.

33. B'Tselem, "Land Expropriation & Settlements," at http://www.btselem.org/english/settlements/international_law.asp.

34. Noam Chomsky, *Hopes and Prospects* (Chicago: Haymarket Books, 2010), 148.

35. Ibid., 148–149, 297–298.

36. Gershom Gorenberg, *The Accidental Empire: Israel and the Birth of the Settlements, 1967–1977* (New York: Times Books, 2006), 99–100, 101.

37. Idith Zertal and Akiva Eldar, *Lords of the Land: The War Over Israel's Settlements in the Occupied Territories, 1967–2007* (New York: Nation Books, 2007), 334–335.

38. Noam Chomsky, *The Essential Chomsky*, edited by Anthony Arnove (New York: The New Press, 2008), 371.

39. Alan Dershowitz, *Why Terrorism Works: Understanding the Threat, Responding to the Challenge* (New Haven: Yale University Press, 2002), 221.

40. Ibid.

41. Note: Neither the Geneva Accords on Vietnam of 1954, nor the so-called "Geneva Accord," the model final-status peace agreement negotiated informally by private Israeli and Palestinian participants, are part of international humanitarian law.

42. "Joint Harvard–M.I.T. Petition for Divestment from Israel," December 5, 2002

43. Alan Dershowitz, *The Case for Israel* (Hoboken: Wiley, 2003), 205.

44. Ibid., 206. Note the utility once again here of Dershowitz's claim that Arafat rejected the allegedly generous peace offers from Israel at Camp David and Taba and immediately thereafter initiated a terrorist war against Israel.

45. Alan Dershowitz, *The Case for Peace: How the Arab-Israeli Conflict Can Be Resolved* (Hoboken: Wiley, 2005), 143.

46. Ibid.

47. Ibid., 144.

48. Irwin Cotler, "Post-Holocaust and Anti-Semitism: Durban's Troubling Legacy One Year Later: Twisting the Cause of International Human Rights against the Jewish People," *Jerusalem Center for Public Affairs*, August 2002.

49. See the United Nations International Criminal Tribunal for the former Yugoslavia, at www.icty.org.

50. See the United Nations International Criminal Tribunal for Rwanda, at www.unictr.org.

51. See "UN and Cambodia Agree on Court to Try Khmer Rouge," at http://www.hrcr.org/hottopics/UNKhmer.html.

52. See, for example: Noam Chomsky, *The Fateful Triangle: The United States, Israel, and the Palestinians*, updated edition (Boston: South End Press, 1999), 39–40; Noam Chomsky, *Pirates and Emperors, Old and New: International Terrorism in the Real World* (Boston: South End Press, 2003), 21, 22, 23, 29, 59, 62, 168.

53. Alan Dershowitz, *Letters to a Young Lawyer* (New York: Basic Books, 2001), xv.

54. Ibid., 41.

55. Ibid., 148–149.

CHAPTER 7. JIMMY CARTER AND APARTHEID

1. "Dershowitz Helped Keep Carter from Speaking at Democratic Convention," Shalom TV, November 14, 2008, as of March 28, 2011, at http://www.shalomtv.com/pdfs/ShalomTV_DershowitzObama_PR.pdf;

2. "Alan Dershowitz Blasts President Jimmy Carter on Shalom TV," YouTube, March 3, 2008; see also: "Alan Dershowitz Calls Jimmy Carter an 'Anti-Israel Bigot,' Saying That He Has No Sympathy for the Jewish People," Press Release, Shalom TV, March 3, 2008, at http://shalomtv.com/pdfs/ShalomTV_AlanDershowitz_PR.pdf.

3. "It's Not Apartheid," *Guardian*, December 11, 2006.

4. Jimmy Carter, *Palestine Peace Not Apartheid* (New York: Simon & Schuster, 2006), 189–90.

5. Ibid., 215.

6. "The World According to Jimmy Carter," *Huffington Post*, November 22, 2006.

7. "Jimmy Carter Issues Letter to Jewish Community on *Palestine Peace Not Apartheid*," The Carter Center, December 15, 2006.

8. Alan Dershowitz, *The Case against Israel's Enemies: Exposing Jimmy Carter and Others Who Stand in the Way of Peace* (Hoboken, NJ: Wiley, 2008), 11–12.

9. Carter, *Palestine Peace Not Apartheid*, 16–17.

10. "Jimmy Carter Issues Letter to Jewish Community."

11. Dershowitz, The Case against Israel's Enemies, 23.

12. Ibid.

13. Carter, *Palestine*, 215.

14. On December 22, 2009, in an article titled "Jimmy Carter: Forgive Me for Stigmatizing Israel," *Ha'aretz* reported: "Former U.S. president Jimmy Carter has apologized to the American Jewish community for 'stigmatizing Israel' and asked for forgiveness for his actions, the JTA [Jewish Telegraphic Agency] reported on Monday." According to *Ha'aretz*, Carter wrote an open letter to the Jewish American community, in which he also said: "We must recognize Israel's achievements under difficult circumstances, even as we strive in a positive way to help Israel continue to improve its relations with its Arab populations, but we must not permit criticisms for improvement to stigmatize Israel. As I would have noted at Rosh Hashanah and Yom Kippur, but which is appropriate at any time of the year, I offer an Al Het [a Jewish prayer to God asking forgiveness of sins] for any words or deeds of mine that may have done so." While Carter did not specifically retract his use of "apartheid" in the title of his book, *Ha'aretz* reported that "Carter has angered American Jews in the past by likening Israeli policy in the West Bank to apartheid South Africa in his book *Palestine Peace Not Apartheid*."

15. "Implementation of General Assembly Resolution 60/251 of 15 March 2006 Entitled 'Human Rights Council': Report of the Special Rapporteur on the Situation of Human Rights in the Palestinian Territories Occupied Since 1967,

John Dugard," Human Rights Council, Fourth Session, Item 2 of the Provisional Agenda, January 29, 2007, 2.

16. Ibid.

17. Ibid., 14.

18. Ibid., 14.

19. Ibid., 17. See also "Occupied Gaza Like Apartheid South Africa, Says UN Report," *Guardian*, February 23, 2007.

20. "Tutu Condemns Israeli 'Apartheid,'" BBC News, April 29, 2002. See also Desmond Tutu, "Apartheid in the Holy Land," *Guardian*, April 29, 2002.

21. "Against Israeli Apartheid," the *Nation*, June 27, 2002.

22. "Declaration of Conscience by South Africans of Jewish Descent, October 23, 2001," *Palestine-Israel Journal*, vol. 8, no. 4 (2001) and vol. 9, no. 1 (2002) at http://www.pij.org/details.php?id=1097.

23. "'This Is Like Apartheid': ANC Veterans Visit West Bank," *Independent*, July 11, 2008.

24. "Occupation, Colonialism, Apartheid? A Re-assessment of Israel's Practices in the Occupied Palestinian Territories under International Law," Democracy and Governance Programme, Middle East Project, Human Sciences Research Council, Cape Town, South Africa, May 2009, Executive Summary, 2.

25. The principal contributors were Max du Plessis, Professor, Faculty of Law, University of KwaZulu-Natal (Durban) and Senior Research Associate, Institute for Security Studies; Fatmeh El-Ajou, Lawyer, Adalah / Legal Center for Arab Minority Rights in Israel (Haifa); Victor Kattan, Teaching Fellow, Center for International Studies and Diplomacy, SOAS, University of London; John Reynolds, Legal Researcher, Al-Haq (West Bank affiliate of the International Commission of Jurists); Rina Rosenberg, Esq., International Advocacy Director, Adalah / Legal Center for Arab Minority Rights in Israel (Haifa); Iain Scoobie, Sir Joseph Hotung Research Professor in Law, Human Rights and Peace Building in the Middle East, School of Law, SOAS, University of London. The consultants were John Dugard, Extraordinary Professor, Center for Human Rights, University of Pretoria, former UN Special Rapporteur on the Occupied Palestinian Territories (The Hague); Hassan Jabareen, Lawyer and General Director, Adalah / Legal Center for Arab Minority Rights in Israel; Daphna Golan, Director, South African Commission on Human Rights (Pretoria); Stephanie Koury, Research Fellow, Sir Joseph Hotung Programme on Law, Human Rights and Peace Building in the Middle East, SOAS, University of London; Jody Kollaphen, CEO, South African Commission on Human Rights (Pretoria); Stephanie Koury, Research Fellow, Sir Joseph Hotung Programme on Law, Human Rights and Peace Building in the Middle East, SOAS, University of London; Gilbert Marcus, Senior Counsel and Constitutional Lawyer (Johannesburg); Michael Sfard, Lawyer (Tel Aviv); Peter A. Stemmet, Advocate and Senior State Law Advisor, Department of Foreign Affairs, Government of South

Africa (Pretoria). For the lists of contributors and consultants, see "Occupation, Colonialism Apartheid?," 3.

26. "Occupation, Colonialism, Apartheid?," 4.

27. Ibid., 8.

28. United Nations General Assembly Resolution 1514 (XV), "Declaration on the Granting of Independence to Colonial Countries and Peoples," December 14, 1960.

29. Bryan A. Garner (ed.), *Black's Law Dictionary*, 7th edition (St. Paul, MN: West Group, 1999).

30. "Occupation, Colonialism, Apartheid?," 8.

31. Ibid., 8–9.

32. The Israel-Palestinian "customs union," according to B'Tselem, was an agreement ("Paris Protocol") between Israel and the Palestinian Authority that was signed in 1994 as part of Oslo I, and established the interim-period economic relations by preserving the economic relations that existed until then, which was "a Palestinian economy integrated in and dependent on the Israeli economy." According to B'Tselem:

"The Protocol established a joint external border for the interim period. Israel collects the import taxes on the goods and transfers to the Palestinian Authority the taxes on goods that were intended for the Occupied Territories. The Protocol further provides that Israel may unilaterally establish and change the taxes imposed on imported goods. Regarding V.A.T. [Value Added Tax], Israel transfers to the Palestinian Authority, in accordance with a monthly accounting, revenues collected for goods and services sold in Israel and intended for consumption in the Occupied Territories.

"This kind of relationship—unlike economic separation or establishment of a free-trade area—was preferable to Israel, which did not want to establish an economic border with the Palestinian Authority, an act that would give a clear flavor of sovereignty [to the Palestinian Authority] and create a binding precedent on the eve of the final status stage. The Palestinian Authority had no choice but to accept the model set forth in the Protocol, because Israel made acceptance a condition for Israel's continuing to allow Palestinians to work in Israel. Israel imposed the condition at a time that the Palestinian Authority was unable to provide employment within the autonomous areas to the tens of thousands of Palestinians working in Israel."

33. Ibid., 9.

34. Ibid.

35. Ibid.

36. Ibid., 9–10.

37. Ibid., 10.

38. Ibid., 13.

39. Ibid., 14.

40. Ibid., 15.

41. Ibid., 14–15.

42. Ibid., 14.

43. Ibid., 15.

44. B'Tselem, "Land Grab: Israel's Settlement Policy in the West Bank," May 2002.

45. B'Tselem, "Forbidden Roads: The Discriminatory West Bank Road Regime," August 2004.

46. "Analysis: Creating a Bantustan in Gaza," *Haáretz*, April 16, 2004.

47. "Bantustan Plan for an Apartheid Israel," *Guardian*, April 26, 2004.

48. "Israeli Journalist Amira Hass Reflects on Reporting Under Occupation," *Democracy Now!*, April 12, 2005, last accessed on February 5, 2010, at http://www.democracynow.org/2005/4/12/israeli_journalist_amira_hass_reflects_on.

49. "Zionist Federation Cancels *Haáretz* Journalist: Columnist Danny Rubenstein Reportedly Likens Israel to Apartheid South Africa," *Ynet*, August 31, 2007.

50. "Yes, It Is Apartheid," *Haáretz*, April 25, 2008

51. "Yes, There Is Apartheid in Israel: This Road Is for Jews Only," *Counterpunch*, January 8, 2007.

52. Dershowitz, *The Case against Israel's Enemies*, 20, 21, 22.

53. Ibid., 22.

54. Ibid., 24.

55. Ibid., 22.

56. "List of White House 'Enemies' and Memo Submitted by Dean to the Ervin Committee," at http://www.colorado.edu/AmStudies/lewis/film/enemies.htm.

57. Dershowitz, *The Case against Israel's Enemies*, 79.

58. Ibid., 164.

59. Ibid., 168.

60. Ibid.

61. Ibid., 174.

62. Ibid.

63. Alan Dershowitz, *Letters to a Young Lawyer* (New York: Basic Books, 2005), 19.

64. Pamela Constable and Arturo Venezuela, *A Nation of Enemies: Chile Under Pinochet* (New York: W.W. Norton, 1993).

65. Jack Anderson, "Hams in Control," April 4, 1977, at http://news.google.com/newspapers?nid=861&dat=19770404&id=6ocqAAAAIBAJ&sjid=F1sEAAAAIBAJ&pg=7010,671874.

66. Joseph P. McCarthy, "Speech at Wheeling, West Virginia," 1950, at http://us.history.wisc.edu/hist102/pdocs/mccarthy_wheeling.pdf.

67. Dershowitz, *The Case against Israel's Enemies*, 119.

68. Ibid., 39.

69. Ibid., 180.

70. B'Tselem, "Statistics: Fatalities," as of March 28, 2011, at http://www.btselem.org/english/statistics/casualties.asp.

71. Dershowitz, *The Case against Israel's Enemies*, 4.

72. Ibid., 78.

73. Abraham Foxman, *The Deadliest Lies: The Israel Lobby and the Myth of Jewish Control* (New York: Palgrave Macmillan, 2007). A search of *The Deadliest Lies* on amazon.com yields the following number of mentions of the words in question: anti-Semitism (20), anti-Semitic (21), anti-Semite (11), bigotry (10), bigoted (8), bigot (8).

74. Ibid., 171.

75. Dershowitz, *The Case against Israel's Enemies*. A search of *The Case against Israel's Enemies* on amazon.com yields the following number of mentions: anti-Semitism (45), anti-Semitic (42), anti-Semite (25), bigotry (19), bigoted (10), bigot (8).

76. Alan Dershowitz, *The Case for Peace: How the Arab-Israeli Conflict Can Be Resolved* (Hoboken: Wiley, 2005). A search of *The Case for Peace* on amazon.com yields the following number of mentions: anti-Semitism (43), anti-Semitic (31), anti-Semite (10), bigotry (15), bigoted (8), bigot (1).

77. Alan Dershowitz, *The Case for Israel* (Hoboken: Wiley, 2003). A search of *The Case for Israel* on amazon.com yields the following number of mentions: anti-Semitism (27), anti-Semitic (27), anti-Semite (9), bigotry (16), bigoted (4), bigot (3).

78. Dershowitz, *The Case against Israel's Enemies*, 31.

79. Alan Dershowitz, "Has Carter Crossed the Line," *Jerusalem Post*, December 21, 2006.

80. Dershowitz, *The Case against Israel's Enemies*, 47.

81. Ibid., 54.

82. Ibid., 77.

83. Ibid., 52.

84. Ibid., 79.

85. Ibid., 4.

86. Ibid., 90.

87. Ibid., 91.

88. Ibid.

89. "The Israeli Committee against House Demolitions (ICAHD) Statement on Sanctions," U.S. Campaign to End the Israeli Occupation, as of March 28, 2011, at http://www.endtheoccupation.org/article.php?id=1047.

90. Dershowitz, *The Case against Israel's Enemies*, 96.

91. Ibid.

92. Ibid.

93. Alan Dershowitz, "Alan Dershowitz: Alice Walker's Bigotry," *ewish Press*, June 20, 2012.

94. Amnesty International, "Suffocating Gaza: The Israeli Blockade's Effects on Palestinians," June 1, 2010.

95. Ibid.

CHAPTER 8. RICHARD FALK AND SELF-DEFENSE

1. "U.N. Rights Investigator Expelled by Israel," *New York Times*, December 15, 2008.

2. "My Expulsion from Israel," *Guardian*, December 19, 2008.

3. "Israel Denies Entry to High-Profile Critic Norman Finkelstein," *Haaretz*, May 24, 2008.

4. "Noam Chomsky Is Denied Entry into Israel," *Haaretz*, May 16, 2010. For a full account of Chomsky's visit, see "Keeping the Record Straight: About Noam Chomsky's Trip to the Middle East in May 2010," Assaf Kfoury, Znet, July 31, 2010, at http://zcommunications.org/keeping-the-record-straight-by-assaf-kfoury.

5. "Chomsky Barred from West Bank by Israel," *New York Times*, May 16, 2010.

6. Books by Aviva Chomsky, a professor of Latin American studies at Salem State University, include: *A History of the Cuban Revolution* (Wiley-Blackwell, 2010); *Linked Labor Histories: New England, Colombia, and the Making of a Global Working Class* (Duke University Press, 2008); and *They Take Our Jobs! And 20 Other Myths about Immigration* (Beacon Press, 2007).

7. Kfoury, "Keeping the Record Straight: About Noam Chomsky's Trip to the Middle East in May 2010."

8. "Chomsky Barred from West Bank," *Boston Globe*, May 17, 2010.

9. Ibid.

10. Association for Civil Rights in Israel, "ACRI Condemns Noam Chomsky's Entry Denial: Interior Ministry Refuses Entry to U.S. Linguist," May 17, 2010.

11. "ACRI: Chomsky One of Many Stopped," *Jerusalem Post*, May 17, 2010.

12. "Irish Nobel Peace Prize Winner Refused Entry to Israel," *Jerusalem Post*, September 28, 2010.

13. "Shin Bet Deports Spain's Most Famous Clown upon Arrival in Israel," *Haaretz*, May 6, 2010.

14. See the Universal Declaration of Human Rights, at http://www.un.org/en/documents/udhr/index.shtml#a9.

15. "Double Standard Watch: Israel's Entry Ban of Richard Falk," *Jerusalem Post*, December 21, 2008.

16. Ibid.

17. Ibid.

18. Richard Falk, "Slouching toward a Palestinian Holocaust," Transnational Foundation for Peace and Future Research, June 29, 2007, at

http://www.transnational.org/Area_MiddleEast/2007/Falk_PalestineGenocide.html.

19. "Double Standard Watch: Israel's Entry Ban of Richard Falk."

20. Human Rights Watch, "Indiscriminate Fire," June 30, 2007, 31.

21. Ibid., 36.

22. Ibid., 49.

23. Ibid., 51.

24. Stanley Karnow, *Vietnam: A History: The First Complete Account of Vietnam at War* (New York: Penguin, 1984), 198.

25. Ted Morgan, *Valley of Death: The Tragedy at Dien Bien Phu That Led America into the Vietnam War* (New York: Random House, 2010), 212.

26. Final Declaration of the Geneva Conference, July 21, 1954, at http://www.fordham.edu/halsall/mod/1954-geneva-indochina.html.

27. Consultative Council of the Lawyers Committee on American Policy Toward Vietnam, Richard Falk, Chair, John H. E. Fried, Rapporteur, *Vietnam and International Law* (Northampton, MA: Aletheia Press, 1990), 41. Originally published by O'Hare, (Flanders, NJ, 1967).

28. "McCarthy Insists Truman Oust Reds; 57 Communists Still Are on Job at State Department Despite Loyalty List," *New York Times*, February 12, 1950.

29. "McCarthy Terms C.I.A. 'Most' Infiltrated Agency," *New York Times*, June 17, 1954.

30. "Truce in Indochina," *New York Times*, July 21, 1954.

31. David Rudenstine, *The Day the Presses Stopped: A History of the Pentagon Papers Case* (Berkeley: University of California Press, 1996), 28.

32. The Lawyers Committee on Vietnam, *Vietnam and International Law*, 43, 47.

33. Dwight D. Eisenhower, *The White House Years: Mandate for Change, 1953–1956* (New York: Doubleday, 1963), 372.

34. Lawyers Committee on American Policy Towards Vietnam, *Vietnam and International Law*, 135, 136, 137.

35. The full committee members were: Richard Falk (chair), John H. E. Fried (rapporteur), Richard Barnet (Institute for Policy Studies), John H. Herz (City College of New York), Stanley Hoffmann (Harvard), Wallace McClure (Duke), Saul H. Mendlovitz (Rutgers), Richard S. Miller (Ohio State), Hans Morgenthau (Chicago), William G. Rice (Wisconsin), Burns H. Weston (Iowa), and Quincy Wright (Chicago).

36. Lawyers Committee on American Policy Towards Vietnam, *Vietnam and International Law*, 19.

37. United Nations Charter Article 2, paragraph 4, states: "All members shall refrain in their international relations from the threat or use of force against the territorial integrity or political independence of any state, or in any manner inconsistent with the Purposes of the United Nations."

38. Lawyers Committee on American Policy Towards Vietnam, *Vietnam and*

International Law, 19–20.

39. Ibid., 20.

40. Ibid., 21.

41. Ibid., 20–21.

42. Ibid., 21–22.

43. Ibid., 55, 57.

44. Ibid., 57.

45. Ibid., 58.

46. "Double Standard Watch: Israel's Actions Are Lawful and Commendable," *Jerusalem Post*, January 4, 2009.

47. "Double Standard Watch: Israel Is Well within Its Rights," *Jerusalem Post*, January 13, 2009.

48. "Israel's Bombardment of Gaza Is Not Self-Defence—It's a War Crime," *Times* (London), January 11, 2009.

49. Ian Brownlie, *International Law and the Use of Force by States* (Oxford: Clarendon Press, 1963).

50. Richard Falk (ed.), *The Vietnam War and International Law, Volumes 1–3* (Princeton: Princeton University Press, 1968–1976).

51. Human Rights Watch, "Indiscriminate Fire," June 30, 2007.

52. Amnesty International, "Israel/Occupied Territories: Israel Must End Unlawful Killings of Palestinians and Stop Reckless Shelling," June 12, 2006. See also, Human Rights Watch, "Indiscriminate Fire," Appendix I: The Gaza Beach Incident, June 30, 2007, where Human Rights Watch methodically rejects Israel's denial that the lethal explosion on the beach in Beit Lahiya on June 9, 2006 was caused by Israeli artillery.

53. Amnesty International, "Israel/Occupied Territories: Call for International Investigation of Gaza Strikes," June 21, 2006.

54. Amnesty International, "Israel/Occupied Territories: Palestinian Armed Groups Must Release Abducted Israeli Soldier," June 27, 2006.

55. "Palestinian Leader Orders Force to Find Israeli," *New York Times*, June 27, 2006.

56. Ibid.

57. "Israeli Troops Move into Gaza; Bridges Are Hit," *New York Times*, June 28, 2006.

58. Amnesty International, "Israel/Occupied Territories: Deliberate Attacks a War Crime," June 30, 2006.

59. B'Tselem, "Act of Vengeance: Israel's Bombing of the Gaza Power Plant and Its Effects," September 2006.

60. Human Rights Watch, "Gaza: Israeli Offensive Must Limit Harm to Civilians," June 28, 2006.

61. B'Tselem, "Sonic Booms Constitute Collective Punishment," July 3, 2006.

62. "Palestinians Say IDF Arrests More Than 30 Hamas Officials," *Haaretz*, June 29, 2006.

63. "Israel Hits Palestinian PM's Gaza Office," Associated Press, July 1, 2006.

64. "Switzerland Says Israel Violating International Law in Gaza Strip," *Haaretz*, July 4, 2006.

65. Alan Dershowitz, "The Anti-Israel Double-Standard Watch," *Huffington Post*, July 14, 2006.

66. B'Tselem, "Administrative Detention," posted as a permanent category.

67. B'Tselem, "Barred from Contact: Violation of the Right to Visit Palestinians Held in Israeli Prisons," September 2006.

68. Dershowitz, "The Anti-Israel Double-Standard Watch."

69. B'Tselem, "No Minor Matter: Violation of the Rights of Palestinian Minors Arrested by Israel on Suspicion of Stone-Throwing," July 2011.

70. Amnesty International, "Israel/Lebanon: Deliberate Destruction or 'Collateral Damage'? Israeli Attacks on Civilian Infrastructure," August 23, 2006; See also the detailed report by the Lebanese Higher Relief Council at http://www.reliefweb.int/rw/rwb.nsf/db900SID/EKOI-6ST5ZM?OpenDocument.

71. "Hezbollah Lawmaker Says Group Targeted Civilians Only in Reprisal," *Haaretz*, September 14, 2006.

72. Howard Friel, "The Winograd Report v. the New York Times," *Common Dreams*, May 3, 2007.

73. Ibid.

CHAPTER 9. RICHARD GOLDSTONE AND WAR CRIMES

1. Alan Dershowitz, "Goldstone Investigation Undercuts Human Rights," *Jerusalem Post*, September 17, 2009.

2. Ibid.

3. Ian Brownlie et al., "Israel's Bombardment of Gaza Is Not Self-Defence—It's a War Crime," *Times* (London), January 11, 2009.

4. Alan Dershowitz, "Israel's Actions Are Lawful and Commendable," *Jerusalem Post*, January 4, 2009.

5. Alan Dershowitz, "An Anti-Israel Extremist Seeks Revenge through Goldstone Report," *Huffington Post*, February 12, 2010.

6. Hanan Chehata and Desmond Travers, "Exclusive MEMO Interview with Colonel Desmond Travers—Coauthor of the UN's Goldstone Report," *Middle East Monitor*, undated.

7. Dan Harvey, *Peacekeepers: Irish Soldiers in the Lebanon* (Dublin: Merlin Publishing, 2001), 51, 84.

8. Robert Fisk, *Pity the Nation: The Abduction of Lebanon* (New York: Nation Books, 2002), 138.

9. "Mine Kills 3 Irish U.N. Soldiers in South Lebanon," *New York Times*, March

22, 1989.

10. "Irish Soldier with U.N. Killed by Israeli Tank Fire in Southern Lebanon," *Los Angeles Times*, January 12, 1987.

11. Fisk, *Pity the Nation*, 136.

12. Ibid., 135–141.

13. Ibid., 136.

14. "Human Rights in Palestine and Other Occupied Arab Territories: Report of the United Nations Fact Finding Mission on the Gaza Conflict," Human Rights Council, September 15, 2009, 5.

15. Dershowitz, "An Anti-Israel Extremist Seeks Revenge through Goldstone Report."

16. "Siddiqui: Looking for Accountability over Gaza," *Toronto Star*, October 15, 2009.

17. Alan Dershowitz, "Goldstone Report Is an Ad Hominem Attack," *Jerusalem Post*, September 29, 2009.

18. "Dershowitz: Goldstone Is a Traitor to the Jewish People," *Haaretz*, January 31, 2010.

19. Alan Dershowitz, "Legitimating Bigotry: The Legacy of Richard Goldstone," *Jerusalem Post*, May 9, 2010.

20. Richard J. Goldstone, *For Humanity: Reflections of a War Crimes Investigator* (New Haven: Yale University Press, 2000), xix.

21. "Judge Goldstone's Dark Past," *Ynet*, May 6, 2010.

22. "Richard Goldstone: I Have No Regrets about the Gaza War Report," *Haaretz*, May 6, 2010.

23. "Judge Goldstone's Dark Past."

24. "S. Africa Police Blamed in Fatal Shootings of Black Protesters Last March," *Los Angeles Times*, September 2, 1990.

25. "Judge Named to Lead Gaza Inquiry Is Known for Fairness," *Los Angeles Times*, April 8, 2009.

26. William A. Schabas, "Book Review of *For Humanity: Reflections of a War Crimes Investigator* by Richard Goldstone," *American Journal of International Law*, vol. 95, no. 3 (July 2001): 742–744.

27. "Israel Agrees to Gaza Ceasefire," BBC News, June 18, 2008.

28. Amnesty International, "Gaza Blockade: Collective Punishment," July 4, 2008. AI also reported that "in the first five months of 2008 some 380 Palestinians, more than a third of them unarmed civilians and including more than 60 children, were killed by the Israeli army, almost all of them in the Gaza Strip," while "in the same period 25 Israelis, 16 of them civilians, were killed by Palestinian armed groups."

29. Amnesty International, "Freedom of Movement, Right to Education Denied," August 14, 2008.

---

30. Amnesty International, "Further Information on Medical Concern," August 22, 2008.

31. Amnesty International, "Health Professional Actions: Patients from Gaza Are Still Denied Access to Medical Treatment in Israel," August 29, 2008.

32. Amnesty International, "Medical Concern," October 16, 2008.

33. "Israel-Hamas Violence Disrupts Gaza Truce," Reuters, November 6, 2008.

34. Amnesty International, "Gaza Ceasefire at Risk," November 5, 2008.

35. Amnesty International, "Israeli Army Blocks Deliveries to Gaza," November 14, 2008.

36. Andrea Becker, "The Slow Death of Gaza," *Guardian*, November 24, 2008.

37. Amnesty International, "Gaza Reduced to Bare Survival," December 5, 2008.

38. "Israel's 'Crime against Humanity,'" TruthDig.com, posted on *Common Dreams*, December 15, 2008

39. Steve Niva, "War of Choice: How Israel Manufactured the Gaza Escalation," *Foreign Policy in Focus*, January 7, 2008.

40. Amnesty International, "Gaza Ceasefire at Risk"

41. Sara Roy, "If Gaza Falls . . . ," *London Review of Books*, January 1, 2009.

42. Alan Dershowitz, "Israel Is Well within Its Rights," *Huffington Post*, January 13, 2009.

43. Amira Hass, "History Did Not Begin with the Qassams," *Ha'aretz*, January 14, 2009.

44. See, Adam Horowitz, Lizzy Ratner, and Philip Weiss (eds.), *The Goldstone Report: The Legacy of the Landmark Investigation of the Gaza Conflict* (New York: Nation Books, 2011). The editors chronicled the major events of the cease-fire as follows:

June 2008: Egypt brokers a ceasefire between Israel and Hamas. The ceasefire terms reportedly state that Hamas will halt attacks against Israel from groups inside Gaza, while Israel will cease military operations inside of Gaza and ease the blockade.

June–July 2008: Hamas insists that it is committed to keeping the truce, but other militant groups inside Gaza continue firing rockets. Israel fails to ease the blockade and conducts military operations inside Gaza and the West Bank aimed at Hamas. . . .

November 2008: After two months of relative calm, Israel breaks the truce with Hamas in a raid that kills six gunmen in Gaza. Hamas responds by firing rockets into Israel. Attacks by both Israel and armed groups in Gaza escalate in November and December. Nearly 200 rockets and mortar shells are fired into Israel in most of November, up from two in October. . . .

December 2008: Gaza authorities declare an end to the truce with Israel following the continuing blockade on Gaza and multiple Israeli strikes during the first week of December, including one that kills two children and injures two others in Rafah. Israeli authorities say that Gazan forces fired 130 rockets and mortars into Israel in the first 18 days of the month.

45. Brownlie et al., "Israel's Bombardment of Gaza Is Not Self-Defence—It's a War Crime"; "Human Rights in Palestine and Other Occupied Arab Territories: Report of the United Nations Fact Finding Mission on the Gaza Conflict" (hereinafter the "Goldstone report"), Human Rights Council, Twelfth Session, A/HRC/12/48, September 15, 2009, paras. 64, 109, 383, 922, 1212, 1304, 1324, 1526, 1716.

46. Alan Dershowitz, "Using Civilians as Weapons: The Lack of Moral Clarity about Hamas," *Miami Herald*, January 16, 2009.

47. "Israel Attacks Gaza, More Than 155 Reported Killed," Reuters, December 27, 2008.

48. Amnesty International, "Civilians Must Be Protected in Gaza and Israel," December 28, 2008.

49. Norman Solomon, "A Hundred Eyes for an Eye," *Common Dreams*, December 29, 2008.

50. Robert Fisk, "Leaders Lie, Civilians Die, and Lessons of History Are Ignored," *Independent*, December 29, 2008.

51. National Lawyers Guild, "The National Lawyers Guild Condemns Illegal Israeli Massacre of Over 300 Gazans: Calls for Ceasefire and Urges Participation in Protests," December 29, 2008.

52. B'Tselem, "Protect Civilians from the Impact of Hostilities," December 30, 2008.

53. Gideon Levy, "The IDF Has No Mercy for the Children in Gaza Nursery Schools," *Ha'aretz*, January 15.

54. Dershowitz, "Using Civilians as Weapons: The Lack of Moral Clarity about Hamas."

55. Gideon Levy, "Someone Must Stop Israel's Rampant Madness in Gaza," *Ha'aretz*, January 16, 2009.

56. "Investigate Now," *Ha'aretz*, January 22, 2009.

57. Chris Hedges, "Party to Murder," TruthDig.com, as posted on *Common Dreams*, December 30, 2008.

58. Richard Falk, "Israel's War Crimes," *Common Dreams*, December 30, 2008.

59. Alan Dershowitz, "Israel's Policy Is Perfectly 'Proportionate,'" *Wall Street Journal*, January 2, 2009.

60. "Jewish Organizations Call for End to Gaza Bombings," Inter Press Service, December 31, 2008.

61. "Israel's Operation in Gaza: Frequently Asked Questions," Anti-Defamation League, at http://www.adl.org/main_Israel/FAQs_Gaza.htm#1.

62. Dershowitz, "Israel's Policy Is Perfectly 'Proportionate.'"

63. B'Tselem, "B'Tselem's Investigation of Fatalities in Operation Cast Lead," September 9, 2009.

64. "Onslaught: Israel's Attacks on Gaza & The Rule of Law: December 29, 2008–January 18, 2009: Report of the National Lawyers Guild Delegation to Gaza," February 2009, at http://www.nlginternational.org/report/NLG_Final_Report.pdf.

65. "Suspend Military Aid to Israel, Amnesty Urges Obama after Detailing US Weapons Used in Gaza," *Guardian*, February 23, 2009.

66. "Rights Group: Israel Made Illegal Use of Phosphorus Shells in Gaza," *Ha'aretz*, March 5, 2009.

67. Amnesty International, "Gaza: World's Leading Investigators Call for War Crimes Inquiry," March 16, 2009.

68. "Guardian Investigation Uncovers Evidence of Alleged Israeli War Crimes in Gaza," *Guardian*, March 24, 2009.

69. "End This Culture of Israeli Impunity," *Guardian*, March 24, 2009.

70. The three films can be viewed at "Gaza War Crimes Investigation: Clancy Chassay Spent Three Months in Gaza Talking to Civilians, Medics, and Investigators about Allegations of War Crimes during Israel's 23-Day Campaign in Gaza," *Guardian*, March 24, 2009, at http://www.guardian.co.uk/world/series/gaza-war-crimes-investigation.

71. Human Rights Watch, "Rain of Fire: Israel's Unlawful Use of White Phosphorus in Gaza," March 25, 2009, http://www.hrw.org/reports/2009/03/25/rain-fire.

72. The film *Rain of Fire: White Phosphorus in Gaza* can be viewed at http://www.hrw.org/en/features/rain-fire-white-phosphorus-gaza.

73. Sebastian Van As, Alicia Vacas Moro, Ralf Syring, Jørgen Lange Thomsen, and Shabbir Ahmed Wadee, Physicians for Human Rights—Israel, and Palestinian Medical Relief Society, "Fact-Finding Mission into Medically Related Violations in the Gaza Strip during 27.12.2008–18.01.2009," April 2009, at http://www.medico.de/media/die-kurzfassung-abbreviated-version.pdf.

74. "UN Accuses Israel of Gaza 'Negligence or Recklessness,'" *Guardian*, May 5, 2009. See also: Human Rights Watch, "Gaza: Pursuit of the Laws of War," May 8, 2009; "Letter Dated 4 May 2009 from the Secretary-General Addressed to the President of the Security Council: Summary by the Secretary-General of the Report of the United Nations Headquarters Board of Inquiry into Certain Incidents in the Gaza Strip between 27 December 2008 and 19 January 2009," A/63/855, May 15, 2009.

75. "UN Team Arrives in Gaza for War Crimes Probe," *Ha'aretz*, June 1, 2009.

76. "Barak: Israel Won't Assist UN Gaza Probe," *Jerusalem Post*, June 1, 2009.

77. "Amnesty Accuses Israel of Using Human Shields in Gaza," Agence France Presse, July 2, 2009.

78. Amnesty International, "Israel/Gaza: Operation 'Cast Lead': 22 Days of Death and Destruction," July 2009, 1–3.

79. "Amnesty Accuses Israel of Using Human Shields in Gaza."

80. "Bearing the Brunt Again: Child Rights Violations during Operation Cast Lead," Defense for Children International—Palestine Section, September 2009, at http://www.dci-pal.org/english/publ/research/BearingTheBruntAgain.pdf.

81. Ibid.

82. Richard Falk, "The Goldstone Report: Ordinary Text, Extraordinary Event," *Global Governance*, vol. 16, no. 2 (April 2010), http://journals.rienner.com/doi/abs/10.5555/ggov.2010.16.2.139.

83. Goldstone report, para. 43.

84. Ibid., paras. 702–881.

85. Ibid., introduction.

86. Ibid., paras. 50–54.

87. Ibid., para. 1732.

88. Ibid., para. 1733.

89. Ibid., para. 1763.

90. Ibid., para. 1772.

91. Ibid., paras. 108, 1724.

92. Alan Dershowitz, "Goldstone Report Is a Barrier to Peace," *Huffington Post*, September 22, 2009.

93. Michael Oren, "UN Report a Victory for Terror," *Boston Globe*, September 24, 2009.

94. Ehud Barak, "At the U.N., Terrorism Pays," *Wall Street Journal*, September 25, 2009.

95. Moshe Arens, "A License to Kill," *Ha'aretz*, October 6, 2009.

96. Alan Dershowitz, "The Case against the Goldstone Report: A Study in Evidentiary Bias," *Jerusalem Post*, January 31, 2010, at http://www.jpost.com/Israel/Article.aspx?id=167379.

97. Alan Dershowitz, "Hezbollah's Triumph: Israeli Rockets Hits Lebanese Children," *Huffington Post*, July 31, 2006.

98. Ibid.

99. "Israel Suspending Lebanon Air Raids After Dozens Die: Halt of 48 Hours," *New York Times*, July 31, 2006.

100. Human Rights Watch, "Israel/Lebanon: Qana Death Toll at 28: International Inquiry Needed Into Israeli Air Strike," August 2, 2006.

101. Alan Dershowitz, "Hezbollah's Triumph: Israeli Rockets Hits Lebanese Children," *Huffington Post*, July 31, 2006.

102. Joy Gordon, *Invisible War: The United States and the Iraq Sanctions* (Cambridge: Harvard University Press, 2010), 3.

103. Alan Dershowitz, "Lebanon Is Not a Victim," *Huffington Post*, August

7, 2006.

104. Human Rights Watch, "Fatal Strikes: Israel's Indiscriminate Attacks against Civilians in Lebanon," August 3, 2006.

105. "Children Die in Convoy Attack as Israel Widens Lebanon Assault," *Guardian*, July 15, 2006.

106. "Israel Widening Scope of Attacks across Lebanon," *New York Times*, July 16, 2006.

107. Robert Fisk, "The Child Lies Like a Rag Doll—A Symbol of the Latest Lebanon War," *Independent*, July 20, 2006.

108. Robert Fisk, "Marwahin, 15 July 2006: The Anatomy of a Massacre," *Independent*, September 30, 2006.

109. Human Rights Watch, "Why They Died: Civilian Casualties in Lebanon During the 2006 War," September 2007, 8.

110. Amnesty International, "Deliberate Destruction or 'Collateral Damage'? Israeli Attacks on Civilian Infrastructure," August 22, 2006.

111. Ibid.

112. Alan Dershowitz, "The 'Human Rights Watch' Watch, Installment 1," *Huffington Post*, August 21, 2006.

113. Ibid.

114. Human Rights Watch, "Fatal Strikes: Israel's Indiscriminate Attacks against Civilians in Lebanon," August 3, 2006.

115. For a fuller examination of Dershowitz's August 21, 2006 column in *Huffington Post*, "The 'Human Rights Watch' Watch, Installment 1," see Howard Friel and Richard Falk, *Israel-Palestine on Record: How the New York Times Misreports Conflict in the Middle East* (New York: Verso, 2007), 165–175.

116. Alan Dershowitz, "Amnesty International's Biased Definition of War Crimes: Whatever Israel Does to Defend Its Citizens," *Huffington Post*, August 29, 2006.

117. Ibid.

118. Rome Statute of the International Criminal Court, at http://untreaty.un.org/cod/icc/statute/romefra.htm.

119. Dershowitz, "Amnesty International's Biased Definition of War Crimes."

CHAPTER 10. CHOMSKY'S UNIVERSALISM

1. Alan Dershowitz, *Preemption: A Knife That Cuts Both Ways* (New York: W.W. Norton, 2006), 3.

2. Ibid.

3. "Time to End the Conspiracy of Silence Over Drone Attacks: UN Investigator," *Common Dreams*, June 21, 2012.

4. American Civil Liberties Union, "U.S. Targeted Killing Program: A Dangerous Precedent," June 20, 2012, at http://www.aclu.org/blog/national-

security/us-targeted-killings-program-dangerous-precedent.

5. "Secret 'Kill List' Proves a Test of Obama's Principles and Will," *New York Times*, May 29, 2012.

6. Glenn Greenwald, "What Might Cause Another 9/11," *Salon*, June 13, 2012.

7. Jonathan Turley, "10 Reasons the U.S. Is No Longer the Land of the Free," *Washington Post*, January 14, 2012. See also: Jonathan Turley, "Obama: A Disaster for Civil Liberties," *Los Angeles Times*, September 30, 2011; "Final Curtain: Obama Signs Indefinite Detention of Citizens into Law as Final Act," Jonathan Turley's Blog, January 2, 2012.

8. Bill Quigley, "Twenty Examples of the Obama Administration Assault on Domestic Civil Liberties," *Common Dreams*, December 1, 2011.

9. Bill Quigley, "Thirteen Ways Government Tracks Us," *Common Dreams*, April 9, 2012.

10. Ralph Nader, "Obama at Large: Where Are the Lawyers?" *Common Dreams*, May 31, 2012.

11. See, for example: "Further Reflections about John Brennan's Targeted Killing Speech," *Common Dreams*, May 1, 2012; "Obama White House Rejects Request for Targeted Killing Docs," *Common Dreams*, June 21, 2012.

12. See, for example: "Obama White House Rejects Request for Targeted Killing Docs"; "Guantanamo at 10: The Defeat of Liberty by Fear," *Guardian*, January 12, 2012; "Anwar al-Awlaki's Extrajudicial Murder," *Guardian*, October 1, 2011; "Anything Goes: The New FBI Guidelines," *Progressive*, June 23, 2011.

13. See, for example: "Killer Drone Attacks Illegal, Counterproductive," *Common Dreams*, June 25, 2012; "Hope Dies at Guantanamo," *Jurist*, June 21, 2012; "Close the Guantanamo Gulag," *Common Dreams*, January 17, 2012.

14. Chris Hedges, "Someone You Love: Coming to a Gulag Near You," *TruthDig*, April 2, 2012.

15. "NDAA's 'Indefinite Detention' Provisions Unconstitutional, Says Judge," *Common Dreams*, May 17, 2012.

16. Noam Chomsky, "If You Want to Stop Terrorism, Stop Killing Muslims," YouTube, at http://www.youtube.com/watch?v=dW0eiPiuUuk.

17. "Nir Rosen: 'We Managed to Make the Taliban Look Good,'" *Democracy Now!*, December 2, 2009, at http://www.democracynow.org/2009/12/2/nir_rosen_we_managed_to_make.

18. "Terror War Seen Hurting U.S. in Muslim World," Associated Press, November 24, 2004.

19. *The 9/11 Commission Report: Final Report of the National Commission on Terrorist Attacks upon the United States* (New York: W.W. Norton, 2004), 376.

20. "Spy Agencies Say Iraq War Worsens Terrorism Threat," *New York Times*, September 24, 2006.

21. "Mossad Chief: Invasion Has Created a Holy War," *Independent*, November

9, 2003.

22. "Mubarak: Arabs Hate U.S. More Than Ever," Reuters, April 20, 2004.

23. "Hans Blix: War in Iraq Has Made Terrorism Worse, 'It Has Failed Miserably,'" Agence France Presse, October 13, 2004.

24. "Al-Qaeda Boosted by Iraq War, Warns Think Tank," Agence France Presse, May 25, 2004. See also: "Occupation Made World Less Safe, Pro-War Institute Says," *Independent*, May 26, 2004.

25. *Common Dreams* (Agence France Presse). See also: "Poll Finds Hostility Hardening Toward U.S. Policies," *New York Times*, March 17, 2004; "Pyrrhus on the Potomac: How America's Post–9/11 Wars Have Undermined US National Security," Project on Defense Alternatives, September 5, 2006; "Losing Hearts and Minds: World Public Opinion and Post–9/11 US Security Policy," Project on Defense Alternatives, September 14, 2006; "War and Consequences: Global Terrorism Has Increased Since 9/11 Attacks," Project on Defense Alternatives, September 25, 2006; "New Peace Index Ranks US Among Worst Nations," Reuters, May 30, 2007; "Do U.S. Drones Kill Pakistani Extremists or Recruit Them," *McClatchy Newspapers*, April 7, 2009. See also: Glenn Greenwald, "What Might Cause Another 9/11," *Salon*, June 12, 2012; Pew Global Attitudes, "US Drone Program Fuels Global Dismay with Obama Presidency," June 13, 2012.

26. Chalmers Johnson, "The Lessons of Blowback," *Los Angeles Times*, September 30, 2001.

27. Chandra Muzaffar, "Decent People Reject Terrorism and U.S. Bombing at the Same Time," *International Herald Tribune*, November 5, 2001.

28. "Disparities of Wealth Are Seen as Fuel for Terrorism," *International Herald Tribune*, December 20, 2001.

29. *The New York Times Guide to Essential Knowledge* (New York: St. Martin's Press, 2007), 516.

30. World War II Casualties, Wikipedia, last accessed on February 12, 2013 at http://en.wikipedia.org/wiki/World_War_II_casualties. This presents probably the most extensively detailed accounting of the casualties of World War II.

31. Noam Chomsky, *9-11* (New York: Seven Stories, 2001), 11–12.

32. Ibid., 23–24.

33. "The War: A Trillion Can Be Cheap," *New York Times*, July 24, 2010; "Report: Iraq, Afghanistan Wars Cost US Nearly $4 Trillion," Voice of America, June 29, 2011; "The True Cost of the Iraq War: $3 Trillion and Beyond," *Washington Post*, September 5, 2010. See also, Linda J. Bilmes and Joseph Stiglitz, *The Three Trillion Dollar War: The True Cost of the Iraq Conflict* (New York: W.W. Norton, 2008).

34. London Charter of the International Military Tribunal, August 8, 1945, Article 6(a), at http://avalon.law.yale.edu/imt/imtconst.asp#art6.

35. Judgment of the International Military Tribunal, September 30, 1946, at

http://avalon.law.yale.edu/imt/judnazi.asp#common.

36. United Nations General Assembly Resolution 177(II), "Formulation of the Principles Recognized in the Charter of the Nürnberg Tribunal and in the Judgment of the Tribunal," November 21, 1947, at http://daccess-dds-ny.un.org/doc/ RESOLUTION/GEN/NR0/038/84/IMG/NR003884.pdf?OpenElement.

37. Principles of International Law Recognized in the Charter of the Nürnberg Tribunal and in the Judgment of the Tribunal, 1950, at http://www.icrc.org/ihl.nsf/full/390.

38. Charter of the United Nations, 1945, Preamble, at http://www.un.org/en/documents/charter/preamble.shtml.

39. Ibid., Article 2 (4), at http://www.un.org/en/documents/charter/chapter1.shtml.

40. Noam Chomsky, *What We Say Goes: Conversations on U.S. Power in a Changing World* (New York: Metropolitan, 2007), 1.

41. Noam Chomsky, *Failed States: The Abuse of Power and the Assault on Democracy* (New York: Metropolitan Books, 2006), 66.

42. A. C. Grayling, *Among the Dead Cities: The History and Moral Legacy of the WWII Bombing of Civilians in Germany and Japan* (New York: Walker & Company, 2006), 234.

43. Howard Zinn, *The Bomb* (San Francisco: City Lights Books, 2010), 31.

44. Mark Selden, "A Forgotten Holocaust: U.S. Bombing Strategy, the Destruction of Japanese Cities, and the American Way of War from the Pacific War to Iraq," in Yuki Tanaka and Marilyn B. Young (eds.), *Bombing Civilians: A Twentieth-Century History* (New York: New Press, 2009), 79.

45. International Committee of the Red Cross, "Protocol I Additional to the Geneva Conventions of 12 August 1949, and Relating to the Protection of Victims of International Armed Conflicts (Protocol I), 8 June 1977, at http://www.icrc.org/ihl.nsf/full/470?opendocument.

46. Noam Chomsky, *American Power and the New Mandarins* (New York: Pantheon, 1969), 167.

47. Errol Morris (dir.), *The Fog of War: Eleven Lessons from the Life of Robert S. McNamara*, Sony Pictures, 2004.

48. "Record Air Attack," *New York Times*, March 10, 1945.

49. Morris (dir.), *The Fog of War*.

50. "New Fire Attack," *New York Times*, March 12, 1945.

51. Warren Moscow, "Japan Is Hit Again," *New York Times*, March 14, 1945.

52. "Many Bombs Loosed," *New York Times*, March 17, 1945.

53. Grayling, *Among the Dead Cities*, 77.

54. Tsuyoshi Hasegawa, "Were the Atomic Bombings Justified?" in *Bombing Civilians*, 117.

55. Bruce Cumings, *The Korean War* (New York: The Modern Library, 2010),

149–150, 151.

56. Ibid., 159–160.

57. Ibid., 161.

58. Grayling, *Among the Dead Cities*, 274–275.

59. Selden, "A Forgotten Holocaust," in *Bombing Civilians*, 89, 93.

60. Alan Dershowitz, "There Will Never Be Peace if Iran Gets the Bomb," *Huffington Post*, November 29, 2010; "WikiLeaks Contradicts Obama Administration on Iran," *Huffington Post*, December 6, 2010; "Israel Has the Right to Attack Iran's Nuclear Reactors Now," *Huffington Post*, March 16, 2011; "Why Deterrence Won't Work against Iran," *Huffington Post*, March 20, 2012.

61. Dershowitz, "Israel Has the Right to Attack Iran's Nuclear Reactors Now."

62. Yonat Friling, Liveshots, "50 Tons of Smuggled Weapons Seized," Fox News, March 16, 2011, at http://liveshots.blogs.foxnews.com/2011/03/16/50-tons-of-smuggled-weapons-seized/.

63. Dershowitz, "Israel Has the Right to Attack Iran's Nuclear Reactors Now."

64. The Israeli military alleged that Iran had sought to smuggle to Hamas the following list of weapons, as reported by Fox News: "The ship's cargo included: 230 mortar shells 120 mm, 2,270 mortar shells 60 mm, 6 C-704 anti-ship missiles, 2 radar systems manufactured in England, 2 launchers, 2 hydraulic mounting cranes for the radar system and 66,960 bullets for AK-47 rifles. All weapons had labels and manuals in Farsi, which links Iran to the arms smuggling attempt." See Friling, "50 Tons of Smuggled Weapons Seized."

65. Dershowitz, "There Will Never Be Peace if Iran Gets the Bomb."

66. See National Intelligence Council, Office of the Director of National Intelligence, "National Intelligence Estimate: Iran: Nuclear Intentions and Capabilities," United States of America, November 2007, at http://www.dni.gov/press_releases/20071203_release.pdf; "U.S. Agencies See No Move by Iran to Build a Bomb," *New York Times*, February 24, 2012; Seymour M. Hersh, "Iran and the Bomb: How Real Is the Nuclear Threat?" *New Yorker*, June 6, 2011; Seymour M. Hersh, "Iran and the I.A.E.A.," *New Yorker*, November 18, 2011; Seymour M. Hersh, "Our Men in Iran?" *New Yorker*, April 6, 2012; "Training Terrorists in Nevada: Seymour Hersh on U.S. Aid to Iranian Group Tied to Scientists' Killing," *Democracy Now!*, April 10, 2012, at http://www.democracynow.org/2012/4/10/training_terrorists_in_nevada_seymour_hersh.

67. National Intelligence Council, Office of the Director of National Intelligence, "National Intelligence Estimate: Iran: Nuclear Intentions and Capabilities," United States of America, November 2007.

68. Ibid.

69. James Risen and Mark Mazzetti, "U.S. Agencies See No Move by Iran to Build a Bomb," *New York Times*, February 24, 2012.

70. Hersh, "Iran and the Bomb: How Real Is the Nuclear Threat?"

71. Risen and Mazzetti, "U.S. Agencies See No Move by Iran to Build a Bomb."

72. Hersh, "Iran and the Bomb: How Real Is the Nuclear Threat?"

73. Alan Dershowitz, *Preemption: A Knife That Cuts Both Ways* (New York: W.W. Norton, 2006), 93–94.

74. Dershowitz, *Preemption*, 94–96.

75. Dan Reiter, "Preventive War and Its Alternatives: The Lessons of History," Strategic Studies Institute, U.S. Army War College, 2006; Dan Reiter, "Preventive Attacks against Nuclear Programs and the 'Success' at Osiraq," *NonProliferation Review*, vol. 12, no. 2 (Summer 2005), at http://www.diplomatie.gouv.fr/fr/IMG/pdf/Osirak.pdf; Dan Reiter, "The Osiraq Myth and the Track Record of Preventive Military Attacks," Policy Brief: Ridgway Center for International Security Studies, University of Pittsburgh, (undated), at http://www.pitt.edu/~gordonm/RW/ReiterPB.pdf.

76. Reiter, "Preventive Attacks against Nuclear Programs and the 'Success' at Osiraq."

77. Ibid.

78. Dan Reiter, "Letter to the Editor," *Atlantic Monthly*, March 2005.

79. Reiter, "Preventive Attacks against Nuclear Programs and the 'Success' at Osiraq."

80. Malfrid Braut-Hegghammer, "Revisiting Osirak: Preventive Attacks and Nuclear Proliferation Risks," *International Security*, vol. 36, no. 1 (Summer 2011): 101–132.

81. Richard K. Betts, "The Osirak Fallacy," *National Interest*, March 1, 2006, at http://nationalinterest.org/article/the-osirak-fallacy-1093.

82. Stephen M. Walt, "Another Bogus Argument for War with Iran," *Foreign Policy*, March 1, 2012, at http://walt.foreignpolicy.com/posts/2012/03/01/another_bogus_argument_for_war_with_iran.

83. Noam Chomsky, Ervand Abrahamian, and Nahid Mozaffari, with David Barsamian (ed.), *Targeting Iran* (San Francisco: City Lights Books, 2007), 37–38.

84. Noam Chomsky, "The Imperial Way," *Huffington Post*, February 15, 2012.

85. Dershowitz, *Preemption*, 182.

86. Ibid., 11.

CHAPTER 11. DERSHOWITZ'S AUTHORITARIANISM

1. Bruce Ackerman, *Before the Next Attack: Preserving Civil Liberties in an Age of Terrorism* (New Haven: Yale University Press, 2006), 2.

2. Ibid., 9. Ackerman credited Michael Ignatieff, *The Lesser Evil: Political Ethics in an Age of Terror* (Princeton: Princeton University Press, 2004). For an analysis of Ignatieff's work, including his "lesser evils" analysis, see Howard Friel and Richard Falk, *The Record of the Paper: How the New York Times Misreports U.S. Foreign*

Policy (New York: Verso, 2004), 51–64, 151–161.

3. Ackerman, *Before the Next Attack*, 3.

4. Ibid.

5. Ibid., 4–5.

6. Bruce Ackerman, *The Decline and Fall of the American Republic* (Cambridge: Harvard University Press, 2010), 168.

7. Gulf of Tonkin Resolution, Joint Resolution of Congress, HJ RES 1145, August 7, 1964.

8. Authorization for Use of Military Force against Iraq Resolution of 2002, Public Law 107–243, October 16, 2002.

9. Ackerman at least seeks to introduce congressional oversight of the president's powers during a national state of emergency, which at the moment apparently is nearly unlimited. On September 14, 2001, President George W. Bush issued Proclamation 7463, a "Declaration of National Emergency by Reason of Certain Terrorist Attacks," which President Bush renewed each year while he was president, and which also has been renewed annually to date by President Obama. Apparently, the annual renewals of the state of emergency following the terrorist attacks of 9/11 were at the sole discretion of presidents Bush and Obama, aside from having to report the decision to the Congress pursuant to the National Emergencies Act of 1976, which was meant to introduce congressional oversight of the president's emergency powers. However, as Ackerman observed, while the act "can't deal with terrorism without fundamental revision," the Congress has "gone on record affirming the need to control the pathologies of emergency power." Ackerman, *Before the Next Attack*, 123.

10. Ackerman, *Before the Next Attack*, 20.

11. Ibid., 21.

12. Ibid., 22.

13. Philip B. Heymann, *Terrorism, Freedom, and Security: Winning without War* (Cambridge: MIT Press, 2003), 17, 161.

14. Ibid., 15.

15. Ibid., 15–16.

16. "Effect of the Gulf War on Infant and Child Mortality in Iraq," *New England Journal of Medicine* (September 24, 1992): 931.

17. "The Effect of Economic Sanctions on the Mortality of Iraqi Children Prior to the 1991 Persian Gulf War," *American Journal of Public Health* (April 2000): 546–552.

18. "Sanctions and Childhood Mortality in Iraq," *Lancet* (May 27, 2000): 1851–1857.

19. "UN Says Sanctions Have Killed Some 500,000 Iraqi Children," Reuters, July 21, 2000.

20. See also, Joy Gordon, *Invisible War: The United States and the Iraq*

Sanctions (Cambridge: Harvard University Press, 2010), 86–102.

21. The U.S.-led economic embargo against Iraq of 1990–2003 was cited by Osama bin Laden in an interview with the *Independent*'s long-time Middle East reporter Robert Fisk. In his 2005 book, *The Great War for Civilisation: The Conquest of the Middle East* (Knopf), Fisk wrote: "Bin Laden had asked me—a routine of every Palestinian under occupation—if Europeans did not resist occupation during the Second World War. I told him no Europeans would accept this argument over Saudi Arabia—because the Nazis had killed millions of Europeans yet the Americans had never murdered a single Saudi. Such a parallel was historically and morally wrong. Bin Laden did not agree: 'We as Muslims have a strong feeling that binds us together. . . . We feel for our brothers in Palestine and Lebanon. . . . When sixty Jews are killed inside Palestine'—he was talking about Palestinian suicide terrorists in Israel—'all the world gathers within seven days to criticize this action, while the deaths of 600,000 Iraqi children did not receive the same reaction.' It was bin Laden's first reference to Iraq and the UN sanctions which were to result, according to UN officials themselves, in the death of more than half-a-million children. 'Killing those children is a crusade against Islam,' bin Laden said." Fisk, *The Great War for Civilisation*, 22.

22. See International Court of Justice, "Legal Consequences of the Construction of a Wall in the Occupied Palestinian Territory," Advisory Opinion, July 4, 2009, in which the ICJ ruled that it "finds that the construction by Israel of a wall in the Occupied Palestinian Territory and its associated régime are contrary to international law"; at http://www.icj-cij.org/docket/index.php?pr=71&code=mwp&p1=3&p2=4&p3=6&ca.

23. Ackerman, *Before the Next Attack*, 172.

24. Gabriella Blum and Philip B. Heymann, *Laws, Outlaws, and Terrorists: Lessons from the War on Terrorism* (Cambridge: MIT Press, 2010), 167–169. The authors also found mixed evidence that Western values, democracy, and freedom were a source of Muslim contempt toward the United States, with American cultural values being viewed in a negative light and the political values of democracy and civil liberties viewed favorably. See, Blum and Heymann, *Laws, Outlaws, and Terrorists*, 166–167.

25. John L. Esposito and Dalia Mogahed, *Who Speaks for Islam? What a Billion Muslims Really Think* (New York: Gallup Press, 2008).

26. Blum and Heyman, *Laws, Outlaws, and Terrorists*, 170.

27. Ibid., 171.

28. U.S. public diplomacy is defined by the U.S. Public Diplomacy Alumni Association as "seek[ing] to promote the national interest of the United States through understanding, informing and influencing foreign audiences."

29. Ibid.

30. David Cole and Jules Lobel, *Less Free, Less Safe: Why America Is Losing the*

War on Terrorism (New York: New Press, 2007), 222.

31. Ibid., 223.

32. Richard Posner, *Not a Suicide Pact: The Constitution in a Time of National Emergency* (New York: Oxford University Press, 2006), 2.

33. Ibid., 2.

34. Ibid., 3.

35. Ibid., 5–6.

36. Ibid., 6.

37. Ibid., 148.

38. Ibid., 10–11.

39. Ibid., 12.

40. Alan Dershowitz, "Toward a More Productive Discourse," *Huffington Post*, August 1, 2006.

41. Ackerman, *Before the Next Attack*, 108.

42. Dershowitz has stated his position on torture in response to what he considers mischaracterizations of his position by critics, in "Toward a More Productive Discourse."

43. Ackerman, *Before the Next Attack*, 108–109.

44. Heymann, *Terrorism, Freedom, and Security*, 111.

45. Ibid.

46. Alfred W. McCoy, "The Myth of the Ticking Bomb," *Progressive* (October 2006): 20–24.

47. Posner, *Not a Suicide Pact*, 38.

48. Ibid., 85–86.

49. Alan Dershowitz, "Big Brother, Where Art Thou? Rethinking Civil Liberties in the Age of Terrorism," *San Francisco Chronicle*, October 28, 2001.

50. Ibid.

51. American Civil Liberties Union, "How the Anti-Terrorism Bill Limits Judicial Oversight of Telephone and Internet Surveillance," October 23, 2001, at http://www.aclu.org/national-security/how-anti-terrorism-bill-limits-judicial-oversight-telephone-and-internet-surveillance.

52. Ibid.

53. Electronic Frontier Foundation, "Let the Sun Shine on Patriot—Section 206," at http://w2.eff.org/patriot/sunset/206.php.

54. FISA Court refers to the Foreign Intelligence Surveillance Act Court, which was established by the U.S. Foreign Intelligence Surveillance Act of 1978.

55. James Bovard, "The FISA Farce," Future of Freedom Foundation, January 8, 2006; Electronic Privacy Information Center, at http://epic.org/privacy/terrorism/fisa/.

56. Center for Constitutional Rights, "The State of Civil Liberties: One Year Later: Erosion of Civil Liberties in the Post 9/11 Era: A Report Issued by the Center

for Constitutional Rights," undated, at
http://ccrjustice.org/v2/reports/docs/Civil_Liberties.pdf.

57. Mike Wiser, "Divided Faculty Panel Debates U.S. Response to Global Terror," *Harvard Law Record*, December 3, 2002.

58. Dick Durbin, United States Senate, "Statement on Durbin-Lee Roving Wiretap Amendment to the Patriot Act," March 10, 2011, at http://durbin.senate.gov/public/index.cfm/statementscommentary?ID=e1c5e6b8-0b6f-4705-a2e2-679eb502eb0d.

59. American Civil Liberties Union, "Statement of the ACLU's Gregory T. Nojeim on the Impact of National ID Cards on Civil Liberties: A National ID Card, National ID Systems, and Their Impact on Civil Liberties: Before the House of Representatives, Committee on Government Reform and Oversight, Subcommittee on National Economic Growth, Natural Resources and Regulatory Affairs," September 17, 1998.

60. Alan Dershowitz, "Why Fear National ID Cards?" *New York Times*, October 13, 2001.

61. American Civil Liberties Union, "Testimony of Legislative Counsel Katie Corrigan on the Establishment of a National ID Card System before the House Government Reform Subcommittee on Government Efficiency, Financial Management and Intergovernmental Relations: House Committee of Government Reform on the Establishment of a National ID Card System," November 16, 2001.

62. Ibid.

63. Alan Dershowitz, *Preemption: A Knife That Cuts Both Ways* (New York: W.W. Norton, 2006), 105.

64. Ibid., 106.

65. Ibid., 118.

66. *Williamson v. United States*, 184 F.2d 280, 282 (2d Cir. 1950).

67. Dershowitz, *Preemption*, 106–108, 114–115.

68. Ibid., 121.

69. Alan Dershowitz, "Torture and Accountability," *Los Angeles Times*, October 17, 2006.

70. Alan Dershowitz, "Democrats and Waterboarding," *Wall Street Journal*, November 7, 2007.

71. Ibid.

72. Larisa Alexandrovna, "Alan Dershowitz: Was He against Nazi Practices before He Was for Them?" *Huffington Post*, November 11, 2007.

73. Alan Dershowitz, "Torture, Accountability, and Name Calling," *Huffington Post*, November 17, 2007.

74. See, "Common Article 3 of the Geneva Conventions: Text," Associated Press (as reported by the *New York Times*), at http://www.nytimes.com/ref/us/AP-Guantanamo-Geneva-Conventions.html.

75. "Convention against Torture and Other Cruel, Inhuman, or Degrading Treatment or Punishment," at http://www.hrweb.org/legal/cat.html.

76. "War Crimes Act of 1996," Wikipedia, at http://en.wikipedia.org/wiki/War_Crimes_Act_of_1996.

77. Alan Dershowitz, *Why Terrorism Works: Understanding the Threat, Responding to the Challenge* (New Haven: Yale University Press, 2002), 135, 138.

78. "Convention against Torture and Other Cruel, Inhuman or Degrading Treatment or Punishment," Article 2, at http://www2.ohchr.org/english/law/cat.htm.

79. Alan Dershowitz, "The Case for Torture Warrants," at http://www.alandershowitz.com/publications/docs/torturewarrants.html.

80. Alan Dershowitz, "Killing Terrorist Chieftains Is Legal," *Jerusalem Post*, April 22, 2004.

81. Alan Dershowitz, "Targeted Killing Is Working, So Why Is the Press Not Reporting It," *Huffington Post*, January 3, 2008.

82. Alan Dershowitz, "Targeted Killing Vindicated," *Huffington Post*, May 2, 2011.

83. Dershowitz, *Preemption*, 121–140.

84. Mary Ellen O'Connell, "Why Obama's 'Targeted Killing' Is Worse Than Bush's Torture," *Guardian*, January 20, 2012.

85. Bill Quigley, "Five Reasons Drone Assassinations Are Illegal," *Common Dreams*, May 15, 2012.

86. Ibid.

87. "Human Rights Group to C.I.A.: End Drone 'Targeted Killing' Program: Statement by Human Rights Watch," *Common Dreams*, December 19, 2011.

88. "Rights Groups File Challenge to Targeted Killing by U.S.: Statement by ACLU and Center for Constitutional Rights," *Common Dreams*, August 30, 2010.

89. Philip Alston, "Report of the Special Rapporteur on Extrajudicial, Summary or Arbitrary Executions," United Nations Human Rights Council, May 28, 2010, at http://www2.ohchr.org/english/bodies/hrcouncil/docs/14session/A.HRC.14.24.Add6.pdf.

90. Alan Dershowitz, "Killing Terrorist Chieftains Is Legal," *Jerusalem Post*, April 25, 2004.

91. Ibid.

92. Amnesty International, "Amnesty International Strongly Condemns the Assassination of Sheikh Yassin," March 22, 2004.

93. B'Tselem, "19 Dec. 06: High Court of Justice Imposes Limitations on Israel's Targeted-Killing Policy," at http://www.btselem.org/firearms/20061219_targeted_killing_ruling.

94. See B'Tselem figures cited in "Israeli Targeted Killings," Wikipedia, at

http://en.wikipedia.org/wiki/Israeli_targeted_killings.

95. The search words used in the Google search engine—"Dershowitz, Bill of Rights, huffpost.com"—showed no results.

The search words—"Dershowitz, First Amendment, huffpost.com"—showed three results. One result referenced an article on *Huffington Post* by Dershowitz titled "Former President George W. Bush Prejudices the Legal Process against Julian Assange," March 3, 2011, in which Dershowitz wrote: "There are strong legal and policy reasons why Julian Assange should not be the subject of any criminal investigation or prosecution. These reasons relate not only to the rights of Assange and WikiLeaks, but as well to the First and Fourth Amendment right of American citizens who follow WikiLeaks and read the materials they have brought to the marketplace of ideas."

A second result referenced an article on *Huffington Post* titled "Conviction of the 'Irvine Ten' Is Constitutionally Sound," September 30, 2011, in which Dershowitz wrote: "Ten students who set out to prevent Israeli Ambassador Michael Oren from speaking to students at the University of California Irvine campus have been convicted of a California misdemeanor and sentenced to probation and a fine. The California statute is designed to protect the First Amendment rights of a speaker and his audience against those who would censor the speaker by deliberately disruptive conduct. The conduct engaged in by the students, acting on behalf of a University of California Muslim group, was more than merely disruptive in the sense of episodic booing or heckling. It was calculated to 'shut down,' in the words of one of the students, Ambassador Oren. In such a case, the First Amendment is clearly on the side of the prosecutor who seeks to prevent the censorship of protected speech, rather than on the side of those who have conspired to censor speech with which they disagree."

A third result referenced an article, "Did Brooklyn College's Political Science Department Violate the First Amendment?" February 12, 2013.

The search words—"Dershowitz, Fourth Amendment, huffpost.com"— showed one result, "Conviction of the 'Irvine Ten' Is Constitutionally Sound."

The search words—"Dershowitz, Fifth Amendment, huffpost.com"—showed two results. One result referenced an article titled "A 'Person of Interest' Can't Be Arrested," September 16, 2009, which was about the murder of Yale University medical student Annie Le.

The second result referenced an article titled "Why Roger Clemens, Even If Innocent, Should Take the 5th," January 11, 2008.

96. Dershowitz, *Preemption*, 55. The full reference reads: "The authority of the justice of the peace to confine dangerous people on preventive grounds persisted even after the adoption of the Constitution and the Bill of Rights, though the duration of the confinement was generally limited, except in the case of the dangerously mentally ill."

97. Ibid.

98. Dershowitz, *Preemption*, ix.

99. Ibid., 24.

100. Ibid., 39–40.

101. Ibid., 58.

102. Ibid., 60–61.

103. Ibid., 61–62.

104. Ibid., ix, 3, 20, 24, 32, 39–40, 58, 61–62, 284, 285, 296, 297, 331.

105. Ibid., 55.

106. Dershowitz writes here about the preventive confinement of "dangerous persons," a classification in which he mixes criminal defendants, the mentally ill, material witnesses, predicted saboteurs or spies during wartime, and suspected terrorists.

107. Ibid., 33.

Chapter 12. Chomsky's Anti-Authoritarianism

1. William F. Buckley Jr. and Noam Chomsky, "Vietnam and the Intellectuals," *Firing Line*, Public Broadcasting System, April 3, 1969, Hoover Institution Video Library, Stanford University, Stanford, California.

2. Alan Dershowitz, *Chutzpah* (Boston: Little, Brown, 1991), 173.

3. Milan Rai, *Chomsky's Politics* (New York: Verso, 1994), 131. See also, Brian Morton, "Chomsky, Then and Now," *Nation*, May 7, 1988.

4. Martin Bormann and Alfred Rosenberg were high-ranking Nazi intellectuals and political officials.

5. Noam Chomsky, *American Power and the New Mandarins: Historical and Political Essays* (New York: Pantheon, 1969), 8–9.

6. Noam Chomsky, *Peace in the Middle East? Reflections on Justice and Nationhood* (New York: Vintage, 1974), 57–58.

7. Noam Chomsky, "Interview," in James Peck (ed.), *The Chomsky Reader* (New York: Pantheon, 1987), 13.

8. Noam Chomsky, "American Foreign Policy," Delivered at Harvard University, March 19, 1985, available at Chomsky.info, at http://www.chomsky.info/talks/19850319.htm.

9. "Truth Commission: Guatemala," United States Institute of Peace, Truth Commission Digital Collection, at http://www.usip.org/publications/truth-commission-guatemala.

10. Noam Chomsky and Edward S. Herman, *The Washington Connection and Third World Fascism* (The Political Economy of Human Rights—Volume I) (Boston: South End Press, 1979), 252.

11. Ibid., 252–253.

12. Ibid., 254–255.

13. Ibid., 255.

14. Ibid.

15. Noam Chomsky, *Deterring Democracy* (New York: Verso, 1991), 27, 33, 41, 51, 83, 229, 308, 313, 334, 335, 341, 342, 349, 391, 396.

16. Dershowitz, *Chutzpah*, 174.

17. Ibid., 176.

18. Werner Cohn, "Chomsky and Holocaust Denial," in Peter Collier and David Horowitz (eds.), *The Anti-Chomsky Reader* (San Francisco: Encounter Books, 2004), 119–120.

19. Ibid., 137.

20. Ibid., back cover.

21. "Drive to Release Polish Jew Gains," *New York Times*, October 14, 1973.

22. "Scholars in West Assail Belgrade," *New York Times*, January 31, 1974.

23. Irving Howe, "The Case Worker: A Brilliant First Novel about Human Refuse in Budapest," *New York Times*, January 27, 1974.

24. Noam Chomsky, "The Case Worker," Letter to the Editor, *New York Times*, February 3, 1974.

25. "U.S. Writers Urge Iran to Release 12," *New York Times*, February 4, 1974.

26. "India Is Accused of Prison Abuses: Petition from 300 Foreign Intellectuals Assails the Detention of Politicians," *New York Times*, September 10, 1974.

27. "Leader of Inmate Rights Drive Is on Governor's Clemency List," *New York Times*, December 17, 1975.

28. Rai, Chomsky's Politics, 131.

29. Robert Barsky, *Noam Chomsky: A Life of Dissent* (Cambridge: MIT Press, 1997), 180.

30. Pierre Vidal-Naquet, "A Paper Eichmann: Anatomy of a Lie," *Esprit*, September 1980, translated by Jeffrey Mehlman, reprinted in Pierre Vidal-Naquet, *Assassins of Memory: Essays on the Denial of the Holocaust* (New York: Columbia University Press, 1992), 1–59.

31. "Faurisson Affair," Wikipedia, at http://en.wikipedia.org/wiki/Faurisson_affair.

32. Vidal-Naquet, *Assassins of Memory*, 65–74, 69.

33. Ibid., 58.

34. Noam Chomsky, "The Faurisson Affair: Noam Chomsky Writes to Lawrence K. Kolodney," Chomsky.Info, at http://www.chomsky.info/letters/1989——.htm.

35. "Faurisson Affair," Wikipedia, at http://en.wikipedia.org/wiki/Faurisson_affair#Petition_signed_by_Chomsky.

36. The petition read in full: "Dr. Faurisson has served as a respected professor of twentieth-century French literature and document criticism for over four years at the University of Lyon 2 in France. Since 1974 he has been conducting extensive

independent historical research into the 'Holocaust' question. Since he began making his findings public, Professor Faurisson has been subject to a vicious campaign of harassment, intimidation, slander, and physical violence in a crude attempt to silence him. Fearful officials have even tried to stop him from further research by denying him access to public libraries and archives. We strongly protest these efforts to deprive Professor Faurisson of his freedom of speech and expression, and we condemn the shameful campaign to silence him. We strongly support Professor Faurisson's just right of academic freedom and we demand that university and government officials do everything possible to ensure his safety and the free exercise of his legal rights." See, "Faurisson Affair," Wikipedia, at http://en.wikipedia.org/wiki/Faurisson_affair#cite_note-5, which is one of the few sources on the subject that has reproduced the petition in full.

37. Noam Chomsky, "Some Elementary Comments on the Rights of Freedom of Expression," Chomsky.Info, at http://www.chomsky.info/articles/19801011.htm.

38. Ibid.

39. Ibid.

40. Philippa Strum, *When the Nazis Came to Skokie: Freedom for Speech We Hate* (Lawrence: University Press of Kansas, 1999), 1–2.

41. "A.C.L.U. Members Resign Over Defense of Nazis," *New York Times*, August 11, 1977.

42. Strum, *When the Nazis Came to Skokie*, 82.

43. Ibid., 83.

44. Alan Dershowitz, *Chutzpah* (Boston: Little, Brown, 1991), 120.

45. Alan Dershowitz, *The Case for Israel* (Hoboken: Wiley, 2003), 213.

46. Noam Chomsky, "His Right to Say It," the *Nation*, February 18, 1981.

47. Alan Dershowitz, *The Case for Peace: How the Arab-Israeli Conflict Can Be Resolved* (Hoboken: Wiley, 2005), 170.

48. Ibid., 171, 227.

49. Cohn, "Chomsky and Holocaust Denial," in Collier and Horowitz (eds.), *The Anti-Chomsky Reader*, 119–120.

50. Ibid.

51. Dershowitz, *Chutzpah*, 192.

52. Ibid., 191.

53. Anti-Defamation League, "Backgrounder: The Jewish Defense League: About the Jewish Defense League," at http://www.adl.org/extremism/jdl_chron.asp.

54. "Meir Kahane," JpostPedia.com, at http://www.jpost.com/topic/Meir_Kahane.

55. Dershowitz, *Chutzpah*, 194.

56. Ibid., 192.

57. Ibid., 191.

58. Ibid.

59. Dershowitz, *The Case for Israel*, 212.

60. "Talk by Noam Chomsky, Harvard Anthropology Department," November 25, 2002.

61. Dershowitz, *The Case for Peace*, 170.

62. "Talk by Noam Chomsky, Harvard Anthropology Department," November 25, 2002.

63. Noam Chomsky, "American Foreign Policy," Delivered at Harvard University, March 19, 1985.

64. Americas Watch and other members of the "Watch Committees"—Asia Watch, Africa Watch, and Middle East Watch—became Human Rights Watch in 1988.

65. Amnesty International, "Guatemala: A Government Program of Political Murder," 1981.

66. Americas Watch, "Human Rights in Guatemala: No Neutrals Allowed," 1982, 1–3.

67. Americas Watch, "Guatemala: A Nation of Prisoners," January 1984, iv, 11, 17.

68. Cheryl A. Rubenberg, "Israel and Guatemala: Arms, Advice, and Counterinsurgency," *MERIP Reports* (May-June 1986): 16–22, 43–44.

69. Ibid.

70. Jane Hunter, *Israeli Foreign Policy: South Africa and Central America* (Boston: South End Press, 1987), 113, citing Victor Perera, "Uzi Diplomacy—How Israel Makes Friends and Enemies around the World," *Mother Jones*, July 1985.

71. Hunter, *Israeli Foreign Policy*, 116.

72. Ibid.

73. Rubenberg, "Israel and Guatemala: Arms, Advice and Counterinsurgency."

74. Leslie Gelb, "Israelis Said to Step Up Role as Arms Suppliers to Latins," *New York Times*, December 17, 1982.

75. Hunter, *Israeli Foreign Policy*, 99.

76. Rubenberg, "Israel and Guatemala: Arms, Advice and Counterinsurgency."

77. Hunter, *Israeli Foreign Policy*, 14.

78. This determination is the result of reading the four books with no recollection of any mention of Guatemala, the absence of "Guatemala" listed in the index of any of the four books, and a Google Books online search and an amazon.com online search, both of which showed no results for "Guatemala" in any of the four books.

79. Chomsky and Herman, *The Washington Connection and Third World Fascism*, ix.

80. Edward S. Herman, *The Real Terror Network: Terrorism in Fact and Propaganda* (Boston: South End Press, 1982), 7.

81. Chomsky, *Turning the Tide*, 156.

CHAPTER 13. ON KILL COURTS AND TORTURE WARRANTS

1. "Two-Year Manhunt Led to Killing of Awlaki in Yemen," *New York Times*, September 30, 2011.

2. "Obama on Awlaki Death at Mullen Retirement Ceremony," *New York Times*, September 30, 2011.

3. David Cole, "Killing Citizens in Secret," *New York Review of Books*, October 9, 2011.

4. "Secret 'Kill List' Proves a Test of Obama's Principles and Will," *New York Times*, May 29, 2012.

5. Bryan A. Garner (ed.), *Black's Law Dictionary*, 7th Edition (St. Paul: West Group, 1999), 516–17.

6. "18 USC § 1119—Foreign murder of United States nationals," at http://www.law.cornell.edu/uscode/text/18/1119.

7. "Executive Order 12333, United States Intelligence Activities, (As amended by Executive Orders 13284 (2003), 13355 (2004) and 13470 (2008))," at http://www.fas.org/irp/offdocs/eo/eo-12333-2008.pdf.

8. 020413 DOJ White Paper, 1.

9. Ibid., 2.

10. Ibid., 6.

11. Ibid., 7.

12. Michael Isikoff, "Justice Department Memo Reveals Legal Case for Drone Strike on Americans," NBC News, February 4, 2012, at http://openchannel.nbcnews.com/_news/2013/02/04/16843014-justice-department-memo-reveals-legal-case-for-drone-strikes-on-americans?lite.

13. DOJ White Paper, 2.

14. Mary Ellen O'Connell, "Killing Awlaki Was Illegal, Immoral, and Dangerous," CNN World, October 1, 2011.

15. DOJ White Paper, 2.

16. "S.J. Res. 23 (107th): Authorization for Use of Military Force," Govtrack.us, at http://www.govtrack.us/congress/bills/107/sjres23/text.

17. DOJ White Paper, 3.

18. "18 USC § 1119—Foreign murder of United States nationals," at http://www.law.cornell.edu/uscode/text/18/1119.

19. DOJ White Paper, 10.

20. "Obama's Speech on Drone Policy," *New York Times*, May 23, 2013; "The End of the Perpetual War," *New York Times*, May 23, 2013.

21. DOJ White Paper, 15.

22. "Attorney General Eric Holder Speaks at Northwestern University School of Law," March 5, 2012, at http://www.justice.gov/iso/opa/ag/speeches/2012/ag-speech-1203051.html.

23. Office of the Attorney General, Letter to the Honorable Patrick L. Leahy,

Chairman, Committee on the Judiciary, May 22, 2013, at
http://www.justice.gov/slideshow/AG-letter-5-22-13.pdf.

24. "Obama's Speech on Drone Policy" (transcript), *New York Times*, May 23, 2013.

25. Jeremy Scahill, *Dirty Wars: The World Is a Battlefield* (New York: Nation Books, 2013), 501.

26. "Obama on Awlaki Death at Mullen Retirement Ceremony," *New York Times*.

27. Scahill, *Dirty Wars*, 318.

28. Ibid., 361.

29. Scahill, *Dirty Wars*, 318–19; Gregory Johnsen, *The Last Refuge: Yemen, al-Qaeda, and America's War in Arabia* (New York: Norton, 2012), 247.

30. Scahill, *Dirty Wars*, 319.

31. Alan Dershowitz, "Lebanon Is Not a Victim," *Huffington Post*, August 7, 2006.

32. Ibid., 269.

33. "Obama's Speech on Drone Policy" (transcript), *New York Times*, May 23, 2013.

34. "Exclusive: Nasser al-Awlaki to Obama: Why did You Kill My U.S.-Born Son, Grandson in Drone Strikes," *Democracy Now!*, June 7, 2013, at http://www.democracynow.org/2013/6/7/exclusive_nasser_al_awlaki_to_obama.

35. "Two-Year Manhunt Led to the Killing of Awlaki in Yemen," *New York Times*, September 30, 2011.

36. Scahill, *Dirty Wars*, 507.

37. "One Drone Victim's Trail from Raleigh to Pakistan," *New York Times*, May 22, 2013.

38. "Obama's Speech on Drone Policy" (transcript), *New York Times*, May 23, 2013.

39. "Al-Aulaqi v. Obama: Lawsuit Challenging Targeted Killings," American Civil Liberties Union, October 19, 2011, at http://www.aclu.org/national-security/al-aulaqi-v-obama.

40. Robert Wright, "The Price of Assassination," *New York Times*, April 13, 2010.

41. "Secret 'Kill List' Proves a Test of Obama's Principles and Will," *New York Times*, May 29, 2012.

42. "Obama Drone Oversight Proposal Prompts Concern over 'Kill Courts,'" *Guardian*, May 24, 2013.

43. David Kravets, "Secretive Spy Court Approved Nearly 2,000 Surveillance Requests in 2012," *Wired*, May 2, 2013.

44. Ibid. See also: U.S. Department of Justice, Office of Legislative Affairs, Letter to the Honorable Harry Reid, April 30, 2013, at http://www.wired.com/images_blogs/threatlevel/2013/05/fisacases.pdf.

45. Bill Quigley, "Spying by the Numbers: Hundreds of Thousands Subject to Government Surveillance and No Real Protection," Common Dreams, June 20, 2013.

46. "President Obama Signs FISA Amendment Act Extension," *Lawfare*, January 1, 2013, at http://www.lawfareblog.com/2013/01/president-obama-signs-fisa-amendments-act-extension/.

47. David Kravets, "Secretive Spy Court Approved Nearly 2,000 Surveillance Requests in 2012," *Wired*, May 2, 2013.

48. "NSA Collecting Phone Records of Millions of Verizon Customers Daily," *Guardian*, June 5, 2013.

49. "FISA Court Ordering Verizon to Turn Over Records of All Calls: Center for Constitutional Rights Reacts," June 6, 2013, via Common Dreams, at http://www.commondreams.org/newswire/2013/06/06-0.

50. "NSA Surveillance Is an Attack on American Citizens, Says Noam Chomsky," *Guardian*, June 19, 2013.

51. "Alan Dershowitz on the Legality of NSA Phone Monitoring Program," Newsmax, June 7, 2013, on YouTube at http://www.youtube.com/watch?v=nuoKhjWFiGM.

52. Benjamin Wittes, "What Ben Franklin Really Said," *Lawfare*, July 15, 2011, at http://www.lawfareblog.com/2011/07/what-ben-franklin-really-said/.

53. See Wittes, "What Ben Franklin Really Said," for an informed assessment of the actual context in which Franklin issued the statement in question.

54. "Obama's Speech on Drone Policy" (transcript), *New York Times*, May 23, 2013.

55. See, for example, Alan Dershowitz, "The Case for Torture Warrants," Reuters, September 7, 2011, at http://blogs.reuters.com/great-debate/2011/09/07/the-case-for-torture-warrants/.

56. Alan Dershowitz, "The Case for Torture Warrants," last accessed on June 19, 2013, at http://www.alandershowitz.com/publications/docs/torturewarrants.html. See also Dershowitz, "The Case for Torture Warrants," Reuters, September 7, 2011, wherein Dershowitz wrote: "In the United States we execute convicted murderers, despite compelling evidence of the unfairness and ineffectiveness of capital punishment. Yet many who support capital punishment recoil at the prospect of shoving a sterilized needle under the finger of a suspect who is refusing to divulge information that might prevent multiple deaths."

57. Ingo Müller, *Hitler's Justice: The Courts of the Third Reich* (Cambridge: Harvard University Press, 1991), 178.

58. Noam Chomsky, *American Power and the New Mandarins: Historical and Political Essays* (New York: Pantheon Books, 1967).

59. Howard Zinn, *The Logic of Withdrawal* (Boston: Beacon Press, 1967).

60. Richard Falk, (chair), John H.E. Fried (rapporteur), *Vietnam and*

International Law: An Analysis of International Law and the Use of Force (Flanders, N.J.: O'Hare, 1967).

61. "Noam Chomsky v. Alan Dershowitz: A Debate on the Israeli-Palestinian Conflict" (transcript), *Democracy Now!*, December 23, 2005, at http://www.democracynow.org/2005/12/23/noam_chomsky_v_alan_dershowitz_a
.

62. "How the Magna Carta Became a Minor Carta, Part 1," *Guardian*, July 24, 2012; "How the Magna Carta Became a Minor Carta, Part 2," *Guardian*, July 25, 2012.

63. "Noam Chomsky on Presumption of Innocence," with Jan Wellman, YouTube, March 6, 2013, at http://www.youtube.com/watch?v=o63EjNGGe3A.

64. See Alan Dershowitz, *Preemption: A Knife That Cuts Both Ways* (New York: W.W. Norton, 2006), 105–52, 190–250.

BIBLIOGRAPHY

Books

Ackerman, Bruce. *Before the Next Attack: Preserving Civil Liberties in an Age of Terrorism*. New Haven: Yale University Press, 2006.

———. *The Decline and Fall of the American Republic*. Cambridge: Harvard University Press, 2010.

Albright, Madeleine. *Madam Secretary: A Memoir*. New York: Miramax Books, 2003.

Archer, Richard. *As If an Enemy's Country: The British Occupation of Boston and the Origins of Revolution*. New York: Oxford University Press, 2010.

Arnove, Anthony, ed. *Iraq under Siege: The Deadly Impact of Sanctions and War*. Boston: South End Press, 2000.

Barsky, Robert F. *Noam Chomsky: A Life of Dissent*. Cambridge: MIT Press, 1997.

———. *The Chomsky Effect: A Radical Works Beyond the Ivory Tower*. Cambridge: MIT Press, 2007.

Beilin, Yossi. *The Path to Geneva: The Quest for a Permanent Agreement, 1996–2004*. New York: RDV Books, 2004.

Beinart, Peter. *The Crisis of Zionism*. New York: Times Books, 2012.

Bilmes, Linda J., and Joseph Stiglitz. *The Three Trillion Dollar War: The True Cost of the Iraq Conflict*. New York: W. W. Norton, 2008.

Blum, Gabriella, and Philip B. Heymann. *Laws, Outlaws, and Terrorists: Lessons from the War on Terrorism*. Cambridge: MIT Press, 2010.

Brownlie, Ian. *International Law and the Use of Force by States*. Oxford: Clarendon Press, 1963.

Carter, Jimmy. *Palestine Peace Not Apartheid*. New York: Simon & Schuster, 2006.

Cave, Alfred A. *The Pequot War*. Amherst: University of Massachusetts Press, 1996.

Chomsky, Noam. *American Power and the New Mandarins*. New York: Pantheon, 1969.

———. *At War With Asia*. New York: Pantheon, 1970.

———. *For Reasons of State*. New York: Pantheon, 1973.

———. *Language and Responsibility: In Conversation with Mitsou Ronat*. New York: Pantheon, 1977.

———. *Fateful Triangle: The United States, Israel, and the Palestinians*. Boston: South End Press, 1983.

———. *Deterring Democracy*. New York: Hill and Wang, 1992.

———. *Rogue States: The Rule of Force in World Affairs*. Boston: South End Press, 2000.

———. *9-11*. New York: Seven Stories Press, 2001.

———. *Middle East Illusions: Reflections on Justice and Nationhood*. Lanham, MD: Rowman & Littlefield, 2003.

———. *Hegemony or Survival: America's Quest for Global Dominance*. New York: Metropolitan, 2003.

———. *Failed States: The Abuse of Power and the Assault on Democracy*. New York: Metropolitan, 2006.

———. *Hopes and Prospects*. Chicago: Haymarket Books, 2010.

Chomsky, Noam, and Edward S. Herman. *The Washington Connection and Third World Fascism: The Political Economy of Human Rights—Volume I*. Boston: South End Press, 1979.

Chomsky, Noam, Ervand Abrahamian, and Nahid Mozaffari. *Targeting Iran: Interviews with David Barsamian*. San Francisco: City Lights Books, 2007.

Chomsky, Noam, and Howard Zinn, eds. *The Pentagon Papers: The Senator Gravel Edition: Critical Essays: Volume 5 and Index to Volumes 1–4*. Boston: Beacon Press, 1972.

Chomsky, Noam, and Ilan Pappé. *Gaza in Crisis: Reflections on Israel's War against the Palestinians*. Edited by Frank Barat. Chicago: Haymarket Books, 2010.

Clinton, Bill. *My Life*. New York: Knopf, 2004.

Cohen, Avner. *Israel and the Bomb*. New York: Columbia University Press, 1998.

Cole, David, and Jules Lobel. *Less Free, Less Safe: Why America Is Losing the War on Terrorism*. New York: The New Press, 2007.

Constable, Pamela, and Arturo Venezuela. *A Nation of Enemies: Chile under Pinochet*. New York: W. W. Norton, 1993.

Cumings, Bruce. *The Korean War: A History*. New York: The Modern Library, 2010.

Danner, Mark. *The Secret Way to War: The Downing Street Memo and the Iraq War's Buried History*. New York: New York Review Books, 2006.

Dershowitz, Alan. *Chutzpah*. Boston: Little, Brown, 1991.

———. *Letters to a Young Lawyer*. New York: Basic Books, 2001.

————. *Why Terrorism Works: Understanding the Threat, Responding to the Challenge.* New Haven: Yale University Press, 2002.

————. *The Case for Israel.* Hoboken: Wiley, 2003.

————. *America on Trial: Inside the Legal Battles That Transformed Our Nation.* New York: Warner Books, 2004.

————. *The Case for Peace: How the Arab-Israeli Conflict Can Be Resolved.* Hoboken: Wiley, 2005.

————. *Preemption: A Knife That Cuts Both Ways.* New York: W. W. Norton, 2006.

————. *The Case against Israel's Enemies: Exposing Jimmy Carter and Others Who Stand in the Way of Peace.* Hoboken: Wiley, 2008.

Duffett, John, ed. *Against the Crime of Silence: Proceedings of the Russell International War Crimes Tribunal.* New York: O'Hare Books, 1968.

Eisenhower, Dwight D. *The White House Years: Mandate for Change, 1953–1956.* New York: Doubleday, 1963.

Enderlin, Charles. *Shattered Dreams: The Failure of the Peace Process in the Middle East.* Translated by Susan Fairfield. New York: Other Press, 2003.

Esposito, John L., and Dalia Mogahed. *Who Speaks for Islam? What a Billion Muslims Really Think.* New York: Gallup Press, 2008.

Falk, Richard, ed. *The Vietnam War and International Law, Volumes 1–3.* Princeton: Princeton University Press, 1968–1976.

————. *Unlocking the Middle East: The Writings of Richard Falk.* Northampton: Olive Branch Press, 2003.

————. *The Declining World Order: America's Imperial Geopolitics.* New York: Routledge, 2004.

Falk, Richard, Gabriel Kolko, and Robert J. Lifton, eds. *Crimes of War: A Legal, Political-Documentary, and Psychological Inquiry into the Responsibility of Leaders, Citizens, and Soldiers for Criminal Acts in War.* New York: Random House, 1971.

Falk, Richard, and John H. E. Fried, eds. *Vietnam and International Law: The Consultative Council of the Lawyers Committee on American Policy Toward Vietnam.* Flanders: O'Hare, 1967.

Finkelstein, Norman. *Beyond Chutzpah: On the Misuse of Anti-Semitism and the Abuse of History.* Berkeley: University of California Press, 2005.

————. *Knowing Too Much: Why the American Jewish Romance with Israel Is Coming to an End.* New York: OR Books, 2012.

Fisk, Robert. *Pity the Nation: The Abduction of Lebanon.* New York: Nation Books, 2002.

————. *The Great War for Civilisation: The Conquest of the Middle East.* New York: Knopf, 2005.

Foley, Michael S. *Confronting the War Machine: Draft Resistance During the Vietnam War.* Chapel Hill: University of North Carolina Press, 2003.

Foxman, Abraham. *The Deadliest Lies: The Israel Lobby and the Myth of Jewish Control*. New York: Palgrave Macmillan, 2007.

Gordon, Joy. *Invisible War: The United States and the Iraq Sanctions*. Cambridge: Harvard University Press, 2010.

Gorenberg, Gershom. *The Accidental Empire: Israel and the Birth of the Settlements, 1967–1977*. New York: Times Books, 2006.

Grayling, A. C. *Among the Dead Cities: The History and Moral Legacy of the WWII Bombing of Civilians in Germany and Japan*. New York: Walker & Company, 2006.

Greiner, Bernd. *War without Fronts: The USA in Vietnam*. New Haven: Yale University Press, 2009.

Harvey, Dan. *Peacekeepers: Irish Soldiers in the Lebanon*. Dublin: Merlin Publishing, 2001.

Henkin, Louis. *Constitutionalism, Democracy, and Foreign Affairs*. New York: Columbia University Press, 1990.

Herman, Edward S. *The Real Terror Network: Terrorism in Fact and Propaganda*. Boston: South End Press, 1982.

Herman, Edward S., and David Peterson. *The Politics of Genocide*. New York: Monthly Review Press, 2010.

Herman, Edward S., and Noam Chomsky. *Manufacturing Consent: The Political Economy of the Mass Media*. New York: Pantheon, 1988.

Hersh, Seymour. *Chain of Command: The Road from 9/11 to Abu Ghraib*. New York: HarperCollins, 2004.

Heymann, Philip B. *Terrorism, Freedom, and Security: Winning without War*. Cambridge: MIT Press, 2003.

Horowitz, Adam, Lizzy Ratner, and Philip Weiss, eds. *The Goldstone Report: The Legacy of the Landmark Investigation of the Gaza Conflict*. New York: Nation Books, 2011.

Hunter, Jane. *Israeli Foreign Policy: South Africa and Central America*. Boston: South End Press, 1987.

Jennings, Francis. *The Invasion of America: Indians, Colonialism, and the Cant of Conquest*. Chapel Hill: University of North Carolina Press, 1975.

Johnson, Chalmers. *Blowback: The Costs and Consequences of American Empire*. New York: Owl Books, 2000.

Karnow, Stanley. *Vietnam: A History*. 2nd edition. New York: Penguin, 1997.

Kiernan, Benedict F. *The Pol Pot Regime: Race, Power, and Genocide in Cambodia under the Khmer Rouge, 1975–1979*. New Haven: Yale University Press, 2002.

Kretzmer, David. *The Occupation of Justice: The Supreme Court of Israel and the Occupied Territories*. Albany: State University of New York Press, 2002.

Mailer, Norman. *The Armies of the Night: History as a Novel, the Novel as History*. New York: New American Library, 1968.

Mayer, Jane. *The Dark Side: The Inside Story of How the War on Terror Turned into a War on American Ideals*. New York: Doubleday, 2008.

McNamara, Robert S. *In Retrospect*. New York: Times Books, 1995.

McNamara, Robert S., James G. Blight, and Robert K. Brigham. *Argument without End: In Search of Answers to the Vietnam Tragedy*. New York: Public Affairs, 1999.

Miller, Aaron David. *The Much Too Promised Land: America's Elusive Search for Arab-Israeli Peace*. New York: Bantam Books, 2008.

Morgan, Ted. *Valley of Death: The Tragedy at Dien Bien Phu That Led America into the Vietnam War*. New York: Random House, 2010.

Morris, Benny. *1948*. New Haven: Yale University Press, 2008.

———. *One State, Two States: Resolving the Israel/Palestine Conflict*. New Haven: Yale University Press, 2009.

Mullen, Don. *Bloody Sunday: Massacre in Northern Ireland*. Niwot, CO: Roberts Rinehart Publishers, 1997.

National Commission on Terrorist Attacks upon the United States. *The 9/11 Commission Report: Final Report of the National Commission on Terrorist Attacks upon the United States*. New York: W. W. Norton, 2004.

Pappé, Ilan. *The Ethnic Cleansing of Palestine*. Oxford: Oneworld, 2007.

Peck, James, ed. *The Chomsky Reader*. New York: Pantheon, 1987.

Polakow-Suransky, Sasha. *The Unspoken Alliance: Israel's Secret Relationship with Apartheid South Africa*. New York: Pantheon, 2010.

Poniatowska, Elena. *Massacre in Mexico*. Translated by Helen R. Lane. Columbia: University of Missouri Press, 1991.

Posner, Richard. *Not a Suicide Pact: The Constitution in a Time of National Emergency*. New York: Oxford University Press, 2006.

Pringle, Peter, and Philip Jacobson. *Those Are Real Bullets: Bloody Sunday, Derry, 1972*. New York: Grove Press, 2000.

Rai, Milan. *Chomsky's Politics*. New York: Verso, 1994.

Risen, James. *State of War: The Secret History of the CIA and the Bush Administration*. New York: Free Press, 2006.

Ross, Dennis. *The Missing Peace: The Inside Story of the Fight for Middle East Peace*. New York: Farrar, Straus, and Giroux, 2004.

Roy, Sara. *Failing Peace: Gaza and the Palestinian-Israeli Conflict*. London: Pluto Press, 2006.

Rudenstein, David. *The Day the Presses Stopped: A History of the Pentagon Papers Case*. Berkeley: University of California Press, 1996.

Said, Edward W. *The End of the Peace Process: Oslo and After*. New York: Vintage, 2001.

Salisbury, Neal. *Manitou and Providence*. New York: Oxford University Press, 1982.

ands, Philippe. *Lawless World: America and the Making and Breaking of Global Rules from FDR's Atlantic Charter to George W. Bush's Illegal War*. New York: Viking, 2005.

———. *Torture Team: Rumsfeld's Memo and the Betrayal of American Values*. New York: Palgrave Macmillan, 2008.

Scahill, Jeremy. *Dirty Wars: The World Is a Battlefield*. New York: Nation Books, 2013.

Shlaim, Avi. *The Iron Wall: Israel and the Arab World*. New York: W. W. Norton, 2001.

Strum, Philippa. *When the Nazis Came to Skokie: Freedom for Speech We Hate*. Lawrence: University Press of Kansas, 1999.

Swisher, Clayton E. *The Truth about Camp David: The Untold Story about the Collapse of the Middle East Peace Process*. New York: Nation Books, 2004.

Yuki, Tanaka, and Marilyn B. Young, eds. *Bombing Civilians: A Twentieth-Century History*. New York: The New Press, 2009.

Zertal, Idith, and Akiva Eldar. *Lords of the Land: The War Over Israel's Settlements in the Occupied Territories, 1967–2007*. New York: Nation Books, 2007.

Zinn, Howard. *The Bomb*. San Francisco: City Lights Books, 2010.

———. *Vietnam: The Logic of Withdrawal*. Boston: Beacon Press, 1967.

Zobel, Hiller. *The Boston Massacre*. New York: W. W. Norton, 1970.

Articles

Agha, Hussein, and Robert Malley. "Camp David and After: An Exchange (2. A Reply to Ehud Barak)." *New York Review of Books*, June 13, 2002.

Ali, Mohamed M., and Iqbal H. Shah. "Sanctions and Childhood Mortality in Iraq." *Lancet*, vol. 355, no. 9218 (May 27, 2000): 1851–1857.

Ascherio, Alberto, M.D., Robert Chase, M.D., and Tim Coté, M.D. "Effect of the Gulf War on Infant and Child Mortality in Iraq." *New England Journal of Medicine*, vol. 327 (September 24, 1992): 931–936.

Betts, Richard K. "The Osirak Fallacy." the *National Interest*, March 1, 2006.

Braut-Hegghammer, Malfrid. "Revisiting Osirak: Preventive Attacks and Nuclear Proliferation Risks." *International Security*, vol. 36, no. 1 (Summer 2011).

Chomsky, Noam. "A Review of B. F. Skinner's *Verbal Behavior*." *Language*, vol. 35, no. 1 (1959): 26–58.

———. "The Responsibility of Intellectuals." *New York Review of Books*, February 23, 1967.

Daponte, Beth Osborne, and Richard Garfield. "The Effect of Economic Sanctions on the Mortality of Iraqi Children Prior to the 1991 Persian Gulf War." *American Journal of Public Health*, vol. 90, no. 4 (April 2000): 546–552.

Dershowitz, Alan. "Terrorism & Preventive Detention: The Case of Israel." *Commentary*, December 1970.

Fall, Bernard. "Vietnam: The Undiscovered Country." *New York Review of Books*, March 17, 1966.

———. "The View from Vietnam." *New York Review of Books*, February 9, 1967.

Finkelstein, Norman. "The Camp David II Negotiations: How Dennis Ross Proved the Palestinians Aborted the Peace Process." *Journal of Palestine Studies*, vol. 36, no. 1 (Winter 2007).

Kasrils, Ronnie, and Max Osinsky. "Declaration of Conscience by South Africans of Jewish Descent, 23 October 2001." *Palestine–Israel Journal*, vol. 8, no. 4 (2001) and vol. 9, no. 1 (2002).

Lacouture, Jean. "Vietnam: The Lessons of War." *New York Review of Books*, March 3, 1966.

———. "Vietnam: The Turning Point." *New York Review of Books*, May 12, 1966.

McCoy, Alfred W. "The Myth of the Ticking Bomb." *Progressive*, October 2006.

Morgenthau, Hans J. "We Are Deluding Ourselves in Vietnam." *New York Times Magazine*, April 18, 1965.

Morris, Benny. "Camp David and After: An Exchange (I. Interview with Ehud Barak)." *New York Review of Books*, June 13, 2002.

Obermeyer, Ziad, Christopher J. L. Murray, and Emmanuela Gakidou. "Fifty Years of Violent War Deaths from Vietnam to Bosnia: Analysis of Data from the World Health Survey Programme." *British Medical Journal* (June 26, 2008): 1482.

Pressman, Jeremy. "Lost Opportunities: *The Missing Peace: The Inside Story of the Fight for Middle East Peace.*" *Boston Review*, December (2004/January 2005).

Pundak, Ron. "From Oslo to Taba: What Went Wrong?" *Survival*, vol. 43, no. 3 (Autumn 2001): 31–46.

Reiter, Dan. "The Osiraq Myth and the Track Record of Preventive Military Attacks." *Nonproliferation Review*, vol. 12, no. 2 (July 2005).

Roy, Sarah. "If Gaza Falls . . ." *London Review of Books*, January 1, 2009.

Rubenberg, Cheryl A. "Israel and Guatemala: Arms, Advice, and Counterinsurgency." *MERIP Reports*, May–June 1986.

Schabas, William A. "Book Review of *For Humanity: Reflections of a War Crimes Investigator* by Richard Goldstone." *American Journal of International Law*, vol. 95, no. 3 (July 2001): 742–744.

Stone, I. F. "Vietnam: An Exercise in Self-Delusion." *New York Review of Books*, April 22, 1965.

———. "Fulbright: From Hawk to Dove (Part 2)." *New York Review of Books*, January 12, 1967.

Walsh, Elsa. "The Prince: How the Saudi Ambassador Became Washington's Indispensable Operator." *New Yorker*, March 24, 2003.

Walt, Stephen M. "Another Bogus Argument for War with Iran." *Foreign Policy*, March 1, 2012.

Reports

"Legal Consequences of the Construction of a Wall in the Occupied Palestinian Territory: Summary of the Advisory Opinion of 9 July 2004." International Court of Justice, The Hague, The Netherlands, July 9, 2004.

"National Intelligence Estimate: Iran: Nuclear Intentions and Capabilities." National Intelligence Council, Office of the Director of National Intelligence, United States of America, November 2007.

"Occupation, Colonialism, Apartheid? A Re-assessment of Israel's Practices in the Occupied Palestinian Territories under International Law." Democracy and Governance Programme, Middle East Project, Human Sciences Research Council, Cape Town, South Africa, May 2009.

United Nations Agencies Consulted

General Assembly Resolutions
Human Rights Council Special Rapporteur on Israel-Palestine
Security Council Resolutions

Rights Organizations Consulted

American Civil Liberties Union
Amnesty International
Anti-Defamation League
Association for Civil Rights in Israel
B'Tselem
Center for Constitutional Rights
Defence for Children International
Human Rights Watch
International Committee of the Red Cross
National Lawyers Guild
Physicians for Human Rights—Israel

News Organizations Consulted

BBC News
Boston Globe
Global Post
Guardian
Ha'aretz
Harvard Crimson
Independent
Irish Times
Jerusalem Post
New York Times

Los Angeles Times
MIT News
St. Louis Post–Dispatch
Toronto Star
Wall Street Journal

Web Sites Consulted
Common Dreams
Counterpunch
Democracy Now!
Foreign Policy in Focus
Huffington Post
Mondoweiss
The Nation
Salon

INDEX

Baltimore Interfaith Peace Mission 27
Ban Ki-moon 185
Bandar (Saudi Prince) 97-98
Banks, McDowell 20
Bantu Building Workers Act (1951, South
    Africa) 137
Bantu Education Act (1953, South Africa) 137
Bantu (Urban Areas) Consolidation Act (1945,
    South Africa) 138
Bantustans 101, 131, 138, 140-41
Barak, Ehud 82-88, 94, 97-104, 182, 187, 196,
    219
Barnes, William S. 19
Barsky, Robert F. 28, 56-57
Bartlett, Ruhl 19
Bazelon, David 76
Becker, Andrea 179
Begin, Menachem 109
Beilin, Yossi 99
Beit Hanoun 154
Beit Lahiya Elementary School 162, 187
Bell, Daniel 272
Ben-Ami, Shlomo 101
Bentley, Eric 272
Benvinisti, Meron 140
Berrigan, Daniel 27-28, 37
Berrigan, Philip 27-28
Bethlehem 83, 103, 140
Betts, Richard K. 236
Bible 68, 75-76, 78, 262-265
Big Brother 77, 251-54, 262, 288
Bigotry 126, 143, 145-46, 148, 152, 175, 205
Bill of Rights 50, 61, 63, 66, 76, 81, 106, 261-65,
    289, 300
Bishara, Marwan 220
Blackstone, William 51
Blackstone Maxim 51
Blix, Hans 219
Bloody Sunday Massacre 47
Blum, Gabriella 243-46, 251
Board of Rabbis of Greater Phoenix 127
Bok, Derek 30, 57
Borger, Julian 185
Boston Area Faculty Group on Public Issues 19,
    22
Boston Globe 19, 24, 27, 29, 31, 40, 54, 56-58,
    60-61, 63-65, 142, 150, 195
Boston Massacre 43-48, 265
Boston Review 97

Boston University 97
Boudin, Leonard 61
Brandeis University 19, 21, 142
Braut-Hegghammer, Malfrid 236
Breyer, Stephen 57
British Mandate in Palestine 50, 52
British Medical Journal 19
British University and College Union 147
Brookings Institution 220
Browne, Malcolm 22-23
Brownlie, Ian 160-62,172, 180, 191
B'Tselem 12, 108, 114, 139, 145, 164-68, 181,
    183-84, 190, 261
Buckley, William F. 267-68
Buergenthal, Thomas 113
Bundy, McGeorge 18
Bush, George W. 110, 125, 209, 211, 216, 241,
    292, 298
Byrne, Matthew 29
Byron, Samuel 265

C

Cambodia 19, 21 36-38, 56-58, 120-21, 155, 226
Camp David (July 2000) 82, 86-87, 94-95, 98-
    103, 107, 112, 119
Campbell, Tom 255
Cantons 101, 103, 134
Carter Center 125, 127, 144
Carter, Jimmy 13, 97, 117, 125-29, 131, 133,
    139, 141-46, 171, 285-86
Cartesian Linguistics (Chomsky) 34, 267
Caton, Stephen 282
Cave, Alfred 48
Center for Constitutional Rights 213, 253, 257,
    259, 296, 298
Charles, Ray 25
Charney, Jule 17
Chassey, Clancy 185
Chayefsky, Paddy 272
Cheney, Dick 125
Chinkin, Christine 171-74
Chomsky, Aviva 328
Chomsky, Carol 27
Chongjin (Korea) 231
Church, Frank 144
Churchill, Winston 226
Chutzpah (Dershowitz) 56-57, 104, 269, 271,
    278, 280-81, 286
Cicero 75

Extrajudicial killing 66, 80, 139, 209, 258-61, 260, 284, 288, 296
Extraordinary rendition 15, 212

F

Failed States: The Abuse of Power and the Assault on Democracy (Chomsky) 14, 103
Falk, Richard 13, 28-32, 39, 58, 60, 93, 103-04, 144, 149, 152, 154-57, 160, 172, 180, 182, 191, 257, 300
Fall, Bernard 22-23, 40
Fatah 91, 179
Fateful Triangle: The United States, Israel, and the Palestinians (Chomsky) 10, 14
Faurisson, Robert 268-76, 278-80, 282, 289
Faye, Jean-Peirre 279
Federal Bureau of Investigation (FBI) 29, 148, 214, 215, 250, 252-53, 298
Feld, Bernard 143
Ferber, Michael 25, 61
Fernandez, Richard 33
Fielding, Lewis 29
Fifth Amendment (U.S. Constitution) 217, 264, 289-90, 297
Filc, Dani 185
Final Declaration of the Geneva Conference (1954) 156
Finkelstein, Norman 10, 13, 103-05, 150, 151, 171
First Amendment (U.S. Constitution) 29-30, 38, 61-64, 76, 214, 217, 277-78
Fischer, David Hackett 47
Fishman, Irving 20
Fisk, Robert 174, 180, 200-01
Foley, Michael S. 20, 25, 27
Foreign Intelligence Surveillance Court (FISA Court) 15, 212, 253, 297-300
For Reasons of State (Chomsky) 34, 37
Forrest, Katherine 217
Fourth Amendment (U.S. Constitution) 62, 64, 252, 262, 264, 298-99
Fourth Geneva Convention (Geneva IV) 11, 50, 103, 107-22, 161, 163, 165, 192, 193, 225, 227, 244, 247
Foxman, Abraham 146
Frank, Anne 279-280
Frankel, Charles 272
Franklin, Benjamin 299
Fraser, Don 144

Fray, Harold R. Jr. 25
Freud, Sigmund 75
Fried, John H.E. 59
Fulbright, J. William 23, 76

G

Galil assault rifle 285
Gallup 245
Gaza Community Mental Health Center 164
Gaza Strip 11-12, 14, 49, 74, 80, 89, 91-92, 100, 101, 114, 138-39, 143, 148, 154-55, 159-65, 167, 171-72, 177-83, 186, 189, 192-93, 233, 261, 281
Gaza Wastewater Treatment Plant 192
Gelb, Leslie 285
Geneva Accord on Israel-Palestine 11
Geneva Accords on Indochina (1954) 18, 117-18, 155-56, 258
Genocide 19, 41, 120-21, 142, 232, 238, 264, 270, 287
Genocide Convention (Convention on the Prevention and Punishment of the Crime of Genocide) 121, 232
Ghalia family 162
Giacomelli, Giorgio 93
Gilberti, Alan 20
Ginsburg, Allen 272
Glasser, Ira 278
Goering, Hermann 224
Goldberg, Arthur 76
Goldstein, Abraham S. 65
Goldstone Report 171-77, 180, 183-84, 187, 191-96
Goldstone, Richard 13, 171-72, 175, 187, 191
Gonzales, Roberto 67, 209
Goodman, Amy 140
Goodman, Mitchell 61
Gordon, Joy 198
Gorenberg, Gershom 115
Grayling, A.C. 225, 231-32
Green Line 11,112, 30, 133-34, 244
Greenwald, Glenn 210, 299
Greiner, Bernd 21
Grotius, Hugo 68-69
Group Areas Act (South Africa, 1950) 138
Guardian 126, 140, 149, 152, 179-80, 184-86, 191, 199, 201, 258, 297-99
Guatemala 270, 283-87
Gulf of Tonkin 240-41

Gulf of Tonkin incident 18

H

Haddad, Saad 274
Halberstam, David 22-23
Halutz, Dan 169
Hamas 128, 153-54, 160-61, 165, 167, 171-73, 175, 177-80, 182, 185, 187, 189, 195-96, 232-33, 260-61
Hamhung (Korea) 231
Hamilton, Alexander 290
Hamlin, David 278
Haram al-Sharif 82-84, 86, 97, 104
Harburg, E.Y. 272
Haroon, Siddiqui 175
Harris, Barbara 28
Harvard Crimson 22
Harvard University 9, 21, 25, 30, 74-75, 118, 143, 157, 219, 236, 240, 270, 282, 299-300
Harvey, Dan 173-74
Hasan, Nidal 294
Hass, Amira 73, 140, 180
Hedges, Chris 179, 182, 216-17
Hegel, G.W.F. 75
Helal, Gemal 102
Hellfire missiles 184, 188, 289
Henry, Patrick 227, 265
Herman, Edward S. 19, 56, 270, 286-88
Hersh, Seymour 40, 234
Herzog, Chaim 173
Hesburgh, Theodore 144
Heymann, Philip B. 241-51
Heyns, Christof 209-10
Hezbollah 143, 165-69, 196-204, 214
Higher Relief Council (Lebanon) 168
Hilsman, Roger 35
Hiroshima 226, 231
Ho Chi Minh 155, 156
Hoffmann, Stanley 157, 272
Holder, Eric 293
Holocaust 120, 152-54, 251, 268-69, 271, 274, 277-82
Horowitz, David 271
Hossain, Kamal 93
Howard, John 11
Howe, Irving 272
Huffington Post 167-68, 173, 196, 198, 201, 204, 232-33, 258, 261, 295

Human Rights Watch 12, 29, 108, 114, 143-44, 154-55, 164, 184-86, 191, 196-97, 199, 203-04, 259
Human Sciences Research Council (South Africa) 133, 139
Humphrey, Hubert 144
Hungnam (Korea) 231
Hunt, E. Howard 29
Hunter, Jane 285-86
Hussein, Saddam 198, 235-36, 254

I

Indefinite detention 15, 74, 209, 211, 217
International Committee of the Red Cross 108, 113, 119, 120
International Court of Justice 12, 108, 112, 113, 129, 133
International Criminal Tribunal for Rwanda 121
International Criminal Tribunal for the former Yugoslavia 121
International humanitarian law 107, 113-14, 118, 161-62, 164, 167, 183, 185
International Institute for Strategic Studies 219
International Law Commission (United Nations) 224
Iraq 32, 41, 45, 49, 69, 74, 145, 198, 209, 213, 218-19, 222-25, 232, 234-38, 241-44, 246, 260, 300
Isikoff, Michael 290-91, 293
Islamic Jihad 56, 91, 179, 218, 246
Israel Defense Forces (IDF) 43, 89, 93, 96, 130, 154, 165-66, 185, 187, 197, 199, 201, 203-04, 244, 260
Israeli League for Human and Civil Rights 54-56

J

Jack, Alex 25
Jackson, Robert 225, 255-56
Jaffer, Jameel 216, 291
Japan 40, 221, 225-32, 248, 300
Jennings, Francis 48
Jerusalem (see also East Jerusalem) 11, 54, 76, 82-85, 94-95, 97, 98, 100, 105, 106, 109, 115, 127, 140, 179, 247
Jewish National Fund 54
Jilani, Hina 174, 191

Massachusetts Institute of Technology (MIT) 15, 17, 18-23, 26, 28-32, 74, 118-19, 143, 150, 150, 236, 242, 244, 267, 272, 300
Mather, Cotton 41
Mazzetti, Mark 218, 234
McCarthy, Joseph 145, 156
McCoy, Alfred W. 250
McGovern, George 144
McGrory, Mary 143
McLure, Wallace 59
McNamara, Robert S. 19, 21, 32, 228-29
McNaughton, John 32
Mearsheimer, John J. 143, 145-47
Meir, Golda 52
Mengel, James 27
Meron, Theodor 115-17
Miller, Aaron 82, 102
Miller, Richard S. 59
Mitford, Jessica 61
MIT News 75
Mobutu, Sese Seko 286
Mohammed, Jude Kenan 296
Montt, Rios 284
Moratinos Document 99
Morgenthau, Hans 35-37, 39, 59, 157
Morris, Benny 100-02
Morris, Errol 229
Morton, Brian 268
Morton, Louis 227
Moscow, Warren 228
Mubarak, Hosni 219
Muzaffar, Chandra 220
My Lai Massacre 40-41

N

Nablus 83-84
Nader, Ralph 216
Nagasaki 226, 231
Nagoya 228-29
National Defense Authorization Act (NDAA) 216-17
National Intelligence Estimate (NIE, 2007) 233
National Lawyers Guild (U.S.) 1, 181, 184, 216
National Liberation Front 18, 24, 31, 25
National Moratorium on Vietnam 57
National Security Agency (NSA) 214-15, 298-99
Native Laws Amendment Act (South Africa, 1952) 138

Natives (Abolition of Passes and Co-ordination of Documents) Act (South Africa, 1952) 138
Natives (Urban Areas) Amendment Act (South Africa, 1955) 138
Nazis 120, 154, 238, 268-71, 274, 277-79, 282-83, 287, 289
Neier, Aryeh 278
Newman, Paul 143
New York Review of Books 22, 32, 34, 36, 66, 101-02
New York Times 18-19, 21-23, 27-30, 32, 34-35, 37, 61, 65, 83, 86, 101, 116, 149-50, 156, 163, 174-75, 178, 200-01, 210, 215, 218, 228, 254, 272-73, 278, 285, 289, 295-96
Nguyen Dinh Uoc 19
Niva, Steve 179
Nixon, Richard M. 13, 22-23, 29, 39, 57, 61-66, 143-45, 209, 262
Nojeim, Gregory 254
Nuremberg Charter (London Charter of the International Military Tribunal) 223
Nuremberg Principles (Principles of the Nuremberg Tribunal) 224
Nuremberg Tribunal 223-24, 227

O

Obama, Barack 49, 110, 114, 125-26, 209-17, 243, 259, 289-300
O'Connell, Mary Ellen 258, 291
"Occupation, Colonialism, Apartheid? A Re-Assessment of Israel's Practices in the Occupied Palestinian Territories" (Human Sciences Research Council) 133
O'Donnell, Kenneth 59
Old City (East Jerusalem) 82-84, 98
Olmert, Ehud 164-65, 168-69, 197
Olson, A. William 30
Operation Autumn Clouds 189
Operation Cast Lead 184, 186-90
Operation Summer Rains 189
Operation Warm Winter 190
Oren, Michael 195
Orme, William A. 85
Osaka 228-29
Osirak nuclear reactor (Iraq) 234-36
Oz, Amos 9
Ozinsky, Max 132